EMOTIONAL DISTURBANCE AND SCHOOL LEARNING:

a book of readings

EMOTIONAL DISTURBANCE AND SCHOOL LEARNING:
a book of readings

Donald H. Clark, *Hunter College*

Gerald S. Lesser, *Harvard University*

 Science Research Associates, Inc.   Chicago

Contents

INTRODUCTION

THE PROBLEM

Libraries are growing large but colleges are growing larger. It is increasingly difficult to introduce classes of students to research and make the meeting pleasant. One does not get a *feel* for a field by reading the one journal left on the library shelf; and even if one is hearty enough to brave the library at opening time and devour several journals before the rush hour, the reading is of questionable value unless the articles can be discussed with an instructor and classmates.

Journals contain articles that are good and bad, scholarly and superficial, rigorous and naive, interesting and dull. It takes some experience to spot the articles that are likely to be of interest to you, and it takes some instruction to learn to evaluate their content.

It is our hope that the articles collected in this book will serve as a realistic introduction to an exciting field of study. The impact of emotional disturbance on school learning is a topic that generates much feeling. A sixth-grade teacher we met last week in a "disadvantaged" city school said, "There's lots of emotional disturbance in my class. I suppose you're progressive, but I think they need discipline." People take up battle positions easily, but the battles are often pointless. In a young field we need to share ideas rather than sell them.

These battles are made more pointless when we realize that the warriors are shooting blanks—opinions are of very mild interest unless they stand on evidence. It is our hope that these readings will give the student an idea of the kind of research being done on the role of emotional disturbance in school learning, the kind of evidence being accumulated, the criteria being used to evaluate research evidence, and the variety of conclusions being reached. There are certain problems for the researcher in psychology that are peculiar to this area of study. One should begin to appreciate the many and varied difficulties as well as their actual and potential solutions after reading the selections in this book.

These readings are intended as a basis for discussion in class. They were selected as a broad sample of the kinds of articles published in the area. Learning to evaluate research is especially difficult for a student who has not yet done any. Opinion again comes easily. One may happily sort any collection of articles into categories of *good, fair,* and *poor,* but that is a useless occupation. It is more profitable to determine the degree of faith that is justified by the research findings. It is a rare study that teaches nothing and a still rarer one that provides a completely satisfactory answer to a research question.

Now, what should be said of the substantive points discussed in this volume? Tolerance and patience are hard masters when one is surrounded by misery that pleads for help. Those of us who work in this field are eager to help the victims of emotional disturbance find their way out of their dark tangle. We try to help. But the truth is that we operate in the dim of early morning ourselves. Today's *right* answer may prove *wrong* when further illuminated by tomorrow's research. Patience and tolerance. The truth does not really reverse, but it reveals itself slowly. Our working hypotheses shift as we get new glimpses of truth, and truth is never fully revealed because the human situation is changing and the truth must therefore change also.

It is obviously foolish to sit and wait for all of the answers to be discovered. Human misery is around us and we do the best we can to help. An expert is one who weighs the current evidence and formulates a working answer, not someone who knows absolute truth.

THE NATURE OF THE RESEARCH PROCESS

There has been a long-standing dispute over the validity and usefulness of any attempt to define and prescribe the scientific method. One position holds that there should be consensus among scientists on the ground rules of scientific methodology—that a single, accepted system of scientific method would produce a more orderly and more easily communicated scientific product. An opposing position holds that since creative discovery is the essence of science, any single pattern of rules and regulations (no matter how broad) is unrealistically restrictive.

Efforts to specify *the* scientific method applicable to any subject reached a climax about a generation ago, and they have had considerable impact since that time. One popular version of *the* scientific method was formalized as six successive operations:

1. A problem is stated.

2. Observations relevant to the problem are collected.

3. A hypothetical solution of the problem consistent with the observations is formulated.

4. Predictions of other observable phenomena are deduced from the hypothesis.

5. Occurrence or nonoccurrence of the predicted phenomena is observed.

6. The hypothesis is accepted, modified, or rejected in accordance with the degree of fulfillment of the predictions.

Many variations of this formalized treatment have accumulated and have been applied in the social sciences. They do have a certain degree of utility. There is no question that this or any other version of *the* scientific method does work admirably in particular instances, that each of the specified steps is crucial in various phases of scientific research, that agreeing upon some set of ground rules does help scientists communicate with each other, and that explicit statement of scientific methodology does help to distinguish scientific from ascientific forms of inquiry.

But there is also no question that such definitions and prescriptions fail to reflect the untidy, bewildering, exploratory character of scientific research. They ignore the obstacles and questions that demand creative solutions. How does one identify a problem, or decide what observations are relevant and how they should be made? What kinds of hypothetical solutions are reasonable and how do we arrive at them?

There are two additional objections offered to formalized methodologies. They developed very late in the history of science, after many of the significant discoveries had been made without their explicit aid. In addition, current research seldom, if ever, finds it productive to follow *the* method just as it is stated. Science does not progress in carefully designed steps, each having a well-defined beginning and end.

If all these objections to formal methodology are true, how did such a picture of research gain such wide currency? First, the appearance of a finished scientific product is deceiving; it looks neat, logical, complete. But there is an unfortunate confusion between this neat product and the messy process by which it is manufactured. Second, when one attempts to describe a complex process, one is seduced into describing those elements that are visible and easily verbalized. It is easier to talk about previous research, measures, design, and statistics than about origination, development of ideas, and creation. But what is most easily verbalized about research is not necessarily most important.

CRITERIA FOR EVALUATING RESEARCH CONCLUSIONS

We now list some suggested criteria that both instructor and student may find helpful in evaluating the studies presented in this book or elsewhere.

Statement of problem:

1. Are the objectives stated clearly?
2. Is the survey of the literature on the problem complete, relevant, and accurate?
3. In the survey of the literature, are the necessary transitional statements that link the study to previous research included?
4. Has the study already been done? If so, is it worth duplicating? Why?
5. Are incorrect or unnecessary assumptions made?
6. Is the problem stated too broadly or too narrowly?

Hypotheses:

7. Are the hypotheses stated clearly?
8. Are the hypotheses testable?
9. Are the operations necessary to the testing of the hypotheses included?

Definition of variables:

10. Are independent and dependent variables defined clearly?
11. Are the operations used to create conditions stipulated by the variables described clearly?

12. Are the operations appropriate to the variables as defined?

13. To what extent are the variables unitary or unidimensional?

Subjects:

14. Has a rational basis been used in selecting a *population* from which a sample is drawn?

15. Has a rational basis been used in selecting a *sample* from the population?

16. How representative of the total *population* to which the study will generalize is the *sample* employed?

17. What sampling procedures are employed?

18. Are the groups that are to be compared really different?

19. Are identical procedures followed in selecting subjects for a single, homogeneous group?

Method:

20. Do the measures yield a sufficient range of individual differences?

21. Do the measures have sufficient "ceiling" and "floor"? That is, do the measures provide a lower limit that is sufficiently low and an upper limit that is sufficiently high to include all the subjects used in the study?

22. Are the measures relevant to the variables specified in the hypotheses?

23. Are the measures reliable and valid? What form of *reliability* data is presented? What form of *validity* data is presented?

24. Are data on interjudge reliability reported?

25. Are clearly distinct scoring categories employed? If categories overlap, is the nature and degree of overlap indicated and the rules for categorizing the data supplied?

26. Are the administration and scoring of the measures described clearly and unequivocally?

Design:

27. Have proper and adequate controls been established?

28. Have extreme scores, or the total range of scores, been utilized? Is the justification for the chosen procedure adequate?

29.   Have extraneous variables been identified and controlled?

30.   Has an appropriate and powerful experimental design been used?

Results:

31.   Does the evidence presented provide a direct test of the problem?

32.   Is the data analysis complete in the light of the stated objectives?

33.   Are the statistical operations identified?

34.   Are the statistical operations justified?

35.   Are there discernible errors in the statistical analysis?

36.   Are all statistical comparisons reported?

Discussion and conclusions:

37.   Are the interpretations overgeneralizations or undergeneralizations of the results?

38.   Do the interpretations make theoretical sense in the light of other known principles?

39.   Are the results compared with those of other studies?

40.   Are all plausible alternative interpretations of positive results considered?

41.   Are nonsignificant and negative results explained?

42.   Are opinions and conclusions based on evidence differentiated clearly?

43.   Are correct meanings assigned to statistical analyses?

Presentation of study:

44.   Is the study presented clearly and completely? Could it be duplicated from the description presented?

45.   Are errors such as misspellings, incorrect numbering, and inaccurate labeling included in the published report?

FORM OF THE BOOK

This book is presented in six sections. There is a brief introduction to each section. In the final chapter we tie up a few of the many loose strings and indulge in some crystal-ball gazing. Technical terms and symbols are, we hope, translated into relatively plain English in a glossary at the back of the book. We hope that it will not be necessary for the reader to use this glossary rigidly, for it is our belief that one can learn something of use from a study even if he does not understand the complexities of statistics or the jargon of psychologists. One should never fear a casual look through a technical journal.

The studies in this book are not evaluated for you. One must chew his own food to taste it. But we hope you will chew well and discuss these studies, keeping in mind that the chore is not to judge but to evaluate. There is a difference.

We have also appended a long list of references because we hope that some students will become interested in a particular facet of this problem and want to read more. We need hardly state that the list is incomplete, but there are studies to start the student on any aspect of this research topic.

Finally, we introduce you briefly to the men and women who are responsible for these articles, because we want to remind you that they were written by people, like yourself, who care about this problem.

We wish you interested reading.

DEFINITION: emotional disturbance, mental illness, and other labels

"Sticks and stones will break my bones but names will never hurt me." We have all heard children chant something similar to this hasty antidote for the evil spell of words placed on them by someone else. Children understand that words have a certain magic. They fear being called a tattletale for much the same reasons that adults in our culture fear being called a communist: such a label can seriously affect the perception of one's peers. Adults may threaten to take someone to court if he does not retract his slanderous words. Words have magic.

Any person who has ever been labeled "emotionally disturbed" or "mentally ill" can tell you what a profound effect the label has had on the course of his life. Before assigning a label to anyone it is wise to determine the reasons for doing so. Sometimes it is done in an effort to make the name giver more comfortable. If one cannot solve a puzzle, he can feel more in control of it by placing it in a category with a proper name. Instead of saying "I don't understand why Johnny behaves that way," one can say "Johnny is psychotic." If placing the name "psychotic" helps Johnny by helping you to understand him and to help him, fine. If the puzzle is no nearer solution, we have done Johnny a disservice.

The articles in this section are placed here to stimulate thinking about definitions and labels. Our point of view is that it is less profitable to think in terms of a *problem child* than to think in terms of *a child having these problems now*. The report of Macfarlane and her group (of which we are printing only the concluding chapter) makes it clear that all children show "symptoms of mental illness" in the course of growing up.

Clancy and Smitter point out that boys show more "symptoms" in school than girls and that "disturbed" children seem to display a lower than average I.Q. This should make us think about the differences in the way school is experienced by boys and by girls in our culture. It should also stimulate us to take a closer look at the I.Q. and find out about the manner in which it is defined and determined.

And, lest we comfort ourselves with the long road of progress between 1713 and 1965, when reading the account of Emerentia in Kanner's review, we might ask how a visit to a child in one of our present-day state mental hospitals might be described in the year 2217.

In "The Myth of Mental Illness" Szasz reminds us to examine our concept of "illness" before pursuing the source of infection.

The next section, on antecedents, will examine the question of why problems more often occur for one child than for another, and why more problems occur at one time in life than another.

Emotionally Disturbed Children: A Historical Review [1]

Leo Kanner

It is customary to begin a historical account with the search for the earliest observations, ideas, and practices pertaining to the topic under consideration. Ancient and medieval sources are consulted; discovered references are interpreted in the light of the over-all culture of the times and locale; eventually, an evolutionary pattern emerges which links the gradual steps from primitive origins to the facts and theories available when the quest is undertaken.

Similar efforts concerned with emotional disorders of children lead to the amazing disclosure of the total absence of an allusion, however casual, before the eighteenth century. Folklore, which seizes upon every conceivable aspect of human life, is peculiarly silent. Theologic, medical, and fictional writings have nothing to say. This does not warrant the assumption that infantile emotions always ran a smooth course in the

---

[1]Presented in a symposium, "Research on Emotionally Disturbed Children," at the biennial meeting of the Society for Research in Child Development, Pennsylvania State University, March, 1961.

past and that the occurrence of their disturbances is a relatively recent phenomenon. The truth is that, aside from occasional pious pleas for nondescript philanthropy, our ancestral lawgivers, physicians, and philosophers seem to have been indifferent toward the afflicted among many categories of the young and, for that matter, of the grown-ups as well. It was not until the decades immediately before and after the French and American revolutions that the new doctrine of the rights of the individual engendered an unprecedented spurt of humanitarian reforms. Vigorous spokesmen arose for the active alleviation of the plight of the slaves, the prison inmates, the insane, the blind, the deaf, and the mental defectives. For the first time, handicapped children were seen and heard. Young enthusiasts, mostly men in their twenties, undeterred by the skepticism of their renowned mentors, began to experiment with remedial and educational methods.

There was still no comprehension of the kind of children's difficulties which manifested themselves in disorganized feeling, thinking, and acting. Here and there sporadic sketches made their appearance, mostly with the implication of inherent evil. A few examples may suffice to give the flavor of these reports from the pens of outstanding alienists. I should like to precede them with the story of little Emerentia, as chronicled in a clergyman's diary which is cited in the masterful autobiographic novel, *Der grüne Heinrich* by Gottfried Keller (11), in whose native village the incident had taken place in 1713:

> This 7-year-old girl, the offspring of an aristocratic family, whose father remarried after an unhappy first matrimony, offended her "noble and god-fearing" stepmother by her peculiar behavior. Worst of all, she would not join in the prayers and was panic-stricken when taken to the black-robed preacher in the dark and gloomy chapel. She avoided contact with people by hiding in closets or running away from home. The local physician had nothing to offer beyond declaring that she might be insane. She was placed in the custody of a minister known for his rigid orthodoxy. The minister, who saw in her ways the machinations of a "baneful and infernal" power, used a number of would-be therapeutic devices. He laid her on a bench and beat her with a cat-o'nine-tails. He locked her in a dark pantry. He subjected her to a period of starvation. He clothed her in a frock of burlap. Under these circumstances, the child did not last long. She died after a few months, and everybody felt relieved. The minister was amply rewarded for his efforts by Emerentia's parents.

Such was the general milieu in which the alienists of those days came upon specimens of childhood psychosis. The great Esquirol (7, pp. 384-385) reported in 1838 the cases of three "little homicidal monomaniacs." Of an 11-year-old girl who pushed two infants into a well he had nothing more to say than that she "was known for her evil habits." An 8-year-old girl who threatened to kill her stepmother and her brother was returned to her grandparents who had violently disapproved of her father's remarriage. A 7½-year-old girl who had been tossed about among relatives refused to play, had temper tantrums, masturbated excessively, and expressed regret that her mother did not die; the neighbors, to teach her a lesson, put flour into a glass of wine, told her it was arsenic, and forced her to swallow it. On psychiatric advice, she was sent to a convent, where she promptly developed pediculosis. Eventually, she was apprenticed to a jewel cutter and was said to be submissive and to attend church services on Sundays.

In 1841, Descuret (4) told of a boy who lived with a nurse during the first two years of his life. When he was taken to his home, he grew pale, sad, and morose, refused to eat, and did not respond to his parents. The usual toys and diversions had no effect. On medical advice, the nurse was called back and, in the father's words, "from that moment on he began to live again." Eventually, he was separated from the nurse, first for a few hours, then for a whole day, then for a week, until finally the child was accustomed to her absence.

This last example indicates an emerging desire to look for possible explanations of deviant child behavior on other than pseudotheologic and pseudomoralistic grounds.

Around the middle of the nineteenth century, a growing number of such anecdotal bits was published, and a few psychiatrists were no longer satisfied with the mere mechanical recording of observed or quoted instances. In 1867, Maudsley included in his *Physiology and Pathology of Mind* a 34-page chapter on "Insanity of Early Life." In it, he tried to correlate symptomatology with the developmental status at the time of onset and suggested a classification of infantile psychoses. There was objection on the part of those who persisted in denying the existence of mental illness in children. In the 1880 revision of his book, Maudsley (16) felt compelled to counter such criticism with an introductory paragraph, which said, somewhat apologetically:

How unnatural! is an exclamation of pained surprise which some of the more striking instances of insanity in young children are apt to provoke. However, to call a thing unnatural is not to take it out of the domain of natural law, notwithstanding that, when it has been so designated, it is sometimes thought that no more needs to be said. Anomalies, when rightly studied, yield rare instruction; they witness and attract attention to the operation of hidden laws or of known laws under new and unknown conditions; and so set the inquirer on new and fruitful paths of research. For this reason it will not be amiss to occupy a separate chapter with a consideration of the abnormal phenomena of mental derangement in children (p. 259).

In the last two decades of the nineteenth century, courageous attempts were made to collect and organize the existing material in monographs on "psychic disorders," "mental diseases," or "insanity" of children. These were the texts of Emminghaus (6) in Germany, Moreau de Tours (17) and Manheimer (15) in France, and Ireland (9) in Great

Britain. There was a tendency toward fatalism which saw in the dis-orders the irreversible results of heredity, degeneracy, masturbation, overwork, religious preoccupation, intestinal parasites, or sudden changes of temperature.

Thus, around 1900, there was an assortment of publications, rang-ing all the way from single case reports to elaborate texts and announc-ing to an astonished world that children were known to display psy-chotic phenomena.

It was the year 1900 in which Ellen Key (12), the famous Swedish sociologist, made her much-quoted prophetic announcement that the twentieth century was destined to be "the century of the child." It is indeed remarkable that in the next few years many efforts converged on the interest in the doings and experiences of infants and children. The diaries of Preyer, Darwin, Pestalozzi, Tiedemann, and other writers, expanded by Stanley Hall's questionnaires, had paved the way for the new science of developmental psychology and the monumental work of Binet, whose first draft of the psychometric scale was made public in 1905. This was the year in which Freud, on the basis of elicited adult patients' reminiscences, gave literary form to his theory of infantile sexuality. Three years later, Clifford Beers introduced the idea of the prevention of mental illness, focusing on the need to intercept behavioral deviations at the time of their earliest appearance. The establishment of juvenile courts, inaugurated in 1899 in Denver and in Chicago, led eventually to Healy's contributions in the teens of this century. Educa-tors joined in by building into the school systems special instructional facilities for pupils with visual, auditory, neuro-orthopedic, and intellec-tual handicaps.

Yet it was not until the 1930's that consistent attempts were made to study children with severe emotional disturbances from the point of view of diagnosis, etiology, therapy, and prognosis. When the change did occur, it was centered around the concept of childhood schizophrenia. By that time, general agreement had been reached that children were not altogether immune against the illness described by Kraepelin as dementia praecox and referred to by Bleuler as the group of the schizo-phrenias. Ziehen (23) and Homburger (8) had given in their textbooks (both in 1926) ample space to a discussion of its incidence in preadoles-cence and adolescence. De Sanctis (3), at about the same time, had suggested the term "dementia praecocissima" for an assortment of marked disturbances appearing in preschool age. Increasing awareness of the looseness with which childhood schizophrenia was diagnosed or failed to be diagnosed caused Potter (18) in 1933 to delineate the concept so that there might be a consensus with regard to the nosologic assignment of any individual child. In the framework of this and similar definitions, the next step consisted of the search for a clear demarcation of existing variations in onset, symptoms, and course. Ssucharewa (21) in Russia, Lutz (13) in Switzerland, and Despert (5) in this country distinguished between cases with acute and insidious onset, with the implication that the peculiarities of the beginning determined the phenomenology and the progress of the illness.

In the 1940's, a period of controversy and confusion was inaugurated because of the parallel advocacy of two antithetical trends. On the one hand, there was a tendency to revert to pre-Kraepelinian indefiniteness. Beata Rank (19) introduced the notion of the "atypical child," with intended disregard of any distinctions between childhood psychosis, mental defect, and any other form of "severe disturbances of early development." Problems of mother-child relationship were declared to be a common causative denominator. Szurek proclaimed categorically: "We are beginning to consider it clinically fruitless, and even unnecessary, to draw any sharp dividing lines between a condition that one could consider psychoneurotic and another that one could call psychosis, autism, atypical development, or schizophrenia" (22, p. 522).

On the other hand, there was a decided disinclination to house an assortment of heterogeneous clinical entities under one supposedly common etiologic roof. Kanner (10), in 1943, outlined the syndrome of early infantile autism. Mahler (14), in 1949, described a form which she named symbiotic infantile psychosis. In the same year, Bergman and Escalona (2) called attention to what they called children with unusual sensitivity to sensory stimulation. In 1954, Robinson and Vitale (20) added the group of children with circumscribed interest patterns. Bender (1), seeing the origin of childhood schizophrenia in a maturation lag at the embryonic level, subdivided the condition into three clinical types: (a) the pseudodefective or autistic type; (b) the pseudoneurotic or phobic, obsessive, compulsive, hypochondriac type; (c) the pseudopsychopathic or paranoid, acting-out, aggressive, antisocial type.

It is strange, indeed, that a historical review of emotional disturbances of children should occupy itself predominantly, or almost exclusively, with psychoses and, more specifically, with schizophrenia. It is equally strange that, seek as one may, it is impossible to find anywhere a definition of the term "emotionally disturbed children" which had somehow crept into the literature some 30 years ago and has since then been used widely, sometimes as a generality with no terminologic boundaries whatever and sometimes with reference to certain psychotic and near-psychotic conditions. This is extremely important in the consideration and evaluation of past, ongoing, and planned research. It can be said that these studies do exclude such emotional disorders as occasional temper tantrums or night terrors of otherwise well-adjusted children;

chronicity is apparently a paramount requirement. Also left out are emotional problems associated with, or secondary to, inherent mental deficiency or demonstrable organ pathology. But this still leaves a wide variety of heterogeneous conditions which, if thrown together indiscriminately, impart no greater meaning to a study than did the sixteenth century treatises on the fevers or the nineteenth century studies of the blood pressure of "the insane" or of the heredity of "feeblemindedness." It may perhaps be legitimate to link them together from the standpoint of practical epidemiology and the improvement of public health facilities but, beyond this, it would hardly do to claim scientific validity for any research which sets out to look for unitary features in disparate conditions.

A historical survey teaches us that progress has always consisted of a breaking down of diffuse generic concepts into specific categories. We no longer speculate about fevers generically; bacteriology knows of totally different varieties of febrile illness. We no longer speak about insanity generically; we recognize a variety of psychotic reaction types. We no longer speak about feeblemindedness generically; we know that there is a vast difference between mongolism, microcephaly, and phenylketonuria; it would not occur to anyone to lump them together in any meaningful investigation. I believe that the time has come to acknowledge the heterogeneity of the many conditions comprised under the generic term, "emotionally disturbed children." We shall then be in a position to study each of these varieties with true precision. A symposium on the use of the term in scientific publications would, at this juncture, be a major contribution to clarity and mutual understanding.

References

1. BENDER, L.   Current research in childhood schizophrenia. *Amer. J. Psychiat.,* 1954, **110,** 855–856.

2. BERGMAN, P., & ESCALONA, S.   Unusual sensitivities in very young children. *Psychoanal. Stud. Child,* 1949, **3-4,** 333–352.

3. DE SANCTIS, S.   *Neuropsichiatria infantile.* Rome: Stock, 1925.

4. DESCURET, J. B. F.   *Médecine des passions.* Paris: Béchet et Labé, 1841.

5. DESPERT, J. L.   Schizophrenia in children. *Psychiat. Quart.,* 1938, **12,** 366–371.

6. EMMINGHAUS, H.   *Die psychischen Storüngen des Kindesalters.* Tübingen: Laupp, 1887.

7. ESQUIROL, J. E. D.   *Maladies mentales.* Vol. I. Paris: Baillère, 1838.

8. HOMBURGER, A.   *Vorlesungen über die Psychopathologie des Kindesalters.* Berlin: Springer, 1926.

9. IRELAND, W. W.   *The Mental Affections of Children.* Blakiston, 1898.

10. KANNER, L.   Problems of nosology and psychodynamics of early infantile autism. *Amer. J. Orthopsychiat.,* 1949, **19,** 416–426.

11. KELLER, G. *Der grüne Heinrich,* Vol. 1. Munich: Deutsch-Meister-Verlag, 1921.

12. KEY, E. *The Century of the Child.* (English Rev.) Putnam, 1909.

13. LUTZ, J. *Über die Schizophrenie im Kindesalter.* Zurich: Füssli, 1937.

14. MAHLER, M. S. On child psychosis and schizophrenia. *Psychoanal. Stud. Child,* 1952, **7,** 286–305.

15. MANHEIMER, M. *Les troubles mentaux de l'enfance.* Paris: Société d'Éditions Scientifiques, 1899.

16. MAUDSLEY, H. *The Pathology of the Mind.* Appleton, 1880.

17. MOREAU DE TOURS, P. *La folie chez les enfants.* Paris: Baillère, 1888.

18. POTTER, H. W. Schizophrenia in children. *Amer. J. Psychiat.,* 1933, **89,** 1253–1270.

19. RANK, B. Adaptation of the psychoanalytic techniques for the treatment of young children with atypical development. *Amer. J. Orthopsychiat.,* 1949, **19,** 130–139.

20. ROBINSON, F. J., & VITALE, L. J. Children with circumscribed interest patterns. *Amer. J. Orthopsychiat.* 1954, **24,** 755–766.

21. SSUCHAREWA, G. Über den Verlauf der Schizophrenien im Kindesalter. *Ztsch. f. d. ges. Neurol. & Psychiat.,* 1932, **142,** 309–321.

22. SZUREK, S. A. Psychotic episodes and psychic maldevelopment. *Amer J. Orthopsychiat.,* 1956, **26,** 519–543.

23. ZIEHEN, T. *Die Geisteskrankheiten des Kindesalters.* Berlin: Reuther & Reinhard, 1926.

The Myth of Mental Illness

Thomas S. Szasz

My aim in this essay is to raise the question "Is there such a thing as mental illness?" and to argue that there is not. Since the notion of mental illness is extremely widely used nowadays, inquiry into the ways in which this term is employed would seem to be especially indicated. Mental illness, of course, is not literally a "thing"—or physical object—and hence it can "exist" only in the same sort of way in which other theoretical concepts exist. Yet, familiar theories are in the habit of posing, sooner or later—at least to those who come to believe in them—as "objective truths" (or "facts"). During certain historical periods, explanatory conceptions such as deities, witches, and microorganisms appeared not only as theories but as self-evident *causes* of a vast number of events. I submit that today mental illness is widely regarded in a somewhat similar fashion, that is, as the cause of innumerable

"The Myth of Mental Illness," by Thomas S. Szasz, *American Psychologist,* No. 15. 113–118. © 1960, American Psychological Association.

diverse happenings. As an antidote to the complacent use of the notion of mental illness—whether as a self-evident phenomenon, theory, or cause—let us ask this question: What is meant when it is asserted that someone is mentally ill?

In what follows I shall describe briefly the main uses to which the concept of mental illness has been put. I shall argue that this notion has outlived whatever usefulness it might have had and that it now functions merely as a convenient myth.

MENTAL ILLNESS AS A SIGN OF BRAIN DISEASE

The notion of mental illness derives its main support from such phenomena as syphilis of the brain or delirious conditions—intoxications, for instance—in which persons are known to manifest various pecularities or disorders of thinking and behavior. Correctly speaking, however, these are diseases of the brain, not of the mind. According to one school of thought, *all* so-called mental illness is of this type. The assumption is made that some neurological defect, perhaps a very subtle one, will ultimately be found for all the disorders of thinking and behavior. Many contemporary psychiatrists, physicians, and other scientists hold this view. This position implies that people *cannot* have troubles—expressed in what are *now called* "mental illnesses"—because of differences in personal needs, opinions, social aspirations, values, and so on. *All problems in living* are attributed to physicochemical processes which in due time will be discovered by medical research.

"Mental illnesses" are thus regarded as basically no different than all other diseases (that is, of the body). The only difference, in this view, between mental and bodily diseases is that the former, affecting the brain, manifest themselves by means of mental symptoms; whereas the latter, affecting other organ systems (for example, the skin, liver, etc.), manifest themselves by means of symptoms referable to those parts of the body. This view rests on and expresses what are, in my opinion, two fundamental errors.

In the first place, what central nervous system symptoms would correspond to a skin eruption or a fracture? It would *not* be some emotion or complex bit of behavior. Rather, it would be blindness or a paralysis of some part of the body. The crux of the matter is that a disease of the brain, analogous to a disease of the skin or bone, is a neurological defect, and not a problem in living. For example, a *defect* in a person's visual field may be satisfactorily explained by correlating it with certain definite lesions in the nervous system. On the other hand, a person's *belief*—whether this be a belief in Christianity, in Communism, or in the idea that his internal organs are "rotting" and that his body is, in fact, already "dead"—cannot be explained by a defect or disease of the nervous system. Explanations of this sort of occurrence—assuming that one is interested in the belief itself and does not regard it simply as a "symptom" or expression of something else that is *more interesting*—must be sought along different lines.

The second error in regarding complex psychosocial behavior, consisting of communications about ourselves and the world about us, as mere symptoms of neurological functioning is *epistemological*. In other words, it is an error pertaining not to any mistakes in observation or reasoning, as such, but rather to the way in which we organize and express our knowledge. In the present case, the error lies in making a symmetrical dualism between mental and physical (or bodily) symptoms, a dualism which is merely a habit of speech and to which no known observations can be found to correspond. Let us see if this is so. In medical practice, when we speak of physical disturbances, we mean either signs (for example, a fever) or symptoms (for example, pain). We speak of mental symptoms, on the other hand, when we refer to a patient's *communications about himself, others, and the world about him*. He might state that he is Napoleon or that he is being persecuted by the Communists. These would be considered mental symptoms *only* if the observer believed that the patient was *not* Napoleon or that he was *not* being persecuted by the Communists. This makes it apparent that the statement that "X is a mental symptom" involves rendering a judgment. The judgment entails, moreover, a covert comparison or matching of the patient's ideas, concepts, or beliefs with those of the observer and the society in which they live. The notion of mental symptom is therefore inextricably tied to the *social* (including *ethical*) *context* in which it is made in much the same way as the notion of bodily symptom is tied to an *anatomical* and *genetic context* (Szasz, 1957a, 1957b).

To sum up what has been said thus far: I have tried to show that for those who regard mental symptoms as signs of brain disease, the concept of mental illness is unnecessary and misleading. For what they mean is that people so labeled suffer from diseases of the brain; and, if that is what they mean, it would seem better for the sake of clarity to say that and not something else.

MENTAL ILLNESS AS A NAME FOR PROBLEMS IN LIVING

The term "mental illness" is widely used to describe something which is very different than a disease of the brain. Many people today take it for granted that living is an arduous process. Its hardship for modern man, moreover, derives not so much from a struggle for biological survival as from the stresses and strains inherent in the social intercourse of complex human personalities. In this context, the notion of mental illness is used to identify or describe some feature of an individual's so-called personality. Mental illness—as a deformity of the personality, so to speak—is then regarded as the *cause* of the human disharmony. It is implicit in this view that social intercourse between people is regarded as something *inherently harmonious,* its disturbance being due solely to the presence of "mental illness" in many people. This is obviously fallacious reasoning, for it makes the abstraction "mental illness" into a *cause,* even though this abstraction was created in the first place to serve only as a shorthand expression for certain types of human behavior. It now becomes necessary to ask: "What kinds of behavior are regarded as indicative of mental illness, and by whom?"

The concept of illness, whether bodily or mental, implies *deviation from some clearly defined norm.* In the case of physical illness, the norm is the structural and functional integrity of the human body. Thus, although the desirability of physical health, as such, is an ethical value, what health *is* can be stated in anatomical and physiological terms. What is the norm deviation from which is regarded as mental illness? This question cannot be easily answered. But whatever this norm might be, we can be certain of only one thing: namely, that it is a norm that must be stated in terms of *psychosocial, ethical,* and *legal* concepts. For example, notions such as "excessive repression" or "acting out an unconscious impulse" illustrate the use of psychological concepts for judging (so-called) mental health and illness. The idea that chronic hostility, vengefulness, or divorce are indicative of mental illness would be illustrations of the use of ethical norms (that is, the desirability of love, kindness, and a stable marriage relationship). Finally, the widespread psychiatric opinion that only a mentally ill person would commit homicide illustrates the use of a legal concept as a norm of mental health. The norm from which deviation is measured whenever one speaks of a mental illness is a *psychosocial and ethical one.* Yet, the remedy is sought in terms of *medical* measures which—it is hoped and assumed—are free from wide differences of ethical value. The definition of the disorder and the terms in which its remedy are sought are therefore at serious odds with one another. The practical significance of this covert conflict between the alleged nature of the defect and the remedy can hardly be exaggerated.

Having identified the norms used to measure deviations in cases of mental illness, we will now turn to the question: "Who defines the norms and hence the deviation?" Two basic answers may be offered: (*a*) It may be the person himself (that is, the patient) who decides that he deviates from a norm. For example, an artist may believe that he suffers from a work inhibition; and he may implement this conclusion by seeking help *for* himself from a psychotherapist. (*b*) It may be someone other than the patient who decides that the latter is deviant (for example, relatives, physicians, legal authorities, society generally, etc.). In such a case a psychiatrist may be hired by others to do something *to* the patient in order to correct the deviation.

These considerations underscore the importance of asking the question "Whose agent is the psychiatrist?" and of giving a candid answer to it (Szasz, 1956, 1958). The psychiatrist (psychologist or nonmedical psychotherapist), it now develops, may be the agent of the patient, of the relatives, of the school, of the military services, of a business organization, of a court of law, and so forth. In speaking of the psychiatrist as the agent of these persons or organizations, it is not implied that his values concerning norms, or his ideas and aims concerning the proper nature of remedial action, need to coincide exactly with those of his employer. For example, a patient in individual psychotherapy may believe that his salvation lies in a new marriage; his psychotherapist need not share this hypothesis. As the patient's agent, however, he must abstain from bringing social or legal force to bear on the patient which would prevent him from putting his beliefs into action. If his *contract* is with the patient, the psychiatrist (psychotherapist) may disagree with him or stop his treatment; but he cannot engage others to obstruct the patient's aspirations. Similarly, if a psychiatrist is engaged by a court to determine the sanity of a criminal, he need not fully share the legal authorities' values and intentions in regard to the criminal and the means available for dealing with him. But the psychiatrist is expressly barred from stating, for example, that it is not the criminal who is "insane" but the men who wrote the law on the basis of which the very actions that are being judged are regarded as "criminal." Such an opinion could be voiced, of course, but not in a courtroom, and not by a psychiatrist who makes it his practice to assist the court in performing its daily work.

To recapitulate: In actual contemporary social usage, the finding of a mental illness is made by establishing a deviance in behavior from certain psychosocial, ethical, or legal norms. The judgment may be made, as in medicine, by the patient, the physician (psychiatrist), or others. Remedial action, finally, tends to be sought in a therapeutic—or covertly medical—framework, thus creating a situation in which *psychosocial, ethical,* and/or *legal deviations* are claimed to be correctible by (so-called) *medical action.* Since medical action is designed to correct only medical deviations, it seems logically absurd to expect that it will help solve problems whose very existence had been defined and established on nonmedical grounds. I think that these considerations may be fruitfully applied to the present use of tranquilizers and, more generally, to what might be expected of drugs of whatever type in regard to the amelioration or solution of problems in human living.

THE ROLE OF ETHICS IN PSYCHIATRY

Anything that people *do*—in contrast to things that *happen* to them (Peters, 1958)—takes place in a context of value. In this broad sense, no human activity is devoid of ethical implications. When the values under-lying certain activities are widely shared, those who participate in their pursuit may lose sight of them altogether. The discipline of medicine, both as a pure science (for example, research) and as a technology (for example, therapy), contains many ethical considerations and judgments. Unfortunately, these are often denied, minimized, or merely kept out of focus; for the ideal of the medical profession as well as of the people whom it serves seems to be having a system of medicine (allegedly) free of ethical value. This sentimental notion is expressed by such things as the doctor's willingness to treat and help patients irrespective of their religious or political beliefs, whether they are rich or poor, etc. While there may be some grounds for this belief—albeit it is a view that is not impressively true even in these regards—the fact remains that ethical considerations encompass a vast range of human affairs. But making the practice of medicine neutral in regard to some specific issues of value need not, and cannot, mean that it can be kept free from all such values. The practice of medicine is intimately tied to ethics; and the first thing that we must do, it seems to me, is to try to make this clear and explicit. I shall let this matter rest here, for it does not concern us specifically in this essay. Lest there be any vagueness, however, about how or where ethics and medicine meet, let me remind the reader of such issues as birth control, abortion, suicide, and euthanasia as only a few of the major areas of current ethicomedical controversy.

Psychiatry, I submit, is very much more intimately tied to problems of ethics than is medicine. I use the word "psychiatry" here to refer to that contemporary discipline which is concerned with *problems in living* (and not with diseases of the brain, which are problems for neurology). Problems in human relations can be analyzed, interpreted, and given meaning only within given social and ethical contexts. Accordingly, it *does* make a difference—arguments to the contrary notwithstanding—what the psychiatrist's socioethical orientations happen to be; for these will influence his ideas on what is wrong with the patient, what deserves comment or interpretation, in what possible directions change might be desirable, and so forth. Even in medicine proper, these factors play a role, as for instance, in the divergent orientations which physicians, depending on their religious affiliations, have toward such things as birth control and therapeutic abortion. Can anyone really believe that a psychotherapist's ideas concerning religious belief, slavery, or other similar issues play no role in his practical work? If they do make a difference, what are we to infer from it? Does it not seem reasonable that we ought to have different psychiatric therapies—each expressly recognized for the ethical positions which they embody—for, say, Catholics and Jews, religious persons and agnostics, democrats and communists, white supremacists and Negroes, and so on? Indeed, if we look at how psychiatry is actually practiced today (especially in the United States), we find that people do seek psychiatric help in accordance with their social status and ethical beliefs (Hollingshead & Redlich, 1958). This should really not surprise us more than being told that practicing Catholics rarely frequent birth control clinics.

The foregoing position which holds that contemporary psychotherapists deal with problems in living, rather than with mental illnesses and their cures, stands in opposition to a currently prevalent claim, according to which mental illness is just as "real" and "objective" as bodily illness. This is a confusing claim since it is never known exactly what is meant by such words as "real" and "objective." I suspect, however, that what is intended by the proponents of this view is to create the idea in the popular mind that mental illness is some sort of disease entity, like an infection or a malignancy. If this were true, one could *catch* or *get* a "mental illness," one might *have* or *harbor* it, one might *transmit* it to others, and finally one could get *rid* of it. In my opinion, there is not a shred of evidence to support this idea. To the contrary, all the evidence is the other way and supports the view that what people now call mental illnesses are for the most part *communications* expressing unacceptable ideas, often framed, moreover, in an unusual idiom. The scope of this essay allows me to do no more than mention this alternative theoretical approach to this problem (Szasz, 1957c).

This is not the place to consider in detail the similarities and differences between bodily and mental illnesses. It shall suffice for us here to emphasize only one important difference between them: namely, that whereas bodily disease refers to public, physicochemical occurrences, the notion of mental illness is used to codify relatively more private, sociopsychological happenings of which the observer (diagnostician) forms a part. In other words, the psychiatrist does not stand *apart* from what he observes, but is, in Harry Stack Sullivan's apt words, a "participant observer." This means that he is *committed* to some picture of what he considers reality—and to what he thinks society considers reality—and he observes and judges the patient's behavior in the light of these considerations. This touches on our earlier observation that the notion of mental symptom itself implies a comparison between observer and observed, psychiatrist and patient. This is so obvious that I may be charged with belaboring trivialities. Let me therefore say once more that my aim in presenting this argument was expressly to criticize and counter a prevailing contemporary tendency to deny the moral aspects of psychiatry (and psychotherapy) and to substitute for them allegedly value-free medical considerations. Psychotherapy, for example, is being widely practiced as though it entailed nothing other than restoring the patient from a state of mental sickness to one of mental health. While it is generally accepted that mental illness has something to do with man's social (or interpersonal) relations, it is paradoxically maintained that problems of values (that is, of ethics) do not arise in this process.[1] Yet, in one sense, much of psychotherapy may revolve around nothing other than the elucidation and weighing of goals and values—many of which may be mutually contradictory—and the means whereby they might best be harmonized, realized, or relinquished.

The diversity of human values and the methods by means of which they may be realized is so vast, and many of them remain so unacknowledged, that they cannot fail but lead to conflicts in human relations. Indeed, to say that human relations at all levels—from mother to child, through husband and wife, to nation and nation—are fraught with stress, strain, and disharmony is, once again, making the obvious explicit. Yet, what may be obvious may be also poorly understood. This I think is the case here. For it seems to me that—at least in our scientific theories of behavior—we have failed to *accept* the simple fact that human relations are inherently fraught with difficulties and that to make them even relatively harmonious requires much patience and hard work. I submit that the idea of mental illness is now being put to work to obscure certain difficulties which at present may be inherent—not that they need be unmodifiable—in the social intercourse of persons. If this is true, the concept functions as a disguise; for instead of calling attention to conflicting human needs, aspirations, and values, the notion of mental illness provides an amoral and impersonal "thing" (an "illness") as an explanation for *problems in living* (Szasz, 1959). We may recall in this connection that not so long ago it was devils and witches who were held responsible for men's problems in social living. The belief in mental illness, as something other than man's trouble in getting along with his fellow man, is the proper heir to the belief in demonology and witchcraft. Mental illness exists or is "real" in exactly the same sense in which witches existed or were "real."

[1]Freud went so far as to say that: "I consider ethics to be taken for granted. Actually I have never done a mean thing" (Jones, 1957, p. 247). This surely is a strange thing to say for someone who has studied man as a social being as closely as did Freud. I mention it here to show how the notion of "illness" (in the case of psychoanalysis, "psychopathology," or "mental illness") was used by Freud—and by most of his followers—as a means for classifying certain forms of human behavior as falling within the scope of medicine, and hence (by *fiat*) outside that of ethics!

CHOICE, RESPONSIBILITY, AND PSYCHIATRY

While I have argued that mental illnesses do not exist, I obviously did not imply that the social and psychological occurrences to which this label is currently being attached also do not exist. Like the personal and social troubles which people had in the Middle Ages, they are real enough. It is the labels we give them that concerns us and, having labelled them, what we do about them. While I cannot go into the ramified implications of this problem here, it is worth noting that a demonologic conception of problems in living gave rise to therapy along theological lines. Today, a belief in mental illness implies—nay, requires—therapy along medical or psychotherapeutic lines.

What is implied in the line of thought set forth here is something quite different. I do not intend to offer a new conception of "psychiatric illness" nor a new form of "therapy." My aim is more modest and yet also more ambitious. It is to suggest that the phenomena now called mental illnesses be looked at afresh and more simply, that they be removed from the category of illnesses, and that they be regarded as the expressions of man's struggle with the problem of *how* he should live. The last mentioned problem is obviously a vast one, its enormity reflecting not only man's inability to cope with his environment, but even more his increasing self-reflectiveness.

By problems in living, then, I refer to that truly explosive chain reaction which began with man's fall from divine grace by partaking of the fruit of the tree of knowledge. Man's awareness of himself and of the world about him seems to be a steadily expanding one, bringing in its wake an ever larger *burden of understanding* (an expression borrowed from Susanne Langer, 1953). *This burden,* then, *is to be expected and must not be misinterpreted.* Our only *rational* means for lightening it is *more understanding,* and appropriate *action* based on such understanding. The main alternative lies in acting as though the burden were not what in fact we perceive it to be and taking refuge in an outmoded theological view of man. In the latter view, man does not fashion his life and much of his world about him, but merely lives out his fate in a world created by superior beings. This may logically lead to pleading nonresponsibility in the face of seemingly unfathomable problems and difficulties. Yet, if man fails to take increasing responsibility for his actions, individually as well as collectively, it seems unlikely that some higher power or being would assume this task and carry this burden for him. Moreover, this seems hardly the proper time in human history for obscuring the issue of man's responsibility for his actions by hiding it behind the skirt of an all-explaining conception of mental illness.

CONCLUSIONS

I have tried to show that the notion of mental illness has outlived whatever usefulness it might have had and that it now functions merely as a convenient myth. As such, it is a true heir to religious myths in general, and to the belief in witchcraft in particular; the role of all these belief-systems was to act as *social tranquilizers,* thus encouraging the hope that mastery of certain specific problems may be achieved by means of substitutive (symbolic-magical) operations. The notion of mental illness thus serves mainly to obscure the everyday fact that life for most people is a continuous struggle, not for biological survival, but for a "place in the sun," "peace of mind," or some other human value. For man aware of himself and of the world about him, once the needs for preserving the body (and perhaps the race) are more or less satisfied, the problem arises as to what he should do with himself. Sustained adherence to the myth of mental illness allows people to avoid facing this problem, believing that mental health, conceived as the absence of mental illness, automatically insures the making of right and safe choices in one's conduct of life. But the facts are all the other way. It is the making of good choices in life that others regard, retrospectively, as good mental health!

The myth of mental illness encourages us, moreover, to believe in its logical corollary: that social intercourse would be harmonious, satisfying, and the secure basis of a "good life" were it not for the disrupting influences of mental illness or "psychopathology." The potentiality for universal human happiness, in this form at least, seems to me but another example of the I-wish-it-were-true type of fantasy. I do believe that human happiness or well-being on a hitherto unimaginably large scale, and not just for a select few, is possible. This goal could be achieved, however, only at the cost of many men, and not just a few being willing and able to tackle their personal, social, and ethical conflicts. This means having the courage and integrity to forego waging battles on false fronts, finding solutions for substitute problems—for instance, fighting the battle of stomach acid and chronic fatigue instead of facing up to a marital conflict.

Our adversaries are not demons, witches, fate, or mental illness. We have no enemy whom we can fight, exorcise, or dispel by "cure." What we do have are *problems in living*—whether these be biologic, economic, political, or sociopsychological. In this essay I was concerned only with problems belonging in the last mentioned category, and within this group mainly with those pertaining to moral values. The field to which modern psychiatry addresses itself is vast, and I made no effort to encompass it all. My argument was limited to the proposition that mental illness is a myth, whose function it is to disguise and thus render more palatable the bitter pill of moral conflicts in human relations.

References

HOLLINGSHEAD, A. B., & REDLICH, F. C.   *Social Class and Mental Illness.* New York: Wiley, 1958.

JONES, E.   *The Life and Work of Sigmund Freud.* Vol. III. New York: Basic Books, 1957.

LANGER, S. K.   *Philosophy in a New Key.* New York: Mentor Books, 1953.

PETERS, R. S.   *The Concept of Motivation.* London: Routledge & Kegan Paul, 1958.

SZASZ, T. S.   Malingering: "Diagnosis" or social condemnation? *AMA Arch. Neurol. Psychiat.,* 1956, **76,** 432–443.

SZASZ, T. S.   *Pain and Pleasure: A Study of Bodily Feelings.* New York: Basic Books, 1957.   (a)

SZASZ, T. S.   The problem of psychiatric nosology: A contribution to a situational analysis of psychiatric operations. *Amer. J. Psychiat.,* 1957 **114,** 405–413.   (b)

SZASZ, T. S.   On the theory of psychoanalytic treatment. *Int. J. Psycho-Anal.,* 1957, **38,** 166–182.   (c)

SZASZ, T. S.   Psychiatry, ethics and the criminal law. *Columbia Law Rev.,* 1958, **58,** 183–198.

SZASZ, T. S.   Moral conflict and psychiatry. *Yale Rev.,* 1959, in press.

A Study of Emotionally Disturbed Children in Santa Barbara County Schools

Norah Clancy and Faith Smitter

A study of the special needs of all elementary children in the Santa Barbara County schools was initiated in March 1952 and completed in October. The reasons for the study were twofold: First, to obtain factual information for the guidance department as to the extent and the nature of the special needs of elementary school children in the county. Secondly, it was hoped that the process of identifying children with special needs and considering their problems would assist the teachers in under-

"A Study of Emotionally Disturbed Children in Santa Barbara County Schools," by Norah Clancy and Faith Smitter, *California Journal of Educational Research,* Vol. IV, No. 5, November 1953, pp. 209–218.

standing these children and might lead to desirable changes in the teaching practice.

PROCEDURES OF THE STUDY

To insure uniform procedures in reporting children with special needs, the Bureau of Special Education of the California State Department of Education and the supervisory and guidance staffs of the County Superintendent's Office and the Public Health Nurses assisted the teachers in identifying such children. This assistance was given to teachers either individually or through the several regional meetings held throughout the county. To further reduce variations in teachers' reports and the possible effects of the teachers' own personalities upon their judgment, descriptions from the research literature regarding children's problems were given teachers as guides to identification of children with special needs. In order to give the study further validity the teachers were asked to describe the behavior which indicated a special need on the part of each child listed. Any child whose behavior according to the description given by the teacher did not seem to warrant inclusion in the study was not listed. The study included children whose behavior placed them in the following categories:

Gifted and talented children	Serious reading difficulties
Mentally retarded	Special family conditions
Emotionally disturbed	Serious health problems
Defective speech	

A summary report of the total study appeared in the March 1953 issue of this Journal. This article is a report on the findings of children who were identified by teachers as being seriously emotionally disturbed.

RELATED RESEARCH

During the past two decades a tremendous amount of research has been published regarding the emotional difficulties of children. The perspective of related research gives direction to the study of any problem and throws significant light upon the findings. The following factors stand out in the results of these studies as significant in relation to the emotional disturbance of children.

Parental influence as an important source of behavior maladjustments among children has been studied by a number of investigators. Levy (1) studied the effect of excessive mothering on children. In his now well-known book entitled *Maternal Overprotection,* Levy emphasized that children who have indulgent overprotective mothers have a difficult time in their emotional adjustment. When a mother does not require respect and submission to ordinary household tasks this weakness on her part produces disobedience and impudence in the children at home accompanied by bullying, fighting and rebellious behavior at school and with age mates.

During the late 1930's, several students of child behavior (2,3,4) were impressed by the frequency with which children who were delinquent seemed to have no deep feelings for anyone. These children were difficult to treat, and were found to have seriously disturbed relationships with their mothers during their early years.

Since these early studies, effects of deprivation of mother love in early years have been studied by a large number of pediatricians, psychologists, and child psychiatrists. Goldfarb (5), Spitz (6), Bakwin (7), Gesell and Armatruda (8) are in agreement from their studies of infants and young children that deprivation of mother love can have a seriously adverse effect on the emotional well-being of children. Goldfarb points out that the earlier the age at which depriving experiences are initiated and the longer the duration, the greater the extent the maladjustment is likely to be.

In studying the emotional aspects of the parent-child relationship several investigators have studied the effect upon children when the father is absent from home. These studies, particularly those of Bach (9), Stolz (10), Sears and Pitner (11), seem to point to the fact that when the father is absent from the home that children have less tendency to aggression than children whose fathers were at home. With the fathers at home, there is a possibility, according to Stolz "that even in America, fathers may be more punishing than mothers, and the conflicts in mother and father discipline may become frustrating for young children."

Several investigators have studied the broken home as an influence upon the emotional well-being of children. Many studies show that children from broken homes develop less favorably than do others who are not deprived of a normal home life. However, as Wallenstein (12) has pointed out, too many factors are inherent in the situation to give validity to the concept that the broken home per se is a cause of emotional maladjustment. Parents' conflicts, parents' emotional immaturity, and the deprivation of affection are likely to be important influences in a broken home.

The effect on the emotional well-being of young children of a mother's employment outside the home has been the basis for numerous popular articles and some research studies. The reasons why mothers seek employment outside the home seems to be the key to whether or not children are adversely affected. It has been pointed out in several studies (13, 14) that it is not alone the time which a mother spends with her child, but the emotional response she gives him within the time spent that is most significant. Certain mothers are better mothers because they work. They are happier and therefore are able to give greater emotional gratification to children.

Many other causal factors exist besides a child's relationship with his parents which contribute to emotional maladjustment. It has been well established that children who come from homes in which a foreign language is predominantly spoken frequently have problems of an emotional nature. Factors in the school situation itself often contribute to or increase children's maladjustment. As Rivlin (15) has pointed out, the exaggerated importance which schools attach to marks, the overemphasis placed on speed, overemphasis on subject matter, and unnecessary examinations are procedures which frequently contribute to the emotional disturbance of children.

The emotional factors in learning are being studied with increasing frequency by psychologists. Failure to learn what is expected may lead to frustration or fear. Many studies have been made on reading failure as a cause of emotional difficulty, but as Robinson (16) points out emotional difficulties may contribute to reading disability in the beginning and may in turn cause further blocks in learning which in turn further intensifies the frustration. Gates (17) in a recent summary of studies of emotional and personality problems in relation to reading disability, expresses the opinion that emotional problems are present in about 75 per cent of retarded readers, but that in only one-fourth of these is it a sole cause of the disability.

FINDINGS REGARDING EMOTIONALLY DISTURBED CHILDREN

Santa Barbara County teachers reported 846 children or 11 per cent of the school population as emotionally disturbed. Of this number 544 are boys and 302 girls, showing a consistent difference in the problems of boys and girls. Not all school districts reported the same degree of emotional disturbance among the children. Certain school districts reported as high as 35 per cent disturbed, while others as low as 5 per cent. In interpreting these figures certain factors must be taken into account. Districts vary in living conditions, community problems, and recreational facilities, which affect the emotional health of children. Teachers also vary in their sensitivity to children's problems and their awareness of children's needs. School procedures vary with regard to their adaptability to the needs of children. However, on the whole the report of emotional disturbance shows a certain consistency in the per cent listed by grade. The following table shows the number and per cent of emotionally disturbed children reported at each grade level:

TABLE 1
NUMBER AND PERCENT OF EMOTIONALLY DISTURBED CHILDREN
REPORTED IN EACH GRADE

GRADE	NUMBER OF EMOTIONALLY DISTURBED CHILDREN		PERCENT OF THE TOTAL GRADE ENROLLMENT
	Boys	Girls	
Kindergarten	33	18	5
First Grade	71	51	11
Second Grade	75	45	11
Third Grade	76	43	11
Fourth Grade	78	41	12
Fifth Grade	57	34	11
Sixth Grade	48	28	11
Seventh Grade	33	20	10
Eighth Grade	47	16	13
Special Training Classes	22	5	21
No Grade Reported	4	1	
Total	544	302	

The above table raises several significant questions: "Is the low per cent of children described as emotionally disturbed in the kindergarten due to an actual smaller per cent of emotionally disturbed at this age level?" or "Do kindergarten procedures allow for greater flexibility with a consequent fewer number of adult-child conflicts or child-child conflicts?" The per cent of emotionally disturbed children in the eighth grade shows a slight increase over other grades. This may be due to the problems of adolescence or to community and school pressures, which have increased at this age level. The high per cent of children who are emotionally disturbed in the special training classes is significant. The emotional disturbance of many mentally deficient children seems to be inherent in the problem of mental deficiency. Although 21 per cent of mentally retarded children enrolled in special training classes are reported as emotionally disturbed, 42 per cent of the mentally retarded enrolled in the regular grades were reported as emotionally disturbed. These findings would seem to indicate that mentally retarded children adjust more satisfactorily in special training classes than they do in the regular classroom. The results of these findings also are in agreement with the research on the adjustment of mentally retarded children who are in the regular classroom.

Less than half or 344 children reported because of emotional disturbance had IQ's recorded. The following table shows the distribution of IQ's of the emotionally disturbed children for whom test data were available:

TABLE 2
NUMBER AND IQ DISTRIBUTION OF
EMOTIONALLY DISTURBED CHILDREN

IQ	NUMBER
140 +	3
130 — 139	2
120 — 129	12
110 — 119	27
100 — 109	57
90 — 99	68
80 — 89	83
70 — 79	56
60 — 69	31
50 — 59	3
— 49	2
Median — 89	

No IQ given for 502

Table 2 shows that emotional disturbance is not associated solely with a particular IQ level. Deficient, average, and superior children are reported as emotionally disturbed. However, the median IQ of 89 does indicate that dullness and emotional disturbance have a positive relationship. Teachers should consider the mental hygiene hazards of dullness and should assist the dull child to develop all the competencies possible in meeting the problems of life.

Of the children who were reported as emotionally disturbed 272 or 32 per cent came from broken homes. This is more than twice the per cent of children in the total school population who come from broken homes. Obviously, a relationship exists between a broken home and an emotionally disturbed child. Whether the same factors that cause the broken home also cause the emotional disturbance of the children is not known. However, it is clear that a broken home is a danger signal for teachers. Teachers should be aware of the strains in relationships in a broken home, the anxieties and insecurities which these create in children. The knowledge of a broken home should indicate to a teacher that the child coming from such a home needs more reassurance and support than children from normal homes.

Twenty-three per cent or 194 of the emotionally disturbed children had mothers who worked on a full-time basis. Only 14 per cent of the total school population had mothers who worked full time. These figures indicate a relationship between the full-time employment of mothers and the emotional disturbance of children. Again, it is not clear from these data whether the employment of mothers actually caused the disturbance or whether the same factors that caused the emotional disturbance of children also caused the necessity for the employment of mothers. But again, the full-time employment of a mother should be a signal to teachers that a child whose mother is employed needs greater support, greater reassurance, and more attention if emotional problems are to be avoided

Of the children reported as being emotionally disturbed 21 per cent or 178 were reported to come from homes having conditions inimical to the welfare of these children. Alcoholism, overcrowded conditions, and poverty were the most frequent conditions described by teachers.

Only 5 per cent of the total child population was described as coming from homes in which such serious conditions prevail. Obviously, a positive relationship exists between emotional disturbance and serious home conditions, although again it is not clear just what this relationship implies. However, information on the child's cumulative record indicating that such conditions exist in the child's home is a signal to teachers that special compensations must be made at school to overcome the inadequacy of the home life.

A comparison of the per cent of children reported as emotionally disturbed, who have unusual home conditions, and the per cent of others of the school population having similar home conditions is shown in Table 3.

TABLE 3
A Comparison of the Per Cent of Emotionally Disturbed Children Who Have Unusual Home Conditions to Others of the School Population with Similar Home Conditions

Home Conditions	Per Cent of Emotionally Disturbed	Per Cent of Others
Broken Homes	36	11
Mothers Employed Full Time	23	12
Serious Neglect or Deprivation	21	3
Foreign Language Background	20	10

Analysis of the types of broken homes from which emotionally disturbed children were reported yielded the information in Table 4.

TABLE 4
The Number and Per Cent of Children from Certain Types of Broken Homes Who Showed Emotional Disturbance

Type of Broken Home	Number of Children	Per Cent
Foster Parents	21	30
Adopted	17	45
Mother Alone	59	24
Father Alone	11	30
Stepparent and Mother or Father	80	21
Relatives and Mother or Father	30	33
Relatives Alone	47	29
No Type Stated	47	
Total	312	

Although the numbers are small, the above findings seem to indicate that children who are adopted show a higher per cent of emotional disturbances than children from other types of broken homes. Children

from homes in which a real parent has remarried show a lower incidence
of emotional disturbance than those from other broken homes.

Teachers' descriptions of all the emotional disturbances reported fell
into the categories shown in Table 5.

TABLE 5
TYPES AND PER CENT OF EMOTIONAL DISTURBANCE REPORTED

TYPES OF DISTURBANCE	BOYS		GIRLS	
	Number	Per Cent	Number	Per Cent
Withdrawn	132	24	131	43
Unable to Get Along with Age Mates	162	30	95	31
Aggressive	134	25	43	14
Immature	74	12	44	15
Excessive Nervousness	85	16	27	9
Short Attention	82	15	21	7

In addition to these categories, teachers mentioned such behavior as
overly conscientious and docile, extremely negative, overly interested in
sex, moody, erratic, confused, no interest in school, cheats, lies, steals,
cruel, enuretic, epileptic, and the like. The major complaints by teachers
were withdrawal from the group with related fears and anxieties and
inability to get along with others. Wickman's[1] study of some twenty-five
years ago pointed out that teachers mentioned the aggressive and belligerent child most frequently as a problem. The fact that Santa Barbara
teachers described the withdrawn and fearful child most frequently indicates a greater sensitivity on the part of modern teachers to the mental
hygiene problems of children than that shown by teachers twenty-five
years ago.

TEACHERS' COMMENTS

The following comments by teachers are typical of the problems of
children reported as emotionally disturbed:

"Inclined to be noisy, inconsiderate, overly aggressive at school. Antagonizes others
in group. Annoys and interrupts classroom procedures."

"Aggressive toward girls. Takes toys and money. Always in difficulty with some member of the class."

"Dreamy and inattentive in school. Immature. Does not seem interested in group
play."

"Timid and insecure. Child fearful of dress in painting or other activities. Was se-

[1] E. K. Wickman, *Children's Behavior and Teachers' Attitudes* (New York: The
Commonwealth Fund, Division of Publications, 1928), pp. 15–17.

verely beaten by mother at one time. Worried and harassed expression. Does not join freely and happily in group activities. Inhibited and self restricted. Plays only after persuasion and then with anxious air about clothes."

"Class rejects child. Numerous serious fights. Child 'hates' school, particularly arithmetic where performance is poor."

"When talking to adults, uses baby talk. Is 'sneaky.' Always probing adult's motives. Constantly fabricates and uses alibis. Fights a good deal. Bed wetting (father reports)."

"Uninterested, bored, listless. At times sullen. Anti-social, 'light fingered,' lies, copies work, seems lazy. Does not care about learning. Hits, pinches, trips up children, throws rocks. Bad influence in group as younger boys imitate and follow. Girls seek him out in games for partners."

"Sucks thumb. Can't sit still. Talks constantly. Overly dependent. Complete busybody and tattletale. Not well liked or chosen by mates."

"Boy is *very* restless, nervous, aggressive, teases and torments other children. Shows need for affection. Academic progress surprisingly good."

"Can't stand discipline. Flies into a temper. Gets attention by pestering all near him — then can't take pestering in return. Used to run away from school when disciplined. No sense of family security."

"He feels insecure. He is a cry baby. Doesn't concentrate well. Will not learn unless material is force-fed to him."

"Has 'far away in the fog' air about him. Can't get through the fog to teach him. Lives with mother. Father was in mental hospital."

"He is a very large boy. He uses his size to pick on others. He likes girls, but mother forbids any association with girls. He is not liked by classmates."

"Child is deeply disturbed emotionally. Poor coordination. Shaky voice. Very nervous. Is so emotionally rattled that he accomplishes little in school. Disliked by other children because of showing off and inability to do anything without breaking or destroying it."

"In a daze. Completely unaware of everything around him. Accepted by other children but pays little attention to them."

"Child pale and listless but works to capacity. Oblivious of other children. Usually shunned because of body odor."

"Loud talking disrupts class often. Attracts attention with unusual hats and ties. Exaggerates actions."

"Doesn't do his work. Bothers others. Always trying to get even with someone."

"Overly interested in sex. Writes compositions that drip with gore. Sketches murders, knives, guns, fires, blood flowing. Sly, not always to be trusted. Is a daydreamer. Has friends among boys. Girls find him too 'bloody' for their tastes. Draws all over his papers."

"The world is too much for him. Cannot do schoolwork. Just doesn't know the score. Tries to look like a student. A perfect picture of defeat."

"Bitter because she is a Mexican. Thinks the world is against her. Learning is affected because she broods instead of working. Has the idea that no one would be her friend — so why try to make friends?"

"Hearing loss. Wears big bulky hearing aid. Lack of knowledge of how to work it. Batteries often dead. Fears to try anything without a great deal of personal help."

CHILDREN FROM HOMES USING FOREIGN LANGUAGE

An analysis was made of the problems which children present, who come from homes in which a foreign language is spoken. Table 6 indicates the per cent of children from homes in which a foreign language is usually spoken who have such problems and the per cent of children from homes in which English is spoken who are reported as having similar problems.

TABLE 6
PER CENT OF CHILDREN HAVING PROBLEMS
FROM FOREIGN- AND ENGLISH-SPEAKING HOMES

	CHILDREN FROM FOREIGN-SPEAKING HOMES	CHILDREN FROM ENGLISH-SPEAKING HOMES
Gifted	0	0.9
Mentally Deficient	16	3
Emotionally Disturbed	20	10
Speech Defective	5	2
Reading Problems	3	1
Receiving Free Nutrition	9	1
Need Free Nutrition	2	0.2
Family on State Aid	9	1
Mothers Employed	18	14
Broken Homes	24	14
Serious Home Conditions	20	3
Health Problems	22	10

The above data make it apparent that these children have many more problems than children from homes in which English is usually spoken. In not one area investigated did the children from foreign-speaking homes have fewer problems than those of the English-speaking children. Obviously, these bilingual children have definite handicaps to adjustment and learning.

IMPLICATIONS OF THE STUDY

The above findings indicate that emotional disturbances of children are frequent enough to constitute a major problem in education. It is also apparent that an approach to these problems cannot be made solely on an individual study basis, as a clinical approach to the problems of 11 per cent of the child population is not feasible. Nearly every teacher in the county reported one or more emotionally disturbed children in his classroom. These facts indicate that teachers must be assisted to deepen their understandings of the causes of behavior and the factors involved in emotional disturbance. The implications are for psychological service which will direct its attention not only to the study of children with serious problems but primarily to the in-service education of teachers in child growth and motivation.

Implications also are inherent in these data for education on an upper grade and high school level directed toward preparation for family life, an understanding of self, and an understanding of the causes of disturbed behavior. Only through an educational program which includes such a mental health orientation can a comprehensive approach be made to such a large problem.

Educators should direct their attention toward eliminating school procedures and curricula which contribute to anxieties, fears, and frustrations of children. It is probable that many emotional disturbances may originate in the home. However, the school should evaluate its program to determine whether it contributes to or compensates for the inadequacies of children's out-of-school lives.

Bibliography

1. LEVY, DAVID, *Maternal Overprotection*. New York: Columbia University Press, 1943, 417 p.

2. GLUECK, S. and GLUECK, E. T., *One Thousand Juvenile Delinquents*. Cambridge: Harvard University Press, 1934, 341 p.

3. ARMSTRONG, C. P., *660 Runaway Boys*. Boston: D. C. Heath, 1932, 208 p.

4. STOTT, D. H., *Delinquency and Human Nature*. Dunfermline, Scotland: Connely Park House, 1950, 460 p.

5. GOLDFARB, W., "Variations in Adolescent Adjustment of Institutionally Reared Children," *American Journal of Orthopsychiatry*, XVII, July, 1947, 449 p.

6. SPITZ, R. A. and WOLF, E. K. M., "The Smiling Response: A Contribution to the Ontogenesis of Social Relations," *Genetic Psychology Monograph*, XXIV, Aug., 1946, 57 p.

7. BAKWIN, H., "Loneliness in Infants," *American Journal Diseases of Children*, LXIII, Jan., 1942, P. 30.

8. GESELL, ARNOLD and ARMATRUDA, C., *Developmental Diagnosis: Normal and Abnormal Child Development: Clinical Methods and Pediatric Applications*, 2nd ed. New York: Hoeber Co., 1947, 496 p.

9. BACH, GEORGE, "Father-Fantasies and Father-Typing in Father Separated Children," *Child Development*, XVII, Mar.-June, 1946. p. 63.

10. STOLZ, LOIS M., "The Effect of Mobilization and War on Children," *Social Casework*, XXXII, No. 3, April, 1951. p. 143.

11. SEARS, ROBERT and PITNER, MARGARET, "Effect of Father Separation on Preschool Children's Doll Play," *Child Development*, XVII, Dec., 1946. p. 219.

12. WALLENSTEIN, N., *Character and Personality of Children from Broken Homes*, Contributions to Education, No. 721. New York: Teachers College, Columbia University, 1937. 86 pp.

13. JOSSELYN, IRENE M. and GOLDMAN, RUTH S., "Should Mothers Work?," *Social Service Review,* XXIII, Mar., 1949. p. 74.

14. ESSIG, M. and MORGAN, D. W., "Adjustment of Adolescent Daughters of Employed Women to Family Life," *Journal of Educational Psychology,* XXXVII, 1946. p. 219.

15. RIVLIN, HARRY N., *Educating for Adjustment,* New York: D. Appleton-Century Co., 1936. 419 pp.

16. ROBINSON, HELEN, *Why Pupils Fail in Reading,* Chicago: University of Chicago Press, 1946. 257 pp.

17. GATES, ARTHUR I., "The Role of Personality Maladjustment in Reading Disability," *Journal of Genetic Psychology,* LIX, Sept., 1941. p. 77.

A Developmental Study of the Behavior Problems of Normal Children Between Twenty-One Months and Fourteen Years

Jean W. Macfarlane, Lucile Allen, and Marjorie P. Honzik

SUMMARY AND FINAL COMMENTS

The major objective of this report has been to present materials on the frequencies of certain behaviors labeled "problems," found in a sample of fairly representative children. We felt when we began the study that there had been gross overgeneralization from highly selected samples of "problem children" and believed that facts on a sample of children selected on a nonproblem basis would, in conjunction with the findings of selected-for-problems samples, give a more balanced picture and reduce current overgeneralization. A more basic objective, but one subsidiary to the main object of this report, has been to sharpen personality development theory. Our larger undertaking is committed to this end, but we hope that even this report will raise questions about some aspects of contemporary personality development theory.

The sample used as the basis of this report is the control or uncontaminated group of our larger study. It was selected as being more representative than the group in which intervention had occurred. With

From *Behavior Problems of Normal Children,* by Jean W. Macfarlane, Lucile Allen, and Marjorie P. Honzik. Copyright 1954, University of California Press.

respect to its representativeness, the following facts should be stated. It is a subsample of every third child born in Berkeley, California, during an eighteen-month period from January 1, 1928, through June 30, 1929. At the beginning of the study, before sample shrinkage during fourteen years, it represented families of somewhat higher education and, being young families, somewhat lower per capita income than the population at large. By age 14, the last year used in this report, more of the lower socioeconomic level had dropped out so the sample becomes more biased toward the high-middle socioeconomic-educational level. The size of the group studied also presents limits to generalizability, especially in the later years, although limitations are not so great as if these were completely different cross-section samples. The fact is that for the per-centage frequency figures, other fairly representative samples would unquestionably vary somewhat from these, but these figures are a much needed beginning on the long road of filling a major gap of empirical fact with respect to nonpathological groups.

The method was that of simple, open-ended inventory questioning of mothers. The data, therefore, are exclusively from mothers' reports which depend upon what they were able to observe and willing to report. One of the important results of this study is that from this non-going-beneath-the-surface method, significant facts were secured as determined by a number of criteria. This makes for greater accessibility of much needed data on a larger sample than ours so that greater generalizability is possible.

The methods of data organization were based upon the development of empirically derived scales of descriptive continua which permitted the securing of changing distributions of behavior over time, so that ages could be compared in degree and frequency of specified behaviors. Problem and nonproblem categorization was obtained by the establishment of sensible (we hope) but arbitrary cutoff points on these continua.

Our findings will be very briefly summarized. Problem frequencies were of five varieties: (a) problems which declined with age; (b) problems which increased with age; (c) problems which reached a peak and subsided; (d) problems which showed high frequencies, early declined, and later rose again; and (e) problems which showed little or no relationship to age.

(a) Among the problems which declined in frequency with age there were differences in the age at which, and the rate at which, these declinations occurred. Also the declinations on many problems varied with sex and sib order (first- and non-first-born). Among early and rapid drops in frequency were the problems associated with *elimination* controls. *Speech problems, fears,* and *thumbsucking* started their declines somewhat later. At still a later age, and at a slower rate, a decline occurred in *overactivity* and such explosive behaviors as *destructiveness* and *tempers*. Especially with the boys the decline in *tempers* was gradual, a third of them still having temper explosions at year 13.

(b) Only one problem increased systematically with age, namely, *nailbiting,* which had reached its peak and had begun to subside at the end of pubescence in girls and, unquestionably, would have declined for boys had our data extended beyond 14 years.

(c) Problems which reached a peak and subsided had among them *insufficient appetite* associated with the high level of communicable disease, and *lying,* which was tried out as a coping device and then given up for other more effective methods, or occurred in a form less detectable by mothers.

(d) The fourth grouping, which was characteristic of many personality problems, showed two peak elevations of frequency. Often these were at the preschool level and again at late pubescence; such were *restless sleep, disturbing dreams, physical timidity, irritability,* and *attention demanding.* Often the first peak occurred at the age of entering school and at the beginning of adolescence; such were *overdependence, somberness,* and *jealousy,* and in boys, *food finickiness.*

(e) A problem which showed little or no relationship to age after it was once established, was *oversensitiveness,* which, for the girls, stayed up throughout the age period studies; and which, for the boys, flourished until social pressures to "be a man" saw this behavior dramatically drop after age 11. In the section dealing with specific problem patterns, we discussed *oversensitiveness* in detail as one of the most successful coping devices the child evolved in his dealings with parents.

With respect to sib order (first- and non-first-born) substantial differences were found. The first-born boys showed more withdrawing and internalizing patterns, the non-firsts more overt, aggressive, and competitive patterns. The second-born girls exceeded first-born girls in only two respects, *thumbsucking* and *oversensitiveness.* When the first-born were girls, life appeared more difficult than for the other three groups. They showed more problems and more incompatible combinations of both aggression and withdrawing behavior. We speculated about the possible explanation for these differences, but the fact emerges that personality research needs much more detailed investigation into the situational factors and combination of factors including interpersonal relations, same sex and cross-sex expectancies, and child-training processes, disruptions and changes in personal relationships, if we are to point up the important factors in personality development which these simple sib order findings have thrown into relief.

Predictive significance as measured by interage correlations reveals several facts of interest. One is how nonpersistent for a long age span most problems are. Even for adjacent age levels, no correlation is higher than .86, which indicates shifts even for short periods. The most predictive for the 5- to 14-, or 7- to 14-year periods were: *overdependence, somberness,* and *irritability.* It is of interest that considerably higher interage correlations were found for longer periods, for example between 6 and 11 years and 7 and 14, than between shorter periods such as 8 and 11 and 9 and 12, on several personality variables. We interpreted this to mean that events internal and external had caused children to shift around 11 and 12, later to return to more characteristic patterns. These findings are of interest since they are in contrast to our interage correlations for I.Q. where the greater the distance between ages, the lower the correlations.

We have analyzed the interrelationships among problems at two year levels only, namely, 5 and 12 on fourteen problems. It was found that certain problems had more significant behavioral correlates than did others. *Irritability* (a reactivity variable) led in number of correlates, closely followed by *overdependence, moodiness, negativism, somberness,* and *reserve.* Further, many more significant correlates occurred at year 5 for girls than for boys, whereas the reverse was true at 12 when, for the same fourteen problems, boys led substantially in the number of significant correlates. This permitted us the statement that tensional ages for boys and girls apparently vary and led us to speculate about the differential cultural pressures upon boys and girls with respect to age demands for inhibition of certain overt patterns of reaction or expression, which in turn is associated in the two sexes with different age periods of tension while internalization is being learned. All this may be related to biological differences that make possible the earlier establishment of overt conformity patterns in girls.

The other findings relating to problems of health, nutritional, and maturational status, I.Q., and I.Q. variability, and to characteristics of the mothers are too fragmentary and too unsystematically covered in this report to summarize. Even these fragmentary data seemed worth including if for no other reason than to point out the multifactor nature of personality and behavior dynamics, and to emphasize the necessity of avoiding overgeneralization at the present state of our limited knowledge, and of avoiding premature theoretical closure until, from more samples of growing children, a representative sample of biosocial facts is available and integrated.

It seems to us that more (and perhaps better conceived and executed) longitudinal studies than this pioneering attempt are essential if we really are to understand the relationships of early experiences and behavior to later behavior and personality and the processes by which stable personality patterns are achieved, and to understand the critical combinations of biosocial facts throughout the developmental period which disrupt or facilitate the progression to effective maturity.

Epilogue

May we pay our respects to the adaptive capacity of the human organism, born in a very unfinished and singularly dependent state into a highly complex and not too sensible world. Unless handicapped by inadequate structure and health and impossible and capricious learning situations, he threads his way to some measure of stable and characteristic patterning. We see, even in the raw frequency figures presented in this report, the variety of coping devices he uses for his complex set of tasks. He starts out with overt expression of his needs and feelings and attempts immediate and direction solutions to his problems. Many of his overt and direct problem-solving attempts are not tolerated, so he learns when necessary to side-step, to evade, to withdraw, to get hurt feelings and, also, to submit overtly even while his releases and problem-solving continues internally until controls are established. If he is under fairly stable and not too discontinuous pressures and secures enough approval and support to continue his learning and enough freedom to work out his own compromise overt-covert solutions, he becomes, to use the vernacular, "socialized," and even without this optimum combination, he frequently arrives at stable maturity. When we look at the hazards of the course, we are not sure that we have begun to understand how or why.

We can think of no better way to end this long report than to quote from a very poorly designed and inadequately written master's thesis which ended triumphantly with the following statement: "This thesis can be regarded as successful as it will be stimulating to further research in others, since it leaves so many questions unanswered."

section 3

ANTECEDENTS:
why troubles grow

Having explored attempts to name the psychological troubles that plague human beings as they grow, we now stop to ask how and why these troubles take root and become serious. Although it is impossible to answer this question fully, we can look closely at what precedes the advent of trouble.

It is clear that the human being is an animal who learns and that this learning involves not only the development of psychological strengths but also the development of psychological difficulties. He does not learn in a world by himself, but in a world of other people, many of whom feel that they have some degree of responsibility for him. These people feel their responsibility heavily when he experiences psychological difficulty.

Perhaps this haunting feeling of responsibility explains why we exhibit such a passion for placing blame. Is mental illness the parents' "fault," the child's "bad seed," or a reflection of a "sick society"? Who is to *blame?* We do not try to place blame when a houseplant fails to develop properly. We patiently look for reasons such as amount of moisture, temperature, type of soil, or amount of light. We know that each kind of plant has its own needs. But then, houseplants are not learning animals and therefore do not make us feel so responsible for what happens to them. A family pet makes us feel responsible, but nothing can make us feel as responsible as the troubles of a human infant or child.

If we forget blame and look simply at the conditions that influence human growing, we see a wide assortment of variables that may help or hinder. A child is born into a particular culture that may suit his individual needs relatively well or poorly. Nature or society assigns someone to mother him. His socioeconomic status may well be deter-

41

mined prior to birth. He is a first child, a middle child, or a youngest child. He may be the evidence of his parents' love or bear the responsibility of their attempt to heal an unhappy marriage. He must learn a complex network of social rules without losing his individual identity. He must learn those things that his culture values, whether they interest him or not. There are many possible antecedents to trouble and we cannot change the growing conditions as easily for a human being as we can for a houseplant. We can try to help, but *he* must usually make the adjustment by using his abilities to think and learn. Studies of the antecedents of human troubles are numerous. We present a very small sample here. Researchers in this area are not the blind men who tried to compare their limited understanding of the elephant. Our researchers have only small pieces of understanding, but they know it, and so they patiently relay their information to colleagues and hope that soon the pieces of this elephant of "emotional disturbance" will fall together in a form that can be understood.

Perhaps one day accumulated research evidence will free us to respond to the human as helpfully as we do to the houseplant. With humans it may prove impossible to provide just the right growing conditions, but then humans are known for their great ability to adjust. In Section 4 we shall take a closer look at a few of these human beings trying to adjust.

Effects of Child-Rearing Patterns on Mental Health

Lois Barclay Murphy

We have more of almost anything you want to mention than any other country in the world—more property, more gadgets, more food, more science, more medicine, more vitamins, more music, more school—but we don't have better mental health or freedom from problems.

Longitudinal studies like those of Jean MacFarlane (1) at Berkeley demonstrate for the generation she studied in a carefully selected sample that "behavior of the child's needs and of the relation of the culture problems," as we conceive them in professional work with children, are normal for normal children in a moderate-sized city. If by problems we mean enuresis, speech .difficulties, tempers, nail biting, transitory lying or stealing, no child grows up without any problems. However, since these problems often bother parents more than children, and since they are often outgrown, they do not as such reflect seriously on our children's mental health.

Neurotic disturbances can be inferred only from prolonged or severe problems, an accumulation of more than one, interference in development, or a child's failure to participate in the life of his age group. Maladjustments to society, expressed in delinquency or character disorders, and the more blatant difficulties in growing up which we see in borderline-psychotic and psychotic children are rooted in multiple pathological conditions, interactions between vulnerability in the child, disturbance in the family, and other stressful experiences.

It is a large order to discuss child-rearing patterns in relation to all normal tension outlets and to all extreme threats to mental health. Such considerations are complicated further by the fact that child-rearing patterns are not fixed but vary from one area to another, and from one period to another.

The revolution in child-care patterns in the last 15 years testifies to the fluidity of our culture, its capacity for change, and the opportunity both provide for influencing the culture if we can be sure of our ground in doing so. Difficulties in being sure come from disillusionments resulting from one-sided views of the effects that given patterns have on child development. The rigid routines of feeding, toileting, and sleeping, advocated in the thirties, grew out of an oversimplified concept of condition-

"Effects of Child-Rearing Patterns on Mental Health," by Lois Barclay Murphy. Reprinted from *Children,* November-December 1956, 213–218, U.S. Department of Health, Education, and Welfare, Social Security Administration, Children's Bureau.

ing plus pediatric concepts that dealt with nutrition and physical hygiene generally without regard to the emotional consequences of the techniques of imposing these routines. During the forties, there was a tendency to go to the opposite extreme. Both excessive coercion and excessive indulgence brought problems for children.

There is no sure guarantee that we won't make just as many mistakes in the future. But the best insurance against that seems to lie in developing as comprehensive and balanced a picture as possible of the child's needs and of the relation of the culture both to these needs and to the child's ability to satisfy them. It has taken dramatic and painful experience to force our attention to some of the most obvious interactions of culture and child needs. For instance, the studies (2) of Anna Freud, Bowlby, and Spitz are significant in relation to children's problems of separation not only in wartime but also in our peacetime patterns of babysitting, hospitalization, and frequent moving, which uproots little children from the home, neighborhood, and friends with whom they have tried to establish firm relationships.

Several absorbing new books (3) show us in very different ways how complex these interactions are and how many factors both in the culture and in the child are involved in thinking about child-rearing practices. To these I would add various significant studies (4) of factors involved in the development of anxiety and breakdown in reaction to stress in childhood.

A COMPLEX PHENOMENON

All these studies make clear that mental health is always mental health in *a given setting* with each setting's special demands, resources, stresses, and rewards. Mental health is also relative to the *kind of person* we are dealing with; there is no one standard of mental health for everyone. It is also relative to our *concept* of mental health. Children of head-hunters learn ways of using their aggressive drives that are consistent with good mental hygiene in their culture but not in ours. Our child-rearing patterns and concepts of mental health have to be looked at in relation to the culture as a whole—its values, acceptable goals, and the things it disapproves or won't stand for.

Child rearing includes all the cultural influences within and without the family that condition and canalize the child's energies—emotional, motor, intellectual, and so on. Physiological levels of conditioning by feeding and toilet-training experiences are among the first and are very important, but they become interwoven with, offset by, and overlaid by many other levels which are influenced not just by the mother, or even by the family as a whole, but by the whole neighborhood and larger culture as it impinges on the child. For example, one child we studied was quite free from early toilet-training pressure, but when the family moved into a new neighborhood the other children and parents laughed at her because, at 2, she was still wearing diapers. At the Sarah Lawrence College Nursery School in the late thirties and early forties, there were many children whose mothers began toilet training "too early" but who were still happy children, doubtless because they were enjoyed, cared for tenderly, and loved.

In addition to watching the family and the culture as a whole, we need to give separate consideration to the positive and negative aspects of the problem: building mental health and preventing mental break-down, as well as the remedial approaches needed to handle breakdown when it occurs. Building mental health is a matter of building areas of satisfying life in warm relationships with people, and in work and play (5), and in *building ways of solving inner and outer problems*. Preventing mental breakdown is a matter of preventing cultural stress beyond the point that can be handled by individuals, and along with this, *increasing the individual's capacity to cope with stress*. Remedial approaches use both positive rebuilding and preventive, or stress-reducing, techniques.

Building positive strength involves a series of stages or steps which we need to clarify before we talk concretely about child-rearing patterns in the culture—steps partly formulated by Erikson in *Childhood and Society* (6):

1. Finding that life is good and that needs can be met: *trust*.
2. Finding that you can meet them yourself: *autonomy, initiative,* and *industry*.
3. Finding that you can work with others toward meeting group needs: *cooperation*.
4. Finding that threats and danger can be handled, through *avoidance* or *mastery*.

CULTURAL INFLUENCES

We must look at cultural and child-rearing patterns as they affect the needs of the child at each age-level—infancy, preschool, school-age, adolescence—and his ability progressively to tolerate and cope with stress. A balanced approach also involves thinking about "emotional needs" and "ego development," and their integration both as positive interests and areas of satisfaction, and as methods of control and defense. In our thinking, then, about child-rearing patterns and the impacts of the culture on them we will want to keep in mind these questions: What does this pattern or group of patterns mean to the child emotionally? What do they mean to the development of his skill in handling the environment? What do they mean for his image of himself and of the world in which he lives?

Among the many obvious aspects of the culture affecting children in the United States are:

1.   The small family with its individualistic and competitive, but cooperative, values; its areas of spontaneity and rigidity; its mobility; its reliance on babysitters; its excitement about, but often sense of being burdened by, the babies;

2.   Medical guidance, which dominates hygiene, feeding-elimination-sleep routines, inoculations, vitamins, separation of mother from the child immediately after birth and during hospitalization;

3.   Property with its competitive values and its stimulus to interference with the freedom of the child; its comforts, play resources, creative stimulus;

4.   The culturally heterogeneous and conflictful life of many communities—religiously, morally, sexually, aggressively, and structurally—in relationships between classes and shifts from one class to another;

5.   Educational ambition which includes the requirement to meet standards of performance in every area, as well as to develop an understanding of oneself and the world one lives in;

6.   Measurement consciousness, with its stimulus to growth and also to standardization of the child by pressure to conform to norms which generally ignore or minimize the wide range of individual differences in normal samples;

7.   Confusion regarding discipline, values, and demands made on the child;

8.   Mobility: the frequency of moving which can increase confusion in values, make it hard for the child to sink in roots and develop a sense of stable harmony between his inner self and a familiar world outside; which at the same time may acquaint the child with a wider range of people and communities, and lead to broader awareness of ways of life;

9.   Distorted or deprived parent-child relations growing out of the deprivations of the previous generation, in which the cumulative effects of two world wars are exacting an increasing toll; parents' compensatory efforts to create happy experiences;

10.   The increasing dominance of irreality and secondhand experience as TV, added to movies and radio, becomes an easy pacifier for children from the age of 2 on, along with the increased information that TV brings to children.

These influences do not come one by one but are fused in the experience of the baby who is greeted with enthusiasm and cared for thoughtfully. A typical middle-class suburban or metropolitan child is born in a hospital, fed from a bottle and often with a bottleholder as soon as he is steady enough to get his milk that way. He is brought up in a buggy, crib, high chair, playpen, and other furniture. He may be toilet trained early or late, but the chances are that his mother hates diapers. Babysitters substitute for mother when she goes shopping. Muscles and large-muscle activity are encouraged from his earliest months by both his parents, who get excited as he learns to sit up, stand, walk, and climb. Yet as he begins to get into, onto, and under furniture and to grab it, he is generally interrupted, scolded, or slapped for the exercise of the very functions his parents stimulated. Father's professional training may make him quite preoccupied in getting his M.D. or Ph.D., or getting "ahead," and leave him with little chance to play. Probably our typical child's mother doesn't sing him any lullaby, but he does see television early. If his father is in the Army or Navy or is with a big corporation that manufactures and sells on a national scale, his family may move from one place to another too frequently for him to establish roots anywhere.

STRESS PRODUCING FACTORS

These things all sound familiar enough and certainly in and of themselves are not likely to create pathology. We all know plenty of children who get along all right in exactly this kind of life, especially when parents feel comfortable with their own design for living and can give the growing child the support he needs at crisis points or transition points. When does trouble arise? What do these things have to do with hyperactivity, nervous habits, autism, psychogenic retardation, phobias, uncontrollable aggression and other problems brought to our clinics?

We are far from having the necessary data for dealing with such troubles empirically. As professional people we have tended to focus on a few central areas: feeding and toilet-training experiences; discipline; separation from mother; frustrations in the mother-child relation as a whole. But many other factors are involved, most of which have not been studied fully.

We agree that mental health suffers from:

1. *Vulnerability:* exposure to excessive stress;

2. *Emotional deprivation,* traceable to one or more of several sources, and including lack of adequate range of *gratification;*

3. *Anxiety,* also traceable to any combination of a multitude of sources;

4. *Conflict:* lack of integration; and

5. *Lack of adequate defense* against, and compensation for, stress and deprivation.

When factors such as those just mentioned produce anxiety, conflict, or insufficient gratification, particularly in a child who is at a sensitive stage of development or who is naturally vulnerable, we have trouble. The same combination of conditions can be disturbing to one child but not disruptive to another.

VULNERABILITY in the child may arise from unusual sensitivities, uneven growth patterns, specific damage—as a brain damage, illness, or other cause. Vulnerable children make mothers anxious, and this anxiety contagiously makes the children more anxious, lowering their thresholds for response to stress. Children with more than usual sensitivity to sounds or sights or to sensory stimuli in all modalities are more exposed to all the minor and major impacts of the environment.

In our culture, the sensitivity of parents to the normal, or rather to the optional and ideal, often makes them tense, or even guilty, at any deviations or failures to reach the ideal. Thus, in a norm-sensitive culture, vulnerability easily creates a cycle of mutually reinforcing anxiety. Such parents need help in developing more tolerance for deviations from the ideal all along the line.

With babies who have severe colic, diarrhea, and other physiological misery in their first 3 to 6 months there is, in addition to the anxiety of the mother, her fatigue, even exhaustion, which in our small-family culture means that the baby is cared for by a mother who hasn't the strength constantly to give such a baby the extra supply he needs to help the process of establishing inner stability.

EMOTIONAL DEPRIVATION both makes a baby vulnerable, and, as in the types of depressed and anaclitic reactions described by René Spitz, interferes with basic growth drive. This emotional deprivation occurs also in a cultural setting where a mother may have to go to a hospital for a period of time and can leave no familiar mother-substitute with her baby.

Mechanical feeding devices, mechanical nursemaids, like playpens, the culture pattern of isolating the baby from birth, all can contribute to emotional deprivation when they are used to excess or without awareness of what the experience means to the baby. We know from animal studies that deprivation of sensory experience interferes with the development of intelligence, and observations of young children give plenty of evidence that they use sensory or other basic gratifications to offset frustrations and disturbed feelings. Isolating devices, like playpens, can in effect reduce needed sensory gratification and comfort.

Cultural factors which interfere with a rich infantile sensory experience can be expected to leave the child without reserves in his mental-health bank to balance up the withdrawals by deprivation and trauma. Such factors include all the conditions in middle-class life which over-sanitize, overorganize, overstructure the life of the young child so that he is unable to obtain the natural primitive gratifications which build this balance in the emotional bank—from mud pies to war whoops.

ANXIETY may be generated by many factors. Some major ones are these:

—irregularities in the child's growth pattern, such as in children who are verbally advanced but, slow in motor development, or the reverse, in a subculture which emphasizes the importance of meeting standards or normality in a family that expects the child to meet high standards in every area.

—difficulties in coordination which produce frustrations to the child attempting to master his environment;

—blocks, interruptions, and frustrations in exercising autonomy at the age when he has his autonomy spurt; interferences which are an every-day matter in the city where middle-class children are often harnessed, held by the hand, and hovered over until kindergarten age or later;

—traumata from operations, accidents, and such, particularly when these occur before the age of 3, and in quick sequence, or at a time when the child is making other difficult adjustments;

—autonomic instability, aggravated by overstimulation, illness, or emotional stress;

—physiological pressures, due to problems in feeding, tense toilet training, skin or temperature sensitivities, and such;

—inadequacy in coping with physical threats from peers or adults, due to low muscle tonus, small size in relation to the rest of the family;

—sudden disturbances in established relationships due to illness in a parent, conflict between parents, or long absences.

All of these factors need to be seen from a cultural or child-rearing point of view in relation both to adult attitudes and handling of the child, and to the concrete experience of the child in the environment.

Normative pressures in our culture add to the anxiety around growth irregularities ("my 15-month-old boy is walking but he isn't talking yet"). Property emphases in our culture that lead to constant protection of things from the child ("nothing is safe in our house") involve frequent interruption of the child's drive to be active and explore which creates anger between mother and child. Cultural patterns of doing things *to* the child (inoculations, operations, and other body violations) at an age when the child is old enough to suffer and remember but not old enough to understand or master the threat also cause anxiety in children, especially those under 4 or 5. Cultural anxiety about nutrition, quantity of food intake ("why doesn't he finish that bottle?"), and about elimination ("he didn't have a bowel movement today") contributes to physiological tension and uneasiness about eating and related basic functions. At a later age, grossly contrasting patterns of approval and disapproval in different social classes can create anxious conflicts: to fight, in the lower-class groups studied by Havighurst and Davis (7) or not to fight, in middle-class groups.

In the heterogeneous culture of large cities, it is the rule rather than the exception for the child to be exposed to widely differing values and standards in the home and neighborhood. "What mother forbids, the mother next door permits," and vice versa, "Grown-ups don't do what they preach. Public leaders tolerate gangsters or connive with them." "Families expect one standard; schools expect a different one; schools try to adapt learning demands to the child's growth rate, while parents want the child to learn to read at 6," or vice versa. Many strands of influence are tying each other into knots with the child in the middle.

CONFLICT and lack of integration also arise from deeper sources. With the high divorce rate and the prevalence of home tension, from early months the child may have conflicting identifications; that is, conflicts in identifying with two people who can't achieve integration in their mutual life. Oedipal conflicts and sibling rivalries are often increased by the intensity of emotional relationships in a small family, made smaller by the mobility of American life which separates children from potentially comforting grandparents.

For comparison, we might look at a village child in India whose mother has an easy experience at childbirth, nurses her baby until he is 2 or more and old enough to lose interest in nursing because of the competition of other activities, carries him with her wherever she goes so that he does not know what separation is. Her child is carried by an older sibling when a new baby takes over his mother's arms. He receives no toilet training until he is old enough to get around on his own feet and learns where to go. When he begins to run around for himself, he has the freedom of the house and the village with nothing to daunt or disturb his budding autonomy since there is nothing breakable or damageable. With many of these children no severe separation, isolation, or deprivation is experienced.

We can see that we have here a rich complex of factors among which the specific feeding and toilet-training experiences are only two, however fundamental they are, because of the opportunity for massive emotional reactions and conditionings in these settings.

DEFENSES AGAINST STRESS AND DEPRIVATION have already been mentioned in relation to emotional deprivation, but more is needed here. Everything in the subculture, including the neighborhood as well as the family, which builds confidence, pride, skills in mastery, security in

problem solving, flexibility, and perspective on emotional disturbance—
including such expectations as are implied in clichés like "every cloud
has a silver lining" or "tomorrow will be another day" (as contrasted
with "it never rains but it pours")—is part of the total child-rearing
experience and contributes to the child's equipment to deal with the
stresses of his life (8).

With the opportunities provided by the subculture for the optimal
development of the resources of the individual, we can also include
intelligence. Children in slum areas, bad schools, deprived neighbor-
hoods, may or may not be deprived of the emotional nourishment they
need, but they are likely to be deprived of the experience of seeing how
people cope with problems. They may thus be left more helpless than
middle-class children who can observe and participate in a wider range
of learning experiences that are useful in coping with emotional and
environmental problems. The more our schools can provide genuine
experiences in real-life situations, the more confidence children can
develop in their ability to handle problems.

Dr. Margaret Fries in this country, Dr. D. R. MacCalman reporting
on British children, and Rhoda Metraux reporting on German child-
rearing patterns (9) have, in different ways, emphasized the importance of
learning to cope with frustration or life's problems as such—an approach quite distinct from that of measuring up to norms for "successful
performance" in all areas. Learning to stand up for oneself, to think for
oneself, to find solutions of one's own, are very important ingredients of
coping.

Roger Barker's research (10) on a small rural town in the middle west,
where delinquency is unknown and children are by and large relaxed
and healthy, records a comfortable tempo, much time for exploring and
mastering one's environment, much companionship between adults and
children, and warm support and encouragement when a child fails in
some effort like learning to fly-cast.

STRENGTH BUILDING FACTORS

Mental health develops when most of the following are present:

(a) *Good start physiologically*—freedom from gastrointestinal discomfort, frustrating defects in coordination, perception, integration;

(b) *Emotional nourishment;*

(c) *Adequacy of sensory stimuli;*

(d) *Opportunity for motor development* and freedom from excessive
pressure for performance;

(e) *Range of experience;*

(f) *Stable relations with mother* during the period of establishing clear concepts of self and other persons;

(g) *Stable, respected interests, possessions* (cathexis);

(h) *Opportunity to exercise autonomy,* initiative, industry, to achieve mastery over various areas of the environment;

(i) *Feeling supported,* accepted, a source of pride and satisfaction to parents;

(j) *Opportunity to cope* with gradual doses of frustration and difficulty;

(k) *Participation in group life* with some recognizably consistent pattern (freedom from demoralizing value conflicts).

TO SUMMARIZE

The complexity, conflict of values, pressure to perform, and emphasis on protection of property make it impossible to give any simple answers to the question of what is the effect of child-rearing patterns on mental health today. Mental health for a lifetime cannot be guaranteed by self-demand feeding in the first year of life, nor does mental breakdown inevitably occur as a result of early toilet training. Children who are shy at the age of 4 are not necessarily on the way to schizophrenia. It becomes more and more clear that mental health and mental disturbance are the resultants of a complex and varied group of influences from within and without the individual child, and that the part of wisdom is to become increasingly aware of what this total interplay actually is in the case of individual children. This means thinking of the equipment of the individual child and what his resources are for coping with the pressures of his situation, as well as thinking of what those pressures are as he experiences them. One child thrives on a routine which cramps the style of the next. One child goes haywire with a degree of freedom which another child uses creatively.

This brings us to the concluding question: What child-rearing help does each individual child need in order to build more strength to handle the problems he finds in his own subculture situation?

1. MACFARLANE, JEAN, et al: Developmental Study of the Behavior Problems of Normal Children Between 21 Months and 14 Years. Berkeley: University of California Press, 1954.
2. FREUD, ANNA; BURLINGAME, DOROTHY T.: War and Children. New York: Medical War Books, 1943.
  BOWLBY, JOHN: Maternal Care Mental Health. Geneva: World Health Organization, 1952.
  SPITZ, RENÉ: Hospitalism. In Psychoanalytic Study of the Child. Vol. 1. New York: International Universities Press, 1945.

3. SODDY, KENNETH, editor: Mental Health and Infant Development. New York: Basic Books, 1956.

   CAPLAN, GERALD, editor: Emotional Problems of Early Childhood. New York: Basic Books, 1955.

   MEAD, MARGARET; WOLFENSTEIN, MARTHA, editors: Childhood in Contemporary Cultures. Chicago: University of Chicago Press, 1955.

4. GREENACRE, PHYLLIS: Trauma, Growth and Personality. New York: W. W. Norton & Co., 1952.

   LEVY, DAVID: Psychic trauma of operations in children. American Journal of Diseases of Children, January 1945.

   GRINKER, R. R.: Effect of infantile disease on ego patterns. American Journal of Psychiatry, October 1953.

   SELYE, HANS: The Physiology and Pathology of Exposure to Stress. Montreal: Acta, Inc., 1950.

5. MAYMAN, M.: On the concept of psychological health. Unpublished paper read at American Psychological Association, 1955.

6. ERICKSON, ERICK H.: Childhood and Society. New York: W. W. Norton & Co., 1950.

7. HAVIGHURST, ROBERT J.; DAVIS, W. ALLISON: Father of the Man. Boston: Houghton Mifflin Co., 1947.

8. MURPHY, LOIS BARCLAY: Personality in Young Children. Vol. 2, Colin, A Normal Child. New York: Basic Books, 1956.

9. METRAUX, RHODA: Parents and children: an analysis of contemporary German child-care and youth-guidance literature. Chapter 12 *in* Mead, M., and Wolfenstein, M., op. cit.

   MACCALMAN, D. R.: Background to child development patterns in the United Kingdom I and II *in* Soddy, K., op. cit.

10. BARKER, ROGER: One Boy's Day. New York: Harper & Bros., 1951.

Masculinity, Identification and Father-Son Relationships

Paul Mussen and Luther Distler

By identifying with his parents—i.e., endeavoring "to mold (his) own ego after the fashion of one that has been taken as a model" (S. Freud, 1949, p. 63)—the child begins to acquire his parents' personality characteristics, behavior, values, motivations, and attitudes. Two of the major consequents of the processes of identification are the development of the superego, or conscience, and the acquisition of behavior and personality characteristics appropriate to his own sex (sex-typing).

It has been hypothesized that both boys and girls form their first

"Masculinity, Identification, and Father-Son Relationships," by Paul H. Mussen and Luther S. Distler, *Journal of Abnormal and Social Psychology*, No. 59, 350–356. © 1959, American Psychological Association.

identification with a female, the mother, because she is likely to be the most gratifying and affectionate person with whom the child has contact (Mowrer, 1950; Sears, Maccoby, & Levin, 1957). Continued identification with the mother is appropriate for a girl, for she must acquire feminine personality characteristics and interests, but the boy "must shift to a masculine identification, sometime in his early years, if he is to develop normally masculine personality" (Sears et al., 1957, p. 373).

According to psychoanalytic theory, the boy's shift to identification with his father begins during the Oedipal phase of development and is motivated by fears and anxieties related to his hostility toward that parent. By identifying with his father, the boy's fears of counter-aggression are reduced and, at the same time, he vicariously obtains his mother's attention and affection. This is the defense mechanism that has been called "identification with the aggressor" (A. Freud, 1937) and "defensive identification" (Mowrer, 1950).

In contrast to this, the developmental hypothesis states that identification with the father depends on a positive, affectionate relationship between father and son (Mowrer, 1950; Payne & Mussen, 1956). If the father is an important source of nurturance, reward, and satisfaction, his responses and characteristics acquire secondary reward value and the boy imitates his father's behavior in order to "reproduce bits of the beloved and longed for parent" (Mowrer, 1950, p. 615).

Although the two hypothesized explanations of the dynamics underlying identification with the father seem to be vastly different from each other, there is some supportive evidence for each of them. The validity of the developmental identification hypothesis has been tested in a number of recent studies (Levin & Sears, 1956; Payne & Mussen, 1956; P. Sears, 1953; Sears et al., 1957; Sears, Pintler, & Sears, 1946). Thus in one study, five-year-old boys with warm and affectionate fathers (as judged by home interviews) showed stronger father identifications than did boys with "cold" fathers (P. Sears, 1953). It has also been reported that adolescent boys who perceive their fathers as nurturant (according to projective tests) are more likely to identify strongly with this parent than are boys who do not perceive their fathers as rewarding (Payne & Mussen, 1956). Moreover, certain characteristics of boys generally regarded as consequents of identification with the father—sex-typed behavior such as aggression (Levin & Sears, 1956), masculine interests and attitudes (Payne & Mussen, 1956), and highly developed conscience (Sears et al., 1957)—tend to be associated with favorable father-son relationships.

The hypothesis of defensive identification is a complex one that is difficult to investigate empirically. However, there are extensive clinical observations indicating that, as this hypothesis would predict, many children attempt to reduce their anxieties by adopting the aggressive characteristics of individuals whom they perceive as threatening to them (A. Freud, 1937; Mowrer, 1950).

It is quite possible, of course, that the two hypothesized identification processes are not mutually exclusive but may function together to facilitate the boy's shift from a feminine to a masculine identification (Sears et al., 1957). This view is consistent with that of the role theorists who equate identification with the father with "father role playing" (Brim, 1958; Cottrell, 1942; Parsons, 1955). These theorists maintain that identification, or role-playing, depends on the *power* of the identificand—a combination of his reward value *and* his threat or punishment potential. More specifically:

> Given two . . . persons with whom one interacts and who differ in power over the actor (the identifier), i.e., differ in the degree to which they control rewards and punishments for the actor, one would predict that the actor would adopt many of the characteristics of the powerful as contrasted to the less powerful other person. This follows from the fact that it is more important to the actor to predict the behavior of the powerful figure, that he is motivated more strongly to take his role (i.e., to identify), that rewards and punishments are more impressive and the learning consequently better (Brim, 1958, p. 3).

The present paper reports the results of an investigation that attempted to evaluate the validity of the three hypothesized explanations of identification—developmental, defensive, and role-playing. It was assumed that, for young boys, appropriate sex-typing of interests is an indication of identification with the father, and that amount of identification can be estimated from the degree of sex-typing. The rewarding-nurturant and threatening-punitive qualities of the father were evaluated in terms of the child's *perceptions* of the father, rather than in terms of the father's actual behavior, the criterion used in some previous studies (Levin & Sears, 1956; P. Sears, 1953; Sears et al., 1957).

There were several central questions. How do boys who are strongly identified with their fathers, i.e., highly masculine in their interests, perceive their fathers: as basically nurturant and rewarding, as would be predicted from the developmental identification hypothesis, or as punitive and threatening, in accordance with the defensive identification hypothesis? Or are they viewed as powerful agents of both reward and punishment, as the role-playing hypothesis of identification maintains?

METHOD

Subjects. According to psychoanalytic theory and observational data, the late preschool period is a critical time in the boy's shift from feminine to masculine identification. For this reason, it seemed best to use kindergarten boys as *S*s for this investigation.

Initially, 38 white five-year-old boys in two kindergarten classes of a predominantly middle-class public school[1] were given the IT Scale for Children (ITSC), a projective test of sex-role preference (Brown, 1956). The test consists of 36 picture cards depicting various objects, figures, and activities commonly associated with masculine or feminine roles. The child is given a card with a figure drawing unstructured as to sex and referred to as IT. He is then presented with groups of pictures of toys and with paired choices of activities, and asked to choose what IT would like.

"In using IT the assumption is made that the child will project himself or herself into the IT-figure on the basis of his own or her own sex-role preference, and will attribute to IT the child's own role preference." (Brown, 1956, p. 5). The possible range of scores on the test is from zero, an exclusively feminine score, to 84, an exclusively masculine score.

The 10 boys with the highest scores (range 79–84, with a mean of 83) and the 10 boys with the lowest scores (range 30–63, with a mean of 53) were selected for further study.[2] The two groups were matched in socioeconomic status, each of them having the same number of upper-lower, lower-middle, and upper-middle class boys. Ten of the Ss, 5 high scorers and 5 low scorers, came from one kindergarten class, and 10 from the other.

Measures of parent-child relations.   Between one and four weeks after he had taken the ITSC, each of the 20 boys was tested individually in a structured doll-play session. Early in the session, the child familiarized himself with three easily manipulated dolls, representing a mother, a father, and a boy doll, and some very simple toy furniture, which were on a low table in the testing room. S was told that these were to be used in a story-telling game in which the examiner would make up the first part of the story and S would complete it.

The examiner then presented, with appropriate manipulations of the dolls, a series of nine incomplete, family situation stories, and the child was asked to complete each one in play. The stories were structured in such a way that the child could depict either or both parents as nurturant and/or punitive. Five of the incomplete stories follow:

1. The child wants a certain toy. He can't reach it. He goes into the living room to get help. Both Mommy and Daddy are busy reading. What happens?

[1]The authors wish to express their appreciation to A. B. Campbell, Assistant Superintendent of Schools of Berkeley, C. B. Johnson, Principal of the Jefferson School, and C. B. Holmes and E. P. Light, kindergarten teachers, for their cooperation in this study.

[2]While the Ss were selected only on the basis of masculinity score on the ITSC, there is some suggestive evidence that those scoring low on the test were also somewhat more feminine in personality characteristics. Their teachers rated the Ss on 20 scales of personality characteristics, adapted, with slight modifications, from the Fels Child Behavior Scales. These characteristics were: aggression, affection, cheerfulness, competition, conscience, curiosity, emotional control, gross activity, friendliness, gregariousness, kindness, leadership, obedience, patience, physical apprehensiveness, quarrelsomeness, sensitivity, shyness, suggestibility, and tenacity (Richards & Simons, 1941).

The two groups of Ss differed significantly (at approximately the .02 level) on 4 of the 20 scales. The low scorers rated significantly higher than the highly masculine on: gross activity, friendliness, cheerfulness, and gregariousness. The latter three characteristics are, according to sociological analyses of sex role, specifically assigned to the expressive or feminine role (Brim, 1958; Cottrell, 1942; Parsons, 1955). The relatively high ratings of gross activity among those low in masculinity may also reflect group differences in these social characteristics. Significant positive correlations between the gross activity scale and the cheerfulness and gregariousness scales have been reported previously (Richards & Simons, 1941). Apparently, the child who is expressive, outgoing, and cheerful is quite likely to be seen as more active.

3. The child lives on a very busy street. Mommy and Daddy told him never to cross the street alone. The child is playing in the front yard, and Mommy and Daddy are not there. A friend is on the other side of the street playing with his new bike. The child wants to cross the street very much. What happens?

4. The child is having fun playing with his toys. Mommy and Daddy say "It's time to go to bed now." The child says "I don't want to go to bed now." Then the child throws a toy on the floor and it breaks. What happens?

5. The child is getting ready to go to school. He has a knot in his shoelace. He can't fix it. What happens?

8. Let's pretend the little boy had a bad dream. Now the little boy wakes up from his bad dream, screaming. He calls for Mommy or Daddy. Which one does he call for, Mommy or Daddy? Then what happens?

If the child failed to respond to one of the stories or said "I don't know," the story was repeated or the question rephrased. If S did not mention the parents in his play, the examiner asked "What did Mommy or Daddy say or do?" When the child did not designate a specific parent in his response, the examiner inquired "Who did that, the Mommy or the Daddy?" Each doll-play session was completely recorded.

Scoring the doll-play responses. The major hypotheses with which the study was concerned dealt with the relationship between boys' masculinity scores and their perceptions of their fathers. The structured doll-play situation, however, permitted evaluations of the child's perceptions not only of his father but also of his mother and his parents as a unit (when mentioned without specific designation of mother or father) as nurturant and/or punishing. [The assumption underlying the use of this technique is that the boy's responses in doll-play reveal his own feelings about his parents' treatment of him.]

Each story was scored for the presence of nurturance or punishment by the father, mother, or "they" (parents undifferentiated). The stories were scored without the scorer's knowledge of the child's ITSC score.

The following scoring categories were used:

Father Nurturance (FN) score was the total number of stories in which the child character in the stories received help, comfort, attention, or reassurance from the father (e.g., "his Daddy gets it for him" in response to Story 1 described above).

A Mother Nurturance (MN) score was derived by counting the number of stories in which the mother was depicted as nurturant. (For example, in response to the story about the dream, "He calls his Mommy and she says it's just a dream and he can sleep with her.")

They Nurturance (TN) score was the number of stories in which the parents as a unit were nurturant. (For example, S, in response to Story 3: "They help him cross the street." E: "Who helps, Mommy or Daddy?" S: "His Mommy and Daddy.")

Total Nurturance (TotN) score was the sum of the MN (Mother Nurturance), FN (Father Nurturance), and TN (They Nurturance) scores.

The total number of stories in which the father, mother, or "they" disciplined, spanked, criticized, or admonished the child in the story constituted, respectively the Father Punishment (FP), Mother Punishment (MP), and They Punishment (TP) scores.

Total Punishment (TotP) score was the sum of the FP (Father Punishment), MP (Mother Punishment), and TP (They Punishment) scores.

It should be noted that a given story could be scored for more than one variable. For example, if the mother in the story spanked the child and later comforted him, the story would be scored both Mother Punishment (MP) and Mother Nurturance (MN).

The total number of stories involving relationships with the father, either nurturant or punitive (i.e., FN plus FP) constituted the Father Power (FPow) score. Analogously, Mother Power (MPow) was the sum of the Mother Nurturance (MN) and Mother Punishment (MP) scores.

RESULTS

The three theoretical formulations of the dynamics underlying the shift from feminine to masculine identification, outlined above, could be evaluated by determining the relationships between masculinity status and perceptions of parents, as measured by the child's responses in doll play. If the developmental hypothesis is valid, highly masculine boys would perceive their fathers as more rewarding and affectionate or, operationally, would have higher Father Nurturance (FN) scores than boys with low masculinity scores. On the basis of the defensive identification hypothesis, however, it would be predicted that boys who were most strongly identified with their fathers—as this is reflected in their highly masculine interest—would regard their fathers as more threatening and punitive, i.e., would have higher Father Punishment (FP) scores than boys whose father identifications are weak. The role-playing hypothesis of identification offers a third prediction. According to this theory, boys with strong tendencies to play the father role or to identify with the father would feel that their fathers were powerful figures and important sources of both rewards and punishments. In terms of the variables of this study, this would mean that highly masculine boys would have higher Father Power (FPow) scores than boys who have not achieved strong masculine identifications.

Since responses to the structured doll-play situation were scored for perceptions of the mother and "they" (parents as a unit) as nurturant-gratifying and/or punitive-threatening, it was also possible to assess the relationships between these variables and strong or weak sex-typing among five-year-old boys.

Table 1 presents the mean scores of the high and low masculinity groups on all the doll-play scores.

In view of the facts that the number of Ss in each group was small and that the distributions of scores on these variables was nonnormal, U tests (Mann & Whitney, 1947) were employed to compare rank transformation scores on all doll-play scores of Ss scoring high and low on the ITSC. The results of these tests and their significance levels are summarized in Table 2.

It is obvious from this table that the two groups of Ss differ significantly in many of their perceptions of their families. Compared with boys low in masculine identification, as measured by the ITSC, those who were high in this characteristic perceived themselves as receiving more Total Nurturance (TotN) (i.e., more nurturance from all sources combined). Evidently, this difference is primarily attributable to differences in one major component of TotN, the perceptions of father's nurturance, for the two groups differ significantly in Father Nurturance (FN) scores but not in the Mother Nurturance (MN) or They Nurturance (TN) scores.[3]

This finding seems clearly consistent with the developmental identification hypothesis. It supports the prediction, made on the basis of this hypothesis, that young boys are more likely to identify strongly with their fathers, and thus to acquire masculine interests, if they perceive their fathers as highly nurturant and rewarding.

The data also appear to lend support to the second, or defensive identification, hypothesis, which predicted that high masculine identification would be related to views of the father as threatening and punitive. Highly masculine boys tended to attribute more punishment to the fathers in their doll-play stories than boys low in masculine identification did, although the difference between the two groups in the father punishment score was not quite as marked as the difference in the father nurturance variable.

The third, or role-taking, hypothesis states that the degree of identification and, consequently, sex-role learning varies with the amount of the child's interaction with the identificand and the degree to which the

TABLE 1

MEAN SCORES OF BOYS HIGH AND LOW MASCULINITY GROUPS ON FAMILY PERCEPTION VARIABLES

VARIABLE	HIGH MASCULINITY GROUP	LOW MASCULINITY GROUP
Mother Nurturance (MN)	2.1	1.7
Father Nurturance (FN)	3.7	2.2
They Nurturance (TN)	.8	.7
Total Nurturance (TotN)	6.6	4.7
Mother Punishment (MP)	1.2	1.5
Father Punishment (FP)	2.8	2.1
They Punishment (TP)	.2	.7
Total Punishment (TotP)	4.2	4.3
Mother Power (MPow)	3.3	3.2
Father Power (FPow)	6.5	4.3

[3]While the use of t tests was not entirely warranted because of the nonnormality of the doll-play scores, these tests were applied to the data of Table 1. The results were very similar to the U test results, i.e., the high and low masculinity groups differed significantly from each other in the variables FN ($p = .01 - .025$), TotN ($p = < .01$), FP ($p = .01 - .025$), FPow ($p = < .005$) and almost significantly in TP ($p = .05 - .10$).

latter has power over him, i.e., controls both his rewards and his punishments. The data of the present study seem to be fully in accord with this hypothesis, since the low and high masculinity groups differ markedly in Father Power (FPow) scores, the high indentifiers giving a significantly greater number of these responses. This finding is exactly what would be anticipated, since this score is composed of the FN and FP scores, and the highly identified group scored significantly higher in each of these.

The high and low masculinity groups were not significantly different in any of the variables related to perceptions of the mother. However, compared with those scoring low on the ITSC, high scorers tended to perceive their parents as a unit as less punitive, i.e., tended to have lower They Punishment (TP) scores ($p = .07$). This would seem to be further confirmation of the findings of another study which concluded that adolescent "boys who feel comfortable in their relationships with their parents adopt more of their father's behavior and attitudes than boys who experience less favorable parent-child relationships" (Payne & Mussen, 1956, p. 361).

It may be that the boy who scores high in They Punishment (TP) views his family milieu as hostile and unfriendly. While he may not feel that either parent is particularly threatening, he may feel generally rejected, unwanted, and unimportant. Insofar as this is true, the child may be expected to attempt to avoid intensive interactions with his parents. Under these circumstances, he should not identify strongly with his father and, consequently, should not acquire highly masculine interests.

DISCUSSION

The data of the present study indicate that for boys, sex-typing of interests is more directly related to their perceptions of their fathers than to perceptions of their mothers. This finding is in accord with the findings of previous studies (Levin & Sears, 1956; Payne & Mussen, 1956; Sears et al., 1957) as well as with an assumption underlying all three of the identification hypotheses outlined above; namely, that the acquisition of masculine interests, attitudes, and patterns of behavior is primarily determined by the boy's interactions with his father.

Some of the findings of this study lend support to the defensive identification hypothesis; others seem to support the developmental hypothesis. Since the two hypotheses generate predictions that are in some respects diametrically opposed, there are also data that are inconsistent with both hypotheses. Thus, since the developmental hypothesis postulates that identification with the father is dependent upon nurturant rewarding interactions with that parent, the finding that boys also identi-

TABLE 2
DIFFERENCES BETWEEN HIGH AND LOW MASCULINITY GROUPS
ON FAMILY PERCEPTION VARIABLES

VARIABLE	U	p	GROUP WITH HIGHER SCORES
Mother Nurturance (MN)	45.5	NS	—
Father Nurturance (FN)	23.5	.02	Highs
They Nurturance (TN)	48.5	NS	—
Total Nurturance (TotN)	16.0	.004	Highs
Mother Punishment (MP)	44.0	NS	—
Father Punishment (FP)	30.5	.06	Highs
They Punishment (TP)	34.0	.07	Lows
Total Punishment (TotP)	47.0	NS	—
Mother Power (MPow)	49.5	NS	—
Father Power (FPow)	18.5	.007	Highs

fy with punitive, threatening fathers must be inconsistent with this hypothesis. Conversely, the finding that boys are more likely to identify with
a nurturant father is inconsistent with the view of defensive identification
or identification with the aggressor.

A high level of masculine identification does not appear to depend
on any one specific type of father-son relationship. From the child's
point of view, the significant factor seems to be the father's *salience*—his
importance in the child's life—rather than the particular techniques he
uses in dealing with his child. Thus, as a group, boys who have made
substantial father-identifications—reflected in their strongly sex-typed
interests—perceived their fathers as both more nurturant *and* more punitive. Hence, masculine sex-role identification cannot be attributed
exclusively to either the reward value or the threat potential of the
father.

For these reasons, it seems to us that the role theory of identification
is most fully consistent with—and most adequately integrates—the present data. The two groups were clearly differentiated on the Father Power
(FPow) score, indicating that, compared with the other group, the highly
masculine boys had—or at least perceived that they had—more intensive interactions with their fathers. This is exactly what is predicted by
the role theory of sex-role identification, which maintains that more
interaction with another individual, e.g., the father, leads to greater
assimilation of his role.

Moreover, role theory states most explicitly that an individual is
most likely to assimilate the role of, or identify with, individuals he sees
as powerful. From the child's point of view, the most powerful individual
is probably the one who most effectively controls his rewards and punishments. In this way, the theory implies that both reward and punish-

ment strongly influence the course of role learning.

It follows from these postulates of role theory that the boy should be most strongly motivated to imitate or to practice his father's role frequently if he has a great deal of interaction with his father and sees him as a powerful source of rewards and punishments. Under these circumstances, the child gets extensive experience playing the father's role and adopts more of the father's characteristics, including those connected specifically with his sex-role. Our data are substantially in accordance with these theoretical predictions. The highly father-identified *Ss*—those who had adopted masculine interests and behavior—did in fact perceive their fathers as more interactive with them and as major providers of rewards *and* punishments.

There is also a psychoanalytic hypothesis which these data seem to confirm. In summarizing psychoanalytic writings on identification, Bronfenbrenner (1958) notes that one of the "syndromes of parent-child relationship . . . predisposing the child to incorporate or introject the parent" is "a relationship based on conditional love, in which the parent, willfully or unconsciously, withholds expression of affection as the price of conformity" (p. 128). This means that the boy is most likely to identify with his father if his feelings toward him are affectionate, while the father's love is given conditionally. According to this hypothesis, high nurturance from the father, together with the threat of withdrawal of his love (high FP) would lead to strong father identification. This prediction seems to be verified by the finding that highly masculine boys have relatively high Father Power scores, indicating a high degree of combined father nurturance and father punishment.

The findings may also be conceptualized in terms of general behavior theory. Among those with whom the preschool boy has intimate associations, the father is the one who has the most adequate knowledge of appropriate masculine behavior. If there is a high level of father-son interaction (high FPow scores), the father should frequently, and fairly regularly, reward the son's sex-appropriate responses and punish sex-inappropriate responses when they occur. Consequently, the boy's masculine responses should be relatively rapidly and effectively strengthened, while his sex-inappropriate responses become extinguished. In short, vigorous application of both rewards and punishments by the father facilitate the son's shift from feminine to masculine identification.

On the other hand, the condition of relatively little father-son interaction implies sporadic, and at best ineffective, rewards and punishments by the father. Under these circumstances, the shift in identification may be a difficult one, and the child's acquisition of sex-typed interests and behavior may be considerably retarded.

It seems that the father's use of *both* reward *and* punishment is his most effective method of "teaching" his son masculine behavior. It must be emphasized, however, that the high masculine and low masculine groups also differed significantly in the individual variables relating to perceptions of father reward and father punishment. From this it may be inferred that sex-appropriate behavior may be "taught" primarily by rewarding appropriate responses *or* punishing inappropriate responses. In short, from the child's point of view, the important factor is the salience of his relationship with his father, not the particular techniques that the father uses in handling him.

Of course, the present data refer *only* to masculinity of interests. Other possible long-range consequents of different processes of identification cannot be evaluated. For example, it is quite possible that boys who learn their sex roles primarily as a result of being punished or threatened by their fathers differ in many ways (e.g., in personality characteristics, self-conceptions, or basic motivations) from those who achieve their masculine identifications by means of developmental identification or through learning based on some combination of reward and punishment by the father. As the data stand, however, we can only state that five-year-old boys may shift from feminine to masculine identification, as measured by the acquisition of masculine interests, as a result of either developmental or defensive identification processes or, as role theory suggests, by some combination of the two.

SUMMARY

The IT Scale for Children (ITSC), a test of sex-typing of interests, was administered to 38 white, middle-class, kindergarten boys. The 10 *S*s scoring highest in the test were assumed to have developed the highest degree of male role identification, while the 10 scoring lowest were considered the least strongly identified with this role.

In order to determine the relationship between parental perceptions and degree of masculine identification, each of the 20 boys was tested in a structured doll-play situation. During the session, the child completed, in play, nine incomplete stories involving parent-child relations. Responses were scored in terms of the amount of nurturance, punishment, and power (nurturance plus punishment) attributed to the mother, father, and parents as a unit.

The study was designed to evaluate three hypothesized processes of identification—developmental, defensive, and role-taking. Analysis of the data provided evidence consistent with all three hypotheses. As predicted from the developmental identification hypothesis, young boys who were strongly identified with the male role perceived their fathers as more rewarding and nurturant ($p = .02$) than their weakly identified peers did. According to the defensive identification hypothesis, the strongly father-identified boys perceived their fathers as more punitive and threatening. This hypothesis was also supported ($p = .06$). Boys high and low in masculinity were also clearly differentiated on the Father Power score ($p = .007$). This finding indicates that those who have made substantial male identifications view their fathers as powerful sources of *both* reward and punishment, and is in accordance with role theory, which maintains that the child is most likely to assimilate the role of an individual with whom he has intensive interactions, especially if this individual is powerful. To the present authors, it seems that role theory, with its explicit emphasis on the importance of both reward and punishment in role-learning, best integrates all these data.

References

BRIM, O. G., JR.   Family structure and sex role learning by children: a further analysis of Helen Koch's data. *Sociometry,* 1958, **21,** 1–16.

BRONFENBRENNER, U.   The study of identification through interpersonal perception. In R. Tagiuri & L. Petrullo (Eds.), Person Perception and Interpersonal Behavior. Stanford, Calif.: Stanford University Press, 1958. Pp. 110–130.

BROWN, D. D.   Sex role preference in young children. *Psychol. Monogr.,* 1956, **70** (14, Whole No. 421).

COTTRELL, L. S., JR.   The analysis of situational fields in social psychology. *Amer. sociol. Rev.,* 1942, **7,** 370–383.

FREUD, ANNA. *The Ego and the Mechanisms of Defense.* London: Hogarth, 1937.

FREUD, S.   *Group Psychology and the Analysis of the Ego.* London: Hogarth, 1949.

LEVIN, H., & SEARS, R. R.   Identification with parents as a determinant of doll play aggression. *Child Develpm.,* 1956, **27,** 135–153.

MANN, H. B., & WHITNEY, D. R.   On a test of whether one of two random variables is stochastically larger than the other. *Ann. math. Statist.,* 1947, **18,** 50–60.

MOWRER, O. H. *Learning Theory and Personality Dynamics.* New York: Ronald, 1950.

PARSONS, T.   Family structure and the socialization of the child. In T. Parsons & R. F. Bales (Eds.), *Family, Socialization, and Interaction Processes.* Glencoe, Ill.: Free Press, 1955.

PAYNE, D. E., & MUSSEN, P. H.   Parent-child relations and father identification among adolescent boys. *J. abnorm. soc. Psychol.,* 1956, **52,** 358–362.

RICHARDS, T. W., & SIMONS, MARJORIE.   Fels Child Behavior Scale. *Genet. psychol. Monogr.,* 1941, **24,** 259–309.

SEARS, PAULINE.   Child-rearing factors related to playing of sex-typed roles. *Amer. Psychologist,* 1953, **8,** 431. (Abstract)

SEARS, R. R., MACCOBY, ELEANOR E., & LEVIN, H. *Patterns of Child Rearing.* Evanston, Ill.: Row, Peterson, 1957.

SEARS, R. R., PINTLER, M. H., & SEARS, PAULINE.   Effect of father separation on preschool children's doll play aggression. *Child Develpm.,* 1946, **17,** 219–243.

An Exploratory Study of the Attitudes of Noncrippled Children Toward Crippled Children in Three Selected Elementary Schools

Helen K. Billings

PURPOSE OF THE STUDY

This study was concerned with the problem of discovering what attitudes are held by noncrippled elementary children of grades 1, 3, and 6 toward crippled children. It was an effort to find whether the factors influencing the formation of certain stereotypes such as race, nationality, and religion tend to become the same factors influencing the formation of stereotypes or prejudices regarding less "culturally important" characteristics, such as physical or mental deficiencies. It was primarily exploratory and descriptive in character.

THEORETICAL POSITION

The major theoretical consideration upon which this study was based was proposed by Roger C. Barker (1:8):

Individuals who differ physically from the majority of individuals around them have the same minority status as minority groups . . . The minority status of the physically disabled, which is due to the negative attitudes of the physically normal majority, is, in almost all respects, similar to the problem of racial and religious, under-privileged minorities, although it may well be that the source of the negative attitudes toward the physically disabled is even deeper and less rational.

HYPOTHESES

The study investigated three major hypotheses:

Hypothesis I—The attitudes of noncrippled children toward crippled children tend to be different from their attitudes toward noncrippled children and these attitudes tend to be "unfavorable."

Hypothesis II—There is a significant increase in the "unfavorableness" of attitudes toward cripples between grades 1 and 6.

"An Exploratory Study of the Attitudes of Noncrippled Children Toward Crippled Children in Three Selected Elementary Schools," by Helen K. Billings, *Journal of Experimental Education*, No. 31, 381–387. © 1963, Dembar Publications, Inc.

Hypothesis III—The degree of "unfavorableness" of attitude toward
cripples is related to the degree of satisfactory social-emotional adjustment of the school child.

DEFINITION OF TERMS

Certain key terms were used in the study. They were defined in the
following way:

Favorable attitudes are those which tend to result in verbal expressions and acts toward crippled children that tend to give them a feeling
of acceptance, security, and worth, as measured by judges' inferences
from the content material contained in the data procured through the
two projective techniques.

Unfavorable attitudes are those which result in behavior toward the
crippled child which tend to give him a feeling of rejection, insecurity,
and worthlessness.

Neutral attitudes are those attitudes which cannot be said, in the
opinion of the judges, to reveal either favorable or unfavorable attitudes
toward the crippled.

Crippled child, for this study, is defined as a child of elementary
school age who is visibly disabled, through congenital or acquired defects, in the use of his legs and body musculature so that he is unable to
compete on terms of equality with a normal individual of the same age
in the matter of locomotion.

Normal child refers only to the normality of not having an obvious
crippling disability as referred to above.

Disability is used throughout this study as a static term, merely
indicating that the child has some defect or impairment.

Handicap is a more dynamic term referring to the degree to which
the defect or impairment interferes with, or limits, the individual's reaching his maximum. (A physical defect may cause a psychological handicap.)

Projective technique, "The essential feature of a projective technique is that it evokes from the subject what is, in various ways, expressive of his private world and personality process." (2:47) "Tell me a
story . . ." and "Finish this sentence . . ." are variations of widely used
projective techniques.

Generalize refers here specifically to the tendency of the noncrippled
to "spread" evaluation of characteristics actually affected by the injury to
other characteristics not so affected.

Adjustment rating is the score given by teachers to indicate the
child's degree of social adjustment to the school situation.

SAMPLE USED IN THIS STUDY

Fifty-four elementary school children were chosen randomly as subjects for this study, eighteen from each of the three grade levels. These were evenly divided among three schools representative of three distinct "socio-economic" levels. Six children from each of the grades in each school comprised the sample.

PROCEDURE

Two projective techniques, especially adapted for this study, were administered to each of the fifty-four subjects in an effort to identify existing attitudes (and to explore possible factors influencing their development) toward crippled children.

1. Instrument A, comprised of two parts, employed a "Tell me a story" technique; a picture of a seven-year-old girl was used as a stimulus. Children were asked to write stories about the girl in the picture. Some time later, a similar picture was shown and was presented in a similar manner. This time, however, the teacher casually referred to the subject in the picture as "a little crippled girl." Differences between the two stories comprised the data for assessing the attitudes.

2. Instrument B was a "Complete this sentence" test wherein three sentence "starters," among the ten in the test, were related to cripples.

Analysis of the data from these two instruments indicated that responses seemed to fall into two rather well-defined classifications:

1. *Social responses,* indicating acceptance or rejection of the crippled person such as: "I play with him"; "She is my friend"; "We won't let him play with us"; etc.

2. *Value responses,* indicating a judgment of the crippled person such as: "He is no good"; "He is bad"; "She can't do anything"; etc.

These general classifications were then formulated by the judges into two scales: 1) Acceptance-Rejection Scale, 2) Worthy-Devalued Scale.

The first term in the name given each of the scales devised was the term indicating the "ideal" attitude toward cripples. The second term in the name given each scale thus indicated the opposite pole in the continuum. Four categories (degrees of intensity of attitude) were set up and coding procedures established. A four-point scale was used because of the widely recognized weakness of odd-numbered scales. The most desirable pole of each scale continuum was given the smallest score, *one* (very favorable attitude), and the least desirable was given the highest score, *four* (very unfavorable attitude). The large number of responses falling in the middle range were differentiated by being given a score of *two* (somewhat favorable) or *three* (somewhat unfavorable).

Each judge worked alone and evaluated the two stories independently. Stories were rated on two counts:

1. The general "feeling tone" of the story. This included an analysis of words and phrases instrumental in setting the "mood." For example, the general feeling tone might be one in which the reader was left with the general impression that the writer was neutral, or at least not unfavorable toward the central character in the story about the crippled girl. However, if the story should be rife with expressions such as "dark, dismal day," "frowning," "weeping," "lonely," etc., then the rating would tend to drop toward a "somewhat unfavorable" rating score.

2. The general "ending" of the story. This involved such questions as: "Is the cripple seen as able to succeed in life, though crippled?" "Does the future look hopeless for the cripple?" "Is the ending 'realistic and acceptable'?" "Does the subject provide a convenient 'miracle' ending so that he does not have to deal with a crippled heroine?"

Inasmuch as these two criteria were difficult to differentiate in some cases, it was decided to find the mean of the scores as a more consistent and dependable measure when the two scores did not agree. Thus, if a judge rated the "feeling tone" a "three" and the ending a "two," his mean evaluation of this attitude as revealed in the story would be a "two-point-five." The general rating in this case would be identical with the judge who rated the "feeling tone" a "two" and the "ending" as a "three." A general rating was given for both A-R and W-D scales.

The Sentence Completion Test was rated, also, on the four-point scales, on A-R and W-D scales. All three of the significant sentences were judged as a group. For example, if the sentences were "Crippled kids are *mean";* "The boy on crutches is *helpless";* and "The girl in the wheelchair is *crying,"* the words "mean," "helpless," and "crying" would provide the rater with the basis for judging the attitude.

Each teacher is required to evaluate a child's general social adjustment periodically throughout the school year. The most recent of these scores was used in testing Hypothesis III. It was an effort to discover if the child whom the teacher rated as "best" adjusted would be the "most favorable" in his attitude toward cripples.

ANALYSIS AND FINDINGS

The analysis of the data gave support to two of the three major hypotheses of this study, namely Hypothesis I and Hypothesis II.

Hypothesis I—Attitudes of noncrippled children toward crippled children are significantly more unfavorable than their attitudes toward noncrippled children.

This hypothesis was tested through the use of a Chi Square Test (3:384). Data in Table I (below) indicate the number of scores in each category on both stories of Instrument A and on Instrument B. Tables II and III indicate the significance of differences between attitudes on Story 1 and Story 2 of Instrument A, which was used to test this hypothesis. Because of the small number of responses falling in categories 1 and 4 (the extremes), categories 1 and 2 were combined as indicating "favorable" responses and categories 3 and 4 were combined as "unfavorable" when computing the significance of the difference between attitudes on Story 1 and Story 2. This procedure was followed in all of the tables used in the testing of all hypotheses.

TABLE I
NUMBER OF A-R AND W-D* RATINGS ON INSTRUMENT A
AND INSTRUMENT B BY GRADE LEVELS (N = 18)

Instrument A	GRADE 1 SCORE				GRADE 3 SCORE				GRADE 6 SCORE				TOTAL			
	1	2	3	4	1	2	3	4	1	2	3	4	1	2	3	4
Story 1																
A-R	0	18	0	0	0	16	2	0	0	17	0	1	0	51	2	1
W-D	0	17	1	0	0	17	1	0	0	15	2	1	0	49	4	1
Story 2																
A-R	1	10	7	0	0	2	15	1	0	1	16	1	0	14	38	2
W-D	1	11	6	0	0	2	15	1	0	2	16	0	1	15	37	1
INSTRUMENT B																
A-R	1	11	6	0	1	2	14	1	0	1	16	1	2	14	36	2
W-D	1	10	7	0	1	3	13	1	0	2	15	1	2	15	35	2

*A-R = Acceptance-Rejection Scale
W-D = Worthy-Devalued Scale

An examination of the data shown in Table I indicates that, in both the A-R and the W-D areas, by far the greater number of "favorable" ratings were found for Story 1 (noncrippled stimulus). An almost equally large number of "unfavorable" ratings were given to Story 2 (crippled stimulus). Conversely, a negligible number of "unfavorable" ratings were given to Story 1 and only a slightly greater number of "favorable" ratings were given to Story 2. (See Tables II and III.)

Thus Hypothesis I appeared to be substantiated from the data secured for this study. Elementary school children grades 1, 3, and 6 expressed attitudes toward crippled children that were significantly more "unfavorable" than their attitudes toward noncrippled children.

TABLE II
COMPARISON OF ATTITUDES ON THE ACCEPTANCE-REJECTION
SCALE TO STORIES 1 AND 2 ON INSTRUCTION A

STORY	UNFAVORABLE ATTITUDES	FAVORABLE ATTITUDES	TOTAL
1	3	51	54
2	40	14	54
Total	43	65	108

$$x^2_c = 40.820 \qquad\qquad df = 1 \qquad\qquad P. = < .01$$

TABLE III
COMPARISON OF ATTITUDES ON THE WORTHY-DEVALUED
SCALE TO STORIES 1 AND 2 ON INSTRUMENT A

STORY	UNFAVORABLE ATTITUDES	FAVORABLE ATTITUDES	TOTAL
1	5	49	54
2	38	16	54
Total	43	65	108

$$x^2_c = 40.401 \qquad\qquad df = 1 \qquad\qquad P. = < .01$$

FIGURE I
GRAPH SHOWING INCREASE IN "UNFAVORABLENESS" AND DECREASE
OF "FAVORABLENESS" IN ATTITUDES TOWARD CRIPPLES BETWEEN
GRADES 1, 3, AND 6

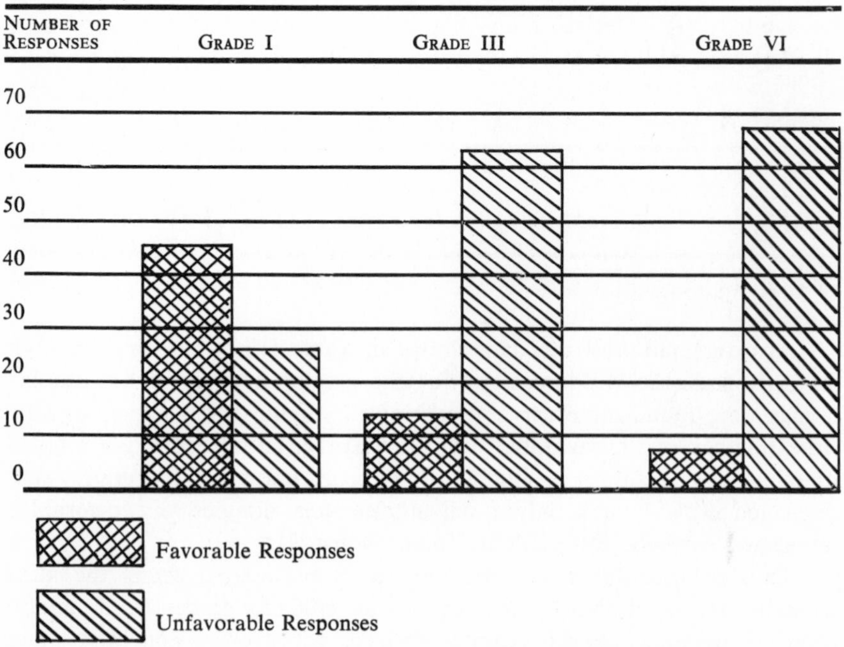

NUMBER OF RESPONSES	GRADE I	GRADE III	GRADE VI

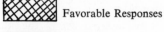

Favorable Responses

Unfavorable Responses

Hypothesis II—Attitudes toward crippled children are a function of the grade level (age) of the child holding the attitudes.

A Chi Square Test (3:384) was applied to the data to test the above hypothesis. Comparisons between the various grades is summarized in Table I. The data revealed that there was a significant difference between grades 1 and 6. However, such a difference was not shown to exist between grades 3 and 6. The slight increase in the number of "unfavorable" responses between grades 3 and 6 indicated the same direction of change as between grades 1 and 3 but the difference was not statistically significant. Figure 1 depicts, in graphic form, the increase of "unfavorableness" and the decrease of "favorableness" as revealed by the data.

Hypothesis III—Attitudes toward crippled children are a function of the social-emotional adjustment of the child holding the attitudes.

This hypothesis was tested by use of the same Chi Square Test (3:384). All responses on Story 2 of Instrument A and all responses to Instrument B, both A-R and W-D scales, were used. The same procedure was applied in the grouping of ratings as for Hypothesis I and Hypothesis II, namely categories 1 and 2 were combined to form the "favorable" attitudes and categories 3 and 4 were grouped to form the "unfavorable" attitudes. A similar procedure was used in classifying the adjustment ratings classroom teachers had made of the subjects. Those scores at or above the median (scores 3, 4, 5) were grouped to form the "high" adjustment ratings and those scores below the median (scores 1 and 2) were combined and considered as "low" adjustment.

Thus the variables for Hypothesis III were the adjustment ratings ("high" and "low") of classroom teachers and the scores on attitudes ("favorable" and "unfavorable") made by the judges in this study. Analysis of the data revealed that the hypothesis was not supported (see Tables IV, V, VI, and VII).

It had been predicted that those children judged to be "high" in adjustment would be found to be most "favorable" in their attitudes toward cripples. Rather than finding a positive relationship between these two variables, however, inspection of the data reveals that a negative relationship exists at the .01 level of confidence. That is, the students judged to be "high" in adjustment were the same students who were most "unfavorable" in their attitudes toward cripples.

Data presented in the tables indicate a markedly greater proportion of subjects rated "high" on adjustment held "unfavorable" attitudes toward cripples. Little difference was found between the "favorable" and the "unfavorable" attitudes of children who rated "low" on adjustment.

TABLE IV
COMPARISON OF ATTITUDES WITH ADJUSTMENT RATINGS ON
ACCEPTANCE-REJECTION SCALE, STORY 2, INSTRUMENT A

ADJUSTMENT RATINGS	UNFAVORABLE ATTITUDES	FAVORABLE ATTITUDES	TOTAL
High	37	6	43
Low	6	5	11
Total	43	11	54

$x_c^2 = 3.972$　　　　　df $= 1$　　　　　P. $= <.05$

TABLE V
COMPARISON OF ATTITUDES WITH ADJUSTMENT RATINGS ON
WORTHY-DEVALUED SCALE, STORY 2, INSTRUMENT A

ADJUSTMENT RATINGS	UNFAVORABLE ATTITUDES	FAVORABLE ATTITUDES	TOTAL
High	38	5	43
Low	5	6	11
Total	43	11	54

$x_c^2 = 7.402$　　　　　df $= 1$　　　　　P. $= <.01$

TABLE VI
COMPARISON OF ATTITUDES WITH ADJUSTMENT RATINGS ON
ACCEPTANCE-REJECTION SCALE, INSTRUMENT B

ADJUSTMENT RATINGS	UNFAVORABLE ATTITUDES	FAVORABLE ATTITUDES	TOTAL
High	38	4	42
Low	7	9	12
Total	45	9	54

$x_c^2 = 4.331$　　　　　df $= 1$　　　　　P. $= <.05$

TABLE VII
COMPARISON OF ATTITUDES WITH ADJUSTMENT RATINGS ON
WORTHY-DEVALUED SCALE, INSTRUMENT B

ADJUSTMENT RATINGS	UNFAVORABLE ATTITUDES	FAVORABLE ATTITUDES	TOTAL
High	38	5	43
Low	5	6	11
Total	43	11	54

$x_c^2 = 7.402$　　　　　df $= 1$　　　　　P. $= <.01$

SUMMARY OF FINDINGS

The data indicated that, in general:

1) Noncrippled children held unfavorable attitudes toward their crippled peers.

2) The oldest group of children (age 11.8 years) were significantly more unfavorable in their attitudes toward cripples than the youngest

group (age 6.5 years).

3) Children judged (by classroom teachers) to be "high" in adjustment were rated (by judges in this study) to be most "unfavorable" in their attitudes toward cripples.

The findings concerning the major hypotheses tended to point up the significance of attitudes displayed toward crippled children as a factor in the social-emotional adjustment of both able and disabled children.

SUMMARY OF IMPLICATIONS FOR THE THEORY

Barker's theory that "individuals who differ physically from the majority of people around them have the status of minority group members and, as such, are subject to the dynamics that hold for any minority group" (1:8), was corroborated by the findings in this study.

Status was made evident by the attitudes of others toward them and it was shown that the noncrippled children (majority group) do hold attitudes that are unfavorable toward crippled children (minority group) and those attitudes tend to reject and devalue the crippled child, forcing him into the position that Barker describes as "ambiguous" and "under-privileged," thus breeding in him insecurity, conflict, and frustration. This study showed that there was a significant difference between attitudes which the elementary school children in this study displayed toward crippled children and those which they displayed toward noncrippled children. Data revealed that crippled children were considered as "inferior" and that they were avoided or rejected by their peers. It further revealed that the older children (grades 3 and 6) were significantly more "unfavorable" in their attitudes than the younger children (grade 1). Hence, for children in grades 1, 3, and 6, the data supported Barker's theory that cripples have the status of minority group members. That they are also subject to the dynamics that hold for any minority group is also supported by this study.

When education in the public schools for all children is the common goal, when equal status is assumed in the classrooms of the elementary school, then the implication seems clear. Ways must be found to reduce prejudice toward cripples if they are not to be further handicapped by the unfavorable attitudes shown them by others in the school.

References

1. BARKER, R. C. "Somatopsychological Significance of Crippling," *Bulletin 55* of the Social Science Research Council, New York, 1953, pp. 59-89.
2. FRANK, L. K. *Projective Methods* (Springfield, Ill.: Charles Thomas Publications, 1948).

3. EDWARDS, A. L. *Statistical Methods for Behavioral Sciences* (New York: Rinehart and Co., 1954).

4. MEYERSON, LEE. "Physical Disability as a Social-Psychological Problem," *Journal of Social Issues,* IV (1948), Editorial Notes.

Dynamics of the Underachievement of Gifted Students

John Curtis Gowan

In recent years, as manpower reserves of talent for scientific and professional occupations have become depleted, more and more attention is being directed to the salvaging of a significant portion of our ablest youth who qualify for the title of gifted underachievers. We are not concerned in this discussion with the economic and social factors which Stice (16) has demonstrated prevented over half of the high-ability high school seniors in our country from going on directly to college. We are rather concerned with the equally depressing fact, demonstrated by Wedemeyer (19), that of those who go, almost 30 percent of the top decile of intelligence fail to attain significant achievement in scholarship because of emotional, educational, personal, financial, or other problems. Faced with the present economic and political rivalry with Russia, a nation turning out scientists at twice our rate, our country cannot afford this waste of its most vital resource—talent.

It is the purpose of this paper, therefore, to explore recent research on the causes and prevention of underachievement in gifted students. Moreover a developmental hypothesis is proposed to account for agreements in research findings and practical implications for education which seem warranted by these results are appended. By "gifted student" we shall refer to a student, two or more standard deviations upward from the mean in general intelligence, loosely—an IQ of 130 or above. Recognizing that practically all gifted children are technically underachievers to some extent, we may define "underachievement" for our purposes as performance which places the student more than a full standard deviation below his ability standing in the same group. Roughly, this works out to about 30 percentiles difference, so that we may call gifted children underachievers when they fall in the middle third in scholastic achievement in grades and severe underachievers when they fall in the lowest third. It should be noted that these definitions are ones made merely for clarity and convenience, and are by no means uniformly used by all those whose research is later to be reported.

It may first be of value to note data concerning the number and percentage of underachievers in secondary schools represented by the previous definitions. Figures have elsewhere (10) been presented to show that in one California high school where seven percent of the students were gifted, 42 percent of these were underachievers. In another high school where two percent of the students were gifted, 16 percent of these were underachievers. In an outstanding independent secondary school, 12 percent of the students were gifted, and nine percent of these were underachievers. In the same paper, it was suggested that "where the percent of underachievers runs much higher than 15 percent, there may be problems of morale, antisocial trends, or other factors in the school which should receive special attention" (10).

There is considerable research evidence to indicate that achievement both in high school and later stems from habits, interests, attitudes, and motivation established in elementary school. With gifted children, these latter factors seem to be facilitated by special curriculum adjustments.

Terman (18), for example, reported that gifted youth who were accelerated in school outstripped those who had not been accelerated, both in college and in later life success. He concluded that "the exceptionally bright student kept with his age group finds little to challenge his intelligence, and all too often develops habits of laziness that later wreck his college career." The Los Angeles School District (11) in 1931 reported a high school comparison between 284 opportunity A students and 381 equally gifted controls; the opportunity A group, which had been segregated in the fifth-seventh grades, had higher high school grade averages, earned more honor grades, and had fewer failures. Cohler (4) found in a similar study that the effect of acceleration was improved performance, and stressed the need for vital school experiences to motivate the child. Sanford (15), after a discussion of the bright child who fails, considered boredom, lack of motivation, and home problems as major causes of underachievement. Engle (6), in another study of accelerants, found acceleration generally conducive to more favorable educational and vocational results than non-acceleration. The same results in even more specific terms were reported recently for the Ford scholarship holders (8). It seems evident from the weight of the foregoing reports either that special curriculum methods for the gifted have some value in themselves in reducing underachievement, or that the increased attention, interest, recognition, and personal contact which accompany them result in increased motivation and consequent increased achievement.

A number of investigators have reported on college level achievement and underachievement of gifted students. Nason (13) found achievement at this level more related to clearness and definiteness of academic and vocational plans and to parental influences than to personal adjustment. Burgess (3), in a study of engineering underachievers, described them in these terms: "less intellectually adaptive . . . less emotional control . . . more dependent in attitudes toward others . . . motivation weak . . . tend not to enjoy the school situation . . . unable to see the value of an education." Dowd (5), in a college study of underachievers in the top decile, found no personality difference, but more incidence of males, and concluded that the factors are operative before college entrance. Morgan (12) in a similar study concluded generally that college achievement of high ability students is "related to 1) maturity and seriousness of interests, 2) awareness and concern for others, 3) a sense of responsibility, 4) dominance, persuasiveness, and self-confidence, and 5) motivation to achieve." Similar results were secured by Pearlman (14).

Studies on younger gifted underachievers have tended to emphasize home backgrounds, parental problems, and emotional immaturity. A study by Bonsall and Stefflre (2) emphasized the importance of not overlooking the socio-economic factor. Basic causes for the behavior of 38 gifted children, referred to a metropolitan clinic as maladjusted and reported elsewhere (9), included disagreements between parents over methods of raising the child, transference of problems of parents to the child, overanxiety or overprotectiveness on the part of the parent, fears of the parents regarding the children's health and safety, divorces and separations, and sibling rivalry. The school problems of these gifted children were seen in such symptoms as: ". . . not interested in school, didn't like teacher, work was too easy, didn't have any friends, liked to stay home with mother." Another inquiry (10) into the family backgrounds of high school underachievers of IQ 130 or better found that they differed significantly from gifted achievers in that the underachievers were predominantly boys, had parents who took little part in community activities, had fewer books in their homes, had less often received private lessons, and expressed a desire in choosing a vocation to get away from the family. The pattern which emerged was one of indifference and rejection on the part of the parent, or behavior so interpreted by the underachiever. In addition he had less time for outside activities, had more problems with time and money, and seemed lacking in ability to conduct himself easily in social situations and to make easy adjustments.

A recent study meriting attention was one made by Barrett (1) in the Toronto, Ontario, high schools. He concluded: the pattern of underachievement is apparent by the fifth grade with weakness in arithmetic characteristic; and parents of underachievers tend to exhibit a neutral or uninterested attitude toward education, to be overanxious, oversolicitous, or inconsistent in their attitude toward the child. In general, such homes show evidence of conflict, authoritarianism by the parent, or domination by the child. In the school situation the underachievers exhibit a predominantly negative attitude toward school, win less acceptance from their classmates, tend to show less interest in reading. While both show feelings of inadequacy, the achievers are aware of their difficulties and constructive in their efforts, while the underachievers withdraw and refuse to compete.

Another study deserving special attention is that of Gough (9). In an effort to construct and validate an achievement scale on the California Psychological Inventory, he investigated personality items among a large number of underachievers. From this group he selected paired groups of gifted achievers and underachievers, dichotomized for both high school and college as well by sex. While there were a number of personality differences, the major ones were that underachievers were significantly higher on the scale for delinquency; and achievers were higher on the scales for social responsibility and academic motivation. The scale for academic motivation correlated over .50 with scales for good impression, lack of dissimulation, social responsibility, tolerance, social participation, antidelinquency, intellectual efficiency, lack of impulsivity. Gough concluded that ". . . academic achievement among intellectually gifted persons is a form of social behavior, and academic underachievement is a form of asocial behavior." He summarizes that underachievement among the gifted is akin to delinquent behavior. A consonant finding had been previously reported by Terman (17) in comparing 150 of his most successful gifted men with 150 least successful. The A group seemed to have greater enthusiasm for living and activity. They read more books, made more collections, engaged in more hobbies, were more successful in school, and popular with classmates and teachers.

The common elements from these research reports indicate that achievement in gifted students versus underachievement seems related to the following factors:

1. Clearness and definiteness of academic and occupational choices versus the opposite
2. Strong ego controls and strength versus weak ones
3. Socialization and social interaction versus withdrawal and self-sufficiency
4. Good use of time and money versus lack of such habits
5. Reading and arithmetic ability versus lack of such competency

6. Positive character integration versus psychotic or neurotic tendency
7. Permissiveness, intraception, and creativity versus authoritarianism in the parental home environment or the gifted individual himself
8. Parents who motivated and took pains or interest versus dominant, autocratic, or laissez-faire parents
9. Some tension in task demands in childhood (the imposition of goals which are clear and possible to attain by parents) versus either no goal or impossible ones
10. Maturity, responsibility, and seriousness of interests versus opposites
11. Awareness of and concern for others versus disinterest
12. Dominance, persuasiveness, and self-confidence versus their opposites
13. Enthusiastic, socialized, activity-oriented view of life versus apathetic withdrawal

As such a summarization is inspected critically it appears to be a description of healthy personal attitudes and behaviors which are associated with the accomplishment of growth patterns on schedule. These skills and attributes are connected with cognitive ego development and singularly related to various developmental stages of childhood. As each new adaption is resolved successfully a new strength and vitality is incorporated into the ego. An excellent description of this developmental process is given by Erikson (7), especially in his "industry" stage which coincides with the early latency period when the child turns outward from the family to peer group recognition in which, in Erikson's words: "He can become an eager and absorbed unit in a productive situation. . . . He develops industry, that is he adjusts himself to the inorganic laws of the tool world. . . . The danger in this stage lies in a sense of inadequacy and inferiority. If he despairs of his tools and skills or of his status among his tool partners, his ego boundaries suffer, and he abandons hope for the ability to identify early with others who apply themselves . . ." Parents who are either too autocratic, too dominant, too protective, or too laissez-faire arrest the child's development into and through this industry stage, where he learns the joy of real work and accomplishment as an aid to status-getting among his peers and with outside authority figures. As a result he is thrown back for libido rewards to the earlier and more primitive satisfactions of the oral, anal, narcissistic, and oedipal periods. Because boys are slightly less mature than girls, and because parents sometimes expect more of them, their introduction to cultural tasks demands may be more difficult, and hence more problems may accrue.

To be sure, public schooling in the primary grades does much for those children whose parents may not have been successful in aiding the child through these critical adjustments; but while doing well by the generality, it frequently misses meeting the needs of two important groups. First is the minority group member who does not identify with the alien culture of the school and second is the gifted child whom it does not challenge during this crucial period. Such a hypothesis explains most of the observed differences between gifted achievers and under-achievers, as well as pointing up the vital necessity of adequate stimulation of gifted children during the primary grades, instead of forcing them to remain bored and inactive.

In contrast to gifted underachievers, the childhood of the gifted achiever appears to involve a constant, but not severe, pressure toward tasks and responsibilities which are perceived by the child as security- or affection-producing and which are neither capriciously administered nor impossible to attain under the aegis of interest-stimulating parental guidance. Thus early experience in realistic goal setting and achieving leads to a personality with strong super-ego demands and strong ego strength to complete these demands. Such a personality tends in adulthood to have a high sense of social responsibility and large performance needs. He is not without anxieties, but these are oriented toward reality, and tend to be ameliorated by his or others' modification of the environment rather than by changes in his attitudes toward it.

The gifted underachiever, on the other hand, appears to be a kind of intellectual delinquent who withdraws from goals, activities, and active social participation generally. As a child his initial attempts at creative accomplishment may not have been seen by others as "worthwhile," but only as "queer" or "different." The blocking of this avenue of rewarding behavior by others, tending as it does to reinforce his often over-critical appraisal of the disparity between his goals and achievements, may blunt his work libido, stifle his creativity, and consign him to a routine of withdrawal and escape as the most tolerable method of insulating his ego from hurt in an alien and disinterested world.

Thus achievement and underachievement in the gifted may be viewed as social and asocial responses of the individual to proper stimulation regarding developmental tasks either tendered or denied by the parental and educational environments.

References

1. BARRETT, H. G., "Underachievement, A Pressing Problem," *Bulletin of the Ontario Secondary School Teachers' Federation,* Oshawa, Ontario, 36:3:111-12, 151-2, (May 31, 1956)
2. BONSALL, MARCELLA and STEFFLRE, B., "The Temperament of Gifted Children," *California Journal of Educational Research,* 6:162-65, 1955
3. BURGESS, ELVA, "Personality Factors of Over- and Under-Achievers in Engineering," *Journal of Educational Psychology,* 42:2:89-99, (Feb., 1956)

4. COHLER, M. J., "Scholastic Status of Achievers and Non-Achievers of Superior Intelligence," *Journal of Educational Psychology,* 32:603-10, 1941

5. DOWD, R. J., "Underachieving Students of High Capacity," *Journal of Higher Education,* 1952, 23:327-30

6. ENGLE, T. L., "Achievement of Pupils Who Have Had Double Promotions in Elementary School," *Elementary School Journal,* 36:185-89, 1935

7. ERIKSON, E. H., *Childhood and Society,* W. W. Norton Co., New York, 1950, 219-33

8. FORD FOUNDATION, Fund for the Advancement of Education, *Bridging the Gap Between School and College,* New York, 1953

9. GOUGH, H. G., "Factors Related to Differential Achievement Among Gifted Persons," (mimeographed), University of California, Berkeley, Cal., 1955

10. GOWAN, J. C., "The Underachieving Gifted Child: A Problem for Everyone," *Exceptional Children,* 21:247-49, (April, 1955)

11. LOS ANGELES CITY SCHOOL DISTRICT, *Fourth Yearbook of the Psychological and Educational Research Division,* #211, Los Angeles, Cal., 1931, 82

12. MORGAN, H. H., "A Psychometric Comparison of Achieving and Non-Achieving College Students of High Ability," *Journal of Consulting Psychology,* 16:292-98, 1952

13. NASON, L. J., "Patterns of Circumstances Related to Educational Achievement of High School Pupils of Superior Ability," Unp. Ed. D. Thesis, U. of So. California, Los Angeles, Cal., 1954

14. PEARLMAN, SAMUEL, "An Investigation of the Problems of Academic Under-achievement Among Intellectually Superior College Students," Unp. Ph.D. Thesis, New York Univ., 1952, (microfilmed, Ann Arbor, Mich., #4149)

15. SANFORD, E. G., "The Bright Child Who Fails," *Understanding the Child,* 21:85-88, 1952

16. STICE, G., MOLLENKOPF, W. G., and TORGERSON, W. S., *Background Factors and College Going Plans Among High Aptitude Public High School Seniors,* Educational Testing Service, Princeton, N.J., 1956

17. TERMAN, L. M., and others, *Genetic Studies of Genius, IV: The Gifted Child Grows Up,* Stanford Univ. Press, Palo Alto, Cal., 1947

18. TERMAN, L. M., "Earmarking the Talented," *Science News Letter* (Apr. 3, 1964), p. 214

19. WEDEMEYER, C. A., "Gifted Achievers and Non-Achievers," *Journal of Higher Education,* 24:25-30, 1953

Interpersonal Relations and Mental Health in the Classroom

Richard A. Schmuck, Margaret B. Luszki, and David C. Epperson

The increasing complexity of conditions under which people in our society live and work has emphasized the importance of effective interpersonal relations. Modern life, particularly in our urban centers, places a premium on the ability to get along with others. In addition, individuals must be prepared to deal with tensions and conflicts—not merely to avoid them but to handle them constructively and creatively—if we are to solve some of the problems of contemporary society.

As a result of changes in our society during the last few years, schools have a heavier responsibility than ever before to help pupils develop behavior patterns which equip them to fill useful roles in society and contribute maximally to group productivity. This means that concurrent with the teaching of subject matter, schools must be concerned with the development of interpersonal relationship skills and positive mental health.

The question has been raised repeatedly, "What is optimal mental health?" Many definitions have been posed and many systematic lists prepared which attempt to delineate criteria or state the characteristics by which mentally healthy people can be identified. One such comprehensive attempt was made by Jahoda (3), who reviewed selected literature on mental health and derived an extensive list of factors which are viewed as indicators of mental health. These were classified into six general areas: (1) Positive attitudes toward the self; (2) Optimal growth, development, and self-actualization; (3) Psychic integration; (4) Personal autonomy; (5) Realistic perceptions of the environment; (6) Adequate environmental mastery.

The research being conducted currently at the Institute for Social Research is concerned with several of these mental health factors. This paper deals with the following:

1. *The pupil's attitudes toward himself.* The child who feels he is liked, valued, and accepted by his classmates, who describes himself in favorable terms, and who feels that he is a part of the classroom group, may be thought to be in a positive state of mental health.

2. *The pupil's perception of reality.* The pupil whose perceptions

"Interpersonal Relations and Mental Health in the Classroom," by R. A. Schmuck, M. B. Luszki, and D. C. Epperson, *Mental Hygiene*, 1963, *47*, 289–299. © 1963, National Association for Mental Health, Inc.

of the classroom are relatively free from distortion has better mental health than the pupil who distorts reality frequently.

3. *The pupil's mastery of his environment.* The child's adequacy in meeting the school's formal learning requirements represents one type of mastery of the environment, while his adequacy in establishing positive relationships with other pupils is another type. Both generally result in a satisfying state of affairs for the pupil and are considered to be indicators of positive mental health.

4. *The pupil's actualization of his potential.* A child with academic abilities he does not use is presumed to have poor mental health. In many such cases, energy is being drained off by excessive anxiety, worry, and hostile feelings, so that the pupil is not free to utilize his ability in performing classroom tasks.

These four elements of mental health refer to the pupil's relationship to and his feelings about people and tasks in the classroom environment. *Mental health here refers to the adequacy of the pupil's relationship to his learning environment and the positiveness of his feelings about himself.* With this orientation to mental health it is evident that the teacher is indeed in a position to influence a pupil's mental health, either positively or negatively. If the teacher possesses the skills necessary to establish a wholesome interpersonal atmosphere and if he can organize learning tasks in a manner which will enhance a pupil's self-esteem, he is contributing, simultaneously, to the improvement of a pupil's mental health.

It seems clear that mental health is influenced to a large extent by the way important people in an individual's environment respond to him. This appears to be true for very young infants, children and adolescents, as well as adults of all ages. An individual's concept of himself is built up through the accumulated reflected appraisals of those with whom he comes in contact.

Every person, in other words, makes use of the reactions of other people in formulating his opinion of himself. He relies on others, to a great degree, for the gratifications and rewards which make him feel worthwhile and esteemed, or for the punishments and disapprovals which make him feel inadequate and worthless. It is primarily other people—in person or in the images one holds of them—who are able to make an individual feel secure and happy or lost and unhappy.

Psychological research indicates that when a person feels anxious or fearful in the presence of another, he has difficulty in accurately perceiving the world. His perceptions may become so distorted that he is unable to behave appropriately. Those who have studied these processes have found that the greater the threat a person feels in the presence of another, the more pronounced the restricting and distorting effect is on his thoughts and perceptions of his surroundings.

An experiment performed by Coombs and Taylor (1) illustrates this phenomenon. Mild degrees of personal threat were introduced to students by belligerent examiners while the students were performing a task requiring intellectual functioning. The researchers predicted that this personal threat would result in an increase of time required to complete the task, as well as an increase in errors in performance.

The 50 participants in this experiment were given the task of translating sentences into a simple code. With only a single exception, the students required longer time periods to complete the coding procedure when they were working under threatening conditions, and they also made a greater number of errors of translation than in a comparable, nonthreatening condition. It is not difficult to predict what might happen to a student who again and again is presented with situations that are threatening to him. The extent to which he actualizes his academic potential is likely to be considerably reduced.

Using some of these general notions, social scientists at the Institute for Social Research have systematically collected information concerning the social atmospheres of classroom settings and the mental health conditions of individual pupils.

Van Egmond (6), for instance, in a study of 640 elementary school children, sought to link ideas concerning a pupil's relationships with other pupils and the extent to which that pupil actualizes his academic potential. He constructed an index of the level of actualization from the relative performance on intelligence tests and achievement batteries. He found that boys who achieve some self-esteem and recognition by being able to influence other boys come closer to actualizing their potential than boys who are not able to gain esteem and recognition through influencing other boys. For these latter boys, conditions of threat undoubtedly prevail when they are in the presence of more powerful, influential boys.

For girls, Van Egmond found that those who were liked by their classmates actualized their potential rather fully, while those who were disliked or liked by very few tended to actualize their potential less fully. For girls, the threatening circumstances of being surrounded by other girls who exhibit dislike for them appears to be disruptive enough to affect their classroom performance significantly.

In another study, Lippitt and Gold (4) found that pupils who are highly liked by others express more liking in their ratings of peers than those who are not liked by their peers. Interestingly, through the course of the school year, this difference in the feelings expressed by liked and disliked children becomes even greater, and the disliked children show more negative feelings toward their fellow classmates at the end of the year than at the beginning, while the highly liked show more positive feelings.

Some systematic observation of pupils' interaction in the classroom also supports these findings. The researchers found that those behavior patterns which indicate aggressive-assertive or passive-hostile activity are more frequently characteristic of the disliked children. These children tend to behave in ways that are likely to disrupt classroom functioning to an increasing degree as they realize how their peers feel toward them. Thus, as pupils are placed in threatening social atmospheres, they tend to react in irrational and nonadaptive ways. Often, by behaving aggressively or with hostility, the disliked pupil creates more dislike for himself, and this can go on and on in a circular fashion. The very nature of the situation must be altered before the individual can hope to regain or build up self-esteem.

In still another study of seven elementary classrooms, Echelberger (2) analyzed teacher ratings of children. These ratings were concerned with conditions of positive and negative mental health, as exhibited by the individual pupil. She found that the more influential and popular children impress their teachers with a significantly more favorable "mental health" picture. They show, for instance, fewer behavior problems, greater social adjustment, and more stable emotional patterns.

The purpose of the current research is to study various aspects of the social atmosphere of the classroom and to relate these group relevant aspects to individual mental health. The data presented in this paper are from four upper elementary classrooms in and around Ann Arbor, Mich. These classrooms are part of a broader study of classroom atmospheres, covering grades four through twelve, in different types of communities in southeastern Michigan.

The particular classrooms used in this analysis were selected because they represented the highest grade in which the pupils were working with the same teacher and classmates throughout most of the school day (sixth grade), and because they also represented two contrasting types of social atmospheres. The four teachers involved were all experienced and well-qualified and were considered to be among the better teachers in their particular school systems.

PROPOSITIONS AND RESULTS

Classroom Affection

Classroom groups, like all other groups, have both formal and informal aspects. The formal aspects have to do with the way the various members work toward carrying out the official or specified goals of the group. In the classroom group, for instance, one formal feature is the way in which any child performs the role of pupil, as it is defined by the teacher and the adult community at large.

The informal aspects of a group, on the other hand, have to do with the manner in which each member relates to other members as persons. In the classroom group one informal aspect is the way affection, or pupils' liking for one another, is distributed. These informal features of a group have an important bearing on the formal aspects, or the way the stated objectives of the group are carried out. Many of them, such as the amount of liking members have for one another or their willingness to help and support each other, may be thought of as conditions for positive or negative mental health.

At least two kinds of informal patterns or group structures of classroom affection can be described. The first of these is referred to as a "centrally structured group," or one with a narrow focus of affection. In such a group, a large number of members agree in selecting a small group of individuals as the ones whom they "like the most," and they also agree in selecting a few other members as the ones whom they dislike. As a result of the narrow focus on a very few members who are most popular and another few members who are most unpopular, there are many members who are neglected and are mentioned by no one as being either liked or disliked.

A second kind of informal pattern is referred to as a "diffusely structured group," or one with a wide focus of popularity. In this kind of group there is a fairly equalized distribution of positive and negative choices. Here almost everyone is most liked or least liked by somebody. There are no distinct subgroups or cliques whose members receive a large proportion of the positive or negative preferences, and there are few neglected members.

Consideration of these two types of structures provides the basis for our first proposition.

GENERAL PROPOSITION I: *Classroom groups with a wide focus of affection (diffusely structured) lead more often to conditions of mental health than groups with a narrow focus of affection (centrally structured).*

Hypothesis 1. *The fact that a pupil is more disliked than liked by his peers is more obvious to him when the group is characterized by a centrally structured liking-disliking distribution than when it is characterized by a diffusely structured distribution.*

The structure of the group and each pupil's position in it is obtained by using a sociometric test. Each pupil is asked to designate four classmates whom he likes most and four whom he likes least. A pupil is given one "positive choice" when he is designated by another pupil as most liked, and one "negative choice" when he is designated as least liked.

A net score is obtained for each pupil by subtracting the total number of negative choices he receives from the total number of positive choices. The mean of this distribution of net scores is equal to zero in every classroom. Classroom groups distinguished by a net score distribution with a "high" variance are designated as centrally structured, while groups distinguished by a net score distribution with a "low" variance are designated as diffusely structured.

A pupil's estimated or perceived position in this sociometric structure is measured in the following manner: Each pupil is asked, "Where would you place yourself in judging how much others in the class like you?" He answers by checking the quarter of the class in which he thinks he belongs. For this analysis, a pupil is designated as occupying a high position if he checks either the first or second quarter, and a low position—that is, considering himself relatively unpopular—if he checks the third or fourth quarter. Table 1 indicates support for Hypothesis 1.

Hypothesis 2. *Pupils in diffusely structured groups evaluate themselves more highly than pupils in centrally structured groups.*

The pupil's self-evaluation, or the way he feels about himself, is obtained from a sentence completion test. The test, as a whole, consists of 46 sentence stems, four of which relate to feelings about the self, as for example, "When I look in the mirror, I . . . . ," and "Sometimes I think I am . . . ." These are rated on a 7-point scale (5) and combined into a self-esteem index. Table 2 indicates support for Hypothesis 2.

TABLE 1
ACCURACY IN PERCEIVING LOW LIKING STATUS IN TWO TYPES OF LIKING STRUCTURES

ACCURACY IN PERCEIVING LOW LIKING STATUS	TYPE OF LIKING STRUCTURE	
	Central	Diffuse
Accurate	20	8
Inaccurate	11	22

Chi-square = 8.80 (p. < .005) df = 1.

TABLE 2
TWO TYPES OF LIKING STRUCTURES AND SELF-ESTEEM

SELF-ESTEEM	TYPE OF LIKING STRUCTURE	
	Central	Diffuse
High	18	34
Low	35	29

Chi-square = 4.66 (p. < .05) df = 1.

GENERAL PROPOSITION II: *When a pupil thinks other pupils do not like him, his mental health is likely to be less positive than when he feels he is liked.*

Hypothesis 3. *Pupils accurate in estimating that they are not well-liked are lower actualizers of academic resources than pupils who are accurate and well-liked.*

A pupil's actual liking status in the classroom social structure is derived from the sociometric test. After a net score is obtained for each pupil by subtracting the total number of negative choices he receives from the total number of positive choices, pupils are rank-ordered according to these scores. This distribution is divided at the median to separate high or low status pupils.

Judgment of whether a child is achieving as well as might be expected is made by the teacher. To obtain this measurement, we divide each class at the median into a higher intelligence group and a lower intelligence group, based on scores from standard intelligence tests. The teacher then divides each group into a high achieving and a low achieving subgroup.

Thus, the class is divided into four ability-achievement groups: high ability-high achievement, high ability-low achievement, low ability-high achievement, and low ability-low achievement. The two high achieving groups are considered to have a relatively high level of actualization of their academic resources, and the two low achieving groups to have a relatively low level of actualization.[1] Table 3 indicates support for Hypothesis 3.

TABLE 3
ACTUAL LIKING STATUS (ACCURATELY PERCEIVED) AND ACTUALIZATION OF ACADEMIC RESOURCES

ACTUALIZATION	ACTUAL LIKING STATUS (ACCURATELY PERCEIVED)	
	High	Low
High	30	5
Low	18	23

Chi-square = 14.19 (p < .001) df = 1.

TABLE 4
PERCEPTION OF LIKING STATUS AND ACTUALIZATION OF ACADEMIC RESOURCES

ACTUALIZATION	PERCEPTION OF HOW WELL-LIKED	
	High	Low
High	50	12
Low	31	33

Chi-square = 14.23 (p. < .001) df = 1.

Hypothesis 4. *Pupils who perceive themselves as not being well-liked are lower actualizers than pupils who perceive themselves as being well-liked.* Table 4 indicates support for Hypothesis 4.

Hypothesis 5. *Pupils who perceive themselves as not being well-liked show lower self-esteem than pupils who perceive themselves as being well-liked.* Table 5 indicates support for Hypothesis 5.

---

[1]This ability-achievement measure, as indicated by the way each class is divided, is the pupil's *relative* position in his class, and not his ability or achievement in relation to all pupils of a particular age or grade.

A Pupil's Conception of Himself in Relation to Others

When a pupil perceives a lack of congruence between his own attitudes and the attitudes of others in the classroom, the environment cannot be considered to provide many opportunities for social rewards. If, for example, a pupil wants to participate actively in classroom activities but believes others in the class would not like this, he is unable to anticipate much needed satisfaction. Under these conditions he is cut off from an important source of gratification. In this sense he can be considered isolated, unsupported, or alienated from potential reinforcing agents.

Since a pupil's conception of himself as a classroom member is formulated, at least in part, by the manner in which he is responded to by his teacher and his peers, one would expect isolation or alienation from them to have an impact on his conception of himself as a learner and as a person.

If a pupil does not think others in the class value him, his image of himself as a participant in classroom learning situations is likely to be negative. Since individuals tend to behave in a manner consistent with their self images, it seems probable that those individuals who see themselves as not being valued as classroom members would be less likely to actualize their potentials as learners than those who consider themselves to be valued.

GENERAL PROPOSITION III: *Pupils whose attitudes are discrepant from those they attribute to others in the classroom also see others as not valuing them. Such pupils experience conflict, which results in reduced personal effectiveness.*

TABLE 5
PERCEPTION
OF LIKING STATUS
AND SELF-ESTEEM

	PERCEPTION OF HOW WELL-LIKED	
SELF-ESTEEM	High	Low
High	50	16
Low	31	29

Chi-square = 7.94 (p. < .005) df = 1.

TABLE 6
SCHOOL ADJUSTMENT AND HOW HE
THINKS OTHERS IN THE CLASS
VALUE HIM

	HOW HE THINKS OTHERS VALUE HIM	
SCHOOL ADJUSTMENT	High	Low
High	29	20
Low	21	42

Chi-square = 7.45 (p. < .01) df = 1.

Hypothesis 6. *When a pupil thinks the teacher and the other pupils do not value him, his school adjustment will be low.*

To determine how he thinks others value him, each pupil is asked to rate himself the way he thinks his teacher sees him and the way he thinks his classmates see him. These ratings are on a nine-point scale ranging from "many things others like about him" to "many things others do not like." The ratings of the teacher and the classmates are combined to form a single index.

The school adjustment items used to test this hypothesis consist of five stems from the sentence completion test such as "Studying is . . . ." and "This school . . . ." Each stem is rated on a 7-point scale (5) and a mean rating computed for each pupil. Table 6 indicates support for Hypothesis 6.

Hypothesis 7. When a pupil thinks the teacher and the others in the class do not value him, his actualization of academic potential is reduced. Table 7 indicates support for Hypothesis 7.

TABLE 7		
ACTUALIZATION AND HOW HE THINKS OTHERS IN THE CLASS VALUE HIM		
	HOW HE THINKS OTHERS VALUE HIM	
ACTUALIZATION	High	Low
High	32	24
Low	18	38
Chi-square $= 7.08$ (p. $< .01$) df $= 1$.		

TABLE 8		
ACTUALIZATION AND CONGRUENCE WITH THE TEACHER		
	CONGRUENCE WITH TEACHER	
ACTUALIZATION	High	Low
High	38	23
Low	25	37
Chi-square $= 5.94$ (p. $< .02$) df $= 1$.		

Hypothesis 8. A lack of congruence between how the pupil feels about classroom relevant behaviors and how he thinks the teacher feels about these same behaviors is accompanied by a low level of actualization.

In order to measure congruence between the pupil's attitudes and those which he attributes to the teacher, each pupil is given a series of statements dealing with classroom standards, as for example, "It is good to take part as much as possible in classroom work," and "If you work very hard others in this class will not like it." He is asked to indicate how he thinks others feel about each of these, putting his answer on a 5-point scale ranging from "almost everyone in the class thinks this," to "only a few in the class think this."

He is also asked to indicate how he, personally, feels, how he thinks the teacher feels, and how his best friends feel. Discrepancy scores are then obtained between his own feelings and the feelings he attributes to his classmates, best friends, and teacher. The discrepancy between his own attitudes and those he attributes to the teacher is the measure of congruence used to test this hypothesis. Table 8 indicates support for Hypothesis 8.

Hypothesis 9. A lack of congruence between how the pupil feels about classroom relevant behaviors and how he thinks the teacher feels is accompanied by a high desire for change in the teacher.

Information regarding desire for change is obtained from the same instrument used to measure classroom standards (described under Hypothesis 8). On it, pupils are asked to indicate how they would like the class and the teacher to change in the opinions they hold. In another instrument, on which they rate the characteristics of their teacher, they are also asked how they would like their teacher to change. The measure used to test this hypothesis was a combination of these two indices: desire for change in classroom standards, and desire for change in teacher characteristics. Table 9 indicates support for Hypothesis 9.

TABLE 9
DESIRE FOR CHANGE AND CONGRUENCE WITH THE TEACHER

	CONGRUENCE WITH TEACHER	
DESIRE FOR CHANGE	High	Low
High	24	42
Low	39	18

Chi-square = 12.58 (p. < .001) df = 1.

TABLE 10
CONGRUENCE WITH THE TEACHER AND ATTRACTION TO THE CLASS

	ATTRACTION TO CLASS	
CONGRUENCE WITH TEACHER	High	Low
High	37	21
Low	22	32

Chi-square = 5.96 (p. < .02) df = 1.

Hypothesis 10. *A lack of congruence between a pupil's own attitudes and those he attributes to the teacher is accompanied by a low attraction to the class.*

In order to establish the pupil's attraction to the class, each was first asked how much time he would like to spend in class. Answers were recorded on a scale ranging from "a lot more" to "a lot less." He was then asked to rank order the different parts of his day, including life in this class, to indicate their relative importance to him, the amount of happiness each brings, and the amount of learning derived from each. Finally, he was asked to check a 6-point scale which ranged from "This class with your regular teacher has mostly good things," to "This class with your regular teacher has mostly bad things." These three sources of data were combined to form an index of attraction to the class. Table 10 provides support for Hypothesis 10.

Hypothesis 11. *A low attraction to the class will be accompanied by a low level of actualization.* Table 11 indicates support for Hypothesis 11.

IMPLICATIONS FOR TEACHERS

These findings emphasize the relevance of positive affect or liking among members of a classroom group for individual mental health and for effective learning. When the pattern of affection is diffuse, so that almost every member is "most liked" by some other member, pupils tend to have more positive feelings toward themselves, perceive the school situation more favorably, and actualize their potentials more fully.

If, as these findings indicate, successful human relations are important to achievement of academic tasks, the teacher should do everything possible to enhance a pupil's ability to obtain emotional support from his peers, not only because good human relations is a value in itself, but also because it contributes importantly to the school's academic goals.

What do findings of this type suggest for teacher behavior? First is the job of obtaining accurate information concerning the distribution of liking choices in the classroom. One way of accomplishing this is through careful and systematic observation.

The teacher might ask himself: Are there some pupils who tend to be left out of most classroom activities? Are there some who are always first chosen, and others who are always last chosen?

He should raise questions such as these in attempting to view his class as objectively as possible, looking at it from time to time as if he were an outside observer. He might also examine his own behavior and attitudes: How do I distribute rewards and punishments in the classroom? Are there certain children to whom I give primarily negative criticism and rebuke, and others who receive a large portion of the praise? In addition to careful observation and self-questioning, the teacher might employ such sociometric techniques as those used in the research reported here in order to find out how interpersonal affect is distributed in his group.

TABLE 11
ACTUALIZATION AND ATTRACTION
TO CLASS

ACTUALIZATION	ATTRACTION TO CLASS	
	High	Low
High	35	21
Low	24	32

Chi-square = 4.37 (p. < .05) df = 1.

Once the classroom distribution of affect is clear to the teacher, and if some change is desirable, he may use various techniques to modify this distribution and develop more positive feelings among the pupils. A co-operative study group, for instance, in which low and high status pupils work together for the achievement of some common goal, is quite often effective in changing inaccurate perceptions and stereotypes about low status children.

Another possibility is to work low status children gradually into roles which are viewed as having considerable status. Some teachers have accomplished this effectively by developing a so-called "steering committee" in which all pupils serve at some time during the school year and through which each achieves some status and self-esteem by being active contributors to classroom decisions.[2]

[2]A report of the case of a "steering committee" in two elementary classrooms, together with other classroom innovations, is contained in *Inventory of Teaching Innovations, Directed toward Improving Classroom Learning Atmospheres,* Institute for Social Research, University of Michigan, December, 1961.

Teachers can enhance the affective tone of the classroom by including information and discussion about the nature of individual differences as a part of the subject matter. An understanding of differences among pupils relative to family background, sex, race, abilities, and interests increases the opportunity for pupils to be more accepting and tolerant of a greater number of their peers. In addition to producing greater acceptance of individual pupils, a classroom standard of acceptance of differences may emerge from such exploration.

Another approach to developing a wider focus of acceptance is through school programs directed toward a greater understanding of behavioral causation, or the "whys" of human behavior. The assumption behind this type of curriculum content is that greater insight into those factors which contribute to a pupil's actions will result in a more accepting classroom atmosphere.

The teacher's own behavior and feeling toward individual pupils can also contribute toward the acceptance of a pupil by his peers. If the teacher himself accepts each pupil as an individual—understanding his limitations and giving him the kind of support he needs to expand his assets and help overcome his shortcomings—members of the class will tend to follow a similar pattern. As a result, there will be a climate of mutual support in the classroom. But if the teacher supports primarily the high achievers and shows rejecting or disapproving behavior to those who are not so successful in classroom learning tasks, a competitive, nonsupportive climate is likely to emerge.

The teacher can give classroom relevant rewards directly by making positive comments about the pupil's performance or indirectly by organizing learning experiences in a manner which will maximize success and reduce failure. In this way, too, he creates the anticipation of future rewards. With more experiences of success, a pupil's self-esteem is enhanced, and concurrently his perception of the school environment should tend to become more positive.

All of these suggestions involve increasing the social-emotional support for all pupils in a classroom group. A second kind of implication emerging from these research findings involves pupil-teacher and pupil-pupil communication of standards and attitudes concerning classroom relevant behavior.

It has been found that when a pupil's attitudes are discrepant from those he attributes to others, he tends to feel he is not valued, his personal effectiveness is reduced, and his school adjustment is low. Often this condition arises from poor communication—that is, when opportunities are not available for an active and public exploration of the interpersonal expectations of both pupils and teacher.

A pupil's own attitudes may actually be quite similar to those of his classmates, but because of inadequate communication he believes they are different. The teacher might be able to correct these erroneous beliefs, or misconceptions, by improving communication in the classroom through discussions of how pupils and he himself feel about learning tasks. By way of such discussions, classroom standards can be clarified and, if necessary, reformulated so that they are made clear and are generally accepted.

SUMMARY

This study attempts to clarify the nature of the relationship between classroom interpersonal relations on the one hand and mental health and academic learning on the other. For the purpose of this exploration, classroom mental health refers to the adequacy of the pupil's relationship to his learning environment and the positiveness of his feelings about himself. Some dimensions of this definition were suggested, and some ways of measuring mental health were described.

Three general propositions were put forward dealing with: (1) The distribution of liking and disliking choices in the classroom; (2) The pupil's perception of how well he is liked; and (3) The pupil's conception of himself in relation to others. The findings suggest that there is an integral relationship between classroom interpersonal relations and pupil mental health. Several implications for improving the classroom learning environment were made on the basis of these and similar findings.

References

1. COOMBS, A. W. and C. TAYLOR, "The Effect of the Perception of Mild Degrees of Threat on Performance," *Journal of Abnormal and Social Psychology,* 47 (1952), 420–24.

2. ECHELBERGER, E., *Relationships Between Personality Traits and Peer Status* (Ann Arbor: University of Michigan, 1959). Unpublished doctoral dissertation.

3. JAHODA, MARIE, *Current Concepts of Positive Mental Health* (New York: Basic Books, Inc., 1958).

4. LIPPITT, R. and M. GOLD, "Classroom Social Structure as a Mental Health Problem," *Journal of Social Issues,* 15 (No. 1, 1959), 40–49.

5. MALPASS, L. F. and F. B. TYLER, *Validation of the Incomplete Sentences Test of School Adjustment* (Carbondale, Ill.: Graduate School, Southern Illinois University, 1961). Unpublished research report.

6. VAN EGMOND, E. E., *Social Interrelationship Skills and Effective Utilization of Intelligence in the Classroom* (Ann Arbor: University of Michigan, 1960). Unpublished doctoral dissertation.

TROUBLED STUDENTS:
case histories

In the last section we examined some of the literature that suggests antecedents of emotional difficulties in schoolchildren. We now turn to a closer look at some children experiencing these difficulties. We know that they come in various sizes, colors, and settings. The small sample found in the following articles hints at their variety.

Behavior representing emotional disturbance appears in the classroom in many forms. There is the fourth-grade boy who cannot take a direct order from a teacher. He will display great temper, leave the classroom, and even kick the teacher if restrained. There is the pretty sixth-grade girl, very bright and a gifted dancer, who simply cannot keep up with the work of her classmates and often fails to hear what the teacher says. There is the first-grade boy who follows his teacher around the room like a puppy and cries if asked to take his seat. There is the high school sophomore who does schoolwork easily though she is often truant, and, when in school, distracts her classmates with her sexually suggestive clothes and mannerisms.

Behavior that is the product of serious emotional turmoil is often described in such vague terms as "lazy," "mean," "stupid," or "undisciplined." The roots of the behavior are usually not visible. The teacher must make an initial decision as to whether the behavior represents disturbance or simply a transient whim that should be discouraged.

Teachers often become adept at sensing the conflicts that lie behind disturbed behavior. Strong conflicts spell more than passing trouble. Experienced teachers gently discourage the unacceptable behavior while assuming a watch-and-wait attitude. If the unusual behavior is not transient, it is likely to represent disturbance emerging from strong conflict.

It is unfortunate that so few case studies are published that clearly illustrate emotionally disturbed behavior in the classroom. The articles that follow were chosen partly because they do give some idea of how a troubled student appears in school. These articles are again representative of the literature available, however, and give far more attention to how the student appears in treatment. Such a description offers the advantage of taking us behind the scene for a glimpsed understanding of what provokes the seemingly inexplicable "disturbed behavior" in a classroom. Herbert's teacher would likely have found it very difficult to explain his ups and downs. We understand such behavior better because of the insights provided in articles such as the one by Ackerman and Lakos. A need remains, however, for case studies that describe evidence of emotional disturbance as it is seen in the classroom.

Edna Mann's article presents students in one of New York City's "600" schools. These schools are set up to educate students who are too difficult to teach or manage in a regular public school. The classes are smaller and the teacher ratio is higher. Special services are often provided. The students represent the kind of "challenge" that many teachers fear. Teachers in a "600" school are not surprised to find a youngster who is already familiar with jail or the psychiatric unit at New York's Bellevue Hospital. We see in her article that these students present some unusual behavior in the classroom, but respond well to help that is especially adapted to the unusual features of their environment.

In this section we are thus concerned with the troubled students and how they appear to a teacher in the classroom, although each article describes some kind of treatment. In Section 5 we shall turn our attention from the students to the treatment process itself.

Rusty: A Brief Behavior Disorder

William K. Boardman

When a child who is a behavior problem is seen for possible treatment, it frequently can be concluded that the relationship between the child and a parent or parent-surrogate is an unhealthy one for the child and has resulted in a behavior disorder. In the majority of such cases there is a good chance that psychotherapy can be used to eliminate the disorder. If the child and at least the most psychodynamically significant adult can be worked with, over a period of time, the desired changes in interpersonal relationships may be achieved.

The "standard" psychotherapeutic approach has proven to be the most effective in the great majority of such cases. Maximum control over the behavioral and emotional expressions of parents and child and their interrelationships is possible. Progress—even without insight—receives regular support and thus has a better chance of being maintained. New information and psychodynamic changes may be integrated into the psychotherapy. Finally, the therapist is in the best position to judge accurately the point at which sufficient progress has been made to terminate treatment.

There is an alternative approach which is effective with certain behavior disorders. It is essentially a "shortcut" involving the application of simple learning theory principles in circumstances where complex psychodynamic factors can be considered to be of minimal concern. Its effectiveness depends upon several conditions: (*a*) The misbehavior in question should be of recent origin or well circumscribed and must be voluntary (this rules out enuresis, tics, stuttering, and various other "neurotic" behaviors). (*b*) It can be assumed that the misbehavior produces a great deal of direct emotional gratification and does not represent to any important degree the disguised expression of repressed affect which requires catharsis through further symptomatic expression. (*c*) It is possible to arrange for desired alternative behavior to lead to immediate rewards, while important gratifications can be withheld during periods of misbehavior. (*d*) It is possible to apply the procedure on a relatively continuous uninterrupted basis. (*e*) The child and the adults involved all appear to have a good potential for rapid behavior change.

The following case illustrates this approach. The history of Rusty's behavior disorder is taken from an account furnished by his mother.

Rusty's behavior problems started when he was 5 years 7 months old and I went

"Rusty: A Brief Behavior Disorder," by William K. Boardman, *Journal of Consulting Psychology,* No. 26, 293–297. © 1962, American Psychological Association.

into the hospital for surgery. There were complications, I had four operations, and was confined in the hospital for 9 weeks. In the daytime, Rusty and his three sisters, ages 10, 8, and 3½, were left in the care of a maid, who has been with me for 8 years, and at night with their grandmother until their father came home from work, usually around 9:00 P.M.

Rusty's first symptoms of being upset were wetting the bed at night, taking money out of his father's wallet, and riding his bike back and forth across a very busy thoroughfare.

(The maid and grandmother could not control Rusty. His grandmother would simply report his misbehavior to his father after Rusty had gone to bed. Climbing on the roof of the house and hammering all the knots out of a neighbor's decorative wood fence were typical of his misdeeds.)

I came home from the hospital and assumed that things would return to normal. Rusty's behavior seemed to get worse, rather than better. He defied me at every opportunity, continued to cross the thoroughfare on his bicycle, and even took matches and scorched furniture in his bedroom one day.

My husband and I decided that the best thing would be to enroll Rusty in a private school in the fall where he could be in the first grade. By public school requirements he was not eligible for first grade because of his birthday. We entered him in a private school and thought that this would help solve our problem because his time would be occupied and he wouldn't have an opportunity to do all of the things he had been doing. The first 3 days of school went beautifully.

The fourth day, Rusty walked out of school and walked over 3 miles home. He told the teacher that he had to go to the bathroom and instead just left school. He was stopped by two men from the school who were out looking for him and asked his name. He gave a false one, so the men let him go. He later told me that he knew the men were from school and that if he told them his right name that they would take him back. He said that he didn't like school and didn't want to get taken back. I did take him back when he got home, though. When we got back to school the teacher began to tell him (in front of me) that a mad dog could have gotten him and torn him to pieces, or that a snake could have jumped out of the weeds and bitten him, and if that didn't happen then the police would get him, put him in jail, keep him on bread and water, make him go to school, and would whip him every time he gave a wrong answer. In spite of this frightening talk, Rusty stayed in school the rest of the day, and also returned to school on the following day where he remained all day. I did visit his room for about 30 minutes on this day.

The next day, Rusty reluctantly went to school. At 9:30 A.M. I received a phone call from my son at school. He said he had a stomach ache. I told him he would feel better later and that I could not come to school because I had nobody to leave the baby with. Around noon I decided to call the school to see if Rusty were still in class. I was informed that he had spent most of the morning in the office trying to call me. They wouldn't let Rusty call, but pretended to call the number for him and kept telling him that the line was busy. Well, about 1:30 P.M. Rusty left school, then went up to a house and asked if he might use the phone. He then called home himself, and finding that I wasn't at home he hung up. He then told the lady who lived there that he had been riding on a bicycle with another boy and fell off, and that the little boy went off and left him and that now he was going to have to walk home. The lady told him it was too far to walk and offered to drive him home. Rusty pointed out three different houses where he told her he lived. She would let him out at the house and wait for him to go in. Instead, he would walk up to the door of each house, look to see if she was watching, but would not go in. So, the lady would take him on to the next house where he said he lived. This went on until finally Rusty showed her the right house. I arrived home just as Rusty did and learned the story from the housewife.

That night the teacher telephoned me and asked how Rusty was. Then she proceeded to tell me that she had told Rusty that day that if he didn't start acting better at school, that his mother might go back to the hospital. That same night we reached a decision—this was not the right school for our son, and this was not the right teacher. So, the next day we registered him for kindergarten in public school (the afternoon session).

He attended kindergarten on Friday. On Monday, he left school after being there only 5 minutes. He had told the teacher he had to go to the bathroom, and when she went to get an older child to stay with her class while she took him, he ran out. This time, though, he did not return home until after 3 o'clock when he saw the other children coming home from school. He knew that I would take him right back to school if he came home.

Tuesday, Rusty was told to stay in the house all morning because he had been leaving school. He was told that when he went to school, then he would be allowed to play with other children. He ran out the front door. Two hours later, he was brought home by a policeman. Rusty had been on his way to his grandmother's house, and was only about two blocks away. He had walked about 2 miles. At this point, he got tired so he went up to a house, rang the bell, and asked to use the telephone. He then called his grandmother to come and pick him up and take him to her house, but she was not at home. The police were then summoned. First he directed the policeman to his grandmother's house and told him that this was his house and that his mother had sent him to the store and told him that if she wasn't at home when he got back he was to go to his friends' house on another street. The policeman told him that he couldn't do that, he had to take him home. So, then Rusty said he would go to his grandmother's house. He brought the officer to his own home, telling him that this was grandmother's house. (Rusty tried to keep the police officer from finding out where he lived, just as he had done previously with the housewife. The officer let him out at a corner and surreptitiously followed him home, telling his mother the circumstances.)

Later that day we had our only direct contact with Rusty and his parents. His mother related the above events, and both parents were concerned with the dangerous nature of some of his antics. From this history, the case appeared to fulfill the necessary conditions described above. Rusty's hostility was open and generalized, with little indication of repression. In fact, he appeared quite skillful in manipulating others in ways which directly satisfied his needs. His parents had not developed rigid patterns of coping with Rusty, and were willing to follow any suggestions which would alleviate the situation. They could thus be used as the agents for accomplishing behavioral change by instructing them in detail as to how to carry out procedures in which Rusty would always be given a choice between unacceptable behavior and clearly defined acceptable behavior and would be punished severely and continuously while he persisted in undesirable acts and rewarded promptly and adequately when he shifted to appropriate behavior. While in such cases it may be assumed generally that a permissive therapeutic relationship unnecessarily prolongs acting-out, an additional factor was also involved here. Some of Rusty's behavior constituted a realistic danger to his physical safety. Permissiveness would allow this danger to continue, and he would even have opportunity to devise *new* forms of dangerous behavior.

While a secretary watched Rusty to prevent his slipping away—he made one half-hearted attempt to walk off down the hall—his parents were told that what they needed most in order to prevent such misbehavior from continuing was courage. They were instructed to buy a screen door latch for Rusty's bedroom door to use, when necessary, to keep him in his room when he had been sent there as a disciplinary measure. Spankings were suggested as appropriate only if they produced the desired results—they had been ineffective up to that point. We pointed out that, unless they literally imprisoned Rusty in his room, he had the power to run away at any time he chose. That since it was impractical from every point of view to make Rusty a permanent prisoner, they must admit to his ability to leave the home or the school, but that they should make the consequences of such behavior so drastic that he would decide for himself to be cooperative. We instructed them to tell Rusty that, if he ran away, he would be locked out of the house and would not be let in until he apologized and promised to behave. We further instructed them to refuse to give Rusty his meals while he misbehaved if it became necessary to do so in order to impress upon him that he could not flaunt authority and enjoy family privileges. They were urged to report regularly by telephone on the progress of their efforts.

Such a regimen appears harsh, but it has a distinct advantage. It is highly unlikely that a parent would not have ambivalent feelings toward a child manifesting a severe behavior disorder. With verbal or other symbolic forms of discipline, ambivalence may be expressed to a degree which seriously reduces or even reverses the intended effect of parental action. When reward and punishment are kept on more basic physical level, there is a much higher degree of efficiency in the learning situation. Both the child *and* the parents understand the rewards and punishments, and are able to recognize and profit from positive changes when they occur.

We spoke to Rusty for only a few minutes. He at first acted the part of a frightened, mistreated, misunderstood child, backing into a corner, hiding his face in his arms, and whimpering. He would not talk. (This was less than 3 hours after he had successfully manipulated a strange housewife and a police officer to suit his purposes.) We pulled him onto our knee and began by commenting that he must be very angry to act the way he had, and that we would guess that he was mad at his mother. We then suggested that his misbehavior was a lot of trouble for him and that it probably wasn't worth the effort. At this point he slid off our lap and began to talk in a very unconcerned manner about something trivial which had happened the day before. We terminated the interview and the family left. His mother reported that as soon as they were in their car, Rusty commented to his parents that they must be pretty mixed up to need to go to a doctor to find out how to make him behave. No attempt had been made to elicit important content during the few minutes spent with Rusty, but it was concluded that this child's ability to shift his behavior and expressions of affect so rapidly and dramatically indicated a minimal loss of emotional control and a good potential for learning from direct interaction with his parents. His mother's account continues.

Wednesday morning Rusty attempted to run away from home, but his father caught him and locked him in his room. He proceeded to try to rip out the window screen and escape. All implements which he could use for this purpose were removed from his room, but he continued to work at the screen with his belt buckle. In late morning, he was let out so that he could be fed and dressed for school. He immediately darted into the bathroom and locked the door, where he stayed for about an hour before the door could be opened. He refused lunch and was dressed by force and carried by his father to school, kicking and screaming, and deposited in the classroom.

The teacher closed the door and Rusty jumped out of the window and left school. He remained away from home just as before until after 3 o'clock. He was locked out of the house because of this until after 5:30 that evening.

At 5:30 he came to the door and apologized. He was let in, fed, and allowed to follow a normal routine through the evening.

Thursday and Friday he stayed in school. Then Friday, after supper (he ate a very large meal) Rusty asked if he could go out and play. When told he couldn't, he left anyway. When he came back and found the door locked (which he had been told before he left would happen) he became pretty upset. He beat on the door with a broom, rang the doorbell, and when he found out this did him no good, he went to the fuse box and proceeded to push all the trippers, thereby turning off all the lights except the one in the garage, where he began playing. He also pushed down the lever which turned off the air conditioner. (His mother telephoned during this period and was quite upset. She was advised to take the other children and leave home for an hour, but she could not bring herself to do so.) He finally went to a neighbor's house and asked to use the phone. He called his daddy at work and told him that he was locked out. His daddy advised him to come apologize, and when he did he was let back into the house.

Saturday (This was Rusty's sixth birthday. His party and presents had been cancelled because of his bad behavior. His mother first greeted him in the morning by singing "Happy Birthday to You." This obviously ambivalent act threw Rusty into a violent fit of anger and precipitated a behavioral crisis which was the turning point in his relationship with his mother.) I told him he had to stay in his room. I locked him in, so he then cut his screen and was going to get out a window. I told him if he wanted out I would let him out the front door, but that he could not get back in. He started to walk away from the house (without socks and shoes.) In about 5 minutes he was back to get his bicycle, but I locked the garage so he couldn't get it. So, he went and turned off the air conditioner at the fuse box. (The box had been padlocked, but he broke the lock.) When I told him I didn't care, he then said that he was going to climb the pole and cut the wires at the pole. He then climbed on the roof and remained there while I got in the car with the other children and drove off. When we returned about an hour later, he was playing in the backyard. (At noon his mother called and reported that she could not go on. Her husband was contacted and told that he was to go home at once and back up his wife. He was instructed to take his wife's side in the battle and to tell Rusty that any more destruction of property would be met by him with extremely severe punishment. Rusty did not come in during the 3 hours his father was at home, but neither did he make a pest of himself. At this point he had missed breakfast and lunch.) He had been given two deadlines—to come in by 12 o'clock in order to receive his lunch and 4 o'clock in order to receive his supper. He was also told by his father that when he came in he would have to spend the rest of the day in his room. He chose to stay outside until 6:15 P.M. at which time it began to rain. When he came in, he was spanked, bathed, and put in bed without supper.

This was putting it mildly. After her husband returned to work, Rusty's mother began to feel really angry for the first time. Whether she was most angry at Rusty, her husband, or the author is a moot question, but when Rusty finally came in she exploded, and he got the whipping of his life. This episode, 4 days after the family's consultation, was the turning point in overcoming Rusty's misbehavior. His mother was learning that she was capable of continuing disciplinary pressure long enough to force Rusty to choose to cooperate, but that she must not initiate hostile, rejecting behavior or it would drive him to further rebellion. Rusty was learning that rebellion, while exciting, was too costly in terms of creature comforts when he went beyond certain limits. The effectiveness of the change in relationship between Rusty and his mother is seen in her final account.

Rusty was an angel all day Sunday and most of Monday. Monday evening while at the dinner table, Rusty and his sister began to get rather wild—giggling and talking—everything except eating. So, they were warned that if they weren't finished by a certain time, their dinner would be thrown out and they would get nothing until breakfast. They continued to misbehave, so the food was thrown out. Well, Rusty was furious. He pushed the table, and in doing so turned over some coffee. He was told to go to his room. Instead he ran and locked himself in the bathroom. He was ignored. In about 15 minutes he came out and went to his room. A few minutes later when I checked on him, I found him sound asleep on the floor.

This was Rusty's final gesture of rebellion. It occurred 6 days after the family's consultation. During the following 11 months, Rusty has remained a spirited but not a rebellious boy. He was tested with the Wechsler Intelligence Scale for Children and found to be of bright-normal intelligence.

A procedure such as this produces rapid results—or none at all. In properly selected cases the probability of success is high, and the major risk involved lies in the assumption that the parent or parents are capa-

ble of initiative, rapid learning, and insight when faced with the responsibility for all of the actions required for repairing the relationship with
their child. Many parents deserve such a vote of confidence.

Cross-sectional Views of the Psychotherapeutic Process with an Adolescent Recovering from a Schizophrenic Episode

Rudolf Ekstein

Alan Gregg once said that an honest narrative of a doctor's treatment attempt
with a patient is one of the best kinds of scientific writing. I believe that no such
narrative can be either scientific or honest unless the writer gives a detailed report
of what he, as therapist, did and said and thought as well as what the patient did
and said, and then tries to relate what effects these complicated interactions between
patient and therapist appeared to have on the progress and outcome of the treatment
attempt. The role played by the therapist is at least half of the story. If an account
of it is omitted from the case report and the patient's productions and behavior are
described and interpreted as if the therapist's role were immaterial or even above
examination, then an honest narrative is not being written.—ROBERT P. KNIGHT, M.D.

The word *treatment* originated in early magical procedures as well
as in medical practice, and implies that something is done to the patient
in order to "fix him up," as exemplified in the administration of drugs
or injections, or the process of surgery. One is induced therefore to
overlook the subtle processes of psychotherapy which constitute interaction rather than a one-sided repair process. A successful psychotherapeutic process is as much the success of the patient as of the psychotherapist. Both are coauthors, as it were, of an interaction. Although it
seems that this interaction takes place solely in the interest of the
patient, we overlook perhaps that the patient too has a profound influence on the therapist—affords him insights and the opportunity for the
development of new techniques which actually constitute a change in the
therapist as well. I believe it is this recognition that may encourage the
psychotherapist to follow Knight's advice and to report about the process
rather than the case, or perhaps more accurately to describe the case by
reporting the process.

"Cross-sectional Views of the Psychotherapeutic Process with an Adolescent Recover-
ing from a Schizophrenic Episode," by Rudolf Ekstein, Ph.D., *The American Journal of
Orthopsychiatry*, Vol. 31, 757–775. Copyright 1961, The American Orthopsychiatric Association, Inc. Reproduced by permission.

He faces many obstacles in such an endeavor. Psychotherapeutic ethics force him to disguise the material, and make him hesitant even then. He does not want to "give away" his patient nor does he find it easy to give away much of himself. The secrecy of the psychotherapeutic session has a dual meaning.

He is also up against the fact that therapy records covering years of treatment do not lend themselves easily to useful communication. What was a living experience between him and his patient may become a boring, repetitive narrative for the reader.

In the face of these obstacles, I have chosen to offer cross-sectional segments of the initial phase in psychotherapy with a 13-year-old girl whose treatment lasted approximately four years. During parts of the treatment she lived in the residential treatment center (an open hospital with school facilities for children), and moved later to a boarding home, remaining there until her final discharge. She was seen three times weekly during the first two years of treatment. Later she was seen semiweekly and during the last year of treatment she was seen only once a week.

A full psychiatric evaluation, including psychological testing and the usual medical and neurological examinations, resulted in a diagnosis of schizophrenia. It was felt then that this girl had sufficient assets to warrant treatment, but that because of the seriousness of her illness this should be undertaken only if long-term residential treatment with individual psychotherapy could be provided by the department and supported by the parents.

In this case we had the unusual help of the child's mother, whose literary talent helped us to reconstruct in vivid terms the patient's tragic flight into illness. Excerpts from the mother's account, which she gave to us as an expression of her relief after we accepted the child for treatment, may serve us perhaps better than a routine case history.

Elaine's favorite song during the preceding months, the theme song for the most delicate period of all, was [a popular song entitled *If*].

[The mother suggests in her autobiographical comments that this theme song proclaimed the deadly clutch which fantasy was gaining on Elaine's life, the lure of the unreal to supplant the real.] Night after night she put it on the record player. Night after night it resounded through the house as, with an eerie expression on her face, she slowly ascended the stairs to the imaginary kingdom of her room. There, behind locked door, she found the love, acceptance, and security of her own making. For now she preferred to regard herself as married, her room as the bridal suite, and life with an imaginary husband more real for her than the give-and-take of high school life.

It is, of course, true that all children indulge in fantasy to some degree; but when a teen-ager goes out and buys a wedding ring and wears it, and she becomes hysterical because by mistake the pillowcase which she wished to wash for her husband has already been washed; when she is wild with grief because she has arrived home a few moments too late to do an adequate cleaning for the reception to be given for her home-coming husband—then this is *illness,* not childlike imagination, but the most elusive of illnesses.

It was impossible to know just how sick Elaine was; to what extent she was aware of her deviation from the normal; how far she had actually moved into the world of her own creating. I felt lost in the unknown. Every hour, every minute I sensed some inexorable force pushing, pushing—pushing her God knows where. And I did not know how to bring her back. I treated her affectionately but casually; referred periodically to the fact that we both understood that she was playing with fantasy, but did not stress it; avoided all possible issues. Life at home became simply a holding action until the right help could be found for her. Her "married" status and her schoolwork were the only things that had any meaning for her. She could not take part in any activity—domestic or social. Much of the time she would not even come down for dinner but would take it (portions for two) upstairs to her room.

On the street Elaine walked with her head turned away from me, her arm crooked as though it were snugly fitted into another's arm. At the movie she would sit exchanging glances, smiles, and even whispers with her phantom. The terrible lure created by the husband of her fancy made living a nightmare because there was no way of estimating his power over her. At times she was like a frantic, caged animal, begging to go walking alone in the late night hours or actually running away through the city streets. And one statement she repeated several times, a strange look in her eyes: "In order to live, one must first die."

How much illness? How much adolescent drama? What thoughts did she control? What thoughts controlled her? I did not know. I just knew that she was headed in the wrong direction.

Each day became more strained, with Elaine removing herself from her group and cramping herself in her room. Everything about her was cramped, her gait, her gestures, her handwriting, her glance. She was a bird in prison in some mysterious cage.

The mother finally yielded to advice and brought the child to the residential treatment center. Since the child at that time had no awareness of her illness, and had fought off professional help in private practice, the suggestion was made by the advising physician that Elaine be brought to us without her knowledge. When she finally came, she felt herself betrayed by her parents.

On record are a number of comments I made then in the staff meeting before I knew that Elaine might be assigned to me for psychotherapeutic treatment. These comments show, perhaps, the initial attitude of the therapist toward his new patient. I said then:

I usually have no quarrels with diagnostic categories, but I am concerned with the label inasmuch as it indicates the kind of treatment we should offer. I would suggest we call her "schizophrenic." I suggest this category to imply that we would have to attempt the kind of analytic treatment which is appropriate for a schizophrenic child rather than for a child within the neurotic range. One of the main difficulties I see in accepting her is to find a way of initiating treatment which is different from the one initiated by her family. If I were responsible for the treatment, I would tell the whole family group that I disapprove of the wrong information the child has been given. She is certainly ill and we feel that she requires treatment, but we can only give it on the condition that we do not start out with a lie. This will prove very painful for the mother, but at the same time I think it would be the only guarantee for successful treatment. If we and they state the truth now from the very beginning we will thus initiate a different type of relationship.

We ought to tell the mother that it will probably take from three to five years to help the child. We should take her only if we know that we can provide her with intensive psychotherapy which ought to be expressive, analytic in orientation, a minimum of three hours per week, and if possible five hours per week.

Elaine was accepted for treatment and a few months later she was assigned to me for treatment.

The social worker brought Elaine for her first psychotherapeutic session with me. Both came up to my office and Elaine entered shyly. She sat down on the couch after taking off her coat, gloves, and hat, all of them obviously new—Christmas presents. The three of us sat for a few minutes talking casually about Christmas, about the gifts Elaine had received. She said that she was very pleased because a number of gifts from her parents came unexpectedly. The gifts from the treatment center were no surprise to her because she said that she knew that she would get gifts from her teachers, and would get exactly what she asked for.

After the social worker left and Elaine was alone with me she continued to impress me in the same way that she did when she was presented in the staff meeting some months earlier and I had addressed a few questions to her. She recalled this incident quite well and even remembered what we had talked about. She had been looking forward to psychotherapy. Then, when I asked whether the feelings she had expressed at the time of her admittance to the treatment center had changed, Elaine told me that at that particular time—while feeling that she had considerable trouble—she was convinced that she could solve them all by herself. Now, four months later, she realized that she could not do it alone and that she needed some help. While she stressed this need and was glad that she could start psychotherapy now, rather than having to wait six months as we had led her to expect, she also told me that she did not think the situation in the treatment center had helped her particularly. She described her difficulties mainly in terms of the external situation. She had roomed at first with two girls, but she and Carol, one of the girls, finally insisted that the younger third girl, who was rather difficult, be removed. Then she and Carol were together, and she feels quite warmly about Carol. However, Carol was soon to go into a foster home and Elaine was afraid that she might have to take back the younger girl, Mary, since the school could not afford to let Elaine have one large room all by herself. Elaine said she could not help thinking of all the new words and slang expressions that she had learned at the Center, and she hinted that she had learned other things there that she should not know and that she had never heard before.

I ventured the thought that this must be quite a burden to her since I knew she was striving to be the right kind of person. She picked this up gratefully, and when I wondered how she could expect any help from the school, being exposed constantly to such temptations, she referred to psychotherapy and called to my attention that she had just made the New Year's resolution that she would give up all her terrible fantasies. While she remained on the couch in a semireclining position, she avoided looking at me, and gave the impression of a dainty, harmless, little fawn. At the same time she told me that the only way she could go to sleep was by having fantasies of torturing someone. She spoke about all the women who were the victims in her cruel fantasies. She thought that this practice was terrible, and had decided that beginning with the New Year she would give up all these fantasies when she went to sleep and would substitute prayers. I suggested that I could see from these remarks how much she was striving to attain a goal of perfection and that I thought she came to see me so that I could help her perhaps to meet this goal. I would surely want to try and see whether I could help her.

At that point I commented that when people strive toward the lofty goal, the top of a high mountain, they may need to travel all kinds of roads, maybe at first roads for automobiles; later they may have to walk on a footpath, then climb on rocks; and finally they may need an ice pick and mountain boots to surmount glaciers and mountain walls. They may need ropes, and even though the goal were the perfect view on the top of the mountain where the air was pure and the view was beautiful, they may have to take all kinds of side paths, climb dangerous cliffs, travel dubious roads. Elaine said she was not quite sure she understood me. As a matter of fact, she thought, after I repeated my idea, that I was implying that it did not make any difference if one were good or bad, because it was as if we at the treatment center were suggesting to her that there was no difference between good and bad. I attempted to correct this impression and stressed again my belief in her goals, but suggested that I was speaking about the method of getting to them. I recalled to her from the original interview at the time she was accepted by the school that she had talked about braces for her teeth, telling us that she wanted a dentist to help her get perfect teeth. She needed to show the dentist what was wrong about her teeth and she needed to wear braces, which perhaps would not look perfect but would help her to get where she wanted to be. She accepted this and continued to speak about some of her inner struggles and about the goals that she saw for herself.

With some misgivings, she said that Carol might enter a foster home; Elaine did not know whether she would want to go to one. She felt she would get used to home life again, but afterwards there would be nothing for her. Since her parents were to be separated she could not return to a home of her own. It was as if her goal of psychotherapy were really an empty one. I indicated simply that we would need time, perhaps a long time, in order to find out together what might be best for her in order to attain the goals that she had set for herself.

After she had left me at the end of the session, I found her standing somewhat anxiously in the waiting room. She told me she did not know whether she should speak to the secretary or to someone else; she had lost a dime which she needed to return to the Center by bus. She asked me whether she could borrow one from me and I gave her the dime. When I asked her whether she could find her way to the office next time, she said half-jokingly and half in sadness that she might get lost, but if she did not come or if she was very late, I should know that she was trying to reach me, and that she would find me.

Freud, in comparing psychoanalysis to "the fine art of the game of chess," suggests that "only the opening and closing moves of the game admit of exhaustive systematic description," and this certainly seems to hold true for the opening gambit of both Elaine and her therapist. Even the innocuous beginning reveals the keen sensitivity of Elaine as she speaks about the Christmas gifts from the treatment center, no surprise to her since she knew she would get exactly what she asked for. This subtle innuendo minimizes the gifts, the nature of which is somehow recognized as technical assistance rather than as evidence for the ideal relationship which she wants to restore between herself and her parents. In spite of the fact that she has seen the psychotherapist only once, and then in a rather large group, she recalls his every word. While admitting she now needs help, she tells the therapist just how afraid she is of this help, and likens it, indirectly through the metaphor of the school milieu which teaches her nasty slang expressions never heard before, to a situation in which she would be permitted, and perhaps encouraged and forced, to think the forbidden, the immoral.

The therapist, rather than translating this directly, responds within Elaine's example; he thus preserves the distance she requests, hints at the burden of psychotherapy but lines himself up on the side of the goal she chooses: to be the right kind of person. As if to check whether the therapist believes what he says, she then talks about her New Year's resolution: "to give up mean and aggressive fantasies of torture."

The therapist again declares himself the ally of her strivings toward goals of perfection and uses then the simile of the mountaintop that one can reach only if one uses all kinds of roads, in order to encourage her to speak freely in the service of her goal. More technically, one might put it this way: The therapist, while agreeing with Elaine's goal of integration, of becoming a moral person, suggests that her illness can only be overcome if she faces the conflicts, the forbidden wishes which she is attempting to repress. The patient, through the New Year's resolution, feels that reintegration is only possible if she is allowed to forget, or at least permitted not to mention, not to think about, that which invades her mind.

Elaine instantly experiences the therapist's example of the different roads that lead to the top of the mountain as temptation, as an invitation to take dubious roads. She tells him indirectly that he does not seem to believe that there is any difference between good and bad.

As soon as he becomes aware of it, he tries to regain lost ground, and attempts to secure his foothold on her tenuous confidence in him by changing the example into a simpler one which he recalled she had used in the initial staff conference a few months earlier. In talking about her request for dental braces, he reintroduces the issue of means and ends on a level which is acceptable to her.

At this moment, she is able to move away from indirect, metaphoric communication, and in comparing herself with the other child, she speaks about her fear that she will not be able to go back to her childhood home because of her parents' pending separation. It is as if she tells us that there really is no available goal for her life, and what is the use of therapy then? The therapist here then introduces time, time with him as the healing factor.

Her request for the dime so that she can return home to the residential center, and her plea for patience with her—her calling to the therapist's attention that she will finally try and reach him—is a prediction, as it were, of a difficult process ahead.

One might also suggest that she tells the therapist how—even before therapy starts—she has made a decision—to suppress the illness and her brutal fantasies, to keep her fantasy world out of the therapist's office, and to invite him to support her ethical goals of perfection. At the same time she speaks about her wish to reach him, and invites his patience. He finds it necessary to ally himself instantly with the goals of her conscience and tries to open the process by stating that many different means, at times risky and perhaps unacceptable at first glance, may be necessary in order to reach this goal. She tries to see her New Year's resolution as the method of therapy while the therapist tries to suggest that the New Year's resolution might be its goal.

The "acting out scene" between the therapist and Elaine can be considered an *action metaphor* in which he gives her the dime to get home while she promises to try to find him and to reach him even though she might get lost on the way. They try to accept one another on each other's terms, without denying the difference in their ways of looking at the nature of the illness.

Elsewhere (1) I have described the transference situation of this initial phase of treatment as follows:

She described how when she walked to the clinic—the traffic light from the distance, shining like a star of hope, had given her assurance that she would not be too late, but would reach him on time. So softly and distantly did she speak that one could not be sure if she spoke of a meeting with the Lord or of being on time for her psychotherapeutic session. And it is likely that her unconscious intent was to prevent just such clarity in her communication. She went on to tell the therapist that for the past two years, at least, she thought of herself frequently in the third person. She would, for instance, write stories in the third person, although she really referred to herself. She discovered that when trying to pray she was unable to communicate with God and that in her inability to reach Him she would have to think about herself. With tear-stained face, she condemned herself bitterly for her inability to make contact with Him and she suggested vaguely that also in contact with people whom she loved she occasionally experienced similar difficulties, although less pronounced than with God. She gave the impression in these sessions of a passionate religious fanatic and only an occasional impromptu gesture would reveal her awareness of herself as an attractive young girl, who could, to use her own words, "turn the charm on."

The struggle between perfection and desire, and Elaine's peculiar way of bringing this into the transference situation can be exemplified best perhaps if we follow her and the therapist into the twelfth session, in the fourth week of treatment:

Elaine started the session with a slight reproach for my being late, hidden behind the comment that she had read quite a number of pages of a book which she held in her hands. After my apology for the unexpected delay, she returned to the book and told me about its content. She felt sad for the heroine, a young woman. (The book, *Faithfully Reporting,* was a Victorian novel by Thomas Hardy about a pure woman who loses her inner peace and her good reputation.)

Elaine told me about the heroine, whose parents insisted that she live with certain rich relatives so that she might perhaps inherit their fortune and marry a man from the better classes. For this reason she was turned against the common people in her community with whom she actually preferred to associate, and all these simple people became angry with her. While she faced one of these situations in which the people's anger was turned against her, a young man who allegedly loved her saved her on his horse. As they were galloping away on the horse, the young, innocent woman was suddenly faced with the demand for a kiss from her rescuer. Elaine hinted then that the kissing led to violence, to rape, and that the victim, after giving birth to a baby, did not know what she was to do while she faced the anger of society. Finally, she decided to face the issue and she carried the baby about openly as if to defy everyone. Her coming out of hiding was her first method of reacting to the loss of her innocence.

Later, the heroine became a milkmaid and met a young man whom she loved dearly. He too expressed interest in her, but she felt compelled to push him away. She did not tell him of her shame and could not respond to his approaches. She turned him away by telling him that there were many other pretty girls and that she did not wish to see him. That is as far as Elaine had gotten in the novel.

I expressed interest in the heroine and I wondered whether she had any other choice. Elaine at first felt that while 1890 was not to be compared with 1950, she saw not much choice for the girl. However, on second thought, she felt she would have advised the girl differently and would have told her to wait until the friendship with this man developed to a certain point, and then face him squarely with the issue and leave it up to him as to what the secret of her life meant to him.

I wondered whether the young man could have done something in order to accelerate the process. How could he have helped this woman to share the secret of her life with him? Did he need to stand by and permit her to ruin herself and thus lose her? Elaine insisted that there was nothing that the man could do. After all, he was no mind reader. All my attempts to assign him a role of helpfulness were warded off by the insistence that the girl did, or should do, nothing to let him in on the deepest secret of her life.

Finally I understood and suggested that Elaine's point meant that only if the heroine of the story offered some effective hint, or was willing to take some help from him or someone else, could she be helped. So much did the heroine assume a natural behavior and hide her secret that even with the best of intentions this young man could do nothing. But I wondered whether he might be helpful provided the heroine dropped a hint here or there. Elaine then told me that at one point of the story the heroine almost did this, and Elaine conceded that this man or anyone for that matter, for example, her minister, could be helpful, but it was up to the girl at first and not to the helper.

I fully agreed with her point, but I regretted that there was so little choice for him.

Some of our conversation then turned to the experience in the life of the heroine which the latter was hiding. Elaine blamed the parents of the heroine entirely, because they had driven her to believe in the rich people, thus getting her into trouble with the simple people in the first place, and therefore indirectly creating this very situation. Thus, the girl fell victim to the man "who took her honor." I wondered whether Elaine spoke about rape, and she took this up, suggesting that the story did not directly tell, but that there was no question about it. But then, she left the question somewhat open since she felt that it was not certain whether this incident was entirely the responsibility of the man or whether the woman participated too. She referred to some violence that must have been used but did not exclude the possibility that the girl gave in actively in this violent conflict.

When I wondered whether there were such parents today who might create a situation like the one in the novel, and which made it practically impossible for the heroine to accept help, Elaine denied that such parents could exist today. I reflected on the difference between 1890 and 1950, but I thought that even today parents at times were snobbish and insisted that their children marry within their own class.

The question arose then whether the heroine might be able to get out of this complete deadlock, and we both, half in earnest and half-jokingly, looked forward to our next session, when Elaine would have completed the novel and might know the outcome.

At the point when we were starting to wonder about the outcome of the story, whether the man ever could help the heroine, Elaine rushed away since she did not wish to miss transportation back to the home.

The experienced clinician cannot fail to see the relevance of this material in terms of the helping situation. Earlier we learned of the child's struggles between wild, destructive, and unacceptable wishes on the one hand and lofty ideals of perfection on the other. But it is also important to notice that the transference allusions divide the helper, the analyst, into two images, equally contradictory and opposed in terms of the purpose of their mission. The first rescuer helps the girl in order to violently take sexual possession of her, while the other, ineffective as a helper, must stand passively by because the girl assumes he does not wish to help her, and would not love her, were he to know the secret of her sin. The problem of different means and different ends of the helping process, stated in the first interview in the simile of the mountain climb or the dentist's braces, is here restated and rediscussed by means of the simile of the half-finished novel. The theme is treated in a way that permits both the patient and the therapist only to allude to it rather than to speak about it directly and without emotional distance.

It may be noted here that the therapist, although always aware of the necessity to maintain distance, and to remain within the metaphor, pushes too much in the end. His attempt to speak about "parents today," and his jokingly suggesting that he was interested in the outcome of the story, was rebuked and again this time through an *action metaphor,* Elaine's way of saying that she did not want to use time talking about the outcome, since if she were to do so, she would not get back home. But her fear that she might not get back home, and "miss the bus" as it were, indeed hints at the outcome of the psychotherapy story itself. However, since the psychotherapist did not entirely remain within the simile of the novel, the patient had to regress to a mode of communication which, rather than returning her to the language of secondary process and reality testing, took her back to action language which interrupted the session and did not answer the problem. Disruptions of this kind are, of course, unavoidable but seem to be excellent indicators of the correctness of interpretive work since they yield clues to the levels of communication which can be utilized by the therapist.

In hours to follow, Elaine's struggle to reveal the secret, as well as to keep it buried, kept up ceaselessly. The attitude of the therapist was one of waiting patiently while occasionally, though only indirectly and with a readiness to withdraw instantly, taking the initiative. Recorded material from the twenty-second interview, in the second month of treatment, will show how the psychotherapeutic process brings us nearer to the "secret," the real dilemma as posed by the nature of Elaine's illness.

During this session she spoke about her struggle for self-control. She did not want to hurt Mary, and to reward herself for not giving in to the temptation to do so, she had manufactured little gold stars "in order to have something so that she could aim towards perfection."

She made some remark as to how she needed to think of God in order to be good. The basic idea was to convey to me that she was bad, but that whenever she accomplished something for which she could pin a gold star on the wall, this was not really the good in her, but rather the expression of the good that came from God. She conveyed to me that in her there was the devil and she suggested that whatever good she could accomplish was only through the help of God. It was really God himself.

I understood her to tell me, and I suggested this, that she felt she had no right to think of her good deeds as emanating from her, but that they were rather directives that she received from God. This was the first time she gave some recognition that I understood her completely.

At this point I compared her attempt to get the message from God, which she would need in order to do good, with the one she used previously when looking at the picture of her father, who also told her through the expression she saw in his face what she was to do.

Her first glance in response was one of utter recognition and acceptance of what I said, but she had to retract quickly because it seemed a sin to her that she would want from her father what really she ought to expect from God.

However, when I referred to the educational functions of parents, and that it was the parents' prerogative to tell their children in what way they ought to live, she accepted it partly but added that her father never took responsibility for it. He kept away from educational problems and it was her mother who seemed to be responsible for education. Her mother was the one to say no and to put limits on her just as the school did in the Center. This was exactly why she hated school—because the school did not permit her to do what she wanted and to have her kind of fun. When I carefully tied this up with the idea that the school took over the function of the mother, for which now she hated the school, and thus hinted at the notion she previously denied, namely, that she hated her mother for putting pressure on her, she did not protest. But she veered off again to the main complaint she had against the school.

The school did not let her have her kind of fun. Her fun, however, was completely different from the fun of other people. What she understood to be fun, for example, was to have the opportunity to prepare herself for Christian service and to be permitted again to go to a certain church in another community as she had done some weeks previously, at the time of the beginning of her treatment. She wanted to attend a group meeting of the church. She called to my attention that she did not dare to impose again on any member of the personnel to go with her. The staff member who went with her the first time might perhaps go again, but she was not sure the same person would be on duty that day. She then quickly and spontaneously asked whether I thought it was wrong that she had that kind of fun, which was so different from the fun other people had.

I thought I was not sure in what way it might be wrong. I wondered whether perhaps she meant that it was wrong to the extent that it was hard to live up to this. Perhaps she really asked me whether she should not take on a burden for which she was not ready as yet.

She then reminded me—although I really could not recall it—of a message which she had received during the last church meeting. The message concerned an example, a picture really, which implied a deeper thought. It concerned a board and a nail. She made some allusion that one could not possibly expect that a nail that would be too big and too strong could fit that particular board.

At first it seemed to me that this was an example used by the speaker, but Elaine told me that this message was actually given to her before the real meeting started, when she was waiting alone, and when she prayed all by herself. I wondered whether she referred to a message which was given to her while she prayed, a message that came from spiritual godly powers. She confirmed this and I, while commenting on the many deep meanings that this message might imply, took from the example of the nail and the board the idea that it might express two different aspects of Elaine. She wondered whether I referred to her inner struggle, the real conflict that she had, and I thought I meant just this. I thought she had really come to me to find out what kind of nail would fit the board. I played with the notion that her allusion of nail and board actually referred to two different aspects of Elaine. It seemed that Elaine's problem in relation to her "fun" was that these two different aspects of her personality did not constitute an equilibrium and were really not suited for each other.

While Elaine went along with this interpretation for a while, she then gave a different meaning, as if to correct me, and I thought she was right, realizing that she felt the board represented her and that the question was whether the burden she would assume, that is the nail, would be appropriate for the kind of board that she was.

As the symbolism of board and nail, female and male, became clearer to me, I understood her wish for help to find the right proportions. I made only indirect and distant comments, but she accepted these fully and also the idea that I should be the one to help her. As a matter of fact, it was perhaps then for the first time that she said this as clearly as she did. She added there were not only she and I working on the problem, but that there were really three of us. It was about time to end the hour and I wondered whether she meant that she and I and God would work on her problem. She affirmed this and it seemed for the first time that I had been accepted into a triangle situation. I could not help but feel that for the first time I had evidence that I had become part of her delusional system. I expressed the thought then that the three of us could do it, even though it would be a long struggle. Elaine left with an indication of inner satisfaction.

Elaine's gold stars really represented the gifts which she expected from God, thus indirectly from the therapist, who then was accepted as the insignificant shadow, as though it were God's, but who, nevertheless, then gained a "real" foothold in the transference psychosis. She would need to be good, to forbid herself cruelty against Mary, and thus would then be allowed to reach Christian perfection (as in her fantasy marriage) which would bring her nearer to God, so that she could have "my kind of fun," which she thought would be forbidden by the school, and the therapeutic setting (the mother).

While the conscious thought was that her kind of fun would be Christian perfection, we understand from the intrusive, auditory hallucination, the message of the nail and the board, that things were much more complicated. The therapist's waiting, a cue he took from their discussion about Thomas Hardy's novel, paid off. She was willing to share the secret of the nail in the board with him. It will become clearer later that the therapist's first idea that the nail and the board constituted two different aspects of Elaine was not wrong. If seen against Elaine's problems in establishing and maintaining object relationships, the message of the board and the nail will lead back to this initial meaning.

The next hour, the twenty-third, just one day later, was described by the therapist "as a culminating experience, full of deepest emotion and the exposure of deepest material in an atmosphere of a mixture of feelings of passion and pain."

This hour started innocently enough, and at first sounded very much the way a counseling interview would sound in a high school counseling department. She spoke about her school program, how well she had done, that she stood a good chance of getting only A's, and reflected on her marks. She felt somewhat guilty for showing off, but felt that these good marks would help her to go to college and this in turn would permit her to do the work that she needed to do as a good Christian. She seemed to be struggling with the meaning of growth and success in school, and saw in it an expression of competitive and exhibitionistic strivings on the one hand, and on the other the meaning in terms of her own development. I tried only mildly suggesting the good points or occasionally the disadvantages in different ways of marking children and she went along with me; I only felt some pressure that she was trying to make me into a sort of moralist, occasionally an educator who was to take an equalizing stand or one of trying to move her away from extreme considerations. Nevertheless, I think the main attempt was to be as noncommittal as possible, but at the same time to fully participate in the exchange of communications.

Thus I provided an accepting atmosphere, and differed from her only inasmuch as the vibrations of my own value judgments, if any could be read into my comments, were less intense than hers.

I do not recall any particular important topic we discussed otherwise, but what follows developed from one facet of the discussion which had to do with the right or lack of right of a person to show what she could do or what she was and how far she could go with it.

It was at this point that Elaine reintroduced the topic about the board and the nail. She told me that she had not forgotten what we talked about the day before and as a matter of fact all of a sudden wanted a piece of paper, a "scrap of paper" on which to show me what she meant to convey. She drew a design which she suggested had to do with bookends for which she wanted to use the idea of the board and the nail. My previous suspicion confirmed itself quickly when I looked at the design she had drawn. It certainly suggested the sign of the cross (and quickly I realized that the board that she had always talked about was also the cross to which Christ was nailed). What was to happen then went so quickly and was so full of drama that I am not sure whether my memory reconstructs the conversation adequately, but perhaps I can convey the effect that broke through.

I told her that I realized when she spoke about the board she may have meant it also as the cross which was made of boards. She told me she did, but as quickly as she could she tried to remove the little design, and to tell me that there was really no particular meaning attached to it. However, when I had quickly recognized the main idea that she wanted to convey to me, she went on to tell me with increasing inner pressure about a story that explains the origin of the red breast of the little robin. The robin, according to this story, attempted to pull the thorn out of the forehead of Christ. It is in this way that the little bird got a red breast, red from blood. She spoke then of a different version, again explaining how the red breast of the bird was in one way or the other a symbolization of the bird's attempt to save Christ, and his having taken on some of the suffering.

I recalled at this point Oscar Wilde's story of "The Nightingale and the Rose." While I recounted the story, thoughts went rapidly through my mind. Her little robin reminded me of Robinhood, her phantom husband whom she had never mentioned during psychotherapy. It became clear to me also that she had been attempting to tell me that she was like Christ, perhaps the bride of Christ, and that the question was whether she was now strong enough to bear the nails, the same as Christ. The sadomasochistic nature of the fantasy became clear in spite of the disguise through the theme of suffering in order to redeem others. At the same time I went on to speak about the two young lovers, described in Oscar Wilde's story. I told her the story about the girl's wish for a red rose. The young man, in order to win her, has but one way to get this rose. A nightingale would have to sing the whole winter night while pushing her chest against the thorn of the rose bush. The loveliness of the nightingale's song, the nightingale's love, and the blood which would slowly flow into the stem of the rose bush, would form the rose. The young man got his rose, but the nightingale was dead and its little chest was covered with blood.

Elaine, who was deeply involved with the story up to this point, suddenly got almost violent. Her body convulsed as if shaken by an orgasticlike experience while tears were flowing down her cheeks. She told me to stop. My comparison was completely wrong. One story had nothing to do with the other.

I mildly suggested that I thought there was something in common in the two stories. I did not know how I had hurt her so much. In both cases, I suggested, the bird had suffered because of love. There was the thorn in both stories. Elaine became almost incoherent. She could not see the comparison at all. The one story had to do with God, with Christ, with something holy. I wondered whether she was holding against me my attempt to connect human love with a religious theme. She said that she did not know what I meant. I wondered whether she resented my having brought into these stories not only tenderness and love, but also that aspect of love which was passion. She protested and told me that it had nothing to do with this at all. She then suggested that her being upset was caused by something entirely different, something that I had said much earlier, before I had talked about the nightingale and the rose.

I could not recall what she might possibly refer to. I asked her to give me a hint and she pointed to the drawing, to the cross. I had spoken in some special way as if I understood her deepest thought which she was attempting to hide from everybody, certainly ought to hide from me—the thought about the cross and the nail. I asked her then whether I had implied that I realized that she thought of herself as being in the same position as Christ. I used some "neutral" word as if to hint that I knew that she was He himself. With bitter tears she told me that this was just what upset her. This was a most horrible idea that she could never tell anyone. She could only bear my knowing about it because in some way I was no person. She was attempting to say that since I had a therapeutic function only, I was just her doctor, I did not count in the same way as did the people who were in her family or were her friends.

I reminded her that only the day before she had told me how He and I and she, the three of us together, would be working on this problem, the problem of the board and the nail. That was true, she said, but it was too terrible and how could she ever suppress the thought, to never have it come again, and there I had brought it out in her. She had always been trying to push it away. She felt that she was a coward, that she was weak because she could not keep it away from even herself. Though she slowly quieted down, we still had to run far overtime. I simply said that in spite of all the pain that I seemed to have caused her, I was glad that she had told me. I indicated that it was not the question of being forced to think that thought, and of being unable to push it away, but that the problem was to help her so that she would not need to push away thoughts. She stressed the forbidden nature of the thought and I did not want to disagree with her on that, but still I thought that it was good for her to have told me. Now, while she was ready to accept this as something that she just had to do, it was terrible for her to think that He would know that she had had the thought again. I reminded her again that to speak about this was a task that the three of us had embarked on together. As she slowly regained her composure, she made ready to leave. She herself mentioned the next hour and left deeply shaken.

The wealth of this material is so overpowering that the basic secret which is communicated in this session might easily get lost. The theme of the board and the nail, the theme of the union with Christ, the theme of the little robin who dies in the attempt to save Christ, the theme of the bisexual and sadomasochistic arrangements suggested, the theme of the struggle against earthly love, almost hide the basic problem: the fear of the loss of identity, and the fear of fusion with the love object. The necessary maintenance of distance, the desirability of suppressing "that horrible thought," emphasizes Elaine's need to keep the therapist diluted, as a shadowlike figure from religious images which constitute not only projected introjections, but also serve to drain the affect from the psychotherapeutic situation, so that she can maintain sufficient middle-ground affect, and not be devoured by triggerlike and overwhelming emotional experience. We do not know whether we ought to censure the therapist for introducing Oscar Wilde's story, for his attempt to change the heavenly theme into an earthly one. To be sure, he must have felt that he went too far, but is this feeling about his own activity not simply his countertransference awareness that Elaine went too far, and could not maintain her identity as she pursued her "goal of Christian perfection," to be accepted by Him, to get His gold stars? Her problem then was that in this struggle to be like the other she became the other and wiped herself out. In order to maintain her individuality, to remain different, she was in danger of wiping out the other. As she regained her composure, she suggested that it was possible to tell the therapist since he did not count, he was not a person, he was simply a machine. This struggle for identity, against fusion, and the dynamics of her object relationships have been discussed more fully elsewhere (1). It is interesting that the therapist's notes do not indicate whether he told his patient the end of Oscar Wilde's story. The sacrifice of the nightingale was in vain. The young man brought his rose but was rejected by the narcissistic girl, who did not accept his sacrifice and did not give him credit for accomplishing the impossible. Does he who works with patients as sick as Elaine not feel frequently like Oscar Wilde's hero after he returned to his garret, the rose in the gutter, and the mission having failed? As in Oscar Wilde's story, the therapist is used only as the unimportant third person while Elaine is searching for Him and confides to the therapist that her confessions mean nothing since he is not "real," the patient's way of denying the perception of human contact.

As Elaine brought her deepest problem into the psychotherapeutic situation, thus revealing her illness, and giving, of course, a much more disturbed impression, she actually made progress in her social adjustment. She mastered the school program, and was soon ready to leave the hospital setting and enter a boarding home. As long as she had regular psychotherapeutic sessions scheduled, there was no interruption in her external adjustment, which looked to the outsider in the residential setting like vast improvement. It was as if the symptomatology of the illness found its main expression in the psychotherapeutic session itself. It was only during planned or unexpected absences of the therapist that the rapid gains registered in her living situation broke down again. Returning after an absence, the therapist learned from the social worker that Elaine had been quite disturbed while he was away. She had gone to the domestic personnel and had discussed her religious problems with some of them in a way which frightened them. She had cried a great deal, had locked herself in the closet of her room, and had been praying for hours on end, not permitting anybody to enter. In the next session she gave no inkling at first as to how upset she had been during the therapist's absence. She had to deny completely his absence or presence, his very existence or nonexistence. The question whether the psychotherapist thought her to be ready for a boarding home brought her back to the nature of the help which she was receiving, or rather which, in her words, she had to take from the therapist. He reports this part of her session with him as follows:

She did not know whether she should tell me what happened to her on Sunday, when she was in tears and when even the Bible could not help her. She wondered whether I could understand or help her inasmuch as I did not have the same religion as she. If I were Catholic, for example, or Moslem or something like that, I certainly could not help her. I wondered whether she thought perhaps that I wanted to convert her, or that I did not believe in the values that she had found in her religion. If this is what she thought, I wanted to tell her there was nothing of the sort in my mind.

Elaine then said that I could only understand her if I could be like her. She seemed to convey that I could only understand her if I were actually her, if I could identify with her to that final extent. She did not pursue the topic of my personal religion any further, but slowly moved again to Sunday, which had been so upsetting to her. She had finally discovered during this weekend that the devil was in her and that she had no power to change this. She said all this with intense emotion, with tears in her eyes, and with a sense of utter despair. I reminded her of the session when she had told me that he who thought that he was clean and had freed himself from the devil would suddenly find that the devil had come back with his seven brothers. This comment on my part re-established contact between Elaine and me. I thought she had been possessed during the weekend with deep doubts about God and about His helpfulness. She did not see it in terms of her doubts but rather in terms of the victorious devil.

She then went on to describe her experience. Her heart was on the side of God and full of sincere religion. It was only her mind, her thoughts, which were possessed by the devil. There was her mind, her heart, and her mouth. The mouth did the speaking, the communicating, but the mouth was most of the time dominated by the mind, which in turn was possessed by the devil. It seemed that the emotions were hopelessly outweighed by the mind, and when I offered to try to help her in this struggle, she felt that neither she nor I could do anything about it. It would actually be up to Him. This confirmed my earlier idea that rather than her being able to reach out for me, I would have to reach out for her. Again, in her example, it was up to Him to help her just as it was up to me to identify myself with her.

I wondered whether her upsetting weekend was not my responsibility. My absence, my inability to see her during the usual session, perhaps had brought about this state of affairs. She quickly said that she should not blame me, but rather be grateful that this opportunity arose since it was only because of my absence that she discovered the devil in herself. Otherwise she never would have known. I did not know whether I could fully agree with her even though it was perhaps necessary for her to discover what she was really up against. She spoke then about an example from the Bible. She spoke about the sheep which was endangered by the wolf and was desperately waiting for the shepherd to save it. There were shepherds who gave merely food to the sheep, food and water, which was not enough. There were others who also gave love. It seemed to me that the sheep that she was describing at this moment got only food and water and Elaine agreed with me. I wondered where the shepherd was, had the shepherd gone away? Had the shepherd deserted the poor sheep? While Elaine needed to stress that the shepherd really would never actually leave the sheep and would be there in time to save it from the wolf, she did admit that perhaps the sheep felt lonesome and deserted by the shepherd, and that therefore it saw the danger of the wolf much more enormously. The sheep had lost all power to jump, had lost the power to run away. It was only through the love of the shepherd that the sheep could regain its strength.

Once during the discussion I wondered how the sheep might have felt in the hour of danger. Elaine said that the sheep felt no resentment against the shepherd because it was so terribly scared. Lonesomeness and longing for the shepherd, overwhelming fear and panic had taken hold of it. I reminded Elaine of a dream which she had told me earlier in which she found herself marching into a concentration camp and waiting for some terrible fate. She woke with terror. I likened the terror that she experienced when she woke up to the terror that the sheep must have felt, and therefore thought for a moment that the shepherd would not come back to help it. I then expressed the feeling that I was convinced that the shepherd always would come back. For a moment perhaps there were too many sheep, or it might seem to the sheep that the shepherd had too many sheep to take care of. But Elaine then herself started to say that the shepherd never could have too many sheep. He could do it. I spoke then about the idea that I was sure he would return in due time. She took up my thoughts in terms of future events even though I was already there and had returned. We spoke of the return, and about her being calm, as if it would happen in the future, and as if we were concerned with the sheep of the Bible rather than with her.

This time she did not mind missing the bus. During the session at a moment when we were as far apart as possible, she reported only about the severe doubts that she had in the Lord and which brought out the devil in her, and at that time she looked out the window and never looked at me. At the end of the interview she turned her head and looked at me again. I made some comment that I was glad she saw me in the room again and looked at me. When she left, the mood of doubt in the Lord and the feeling of being possessed by the devil had given way to a large extent to a feeling that the shepherd would return and would not desert the sheep.

At this point it is clear that the psychotherapist has gained a secure foothold in the therapeutic situation, and that he is fully established in the inner struggle Elaine is in and must resolve. There is even the feeling here and there that the distant material, the disguise through the religious context, the defensive and adaptive meaning of which is elaborated elsewhere (2), gives way to sudden knowledge in Elaine that she is talking about the therapeutic process. In her communication the heroes change, and become more earthly, and less perfect. Hours on end she discusses King David and his relationship to Bathsheba. The therapist stresses here and there the psychology of Bathsheba and, while remaining strictly within Biblical context, helps Elaine to accept the fact that any relationship is a function of the behavior of both participants. King David's wishes toward Bathsheba are partly caused by her.

As soon as Elaine's deepest secret was brought into psychotherapy, she was able to face more and more inner issues of her life and to share them with the therapist. One might well say that with the confession of her inability to maintain her individuality under stress, she had really started treatment. The opening phase was truly over, and a good many features of the therapeutic process, although interrupted by regressive phases, by crises, now show more the conventional features of psychotherapeutic work with adolescents, if one is permitted to see anything conventional in the therapeutic work with adolescents.

I believe I can sum up the meaning of the next period, covering another month of psychotherapeutic work, by quoting one of Elaine's dreams and by relating the dream to the two reference points, one of which I mentioned earlier, the obsessive thought that she was Christ and the one later (2) when she thought I was Christ. Elaine had reported the following dream.

I was in a burning house. I think it was the treatment center. I wondered what I could save out of my possessions in my room. I realized that my father's picture was safe downstairs in the file case and nothing would happen to it. But the Messiah records [I had given her these records as a gift] were still in my burning room and they would be destroyed. I never dream with that many thoughts.

If we refer but to the manifest content of the dream, we notice that in the chaos of the burning house, the destruction that threatened to engulf her, the image of the father, his picture, was safe in the metal file (as there is such a metal file in my office) while the phonograph recordings of the Messiah were destroyed in the burning room. We cannot help but sense that the transference problem has now developed in a new direction. The image of the father could only be saved by projecting it onto the image of Christ. Whenever the attempt was made to approach the father, the therapist, or Christ, tremendous danger was in sight, wiped out her individuality, devoured the object, destroyed all individuality. New attempts were then made to reach the father image. He could not be reached because she assumed that he was Christ. As the transference developed, psychotic aspects of this transference withdrew into the dim past, were burned out in the burning room, and the image of the father could be retained while its substitute, the image of the Messiah, was threatened. This dream was related without undue anxiety, and no comment was made on my part with the exception of the suggestion that she must have felt good in the dream after she woke up, when she thought that the picture of her daddy was saved.

In this period also there was a psychological retest. A year earlier her attempts to draw the picture of a man produced unclear and vague outlines, but this time the picture was clear, fairly concise, and the man who was pictured, wearing a sport outfit, had a big *E* on his sweater. I could not help but think that *E* stands for transference.

The vicissitudes of the child's treatment from then on took a more familiar path. Elaine lived in a boarding home, finished high school with extraordinary success, and even won a scholarship at an excellent university. There were, of course, many ups and downs, struggles in the boarding home, critical situations with the parents, and the usual problems in her social relations with her peer group. She finished treatment after four years, seeing the therapist less and less frequently.

Now, at the time of this writing, approximately four years after the ending of her treatment, she is a successful university student and seems to have a rich and adequate personal life. She has contact with her parents, visits them during her vacations, but looks forward to having her own home someday. She has remained a sensitive person with a sense of social responsibility and adequate religious needs. Her therapist hears from her infrequently, but each time the communication confirms the impression that she is doing well. She seems to be able to bear up well under ordinary stresses of life and has become a valuable and appreciated person with a sense of self-respect and a pride in her individuality. The original shame that she experienced about having to admit to others that she was in need of psychotherapeutic help has given way to a certain pride in the therapist. She now needs to hide neither her past illness nor the fact of her therapy. As a matter of fact, she took it upon herself to introduce the therapist to a certain friend of hers. In a follow-up meeting which she arranged at a time when she spent part of her vacation visiting friends in the same community where she had been treated, she reviewed some of her past experiences in psychotherapy. There is a clear recollection of the experience with the exception perhaps that this experience is viewed now in the very same way that someone who is awake recalls a dream. The original experience could be likened to the one of a dreamer who would talk about the dream while dreaming. This dream which she remembered then does not frighten her any more since she has achieved new integration.

At the beginning of this communication I spoke about the fact that any description of a therapeutic process is really coauthored by the patient and the therapist. If Elaine chanced upon this account, and could recognize herself behind the disguises used, I believe that she would have reason to be proud of her successful struggle in which, to some degree, I was able to help her. She might suggest that the struggle is not quite over yet. I think she would add, as she did during her last session with me, that she feels strong enough to carry on alone, that she will not need to come back for further help. But if a crisis should develop, she also feels strong enough to come back for further help rather than to escape once more into a world of engulfing and deepening illness.

References

1. EKSTEIN, RUDOLF, *Vicissitudes of the "Internal Image" in the Recovery of a Borderline Schizophrenic Adolescent.* Bull. Menninger Clin., 29:86–92, 1955.
2. _____, *A Clinical Note on the Therapeutic Use of a Quasi-Religious Experience.* J. Am. Psychoanal. Asso. 4:304–313, 1956.

The Treatment of a Child and Family

Nathan W. Ackerman and Marcille H. Lakos

INTRODUCTION

Principles of psychotherapy are secondary to a systematized understanding of human problems and defined forms of maladaptation and illness. The specific techniques of psychotherapy are derived, step by step, from an integrated theory of personality development, social interaction, and psychopathology. This theory provides us with a set of normative expectations with regard to the endo-psychic organization of personality, relations of individual, family, and wider society, and a corresponding set of standards for judging a range of deviations from the norm. The purpose of treatment is to correct what is deviant and wrong in a person's life adaptation and in his endo-psychic organization. The treatment process stands or falls according to the validity of this judgment as to what is wrong with a person at a given time and in a given social place.

Our purpose here is to describe the treatment of a disturbed child within the frame of a concomitant program of therapy for the child's family. The treatment of a disturbed child requires us to respect the child's individuality. But the concept of individuality in a child is often incorrectly understood. A child's "individuality" may be healthy or pathological. This distinction is an important one.

The concept of individuality in a child is frequently treated as if it meant everything in the child that is separate or different from his parents. Such an interpretation emphasizes the child's separateness, and even his opposition to parents, while seeming to ignore the principle that healthy separation in the child cannot go forward except in the matrix of healthy emotional union or identification with his parents. In other words, healthy individuality in a child represents a balance between two components: a component of togetherness with parents and family, and another component of autonomous development. Individuality in this sense absorbs within itself much of the social interactional content of family experience. It does not represent exclusively tendencies in the child which are different from or opposite to those of parents and family.

The unfolding of a child's personality is, in great part, the product

Arthur Burton, editor, *Case Studies in Counseling and Psychotherapy*. © 1959, "The Treatment of a Child and Family," by N. W. Ackerman and M. H. Lakos, by permission of Prentice-Hall, Inc., Englewood Cliffs, New Jersey.

of social process. The family is the basic group within which the child is socialized. The child takes into himself something of the mother and something of the father, but also develops something unique and different. The child's uniqueness is influenced, beyond hereditary factors, by differences between the parents and the child's perception of the emotional relations between them. This interaction and merging of mother and father epitomizes the emotional essence of the family as a group; it is the core of the psychological identity of the family.

A child's personality is the end result of a certain fluid balance between tendencies toward psychic union with the parents and separation from them. The secure development of autonomy in the child's personality is thus contingent upon secure identity of the child with parents. Healthy identity with the parents means healthy separation; pathological identity means pathological separation. In circular fashion, whatever is deviant in the process of separation further distorts the pattern of emotional identification with parents and family.

The emotional disturbance of a child cannot be evaluated or treated in a social vacuum. Whatever is deviant in the child's behavior needs to be viewed as a symptom of the social psychopathology of the family group. In this sense, the traditionally demarcated professional field of child psychiatry might justifiably be called, instead, family psychiatry. If the pathological trends in a child's personality are to be successfully treated, the pathological trends within his family group must also be treated concurrently. If the child is to be restored to a path of healthy autonomous development, he must be restored to a position of healthy emotional union with parents and family. The unit of diagnosis and therapy is the child and family as an integral phenomenon rather than the child as an isolated being.

In the field of child psychotherapy, it is often claimed that family therapy is carried out at the same time as the therapy of the child. This usually means treatment of the child and mother, sometimes by separate therapists, sometimes by the same therapist. In a strict sense, however, this is not family therapy. This is an atomistic approach to child and mother as separate individuals, and it does not constitute a true therapy of the family group. Ordinarily, such treatment does not encompass a systematized conceptualization of the child-mother pair as a functional expression of the psychological configuration of the family as a whole. In the setting of traditional child guidance practices, the disturbances of parental attitudes are mainly related to the parents' individual personality, but not to the totality of role relations within the family group.

It is within the framework of viewing the child and family together as the basic phenomenological unit that we try to evaluate a disturbed child. It is within this conceptual orientation that we now describe the treatment of a particular case.

The primary patient is a ten-year-old boy referred with a series of complaints: failure in school work, chronic reading difficulty, depression and withdrawal, fear of father, jealousy of sister, and fears of illness and injury.

The early clinical interviews occurred in the following sequence: interview with both parents, with the child alone, with both parents again, each parent individually; then, interviews of child with both parents together and with each parent separately.

INITIAL INTERVIEWS WITH PARENTS

In the first interview with the parents, the father assumed the initiative. The mother sat by with a stony, impassive face but obviously listening very intently. The father placed himself instantly in the dominant position with a tacit assumption of superiority to his wife. He was clearly worried. There was a note of panic in his voice but his outward demeanor was controlled and reasoned. His wife sat stiff, constrained, frozen, offering only an occasional comment if her husband made a direct inquiry of her. At this time, and for some months thereafter, two significant pieces of information were lacking: the father was in personal analysis; and the school had recommended psychiatric consultation for the child two years back, but the parents delayed action on this recommendation right up to the point where the marriage was about to crumble. It was at the very peak of the family crisis that the parents became urgently motivated to request psychiatric help for the boy.

Sharply in evidence in the first interview was the father's wrath toward the child. He confessed it candidly. He stated that he never liked him, was critical of his intellectual failure, but also revealed his intense personal torment and guilt over the child's rejection. Ostensibly, his son was a severe disappointment to him because he seemed so stupid. The father leaned over backward to take the blame upon himself. He carefully sidestepped any temptation to be openly accusatory to his wife. We learned later, however, that in his own mind the father associated the boy with his mother and chalked them both up as stupid. He seemed to treat the boy exclusively as belonging to his mother. The mother was aware of this and said nothing. But the air between them was thick with unexpressed tension. Being an intellectual perfectionist, the father could not abide even the appearance of stupidity in any member of his family. Mother and son acted dumb, but weren't. It was merely that the father expected them to be so.

In the second interview with parents, the mother thawed out of her frozen state sufficiently to show some intense emotion. She choked up and cried. Only with support and encouragement from the clinician could she express even a small part of her tormented feelings. She felt an enormous guilt for the failure of both her and her son in the father's eyes.

FIRST INTERVIEW WITH THE CHILD PATIENT

Hubert was slightly undersized for his age, but, what is more important, he acted like a much younger child. He appeared blank and withdrawn. He was dull, sluggish, extremely walled-off. His attitude was removed, taciturn, depressed. He was unspontaneous and uncommunicative. He engaged in play in a self-absorbed way, ignoring everyone about him. Using building blocks he constructed a garage which he called a fortress. He admitted on questioning that it would be extremely difficult to get inside the walls of this building. When asked how long it would take, he muttered under his breath, "At least two years." He seemed to be intensely barricaded. His behavior suggested deep preoccupation with inner fantasies of power and destruction. Later, he alluded in a low voice to the toy building as the place where his father worked. His father was the director of an engineering school.

HISTORICAL BACKGROUND

The problems of this boy can hardly be understood except against the background of the disturbed relations of his parents and the twisted path of the development of his family. There was a religious difference between the parents; the father was Jewish, the mother Protestant. There was, beyond this, a further clash of cultural background which created a critical barrier between man and wife. This was especially complicated by the husband's extreme mistrust of the wife, a condition testified to by her husband's family.

Originally, this man and wife met at his place of work. She was a research assistant in the engineering school of which he was director. The courtship was a troubled one. It involved a long struggle with the man's parents to get them to accept the marriage. Throughout this struggle he was torn with conflict—trying, on the one hand, to placate his family, and, on the other, to win acceptance of the woman he wished to marry.

The opposition of his mother continued to be sharp and overt until a particular event occurred involving a bitter verbal battle between his older sister and mother. Out of her vindictiveness the sister declared vehemently that whether her mother liked it or not, her brother would be married. Promptly thereafter the mother collapsed, went to bed, but following this ceased to oppose the marriage.

The first phase of the marriage was tense and difficult. The new wife made an early but unsuccessful attempt to become pregnant. She felt she should have a child to please her husband. She was plagued with fears of sterility. Finally, she had a miscarriage which caused considerable anguish to her and her husband. Somewhat later she became pregnant with our patient, Hubert, but by this time her husband was inducted into the armed services. He left to go abroad with the military during her pregnancy. He arranged for his wife to live with his older sister. This arrangement was motivated strongly by his suspicion of his wife, his jealousy, and his fear that she might be unfaithful.

This jealousy is epitomized in one dramatic episode. On one occasion, the father, on returning home, secretly searched the mother's dresser drawer to be sure that her diaphragm was in its accustomed place. He was unable to find it, became infuriated, and charged his wife with infidelity. She was profoundly hurt and angry. All the time, the diaphragm was exactly where it should have been, but in his anxious haste the father had overlooked it. But the mother, as usual, and despite her humiliation, sided emotionally with her husband against herself. She felt, too, that a woman was not to be trusted. She shared with her husband an attitude of contempt and disparagement toward women. There were several critical episodes in her personal life in which she felt cruelly betrayed by women whom she had trusted as friends.

Hubert's birth took place while the father was abroad in military service. He was the first of four children. Prior to his birth, the mother dreamed idealistically of motherhood but was painfully disillusioned when the child finally arrived. She felt abandoned, utterly alone, and frightened and burdened by the responsibility of the child. She had little communication with the sister-in-law with whom she was then living. She felt tied to the baby but had virtually no other human contacts.

During the first phase of the child's life the mother was isolated and depressed. The child cried constantly. The mother used phenobarbital to quiet his crying and administered enemas to alleviate his cramps. He cried and screamed almost continuously up to the age of four months. She resented the baby's demands and felt estranged from him. She rarely held him in her arms or showed him any affection. His development was slow. It was two years before he spoke his first words. At 18 months he had difficulty with adenoids. He had distressed breathing and drooled at the mouth. Though depressed and deeply guilty, the mother kept her emotions to herself. This was the character of the mother's life situation until the father's return from the military.

Hubert was two years of age when the father returned. When the boy first saw his father, he screamed and refused to have anything to do with him. If he saw his father approaching his mother, he cried out in anguish. He seemed to go into acute panic when he saw his father in bed with his mother. Every member of the family was at this time severely troubled. The mother told the father little of how she felt. She was run down, exhausted, and did not look well. The father himself was morbidly unhappy. The parents felt estranged. The father showed little trust in the mother's affection for him. He escaped to his professional work. He came home late and saw little of his wife or the boy.

This situation continued until the mother became pregnant with the second child, a girl, toward whom Hubert later felt intense jealousy. During this period the boy continued his state of isolation; he did not play with other children. At the age of four or five Hubert became increasingly destructive. He showed no warmth to either parent, teased and struck his sister, and suffered criticism from both his parents. At five years he had a tonsillectomy, after which his mouth breathing and drooling diminished. The mother continued to be stern and cold toward him.

In kindergarten he was slow in learning and socially withdrawn. The teachers were puzzled because of his good intelligence. He daydreamed a good deal. The father, believing he was stupid, treated him harshly. During these years, Hubert had several minor accidents and developed an intense fear of bodily injury. The parents continually disagreed about the way to handle him.

The father tended to be indifferent to the child until his behavior became unbearable. He would then become abusive and insist, "That's enough." After an outburst of irritability, he would feel guilty and apologize to the boy. Otherwise, the father would simply ignore him. The mother resented this, and was critical of the father for not being more strict with the boy. The boy was consistently more difficult when the father was present. Later, two other children were born, making a total of four. The father enjoyed the younger children, and was especially fond of the second child, a girl. This tended, of course, to aggravate the patient's jealousy. These are the salient features of this boy's history.

At the time of referral a severe barrier existed between mother and child, also between father and mother, and father and child. The mother drew back sharply from the boy as if he were the worst part of herself. Both mother and boy felt they were to blame for the father's rejection of them; it was their own doing.

PROGRESS OF THERAPY

It seemed evident that if we were to make progress with this case we would have to confront the family problem as well as the boy's. We would have to move in the direction of dissolving the emotional barrier first between mother and child, after that between the parents, and finally, do something to restore the father's acceptance of the boy. Regardless of the father's involvement in personal analysis, our orientation was to commit both parents to participation in the therapy of the child. The father was involved in his family role as parent to this child and as husband to his wife. The mother was involved as parent to the child and as wife to her husband. The therapy was therefore conducted at several levels; individual sessions with the child, sessions with child and mother, individual sessions with mother, group therapy in a mother's group, and, later, sessions with the child and father. Therapy was mainly conducted by the female therapist, under the supervision of the male psychiatrist. Periodic family conferences were held, in which both male and female clinicians took part.

One event colored the entire course of treatment and should be related first. After about nine months of therapy, the mother terminated her individual sessions. Therapy of the child was continued, but the mother withdrew. The reasons were not immediately clear. The mother had an outburst of anger at the therapist when she discovered in group therapy sessions for mothers that women could enjoy sex and even experience orgasm. She felt bitter that her husband had withheld this information from her all these years. Until now she believed that men had a corner on sex and that women submitted purely out of a sense of duty. She was hurt and angry at her husband, but blew up at her female therapist. This was the precipitating situation.

But there were other reasons. Both she and her husband were suspicious of the therapist and fearful of injurious personal exposure. Her husband supported her decision to quit individual therapy, partly because of his belief that she was too stupid and too fragile, partly because of a submerged fear that she might get out of hand and turn toward another man. His jealousy of his own son was clearly a factor. Though interrupting individual therapy, the mother wished to continue in group therapy. It was judged wise, however, to remove her from group therapy as well, since we would have then no control over her emotional response to the group experience. This she resented. For a relatively short period, we continued the isolated treatment of the child, partly because of our uncertainty as to how this situation would unfold.

With the passing of the summer months, however, the mother returned, confessed that she was in error, expressed resentment regarding her exclusion from group therapy and asked to be reinstated both in the group and individual treatment. She did this on her own, with the father reluctantly assenting.

A quick preview of the sequence of changes in therapy is helpful for purposes of orientation. There occurred first a melting of the emotional barrier between mother and child. A new level of joining and emotional intimacy was established in this family pair. Following this there was improvement both in the boy and the mother. This left the way open for a beginning change in the relations between the two parents. It was the improvement in the parents' sexual relationship and the father's increased receptivity to both mother and boy which ultimately induced him to request a more active participating role in the boy's therapy. He also asked to have individual sessions to guide him in his paternal attitudes. Ultimately, there was substantial improvement in the intimacy of family relations at all levels.

The direct therapy of the boy began slowly. Initially, he appeared both oppressed and depressed. He bowed his shoulders; his movements were laboriously slow. He scuffed his feet as he walked across the room. He rarely looked at the therapist. His eyes were glazed and dull. His face was mask-like. His thought processes seemed to be split off from the movement of his hands. He was extremely reticent; he knelt quietly in a corner of the room and played with blocks in a feeble, detached, lifeless way. From time to time he interrupted his play to simply sit and indulge his fantasies. He seemed to resent any attempt at conversation. The therapist, therefore, sat by quietly, saying extremely little.

This type of relationship persisted for four sessions with almost no verbal communication of any sort. There was only a slight show of interest when the therapist offered candy to the boy.

Beginning about the fourth session, his building activity became somewhat more organized and he showed increasing alertness to the therapist's presence. Now and then he cast sidelong glances at her and asked a few questions concerning the blocks. The therapist recognized his frightened and disguised appeal for her to take part in his game. She responded. He seemed pleased by this and proceeded then to test the therapist's reaction to his urge to destroy the building. When there was no sign of criticism, he proceeded to destroy the house, making a loud bang and relishing it.

In general his behavior continued to be cautious, fearful, suspicious, and walled-off. While believing himself to be stupid, he was nonetheless under compulsion to display his intellect to the therapist. This occurred mainly in the form of reciting to her fragmented pieces of information about current events. Gradually, as he felt safer in this relationship, safer both from criticism and from any compulsion to behave according to her dictates, he became more accessible. The therapist continued warm, friendly, but non-intrusive, waiting for cues from the boy as to the level at which he would accept her participation.

In the sixth session there came another change. He dropped his interest in blocks and proceeded to become interested in ball-playing. He confessed his total failure as an athlete. He said his fingers got in the way; he was awkward. But he seemed to appeal to the therapist to raise his confidence. She responded by joining him in a game of catch. At first his coordination was extremely poor. He was all hands and feet, but he was tenacious and the ball-playing continued. He improved rapidly. After a time, he jumped, and caught and threw the ball quite skillfully. His interest moved to other activities: finger painting, drawing (mostly of submarines), and depicting his own fantasies of outer space. He was ambitious to be the first man to visit Mars. He felt he might be happier there than on earth. The therapist was a full participant in all these activities. She talked only if the boy seemed to welcome it.

During this growing intimacy between boy and therapist, the boy slowly offered small confidences about his parents. This came without any pressure whatsoever. He was aware that his mother was coming to see the therapist once a week. He made clear how utterly alone he felt, how unable to communicate with anyone in the family. He felt incredibly inferior and dumb. He gradually became more assertive and complained of his parents' failure to understand him. He felt stripped of confidence as a result of the mother's alienation from him and also as the result of her guilty over-protection.

The mother, in response to her own conflict, tended to protect him from the father's criticism and tended to do the talking for him; in effect, she put words right into his mouth. She lived his life for him, treating him as a piece of herself rather than as a separate person. This was clearly the effect of her fright of the father's criticisms.

As the boy revealed himself increasingly to the therapist, he cautiously hinted that he would like his mother to join the session with him. He wanted to show her his drawings and display his new facility in ball-playing. But he was frightened. He wanted to ask her if she loved him, but he didn't dare. She would misunderstand and get bossy.

The mother was invited to be part of the boy's sessions. Initially, both boy and mother were extremely awkward with one another. Gradually, he drew her into games with him and hesitantly showed some of his feelings. The mother had previously felt completely rejected by the boy. She was shocked and elated to discover that she was so deeply important to him. When they sensed that each really needed the other, the relationship, at first wooden and blocked, warmed up. Finally, the boy, while caressing a toy animal, sat next to his mother, and took hold of her hand. The mother was touched to the core and could hardly hold back her tears. She seemed stilted, self-conscious, fumbling, and hardly knew what to do or say. Finally, in a labored, awkward manner she put her arm around her boy and they sat quietly together. They agreed later—it felt good! They walked out of the office arm in arm.

The patient responded to this reunion with his mother with an excited, buoyant mood. Their play together in therapeutic sessions became hectically animated. They reached a point where they experienced a climactic shared excitement in a playful fight with water guns. The boy doused the mother from head to foot; while at first self-conscious and scared, she came gradually to love it. Emotional communication became intense. They laughed and cried together.

Let us turn now to a consideration of what was happening in the meantime in individual sessions with the mother. Initially, she seemed frozen, guilt-ridden, defensive, and aloof. Her conversation was almost entirely on the surface. She surrounded herself with this protective wall as though to ward off expected attack. Nevertheless, she was earnest in her desire to help the child. She revealed quite unmistakably her feeling of lack of worth in her husband's eyes, and her tendency to agree with him that she was stupid. Yet, paradoxically, she rose to the challenge to try to prove her good intellect to the therapist, exactly as did the boy. She tried in every conceivable way to build up her sense of worth and importance, and to impress her husband and the surrounding community. Small successes meant nothing to her. The slightest disappointment confirmed her conviction of inferiority. Her whole demeanor seemed to radiate shame for herself and for her son. At first she showed little feeling. This gradually changed. She revealed her fear of admitting openly any closeness with the boy. She wanted to disconnect herself from the boy in her husband's mind.

At another level she discussed her husband's character, his severe suspiciousness, his jealousy, and his accusations of infidelity. Within the family there was no spontaneous joy. All issues were met with a heavy hand. There was little relaxation, no play, no humor. The emotional climate of the entire family group was heavy and depressive.

The therapist's role with the mother was one of sympathetic support and acceptance, providing abundant opportunity for the free expression of her conflicting emotions. The significant parts of her relations with the child and husband were discussed frankly with her. At times she was given direct advice concerning her conduct with the boy. She was encouraged to learn to listen to him as she herself was listened to.

A sharp change occurred when she learned in the mother's group that women had sexual orgasms. This was a real shock. She came to her individual session with anxious, pressured questions. Hitherto, she had carried out her obligation with her husband in a passive, frigid, immobile manner. This, to her, was the normal state of affairs in married life. As she talked, she became increasingly irate at the way she'd been cheated. She exploded at the therapist and quit. As has earlier been indicated, after a lapse of several months she began again where she had left off. The therapist responded earnestly to her urge to explore this sexual discovery. There was candid discussion of the sexual potentials of a woman. The mother was encouraged in the expectation of personal pleasure. Following a particularly tense session in which the mother discussed at length her experiences of treachery at the hands of women and confessed her fear of betrayal by the therapist, she began to show increasing interest in her sex life. She overcame her vindictive feeling toward her husband and participated more freely in sexual love with her husband. Her husband in turn reacted with considerable surprise, but also genuine appreciation. For the first time she had succeeded in winning from him overt, enthusiastic expressions of approval. This was a turning point in the relations between man and wife.

It also marked a change in her attitude toward the therapist. Following this improvement she became much more trusting. She confessed much more frankly her previous suspicions of the therapist, her fear of betrayal, her contempt for women, and her need to cut off her feeling in her dealings with them. About this time, she began to show intense feelings in the therapeutic sessions. She dropped her defensive barricade and literally poured out emotion.

Gradually, the mother's rigidity mellowed. She responded with increasing warmth to the boy; he, in turn, moved closer to her. The melting of the mutual mistrust between mother and son opened the way to a new level of emotional identity. Of particular importance in this newly discovered intimacy were the water fights in which Hubert directed a steady stream against his mother. It was quite striking to note in this connection the boy's increasing freedom in emotional communication with his mother. He dropped his mask. He no longer acted dumb. In place of his previous dull apathy, he now displayed some spark and real intelligence. He showed his most acute fear in connection with an open show of tears. He was convinced that it was weak and foolish of him to cry; but when mother and son cried together, his fear was eased.

As the intimacy between the mother and son unfolded, the boy talked increasingly about what was wrong with his relations with his father. He became guilty concerning this, however, and showed strong reluctance to belittling his father in his mother's eyes. The recognition of the boy's guilt over the temptation to use one parent against another induced the therapist to suggest sessions for the boy and father. While considering this plan, the boy entered a plateau. He seemed for a time to freeze and he was unable to make further progress.

The anticipation of joined sessions with his father induced again a compulsive urge to prove his worth through a display of superior factual knowledge about the world. It was as if the father could tolerate the boy only at this level of intellectual superiority. Ordinarily, conversation between father and son was sparse and impersonal. When it did occur, it took the form of a detached, intellectual discussion, which tended quickly to deteriorate into an irritable argument about who was right or who knew better.

By this time the boy had a clear picture of his father's rejection of him, his suspiciousness, and criticism of his stupidity. With increasing awareness of his father's preference of the other children, the boy's hate and fear of his father emerged quite sharply.

In the therapy sessions with the boy and father, the father was at first reserved and defensive. His intelligence, essential honesty, and desire to really understand came to the fore, however. He listened both to the boy and the therapist with some respect. Gradually, the boy overcame his fear sufficiently to express directly to his father for the first time his conflicting feelings. The father was deeply impressed. He tended partly to justify his attitudes and partly to confess his guilt for failing to understand the boy. He admitted to the boy that he lacked confidence in him, that he preferred the other children, that at times he was disdainful and indifferent. While making these confessions, the father seemed depressed.

For this reason the therapist had several sessions with the father alone. She gave emotional support to the father for his intellectual understanding and his earnest desire to help his son. At the same time, a number of the father's misconceptions of the boy were challenged and discussed freely. When issues arose that had to do with the relations between mother and father, the father showed much more animation. He was at first more interested in his wife than his son. His motivation to improve his marital relations was stronger than his urge to help the boy. In short, he was more preoccupied with his own needs than with his son's needs.

Discouraged in the beginning, he talked of the complete stalemate in his relations with his wife; he did not know which way to turn. After a time, however, he gave recognition to a distinct change for the better in the behavior of both boy and mother. He was impressed with the improvement in his wife's sexual response.

At about this time, a joint conference was arranged which included the man and wife, the male psychiatrist, and female therapist. The purpose of this was to survey progress and decide further steps in therapy. The father admitted a lessening of his hostile feelings toward the mother. They were now finding more satisfactions together, which gave him real hope. Both man and wife agreed that things had been rough but they now expressed a desire to make the marriage a lasting one. The wife remarked, "I've learned something. I feel now that you don't have to know exactly what is going on but if things work out it is satisfying enough." She meant by this that she had dropped her effort to prove her intellectual adequacy, had ceased to cut off the flow of her feeling, and felt more alive. Of particular importance in this interview was the more candid discussion of the difficulties that resulted from the husband's jealousy. The wife was able to "tell her husband off." She expressed more openly her resentment of the father's jealousy and his refusal to allow her to leave the house unattended.

A month later, there was a very distinct change in the attitude of the father. He was more positive, no longer depressed, and spoke enthusiastically of the change in his relations with his wife. She was warmer, he was less suspicious; they found real pleasure in one another's company. This enabled him now to show a genuine interest in the boy.

In the meantime, Hubert responded well to the therapeutic sessions with the father. He regarded the achievement of a new contact with his father as something outstanding. Following this, he showed substantial improvement in his work at school. He was a more spirited, interested student. He continued to be a slow learner but his achievement was distinctly on the upgrade. At the same time he was less hostile toward his sister.

When the mutual hostility and suspiciousness between father and son eased, there were further individual sessions with Hubert. He began now to talk increasingly of his sexual feelings. He confessed his masturbation but was troubled because he got little feeling from it. During one such session Hubert showed considerable agitation and anxiety; he fidgeted and wrung his hands. With encouragement he related his worries. He confessed to several episodes of exploratory sex play with his sister. His reaction after these experiences was one of intense guilt and disgust. He was given every opportunity to talk himself out in these matters and much relieved to discover that his sex urges were by no means unique. They did not make him a bad, perverted person.

This encouraged him to talk more and more of his body experiences. He began to value his body more. His appearance changed; he became neater, and paid more attention to his looks. He began also to learn more of the skills which were required of him in social relations, ball-playing and dancing. Through dancing lessons, he acquired a girl friend.

One day he came to therapy quite depressed and far away. He seemed lonely, and said little. After a considerable period of tortured reticence, he admitted finally that he continued to be worried about his masturbation. He hated to "jerk off," felt very guilty about it, and was sure that it hurt his penis. He complained that it was actually painful. He imagined that the liquid would run dry if his glands were overworked, and that they would cease to function. He had the thought that the semen was infected with germs and was a real danger if allowed to stay on his pajamas.

Discussion of these conflicts and fears led to the realization that he wanted to hear the male psychiatrist's view of these problems. This was arranged for. The problem of his masturbation and associated fears was discussed with female therapist and male psychiatrist together. The discussion was lengthy. The core of this conflict emerged finally: the boy was intensely disappointed because the pleasure of seminal discharge was somehow impaired. In fact, at times, he did not realize that he was having an orgasm unless he looked directly at his penis. It was discovered that in masturbation, he was actually hurting his penis. He rubbed it harshly, angrily. Through various hints, it seemed probable that he was unconsciously equating his penis with his father. In the act of beating his penis, he was attacking his father—a symbolic act of vengeance. He seemed to disconnect himself from his penis, disowning it and treating it as if it belonged to his father. This disguised rage against the penis, the guilt, and fear of retaliation, took the pleasure out of the act. Interpretation of this conflict and further discussion of his anger and competitive battle with his father eased the patient's depression and worry.

This boy and family have been in therapy three years. It continues to the present time. The unity of the family has been preserved and enhanced. There is now no danger of a break-up of the marriage. The parents have a new bond. They enjoy one another. The relations of mother and son are vastly improved. The relations of father and son, though better, are still an area of tension. The boy himself is much happier and no longer withdrawn and depressed. He feels he has made great strides. He now feels accepted at school; he does better both academically and athletically.

You Make Your Own Ideas

A Group Project with Disturbed Adolescent Boys

Edna Mann

In every school there is a large unmet need for psychotherapy. In a 600 school, for the emotionally and socially maladjusted pupils, the need about equals the number of boys on the register—and the personnel to do individual treatment is woefully small.

For that reason, about five years ago, a therapy group of six boys was started and has continued at one of those schools. It soon became apparent that the group, by its very nature, offered a therapeutic instrument especially suited to these boys whose special difficulty was in getting along with people. These boys are suspicious and often worried—about being or being thought "crazy." When they are invited to the "Student Consultation Clubs," they feel it is not because they are "mental" (to quote one of them), but because they "have good ideas." That helps start them out with a new image of themselves.

We have had groups of different ages—six to ten in numbers, ten years to sixteen years in age—with different goals, or different emphases in treatment. For the past three years, we focused on fourteen- to sixteen-year-olds to help them bridge the gap between their relatively protected school setting and the next step—work or high school. The weekly group sessions have frequently been followed by individual sessions, when sought by a member or when the leader felt it was needed.

But the main focus of study was the boys themselves, as they functioned in the group setting. The groups met weekly and, by request of the boys, the meetings were extended to two periods—through and including recess.

An on-the-spot validation of the group process is suggested by some of the boys' actual comments, and some of their changes in action and attitude.

It must be noted that these boys are very wary of showing warmth or trust. Said Bob, when we were talking about the club, taking stock at the end of the year, "In our Boys Club, I learned to get along with others. Now I got some friends—two or three. I see the whole school is not against you . . . *You talk it off your mind.* Everything is confidential."

Another boy, Bill, originally referred to the Bureau of Child Guidance for intensive study, was taken on for group therapy. He has shown a change in his attitude to himself, in his appearance, his behavior and

"You Make Your Own Ideas," by Edna Mann, *Pathways in Child Guidance*, 1964, *6*, 3–9. Dr. Simon S. Silverman, editor. © 1964, Bureau of Child Guidance, New York City.

comments. He was referred by the teacher and principal because he veered between being suddenly hostile or withdrawn (mostly withdrawn). He was suspicious, moody, shy, depressed, and friendless. He can tell this story in a few words:

"I used to be the gloomiest boy in the school—the shy kind. I was by myself all the time—didn't join in any games—always by myself with the punching bag. In the club, the boys began to talk about things I knew—how to act with grown people. I felt I ain't got anything to lose—I need help—we both need help—we give ideas. I need ideas also. I knew what I was saying but I didn't know how to say it before. Once you get talking, the rest is easy. If you can do one thing, you can do another thing. I used to be at the bottom of the hill."

This boy was selected recently to go to the Board of Education with a classmate and teacher to help put up an exhibit about the school. Instead of a gloomy, depressed manner, noted by the Bureau of Child Guidance psychiatrist and psychologist in the original B.C.G. study, this boy has become purposeful, mobile in expression, often smiling, (though, of course, many home problems, including his relation to his step-father, remain).

The case of another difficult boy and how he responded in the group, illustrates a procedure used and also how a session developed:

Jacob—with one psychotic parent and himself encased in a cement front covering his quivering uncertainty—announced the first day at the group, "This club is for nuts; this is a prison. You are a cop." Later in the year, when the boys mentioned a new hole in the playyard fence, Jacob said, "The 3 o'clock boys did it, though the cops are protecting our school for us." (Formerly, a cop was an out and out enemy, and so was the school, and so was the club. This is progress for Jacob, though his adjustment is tenuous and continues precarious.)

In Jacob's earlier sessions in the club, he used to sit and bang out loud rhythms on the desk. The boys yelled "Shut up." He kept on as if he were out of earshot: loud, steady, disruptive banging. Al yelled at him, "You stop." Jacob said, "Make me." Al let loose a string of epithets.

The leader said (and this is the usual procedure whether we are discussing lateness or fighting or cursing, or wearing big belt buckles, or smoking in the subways, or drinking or dope or gambling)—"Why do you think people (not Jacob) make noises and things like that?"

TRANSCRIPT FROM SESSION

A brief transcript from the session follows:

Leader: Why do people act restless, make noises and things like that?

Charlie: They are nervous.

Leader: Why?

Charlie: They never get nervous unless they are worrying about something.

Leader: About what?

Charlie: About troubles.

Leader: Like what?

Harris: About girls.

About school (several other worries cited by group).

Leader: Why do they act restless—How do they *feel?*

Harris: Here's Charlie (sitting next to him). (He points to Charlie's ears.) He's got big ears—not like other boys.

Charlie: (Smiling. There is good feeling between the two boys. Formerly it would have ended in a fight.) I don't care. Everybody's got something.

Al: (Tells about and dramatizes a fat woman walking down the street near his home—making noises, nervous and "goofing.")

The boys had forgotten Jacob in all this, but he was seeing a new image of how his actions strike others. Where orders and threats and insults did not stop his banging, this demonstration did. He stopped, and he never did it again.

Al: (Continuing with his dramatization of the fat woman, careening down the street.) She's crazy.

Leader: Not crazy. Just nervous. Like all of us sometimes.

Al: Sometimes Pete (a classmate, upstairs) acts nervous. (Then he acted out Pete, flipping his lips and making noises.)

Leader: Why do you think he does that?

Harry: Maybe he's unhappy.

Charlie: Don't fight him.

Leader: What do you think you could do?

Charlie: Go over and talk to him, and say something to make him laugh and feel better.

We then decided to act out two approaches to Pete, one ending up in a shadow boxing fight; then the second in which Charlie, who had made the suggestion, goes over to Pete, puts his hand on Pete's shoulder, and tries to distract him with funny stories. The boys watch this role-playing very much interested.

Jacob had been invited to play Pete's part. He refused—but within himself, he began to play a new part, seeing himself more as others in the group saw him, as they saw people like him. He did not like this sudden image of himself.

The group's insights into the "why" of his banging gave it a new meaning for him—instead of seeming strong and defiant and independent (as he pictured himself), he saw himself as one of many who are troubled and show it. His behavior became less destructive to the group, and the group responded by becoming friendlier to him; a benevolent circle in the making instead of a vicious one.

How the boys change comes alive in direct quotes from an early and late session featuring Jacob and Robert.

Jacob, after a few choice insults, distributed impartially to me and the boys, pushes back his chair and lies down on the couch in the room. I ask around the circle:

"Do you think Jacob should sit up or lie down?"

Robert says, "He should drop dead."

I ask, "Lying down or sitting up?"

Robert takes time to deliberate on that one, "Just so long as he drops dead, I don't care if he lies down or sits up."

At a later session of this same group . . .

Robert says, "Nobody could get along with Miss X (a teacher)."

Bill says, "I can get along with anybody." (This is the same Bill who was the lone wolf.)

Robert: "Yes, by kissing the ground they walk on—going on errands for the teachers."

Leader: "Who also goes on errands?"

Lanny says, "I do, but I take privileges for myself on the way. That's the only reason I go."

Leader: "Why is it so hard to say you do something nice?"

Robert explains, "You're afraid if you say you do something nice, you'll be called a faggot or a punk."

Leader: "Who has the courage to say something nice that you do?"

Robert: "I did something nice."

Chorus from the group: "WHAT? WHAT?"

Robert: "A boy felt bad and I went over and talked to him and made him feel better."

Leader: "What did others of you do?"

Stanley: "I went on an errand for a blind man in my house, and didn't finagle the change, and for me—that's something."

New group attitudes have emerged. In the beginning, only rarely, and only one boy alone or two might admit to moral scruples or tender feelings—but when they were in the larger group, they competed for status in seeming tough and callous.

EMERGENCE OF WARM FEELINGS

Gradually, it became more acceptable in this group to express warm feelings, or pangs of conscience, or need for self-control and for outer controls. More often now, a boy was willing to seem "soft" or "good." One of the most clowning and troublesome said, "I used to be flicked in the mind—not normal—sick—when I was so bad, I thought I was having fun—but I was just hurting myself."

Another, "It made me feel funny when I see that boy beat up on the street—inside my heart—soft."

About a teacher, "It's her conscience makes her unhappy. She does things she knows is wrong and don't want nobody to prove she's wrong."

"It's our fault (the boys) that they have to make some of the rules we don't like."

This seemed to be a new kind of learning situation where slowly their emotions and attitudes could be recast in the safe warmth of their own sharing.

THEORETICAL ASPECTS

Certain theoretical aspects of the therapeutic process have emerged from our experience and may be summarized as follows:

1. It appears likely that the small group setting may be a natural base for emotional learning which can carry over to larger groups. Special needs of these boys are to adjust in group settings; to develop; to distinguish between irrational, projective gripes and realistic ones; to empathize with others; to accept themselves; to develop better attitudes to authority; to develop socially acceptable standards; in short, to change their values since values are the most important directive of behavior.

2. Since adolescents are particularly sensitive to the mores of their peers, group setting suits their needs. For instance, in tackling the problems of fighting, it makes practical sense to try to change the attitude of the group which establishes the "You're chicken" goading of the individual to fight or lose face. If the group attitudes remain unchanged, an individual's insight about his own fighting is rendered ineffective.

3. Since authority problems loom large, it is preferable for the boys to be in a situation where they can "tell" each other. They can get to see that regulations are not made out of meanness or whim, but are necessary . . . "I bet if nobody in school wanted to smoke, they would make a rule you must smoke" has changed to "Some rules we don't like are made because the boys force the principal to make them" and "The rule protects us."

4. The group acts as a living mirror for each member. One boy comes in with wild hair, tight dungarees, walks with knees bowed out. Greetings from group member as he walks in the door: "The Wild One" (very apt, and it registers).

There is a measure of cohesiveness and support in the group, a similarity of status, and a chance for each boy to take an insight or to let it lie outside his wall of defenses, as long as he needs to or can. Says John when his friend, Joe, objects to John's criticism with a "just don't worry about me":

"You don't worry about yourself. Somebody has to worry about you. I'm trying to help you. You're slipping. I could leave you there like a no-good dead horse. You're spoiling the club for everybody."

At this time, Joe's clowning was disrupting the club, and they were all against him.

5. A primary function of the group is to substitute talking out for acting out:

"What's good about the club is where guys got trouble home or something, and he comes here and talks it off his mind."

6. The experience of a troubled boy can help others in the group who have similar troubles. Instead of just getting help for himself, as in individual therapy, he sees his experiences extended and gains a measure of ego strength and pleasurable empathy. Example: In the talk about lunchroom food (a popular topic in these emotionally deprived boys), one boy said the food is better at Bellevue. He looked a little startled after he said it. The other boys expressed interest and no surprise. They asked questions about Bellevue, and he was informative and reassuring (to any other possible candidate) in his recounting of what he had done there. The boys acted as objective and interested as the leader.

7. The sessions are a natural place to let off steam on any immediate pressing problems. Sometimes before the meeting starts, two boys are discussing a current gripe—which is then brought to the group. Example: A boy felt outraged by an unfair disposition of his case. "They build you up and let you down." It seemed unfair and many of the boys said so. He railed at the unfairness and said he would go on the hook. That led to a discussion of going on the hook, and several admitted it was no fun "especially if you are alone." This last from a boy whose referral problem was that he seemed to prefer to be alone, apart in his own world. It was a question of whether his withdrawal constituted a neurotic defense or a psychotic retreat. His remark gave a diagnostic clue which has been followed up: that he really does not want to be alone.

In several instances, there has been practical follow-through, such as occurs in individual case studies. For example: change of class as the need was indicated; referral for investigation of boys whose serious problems were indicated in group discussions though they were not members of the club; helping boys go after a job; accompanying a boy to a high school where the group leader had contacted the principal and gained his admission.

8. The relationship between the adult leader and the boys is basic. They are quick to react to non-verbal cues and they sense sincerity. They said about one teacher—and they are right—"He is fair. He is so fair and so nice if he hit me, I'd like him, but he does not hit me." (This teacher remarks about the boys. "They never bear a grudge." Against him, they don't.)

Based on five years of practical experience as a group leader, the following points are suggested as important in the role of a leader.

1. The leader's role is far from passive. He presents to the group a new way of functioning and is himself an active symbol of it.

The leader accepts the group norms, but does not adopt them. He is never personally affronted or indignant, but he stands for his own standards. The boys are accustomed to having their standards either adopted completely—as by their age and gang mates—or rejected completely. The group leader aims to introduce a new learning experience.

It is necessary for the leader to find a balance where he can be permissive enough so the boys will show their feelings and their group mores—and at the same time to offer an example of a different type of behavior with which they can identify.

2. The leader offers active help in group functioning, suggesting as may be necessary, procedures—or topics for discussion, following group rules, and so demonstrating respect for rules and for the boys who made them.

An example of how rules are fashioned: In selecting a chairman for the first meeting, the boys were asked how they wanted to do it—by vote, alphabetically, or any other way. They decided to pick a name out of a hat. We got a hat and picked. The least acceptable boy won. We decided that the chairman for one meeting will pick out of the hat the chairman next meeting—a beginning concession to orderly processes—which each chairman has been zealous to carry on.

This particular session started like this:
Several boys talking loud:
Chairman to Jim: "Shut up."
Jim: "Say 'please.'"
Chairman: "Shut up, please."
Jim: "Thank you, dear."
And we were off.
As to the topics selected—the leader should always be ready with a

topic in case none arises from the group.

All our topics have this in common: they are important to the boys. We have talked about gripes, food, school, girls, fighting, prejudice, gangs, drink, obscenity, mothers, state training schools, dope, playing hookey, teacher selection in a 600 school, resistance to group participation.

A very rewarding gem of a topic is *What Makes A Good Teacher*. Perhaps never have so few boys had so much trouble with so many teachers. This is the first time they qualify as experts—and they do. Their evaluation of teachers in the school is what yours would be—or the Bureau of Child Guidance, or the principal.

3.   The leader helps in problem solving—by making the group aware there is a problem, by formulating it so all can contribute, by focusing on the *why* behind it, and asking what to do about it.

The leader aims to raise the discussion from the level of an emotional orgy, such as the boys could enjoy alone without a leader.

4.   The leader must bear in mind, as in individual therapy, the importance of proper timing in formulating the problem and opening up the field for suggestions on handling it. If the leader is in too great a hurry, he may interrupt the flow: the boys may feel they are being pushed—or blocked. It is important to let them talk enough so they are warmly in the subject—and so they feel you are interested in their ideas and in them. Then they are more ready to accept you and your ideas and feelings.

5.   As to structure, such a group needs it. Lack of structure, the laissez-faire approach by the leader, fits only adult groups which have worked together for an extended period.

These boys are so immature emotionally, so low in self-esteem and self-discipline, that without structure and control, one of two things is likely to happen. Either they revert to their usual self-centered, antisocial patterns, or they become threatened and paralyzed by their own lack of control. They do not like it. They are more comfortable with some structure. A group like this is not suited to a straight psycho-analytic approach. Role-playing is often difficult because of their pre-occupation with themselves and inability to take on alter ego roles.

6.   The leader, while appearing permissive, is working towards inner controls—self-discipline for the boys in the group. The leader aims to create a new situation in which they may come to a new type of behavior on their own rather than being forced or ordered. The leader aims to create, with the invaluable aid of the group members, a live situation in which the boys are free to experiment, to try ways of thinking and feeling they have not tried before, to see a mirror image of themselves in the reaction of others to them, to have the experience of an adult who accepts and likes them without acting like them, and who,

as a member of the group, can lead them to consider and reconsider their old ways.

The leader's overall strategy does not require a choice between the tactics of permissiveness or control, but both are used as measures in building self-control.

7. The leader aims at shared leadership wherever and to the extent the group can take it. Instead of telling the answer, the leader throws the problem back to the group. He may pick up what a boy says, highlight some positives in it, using as far as possible the boy's words, but it is the group response which counts most.

In forming a group, the leader also, as far as possible, shares leadership. We have found, as have other studies, that boys work best with a group which they help select. There is usually a nucleus of "old timers from last year." At least one or two, besides the leader, should be a little more mature than the others to serve as a Super-ego Force, both in its Stop and Go aspects.

CONCLUSION

1. It seems best to limit the group to five or six.

2. It seems advisable to keep younger boys together, and older ones together. Their interests and sophistication are at quite different levels.

3. Particularly with younger groups, structuring of the group session seems important, with group leaders being as directive as necessary. The attention span of the younger group is short, they are often at the mercy of their impulses. It is valuable to have a few clear basic rules. One of the best controls was a sense of their own importance—when they knew what they said would make a difference.

4. The older group also prefers group sessions with a focus. If none arises, the leader should provide it.

5. Role-playing has proved useful, but must be adapted to these boys. Many of them can play the central figure, but are too lacking in empathy to play an alter ego or supporting role. Many are so rooted in the immediate present that is hard for them to project into the future or the past.

6. A special caution is that the confidentiality of the sessions should be safeguarded. The boys seem proud that these meetings are so regarded; to the best of our knowledge they have never in five years reported anything to other boys or teachers, and have thus learned a measure of self-control and mutual trust in a life situation meaningful to them.

7. Since the boys' stability is so tenuous, it is important to keep the time and place of the meeting steady. One group dissolved when a

change was made from morning to afternoon. Besides the "change," it meant their giving up shop, which they liked and these deprived boys don't want to give up anything.

8.   The school must receive the group project sympathetically and respect the confidentiality of the sessions.

9.   The leader should be a familiar figure in the school, but independent of it—as is a Bureau of Child Guidance worker. This is of obvious practical importance and builds trust in the boys.

The leader should be a clinician, well trained in the dynamics of behavior and in group processes, comfortable within himself, and flexible and responsive in his approach to the group. He should really enjoy it.

We would like to end with Jim's words to a new member:

"The talking in the group learns you. You have problems outside and you can't solve them yourself. You come in here and talk about it—you put all ideas together, and *you make your own ideas.*"

section 5

TREATMENT:
attempts to help

The cases cited in the last section described some characteristics of students burdened with emotional problems. We now turn our attention fully to the treatment process. What are some current forms of treatment? A person may be involved in individual psychotherapy, counseling, or casework. There are also group therapy, shock treatment, psychodrama, treatment with drugs, family therapy, and many other forms. One may even be treated as part of a total family in therapy sessions that take place in his own home.

What do most of these forms of treatment have in common? Those that are avowedly psychotherapeutic in intent present one person offering a helping hand to another. The therapist is trying to help the troubled person explore his own thoughts and feelings and define his relation to the world around him. The therapist is helping someone to *learn* about himself, to *unlearn* behavior that has been destructive to himself and others, and to *relearn* ways of relating to his world that will be more satisfying. One person is trying to help another person make his psychological burden less heavy. The "patient" or "client" is trying to learn, to grow, to change his behavior through an improved understanding of himself.

Some forms of treatment, such as the use of tranquilizers, aim for change by starting with the *soma,* or body, of the psychosomatic human. This is often followed by some sort of psychotherapy. And there are forms of treatment such as electro-shock therapy that came into being more or less accidently and are continued and refined because they seem to work for people with particular kinds of psychological trouble.

But what do psychotherapy and the other forms of treatment offer us for the future? For every person receiving help, there are many, many others who need help and are getting little or none. There are many citizens to whom psychotherapy is not available because of poverty, ignorance, prejudice, or simply a difference in ethics, mores, faith, and style of living. Sometimes when psychotherapy is made available to a troubled child or adolescent, he cannot make himself available to the psychotherapeutic process. It is too foreign to his way of life. He is troubled and in need of help, but it must be a kind of help that he can understand and use.

Will treatment answer the pressing need to help our children grow into emotionally mature adults? Can we ever train enough therapists to meet our growing need? How does the kind of learning that takes place in treatment compare with the learning that takes place in the classroom?

In Section 6 we shall look into the classroom. It is an important growing place for children and adolescents.

Therapy with Stuttering Children and Their Mothers

Gertrud L. Wyatt and Helen M. Herzan

BACKGROUND OF THIS STUDY

In an earlier experimental study by G. L. Wyatt (30-32) three significant aspects of the feelings of stuttering children toward their mothers were investigated. The stuttering child has experienced a developmental crisis, a disruption of the patterns of complementary behavior between mother and child which are of vital importance for the learning of language in childhood. A disturbance of the mother-child relationship occurring at the time when the child is in the practicing stage of early grammatical speech results in inability on the part of the child to continue language learning successfully. Stuttering is the overt symptom of this disturbance. The child reacts to this experience with intense "distance anxiety" (fear of losing access to the mother), with increasing

"Therapy with Stuttering Children and Their Mothers" by Gertrud L. Wyatt, Ph.D., and Helen M. Herzan, M.D. *The American Journal of Orthopsychiatry,* Vol. 32, 645–659. Copyright 1962, The American Orthopsychiatric Association, Inc., reproduced by permission.

anger and rage and, in the advanced stage, with depressive anxiety and subsequent defensive mechanisms.

Three principles of importance for therapy were deduced from this earlier study: 1) Therapy with a stuttering child should be initiated as soon as possible after the appearance of compulsive repetition of sounds and syllables; 2) therapeutic techniques should be specific for children of different ages and in different stages of stuttering; 3) the mother of the stuttering child should be included in the therapeutic process. In an attempt to implement these principles a one-year pilot study was carried through at the Wellesley Public Schools, Wellesley, Massachusetts, with partial assistance from the U.S. Public Health Service.[1]

The assumption underlying this study was that stuttering in young children represents a primary disorder in language learning. In older children with a long history of stuttering, however, the conflict has been internalized, rigid defenses have been established, and stuttering has turned into a personality disorder on the one hand, and into a disturbance in interpersonal relations on the other. In view of this dual conception of stuttering, it seemed mandatory to develop different forms of treatment for children at different levels of development.

According to the present state of the field, three forms of research in therapy can be differentiated: prediction studies, differential treatment studies, and studies of therapeutic process (21, 24). This study was primarily one of therapeutic process, the outcome of which should permit the formulation of increasingly more precise hypotheses concerning differential treatment patterns and their appropriateness for different cases.

To state the aim of this study in simpler terms: We hoped to improve the methods of therapy with stuttering children so that we ourselves and others would be able to do better therapy in the future.

RESEARCH DESIGN

The following hypotheses were formulated:

1. Younger children (under 7 years of age) should show marked improvement or return to normal speech after a smaller number of therapeutic sessions than older children (over 7 years of age).

2. Children whose mothers exhibited at the beginning of therapy low-level anxiety concerning speech and low-level irritation concerning

[1]In addition to the authors, the following participated in this research: A. W. Berkeley, Ph.D., Boston University Graduate School, and D. C. Klein, Ph.D., Wellesley Human Relations Service, Inc., as consultants in statistics and in community mental health procedures, respectively; Harriet M. Stanton, M.A., and Elaine Loomis, M.A., as assistant therapists.

aggressive behavior should show marked improvement or return to normal speech after a smaller number of treatment sessions than children whose mothers exhibited high-level anxiety and irritation.

Four therapeutic patterns were planned at the beginning of the research study: Patterns I and II for children under seven years of age, III and IV for children over seven years. A fifth pattern had to be devised later in the study.

Pattern I. In view of the intense unconscious mutual closeness between a mother and her young child, it seemed advisable for the therapist to see the child in the mother's presence, at least in the early stage of treatment. The same therapist saw the child mostly in the mother's presence and also had additional conferences with the mother alone (mother-centered therapy).

Pattern II. One therapist saw the mother and the child separately in alternating sessions. This pattern was devised for therapy with school-age children from kindergarten through the second grade (alternating therapy).

Pattern III. Following our assumption concerning internalization of psychological conflict in the older child, the emphasis in the treatment of children in grades three through six was shifted toward the child. One therapist saw the child once a week and saw the mother once a month (child-centered therapy).

Pattern IV. It was assumed that from preadolescence on, stuttering children would resist sharing their therapist with the mother. Pattern IV was therefore arranged for children over 12 years of age. One therapist saw the child weekly, while another had a monthly conference with the mother; the two therapists coordinated their work with each other (child-centered therapy, divided management).

Pattern V. An additional form of treatment was devised for preschool children whose communication disorder consisted of a combination of severely defective articulation (in the absence of organic deficiency) and of stuttering in its initial form. As in Pattern I, the same therapist worked with mother and child; however, the mother was primarily instructed in teaching the child auditory discrimination of speech sounds. It was expected that improvement of the child's articulation would lead to disappearance of the stuttering symptoms.

The original sample consisted of 26 stuttering children. Of these, 18 were referred through the Wellesley Schools or through public or private schools in neighboring towns, 4 were referred through the parents, and 4 through pediatricians. There were 19 male and 7 female children in the sample; 8 were preschool children, 12 attended kindergarten or primary grades, 5 were in the intermediate grades and 1 attended high school; 2 were only children, 8 were the oldest children in the family, 11 were middle, and 5 were youngest children.

Nine of the mothers were under 30 years of age, 12 were between 30 and 40 years, and 4 were over 40 years.[2] Thirteen mothers had a

---

[2]Cases No. 3 and 4 were twins; consequently the number of mothers and families was only 25.

college education and 12 had finished high school; 21 were homemakers only, while 4 were employed part time. Among the fathers, 5 were professional men, 12 were in business, 3 had clerical positions, 4 were craftsmen or skilled laborers, 1 was unemployed.

In only two cases were the parents separated. Of the 25 families, 20 lived in their own home, 3 rented a home, and 2 lived with relatives; 13 families were Protestant, 6 Catholic, 4 Jewish, and in 2 families the parents belonged to different denominations.

G. L. Wyatt established the diagnosis in all cases, but her findings were used as data in this research study only if they agreed with the judgment of two other adult observers (parent and teacher, or parent and physician). Eventually, 20 children and 19 mothers received treatment over periods ranging from 4 to 12 months. These 20 children fell into two diagnostic groups: Group I consisted of 10 so-called "pure cases," in which stuttering was the only developmental disorder observed. Group II, "mixed cases," contained 10 children in whom stuttering appeared together with other developmental or behavioral disorders. The distribution of additional disturbances was as follows:

4 preschool children: history of delayed language development; defective articulation and initial stuttering.
1 preschool child: bedwetting and stuttering.
1 preschool child: feeding difficulties and stuttering.
1 kindergarten child: delayed language development, general immaturity, anxious and restless behavior, nonparticipation in group activities, and stuttering.
1 child, grade 2: advanced stuttering and history of asthma in early childhood.
1 child, grade 3: treated for stuttering in kindergarten by G. L. Wyatt, relapsed into stuttering after two symptom-free years. Periods of marked stuttering alternated with periods of intense aggressiveness on the playground and in the neighborhood.
1 child, grade 4: stuttering, cluttering, difficulty in articulation of the sounds R and L, severe difficulties in skills depending upon motor coordination, such as writing, drawing or riding a bicycle.[3]

The stage of stuttering in which a child was observed at the beginning of treatment was defined according to the criteria set forth in the earlier study by Wyatt (31). The criteria used and the distribution of cases were as follows:

Stage I. The child speaks with frequent compulsive repetition of initial sounds and syllables (by some authors called "clonic" or "initial" stuttering): 3 cases.

Stage I-II. The child's speech shows repetitions, as in Stage I, and also prolongation of vowel sounds. The child is beginning to show overt signs of frustration and anger in connection with his difficulties in communicating (transitional stage): 5 cases.

Stage II. The child exhibits compulsive repetitions, prolongation of vowel sounds and frequent "blocking" of speech (by some authors called "tonic" and "tonoclonic"

[3]This case, an isolated one within our sample, resembled in many aspects the children with congenital dyspraxia described by Katrina de Hirsch (7).

stuttering): 7 cases.

Stage III. The child exhibits the symptoms listed under Stages I and II; in addition, such symptoms can be observed as displacement of overt verbal symptoms into compulsive movements of parts of the body, avoidance of specific words, stilted sentence structure, long pauses, a tendency to avoid looking at the speech partner, withholding of speech, a tendency to avoid certain speech situations or certain topics, vibration of the nostrils, labored breathing (advanced stage): 5 cases.

Preschool children and their mothers as a rule were seen together by the therapist, either in her office or in the child's home. As the treatment program continued, the therapist in most cases made at least one visit to the child's home. In addition to the mothers, most fathers had at least one interview with the therapist. In Cases 6 and 7 the fathers appeared particularly concerned about the child's condition and participated much more actively in the treatment program than was usual.

Because of the time limit of this study and the need for a representative sample, it was necessary to include out-of-town children in the sample. Of the children in the treatment group, 11 were Wellesley children and 9 came from other towns. As the study progressed it became evident that the difference in geographical origin led to considerable heterogeneity in treatment patterns, which was eventually reflected in the treatment results. Two main differences between the local and the out-of-town groups were observed. The treatment of the local children and their mothers was more flexible and at the same time more continuous than that accorded the out-of-town cases. With growing insight into the nature of the treatment process we found that flexibility of schedule was an important aspect of it.

As soon as a child's speech and behavior improved sufficiently, responsibility for therapy was purposely left primarily with the child's mother and conferences with the therapist were scheduled at longer and longer intervals. However, if and when a child went through an acute phase of stuttering or had a sudden relapse after several weeks or months of normal speech, the event was treated as a "crisis" in the mother-child relationship and therapeutic conferences with the child and the mother were then scheduled very close together for some time, until the therapist was satisfied that the crisis had been worked through in a constructive manner. *Flexibility of scheduling and intensified treatment during periods of crisis turned out to be highly valuable therapeutic tools,* but it was much easier to provide them for local than for out-of-town children. Because of our intimate interaction with the local teaching staff, an acute crisis, reflected in the child's symptomatic stuttering, was often brought to our attention by a Wellesley teacher, while in the case of out-of-town children it was difficult, time-consuming and often impossible to establish cooperation with the child's teacher.

PROCEDURES

In view of the fact that most mothers and some of the older children were anxious and apprehensive at the time of referral, it seem preferable to enter into the treatment process as soon as possible and to collect information about the child's past history and about the current family situation gradually. Observations of the interaction between mother and child were made unobtrusively during their joint visits at the therapist's office or during the therapist's visits at the child's home, where he could be observed interacting not only with his mother but also with his siblings and other relatives. The child's school situation was either inferred from his and the mother's reports, or the therapist made direct observations of the child in the classroom and had conferences with his teacher.

During the initial interviews with the mother information was gained about the child's developmental history, with particular emphasis upon language development, onset of stuttering and possible previous treatment. As the treatment progressed, the therapist gradually gained more insight into the relationship between father and mother, the parents' feelings about the child's stuttering, the position of the child in the family, the parents' feelings for each of their children, and their attitudes toward and methods of discipline. It was also of interest to explore what information concerning stuttering the parents had received previously and from whom, what theories they themselves had developed concerning the origin and treatment of stuttering, and how optimistic or pessimistic they felt in their expectations concerning the child's treatment.

A battery of tests was administered to the school-age children, usually during their first or second interview with the therapist. Tests given to most children were the *Machover Draw-a-Person Test* (16), the *Goodenough Draw-a-Man Test* (13), and the *Duess-Wyatt Mother-Child Relationship Test,* or *MCR Test* (30). Some of the older children were also tested with the *Wechsler Intelligence Scale for Children* (25). The developmental level of the youngest children was evaluated informally through observation of their play behavior, their motor skills, their understanding of social situations, and the level of their vocabulary and sentence structure used in spontaneous speech. On the basis of these tests and observations it seemed reasonable to assume that all children in the treatment group fell within the range of normal to superior intelligence.

The following events were defined as "therapeutic encounters": observation of a child at school; visits at the child's home; therapy sessions and conferences with a child, a mother, a mother and child, a father, a father and mother; conferences with teachers and principals, and extensive telephone conversations with parents which went beyond the mere making of appointments. Such "encounters" varied in time from 30 to 90 minutes, with an average of 45 minutes.

Detailed records were written up after each therapeutic interview. In recording their observations, the therapists took care to differentiate between observations of actual events, behavior or speech of parent or child and second-level inferences made from these observations. Within the limits of their own self-awareness, the therapists also recorded their own behavior, reactions, and feelings during these encounters.

The therapists had one weekly consultation with the consulting psychiatrist.[4] Modifications of therapeutic procedures were usually based upon recommendations made by the consultant.

Evaluation of treatment results and disposition of cases. The regular treatment of each child was considered terminated whenever the child had shown normal speech over a period of several months. At that point, however, it was made clear to the parents that the therapist would maintain her interest in the child's future development and they were encouraged to get in touch with her immediately in case stuttering symptoms should return. The parents were also informed that a follow-up study of all cases was planned and that G. L. Wyatt would contact them from time to time over a period of several years even if no relapse into stuttering had been reported by the parents in the interim.

Evaluation of each child's speech was made at two points: first, in June 1959, at the end of the school year; second, in October 1959, soon after the beginning of the new school year. No treatment was given during school vacations.

The evaluation of each child's speech in June and October was made by the therapist and by at least two other adults who saw the child regularly, usually the parents and a teacher. Children who still exhibited marked symptoms of stuttering were listed as "not improved." Children who spoke fluently most of the time or who showed normal speech at all times were listed as "improved."

RATIONALE OF TREATMENT PROCESS

Patterns of Appropriate Interaction Between Adult and Child

According to the theory underlying this study (31), stuttering was considered to be the result of a disruption of the complementary patterns of verbal interaction between mother and child; the aim of treatment was

[4]H. M. Herzan.

therefore the re-establishment of successful patterns of interaction between them. In addition, we hypothesized that in some cases—for example, in that of young children showing symptoms of poorly developed auditory discrimination and of stuttering—the parent-child interaction might have been either unsatisfactory in kind or not frequent enough to permit successful language learning in the child (18, 28). Following some experiments in therapy of stuttering children which one of us had carried out earlier (29, 32), we intended to use normal and successful patterns of interaction between adult and child as the model for our treatment techniques, particularly in working with young children.

However, looking through the literature on language behavior in childhood we discovered that outside of Piaget's important studies of sensory-motor learning through imitation of a model (20), hardly any systematic observations of verbal interactions between adults and young children existed. In the past, studies in language development have usually focused upon the child alone, while interest in the interpersonal aspects of language learning is of very recent origin (see 17). An impressionistic but very vivid description of verbal interaction between children and older boys and men can be found in Margaret Mead's anthropological study of life in New Guinea (18):

Children are taught to talk through the men's and older boys' love of playing with children. There is no belief that it is necessary to give a child formal teaching, rather chance adult play devices are enlisted. One of these is the delight in repetition. . . .

This random affection for repetitiousness makes an excellent atmosphere in which the child acquires facility in speech. There is no adult boredom with the few faulty words of babyhood. Instead these very groping words form an excellent excuse for indulging their own passion for repetition. So the baby says "me," and the adult says "me." . . . I have counted sixty repetitions of the same monosyllabic word, either a true word or a nonsense syllable. And at the end of the sixtieth repetition, neither baby nor adult was bored.

What is true of speech is equally true of gesture. Adults play games of imitative gesture with children. . . .

So in this atmosphere of delight in repetition and imitation, a new language is taught painlessly by one age group to another. The general set shows not only in the willingness to teach and the enjoyment of the lessons but also in the younger child's continuous practicing (pp. 30-33).

We found that both Mead and Piaget mentioned *games of mutual imitation* of the other's gestures, words and phrases. We are all familiar with the growing child's passion for repetition, an aspect of human development which seems to guarantee the necessary overlearning which is essential for the eventual mastery of speech and language. Furthermore, the *adult's delight* in the child's repetitions and imitations should be noted.

Observing interaction patterns between adults and children within the framework of our study, we came across an example of what we would like to call "therapeutic communication" between a kindergarten teacher and a stuttering child.

Miss B, a very gentle and thoughtful young kindergarten teacher, referred Betsy[5] to Mrs. Wyatt because of the child's marked difficulties in communicating. When observed in the classroom during a "show-and-tell period" Betsy talked with marked hesitancy, frequent repetitions of initial sounds and syllables, occasional prolongation of internal vowel sounds, and in an unusually slow speech tempo, thus presenting symptoms characteristic of stuttering, Stage II. The teacher reported that when Betsy and her mother came to their first child-mother-teacher conference, which preceded school attendance, Betsy had been the only one among 26 children in the same situation who had not said a single word during the whole visit. Later it had taken her several weeks before she began addressing her teacher directly.

Betsy was next seen in another room, in the company of her teacher. The therapist—a stranger to the child—sat quietly in a corner while Betsy's teacher arranged an ideal communication situation, one of intimate closeness between adult and child. Miss B sat down in a deep comfortable chair, holding Betsy close to her, so that the teacher had one arm around the child and the child one arm around the teacher. The teacher held a picture book in her lap, *Green Eyes* (3), the story of a kitten, and she began looking at the book with Betsy, talking about the pictures. Both of them at first excluded the observer from their interaction. The child, a plump and rosy girl, half leaned against the teacher's body.

The teacher began to describe the things that happened to the cat in the pictures. The objects and events in the book were on the child's level of interest and experience and the teacher, to describe the pictures, used "early relational language" (31), namely, simple sentence structure with chain-like linking of one short phrase to another. "And what does the kitty do here? He is getting out of his box, see—out of his box—and here, here he climbs over the box, over the box—here—and here, he jumps down, down into the grass." From time to time Betsy spontaneously fell in with the teacher: ". . . out of his box . . . over the box . . ." and, laughing out loud, ". . . jumps out of the box!"

Turning to another page, the teacher translated an aspect of the picture, roundness, into words: "And here the kitty goes round and round, round and round. . . ." Immediately Betsy moved her hand round and round, following the cat in the picture around the tree. At the same time she intoned in a chanting manner: "Round and round and round and round the tree. . . ."

Teacher and child thus demonstrated the ideal learning situation: Both speech partners were attuned to each other and reciprocal identification between the speech partners was established through acts of mutual imitation (1). From time to time the teacher also participated in the child's motions and gestures as well as in her speech and, in addition, she communicated with the child on the prelinguistic level through mutual body closeness and touch. Thus, a pattern of multilevel communication between adult and child was established in which the teaching and learning of linguistic structures was embedded in the genetically earlier complementary behavior of bodily closeness, touch, and gesture, a matrix out of which the conscious command of symbolic language emerges only gradually.[6]

[5]All names used in this report are fictitious.
[6]For further analysis of preverbal communication, see L. K. Frank (10) and J. Ruesch and G. Bateson (22).

Finally the moment had arrived at which Betsy felt ready to invite the strange new person to participate in this interpersonal game of word matching. She began to look sideways at the therapist, then back at her teacher. The therapist, responding to the clue, "tuned in," asking the child a question formulated on her level of language development: "And what is the kitty doing here? Is the kitty outside in the snow?"

Betsy, not yet looking at the strange person but looking at her teacher, answered: "Yes, the kitty is in the snow. He must be cold—in the snow." After several minutes of such indirect communication, Betsy spontaneously walked over to the therapist ready to talk to her directly. Thus the child was given time to assimilate the stranger gradually and used her teacher, a familiar love object, as an intermediary in relating to a new person.

Inappropriate Interaction

In contrast to this example of successful interaction, instances of disturbed or inappropriate interaction between parent and child were observed during our research study. Two of these will be described here briefly.

A mother of twins was observed in her home looking at a picture book with her two 4 year old boys, Steve and Tom. Both children, sturdy and energetic little boys, were leaning against their mother's body, each on one side of her. Both spoke with immature and defective articulation, but both were most eager to speak and to be spoken to. The following is an excerpt of the conversation between mother and children.

Steve: "How do the ho-do grow?" (How does the hoptoad grow?)

Tom: "How do the ho-do grow?"

Their mother, without repeating or correcting the wording of their question, explained to them in adult language how the hoptoad grows. Then she turned the page to another picture.

Steve: "How do da-ying grow?" (How does that thing grow?)

Mother (unable to understand): "What?"

Steve (getting angry): "Da ying . . . da ying . . . how do . . . how do . . . how do da ying grow?"

The mother (beginning to understand): "Oh, that! That is a prehistoric lizard."

The mother, a bright young woman who was very fond of her children, provided adequate preverbal communication in the form of body closeness, but in using an adult vocabulary which was too remote from the twins' developmental level, did not provide them with the corrective feedback necessary for the improvement of their speech patterns. Little mutual imitation occurred between mother and children, while a great deal occurred between the twins, thus reinforcing their inaccurate speech patterns.

During a visit in the home of Roger, a preschool child, the therapist talked with Roger's father and mother about the modern housing development in which the family lived. Discussing the number of people and children living in the project, the father remarked, "There are approximately two to three children per family."

Roger added: "If . . . if we count the father and the mmmother, the . . . the Watsons have more than three people in the family. How mmmmany?"

The grammatical structure of Roger's sentence and the mathematical concept behind his question must be called advanced for a 5 year old child. In observing Roger with his family it became evident that most of the time the adults were not geared to the child's level of communication, but rather that the very intelligent boy tried to express himself on the advanced linguistic level used by his parents.

After lunch the child and the therapist played together with blocks. While Roger built a house, a game of word matching or of mutual verbal imitation was carried on between them.

Roger: "Here is another house, a house for the animals. . . ."

Therapist: "Oh, the house for the animals. Where are the animals?"

Roger: "Here are the animals . . . a lot of animals. . . ."

Therapist: "A lot of animals. A cow . . . a dog. . . ."

Roger's speech became markedly fluent during this form of interaction. His mother, who had been invited to observe from the adjoining room, remarked later, "With you he seems to speak so much better, you really don't know how bad he can be!"

Principles of Therapy

From these brief examples of appropriate and inappropriate communication between adults and children, several general principles can be deduced.

If a disruption or disorder occurs in the area of complementary verbal behavior between a young child and a significant adult, the disorder affects an individual not yet capable of independent adequate verbalization of experiences and it interferes with his learning of complementary verbal behavior. Once the complementary relationship between child and love object has been disrupted, a contact disorder ensues which will most likely be transferred to other newly forming relationships and will predetermine their meaning.

An adult—parent, teacher or therapist—who is ready and capable of attuning himself to the child's level of communication may, however, succeed in establishing a therapeutic relationship, which will in turn serve the child as a starting point for the development of further complementary relationships. In order to succeed in making this communication a therapeutic one, the more mature "teacher" must adjust his level of communication to that of the less mature "learner." He must respond to the clues given by the learner, be alert to the learner's verbal and nonverbal messages, and provide the learner with a corrective feedback.[7]

It should be mentioned here that these principles, which were developed primarily for the treatment of children with communication disorders, are not unlike some propositions concerning psychotherapy put forth by several investigators. E. V. von Gebsattel (12), for instance, declares that *erlösende Ergänzungsbeziehungen* (the accomplishment of satisfying complementary relationships) are at the core of all successful psychotherapy. F. Deutsch and W. F. Murphy (8), in describing the basic technique used in their sector therapy, suggest that the therapist, after

[7]For further discussion of the nature of feedback, see C. Cherry (6) and B. Sondel (23).

listening carefully to the patient, should consciously incorporate the patient's most often repeated expressions or phrases into his own vocabulary, thus preparing and facilitating the patient's identification with the therapist—a procedure which, on an adult level, resembles the technique of "word matching" here developed for use in the treatment of stuttering children.

In developing these therapeutic procedures, however, we were not only interested in the stuttering child's overt language disorder, we were equally interested in his covert psychological difficulties and in the patterns of interaction between mother and child.

Problems of the child. The stuttering child has in his early life experienced a crucial disruption of the primary feedback circuit between mother and child, which is basic for the acquisition of language. He reacted to this disruption with feelings of loss, bewilderment, and helplessness which gradually turned into anger directed against his mother. In many instances this anger is eventually displaced upon siblings or other relatives, who are experienced as rivals for the mother's love and attention. At the same time the child becomes afraid lest his anger may lead to permanent loss of the love object through rejection or abandonment. The stuttering child's early experiences are preserved symbolically in the fantasy of the "search for the mother."

The core problem in the treatment of the stuttering child is therefore his aggression-anxiety: anger against his mother closely connected with the fear of losing her.

Problems of the mother. The specific problems of the mothers of stuttering children are also grouped around feelings of helplessness and anger. Alarmed by the conspicuous symptoms of the child's language disorder and often confused by wrong advice, the mother experiences strong feelings of helplessness. As times goes by and the child's speech does not improve, or even becomes worse, the mother begins to feel incompetent in her maternal role. At the same time the stuttering child's behavior, with its frequent alternation between possessiveness and jealous hostility, arouses feelings of reactive anger in the mother. Problems of discipline become particularly difficult to handle—the mother fears that any determined stand on her part will cause more intense stuttering in the child.

Therapy with mothers. In working with the mother, the therapist provides her with some explanation of the dynamics of language development and of stuttering and of the manner in which the mother herself became involved in the child's communication disorder. To the mother of young children the therapist demonstrates games of word matching and of mutual imitation. In all cases therapist and mother together evaluate the dynamics of the family and consider the stuttering child's role in the family. The therapist helps the mother understand the symbolic meaning of the child's behavior as an expression of his needs and anxieties. With the therapist's support the mother finds the time and discovers ways in which she can be closer to the child, assure him of her understanding and willingness to help, and set the stage for satisfactory mutual interaction.

Thus the therapist teaches the mother, first, through explanation and analysis of her own behavior and communication patterns; second, through demonstration of communication patterns appropriate for interaction with young children. Finally, the therapist helps the mother understand her own feelings for the stuttering child, which are intimately connected with her ability or inability to communicate successfully.

Therapy with young children. In working with young children, the therapist lends herself as an object for mutual imitation and reciprocal identification. Thus she actually teaches the child patterns of communication adequate for his age level. By working with the mother simultaneously, the therapist makes sure that the child will have continuous satisfactory communication experiences in his home.

Therapy with older children and adolescents. Work with older children and adolescents focuses upon the disturbed relationship between mother and child and upon the stutterer's feelings of anger and aggression. The therapist helps the child recognize that in reality—contrary to his fantasies—his mother is not inaccessible, that his anger against her (and often against siblings or other relatives and authority figures) is not as dangerous as he feels it to be and can be expressed verbally without catastrophic consequences.

As Wittgenstein pointed out (27), the child originally has no words for his feelings of anger or pain. In providing the child with words for them, the adult teaches the child anger or pain behavior. Helping the child to verbalize his undifferentiated feelings of anger and anxiety, the therapist makes these feelings accessible to the child's ego, their repression or denial is prevented, and eventually the child learns to cope with them. The sector chosen for therapy with older children consists of the *difficulties in their relationships and not in their speech.*

Therapy with mother and child. Both mother and child have to undergo a learning experience. The aim of therapy is the re-establishment of a positive mother-child relationship and the acquisition of normal speech by the child.

The therapist's procedures shall be so designed and organized that the mother is not replaced by the therapist in her role as the primary speech model but that the therapist only complements and guides the interactions between mother and child. The mother must have the satisfaction of being competent in helping her child to improve. The therapist must beware of demonstrating that she is a "better mother" than the child's own mother. Thus the therapeutic procedure should provide mother and child with a constructive experience, helping them to improve their mutual communication and adaptation.

As can be seen, therapy does not consist of "speech exercises" or "drills," nor can it be called a form of psychotherapy with the stuttering child alone. We like to consider it the teaching and facilitating of communication between mother and child, carried through within a dynamic frame of reference. This form of "mother guidance" seemed to work best when the therapist succeeded in rapidly establishing and in maintaining a mildly positive transference in the mother. Thus regression on the part of the mothers and overdependency upon the therapist were prevented.[8]

The mothers differed in their readiness to become co-therapists. In general, they fell into two groups, those who showed "therapeutic readiness" and those who were at the time not capable of cooperating effectively with the therapist. The two groups differed markedly in their behavior during the therapeutic encounters.

The mothers in the first group were reasonably concerned about the child's stuttering, some were even bewildered or anxious at the beginning of treatment. They expressed their willingness to be of help to the child if they could only know how to proceed. These mothers were intellectually and emotionally able to profit from explanations and demonstrations, to accept suggestions, and to utilize them constructively. Once these mothers understood the principles of therapeutic communication, they were able to use their own imagination in setting up situations of constructive interaction with the child. They soon learned to understand and to handle the child's anger without retaliating and without feeling guilty or depressed. They established a relationship of trust and confidence with the therapist, and they were willing to work through periods when the child relapsed into stuttering, with courage and consistency. Thus these mothers rapidly became the child's primary therapist.

Mothers in the second group seemed highly irritated by the child's speech and his behavior peculiarities. Their relationship to the child as well as to the therapist was ambivalent and inconsistent. During a conference they seemed to understand and accept the therapist's explanations and suggestions but they followed these suggestions all too literally, often turning them into absurdities. As an example we quote one mother, who complained to the therapist, "You told me I must *never* leave the child alone. How can I exist that way?" Thus, these mothers succeeded in proving to the therapist that her advice had been useless.

---

[8]The techniques of treating developmental difficulties in young children through guidance of their mothers have been the object of several studies published in *The Psychoanalytic Study of the Child* (see 5, 11, 14).

Particularly striking was the behavior of the mothers of this second group when they were asked to observe the therapist working with the child. While the therapist demonstrated "word matching" with the child in a play situation, these mothers showed their lack of attention through restlessness or yawning; or they interrupted the demonstration, talking about their own problems, reminiscing about their own childhood, or making hostile remarks about the child or about other family members in the child's presence. They seemed to rival the child for the therapist's attention. They wavered between excessive praise for the therapist during periods when the child's speech improved and intense hostility against her when the child had a relapse into stuttering. Through their behavior these mothers expressed symbolically that they themselves needed treatment before they would be able to act appropriately in a complementary relationship with the child.

Like E. Furman (11), we found that a mother's capacity for cooperation could frequently not be assessed during the initial interview but only after a period of working with her. The mothers of two young children, for example, seemed at first to be quite understanding, but it soon became evident that they could not deal with the specific area—need for closeness to the mother—in which their children were in particular need of help. Other mothers who appeared rigid or overanxious during the initial stage were amazingly capable of following guidance and of cooperating effectively, often in the face of difficult home situations, after a meaningful understanding of the dynamically significant factors had been obtained.

RESULTS AND CONCLUSIONS

It is not the purpose of this paper to give a detailed account of the results of this study and of the analysis of variables.[9] The results of this pilot study have been encouraging. Ten out of 12 children under seven years of age and 5 out of 8 children over seven years of age showed marked improvement or a return to normal speech within treatment periods ranging from 4 to 12 months. The number of therapeutic encounters ranged from 4 to 14 in the younger group and from 10 to 33 in the older group, a difference which was found to be significant at the 1 per cent level of confidence.[10] Thus our first hypothesis was confirmed. The reasons for nonimprovement varied from case to case. Thus our second hypothesis had to be modified.

Because of the limited time and the lack of additional therapists,

[9]A research report was forwarded to the U.S. Public Health Service, National Institutes of Health. Detailed case histories will be presented in a forthcoming book (34).
[10]*Mann-Whitney U Test*, for two samples.

this research had to be done under great pressure. However, the fact that we had to do research under service conditions strengthened our motivation to search for therapeutic techniques which would be economical in terms of staff time. In observing systematically the relationships between 19 mothers and 20 stuttering children, we gained a deeper understanding of the feelings of these mothers and of their reactions to the child's communication disorder. We were able to follow the vicissitudes of the disturbed relationship between the stuttering child and his mother from the onset of stuttering in early childhood into adolescence. The father's role in the child's communication disorder needs further investigation.

The final results of this treatment plan can be evaluated only through a follow-up study. In the meantime we feel encouraged to make the following recommendations:

Therapy with stuttering children should start from a sound theory concerning the interpersonal aspects of language learning in children. The principles derived from the theory and the techniques employed should be adapted to the age of the child treated. The mother of the stuttering child should be included in the treatment program.

Therapy will be more economical if undertaken as soon as possible after the appearance of compulsive repetitions in a child's speech. For preventive purposes, professional people working with young children and with mothers should be made aware of the possible impact which mother-child separation during the child's second and third year may have upon language development in the child. If separation cannot be avoided, measures should be taken which provide a minimum deviation from the child's familiar patterns of communication, and the continuity of the original pattern should be re-established as soon as possible.

A psychodynamically oriented therapy with stuttering children and their mothers can be carried out successfully within the framework of a public school system, provided the therapist has adequate psychological training or supervision in working with children of all ages and with adults, and provided the administration of the program permits individual treatment and flexibility of schedule. It is advisable that the therapist working with mothers and children should have frequent and regular consultations with a psychiatrist or a qualified mental health consultant.

This study has implications for research in language learning and language deviations in children. It has demonstrated the need to develop standardized methods for the observation, recording and measurement of verbal interaction patterns between preschool children and their parents. Such observations should focus not only upon the frequency but also upon the kind of interaction occurring. So far we do not understand the minimum or the optimum conditions related to successful language learning in children. We need to observe the interaction between parents and children with normal and superior as well as with disturbed speech patterns. Through analysis of the various patterns and through differentiation between them, we should add to our understanding of some of the most significant aspects of language behavior in man.

References

1. BAKER, S. J. *The Theory of Silences*. J. Gen. Psychol. 53: 145-167, 1955.
2. BENDER, L. *A Visual Motor Gestalt Test and Its Clinical Use*. Research Monograph No. 3. New York: American Orthopsychiatric Assn., 1938.
3. BIRNBAUM, A. *Green Eyes*. New York: Capitol Publishing Co., 1953.
4. BOWLBY, J. *Maternal Care and Mental Health*. World Health Organization Monograph No. 2. Palais des Nations, Geneva: WHO, 1951.
5. BURLINGHAM, D. T. "Present Trends in Handling the Mother-Child Relationship during the Therapeutic Process," in *The Psychoanalytic Study of the Child*. New York: Internat. Univ. Press, 1951, Vol. VI.
6. CHERRY, C. *On Human Communication*. New York: John Wiley & Sons, 1957.
7. DE HIRSCH, K. *Tests Designed To Discover Potential Reading Difficulties at the Six-Year-Old Level*. Am. J. Orthopsychiatry 27: 566-577, 1957.
8. DEUTSCH, F., and W. F. MURPHY. *The Clinical Interview*. New York: Internat. Univ. Press, 1955.
9. EDWARDS, A. L. *Experimental Design in Psychological Research*. New York: Rinehart, 1951.
10. FRANK, L. K. *Tactile Communication*. Genetic Psychol. Monographs 56: 209-255, 1957.
11. FURMAN, E. "Treatment of Under-Fives by Way of Parents," in *The Psychoanalytic Study of the Child*. New York: Internat. Univ. Press, 1957, Vol. XII.
12. GEBSATTEL, E. V. VON. *Prolegomena einer medizinischen Anthropologie*. Berlin: Springer Verl., 1954, pp. 279-291.
13. GOODENOUGH, F. L. *Measurement of Intelligence by Drawings*. New York: World Book Co., 1926.
14. JACOBS, L. "Methods Used in the Education of Mothers," in *The Psychoanalytic Study of the Child*. New York: Internat. Univ. Press, 1949, Vol. III/IV.
15. KLEIN, D. C., and A. ROSS. "Kindergarten Entry, A Study of Role Transition," in *Orthopsychiatry and the School* (M. Krugman, Ed.). New York: American Orthopsychiatric Assn., 1958.
16. MACHOVER, K. *Personality Projection in the Drawing of the Human Figure*. Springfield, Ill.: Charles C. Thomas, 1957.
17. McCARTHY, D. *Research in Language Development; Retrospect and Prospect*. Monographs Soc. Res. Child Develop. 24, 5: 3-25, 1959.
18. MEAD, M. *Growing Up in New Guinea*. New York: Mentor Books, 1953.
19. MOOD, A. M. *Introduction to the Theory of Statistics*. New York: McGraw-Hill, 1950.
20. PIAGET, J. *Play, Dreams and Imitation in Childhood*. New York: Norton, 1951.
21. RUBINSTEIN, E. A., and M. B. PARLOFF (Eds.). *Research in Psychotherapy*. Washington, D. C.: American Psychological Assn., 1959.
22. RUESCH, J., and G. BATESON. *Communication: The Social Matrix of Psychiatry*. New York: Norton, 1951.
23. SONDEL, B. *The Humanity of Words*. Cleveland: World Publishing Co., 1958.

24. WALLERSTEIN, R. S., L. L. ROBBINS, H. D. SARGENT, and L. LUBORSKY. *The Psychotherapy Research Project of The Menninger Foundation. IV. Concepts.* Bull. Menninger Clinic 20: 239-262, 1956.
25. WECHSLER, D. *Wechsler Intelligence Scale for Children.* New York: Psychological Corp., 1949.
26. WEISS, D. *Der Zusammenhang zwischen Poltern und Stottern.* Folia Phoniatrica 2: 252-262, 1950.
27. WITTGENSTEIN, L. *Philosophical Investigations* (German and English Edition). New York: Macmillan, 1953.
28. WYATT, G. L. "Mother-Child Relationship and the Acquisition of Language" (Mimeographed), 1952.
29. _____, in *Stuttering: Significant Theories And Therapies* (B. Hahn, Ed.). Univ. California Press, 1956.
30. _____. "Mother-Child Relationship and Stuttering in Children." Doctoral Dissertation, 1958, on file at Boston University Library. Microfilm copy available from University Microfilms, 313 North First Street, Ann Arbor, Michigan (Library of Congress Number Mic 58-3130).
31. _____. "A Developmental Crisis Theory of Stuttering," in *Language and Speech.* Teddington, Middlesex, England: Robert Draper, Ltd., Dec. 1958, Vol. I.
32. _____."Mother-Child Relationship and Stuttering in Children: Theory and Therapy." Paper read at the 1959 Annual Meeting of the American Orthopsychiatric Association, San Francisco, California. (Mimeographed.)
33. _____. *Speech and Interpersonal Relations in Childhood.* (Book in preparation.) Glencoe, Ill.: The Free Press.

Drug Therapy in Child Psychiatry: Psychological Aspects

Barbara Fish

While drugs have been used extensively to treat children with schizophrenia, organic brain disease and the so-called primary behavior disorders, most reports have come from hospitals and residential treatment centers (1). There has been an apparent reluctance to combine drug therapy with out-patient psychotherapy in private psychiatric work with children and in many child guidance clinics (2). Fears have been raised that drugs will dull perception, stifle learning and disrupt the therapeutic relationship (3).

In the author's experience, such fears of drug therapy have proved to be groundless. Drugs increased the effectiveness of the treatment program, and the supposed deleterious effects failed to materialize.

"Drug Therapy in Child Psychiatry: Psychological Aspects" by Barbara Fish, *Comprehensive Psychiatry*, No. 1, 1960, pp. 55-61, by permission of Grune & Stratton, Inc.

METHOD

Since 1952, 85 children under 12 years of age have been given drugs as part of their psychiatric treatment in the author's private practice. Two-thirds of the children were diagnosed as primary behavior disorders; a few had organic brain disease, and the remainder were schizophrenic (see Table 1). The families were all from a socio-economic group which could afford private treatment. There was no attempt to select ideally motivated or cooperative families, but merely to provide as much help as the child needed within the practical limitations set by family circumstances and attitudes.

The children were treated after an initial evaluation period of about four weeks. Psychotherapy, educational measures and family case work were used as indicated. Medication was usually tried early in treatment to see what it could add to the total regimen. The drugs ran the gamut of potency from amphetamine, Benadryl and mild ataractics to the phenothiazines, in daily doses that would be considered conservative according to standards for nonhospitalized adult patients (average mg./Kg. day: amphetamine 0.2, diphenhydramine [Benadryl] 4, chlorpromazine [Thorazine] 2, prochlorperazine [Compazine] 0.2, perphenazine [Trilafon] 0.06, triflouperazine [Stelazine] 0.02).

Weekly visits were continued for two months to three years, as long as psychotherapy or active regulation of drugs was considered necessary and effective. The children with schizophrenia and organic brain disease usually required continued medication after the initial period of treatment, and were then seen at longer intervals to supervise their progress and discuss current problems. Follow-up has extended from one to seven years.

RESULTS

This discussion will focus on the role which drugs played in this total program, and the interaction between drug therapy and the other aspects of treatment, for various types of disturbance. A detailed evaluation of the effectiveness of the different drugs in these children will be reported elsewhere, as well as the criteria which were used to measure effectiveness (4).

1. Drugs provided some help for the 20 children in the most disturbed category who could not benefit from psychotherapy at all. This included all the children with schizophrenia or organic brain disease whose effective functioning on intelligence tests was less than 70 per cent of normal, and half of those with I.Q.'s between 70 and 95. The more potent phenothiazines, particularly Stelazine, stimulated the withdrawn, apathetic, hypoactive children toward more competent locomotion and manual dexterity; heightened their responsiveness to people and the environment, and sometimes even stimulated them to communicative speech. In the very disturbed hyperactive children, the phenothiazines, and sometimes Benadryl, reduced psychomotor excitement and the indiscriminate response to stimuli. Although the underlying pathology

remained, drug therapy enabled half of these severely disturbed children to participate in group activities and special classes, and made it possible for an additional one-fourth to benefit from normal schooling.

TABLE 1
SAMPLE OF CHILDREN GIVEN DRUG THERAPY

DIAGNOSIS	I.Q.	ANXIETY RATING	NUMBER
Schizophrenia	under 70	mild to severe	11
Organic brain disease	under 70	mild to severe	3
Schizophrenia	70–95	moderate to severe	9
Organic brain disease	70–95	moderate to severe	3
Schizophrenia	95–135	severe	8
Behavior disorder	95–135	severe	8
Behavior disorder	95–135	moderate	26
Behavior disorder	95–135	mild	17
Total			85

2. In 6 children who were slightly less disturbed, drugs reduced anxiety to the point where they could participate in psychotherapy. These children came from the group with schizophrenia or organic brain disease whose effective intellectual functioning was between 70 and 95 per cent of normal. Without drugs, they made too little contact to benefit from psychotherapy, in the opinion of this observer as well as the other psychiatrists and psychoanalysts who had examined them previously. When catastrophic anxiety colored every aspect of living, these children experienced themselves as helpless victims of an unpredictable and confusing environment, and they reacted with infantile dependence or total withdrawal. After medication reduced this anxiety, they could identify what set off fears of attack or isolation; they could learn that reality was less terrible than their expectations, and they could be helped to cope with the demands of school, group and independent activities.

The majority of the children were less disturbed than the two groups described above and could participate in psychotherapy without drugs. Adding drugs to psychotherapy appeared to accelerate the improvement of many of these children.

3. In the 8 bright schizophrenic children, and in the 8 children with the most severe behavior disorders, drugs reduced the overwhelming anxiety which distorted the children's perceptions of themselves and of the environment. The distortions were less bizarre than in the more damaged schizophrenic children, and were more available for discussion by the child; the effects of drugs and psychotherapy tended to overlap more in this group. The advantage of medication was its speed; when effective, drugs made the children feel considerably better within days or

even hours.

Once the children felt less anxious and irritable, they were able to start examining their behavior and relationships, whereas before, when they were subject to uncontrollable excitement and aggressive outbursts, they had difficulty in looking at this; they tended to deny their explosiveness, or to blame it on everyone else. With drugs, they experienced "good days" as well as "bad days." This seemed to give them enough distance from their feelings so that they could examine their moods and what precipitated them, and eventually even to recognize their own responsibility for some of the events that troubled them.

4. In 14 children with behavior disorders whose anxiety was less severe, but who had markedly immature, hyperactive, impulsive and aggressive behavior, drugs helped to organize attention and motor activity. This hyperactivity was not associated with youthful exuberance, but with increased irritability and poorly organized behavior; over half of these children had marked scatter in intellectual functioning, two-thirds had reading disabilities and others had less specific disturbances of attention and learning. Benadryl was particularly effective in this group. Anxiety diminished, motility became smoother and less impulsive, and attention span increased. All these effects contributed to an improvement in school performance and to greater self-reliance.

Frequently these children were perplexed by their inability to control what they (and society) called "bad behavior." They did not experience the change in motility effected by medication as being "slowed down"; instead they reported "feeling stronger," apparently because they felt more in command of their own motor impulses. Psychotherapy was then able to deal with their earlier guilt and self derogation and with any continuing problems in relationships. The increase in ego strength resulting from drugs, and the secondary effects on the children of their improved performance and relationships, made brief psychotherapy effective for many in this group.

5. Drugs also accelerated the response to therapy of some of the more mature, better organized children with neurotic features. In 10 prepuberty girls and 2 boys with school phobia, sexual and hypochondriacal preoccupations appeared to be intimately related to the appearance of phobic symptoms. Amphetamine rapidly dispelled the morbid preoccupations, anxiety and phobia in 9 of these children. The rest required phenothiazines and psychotherapy for 2–3 months before their symptoms disappeared; even in these children, however, medication provided enough symptomatic relief so that they could return to school immediately.

Eisenberg has demonstrated that the prompt return to school, even with force if necessary, is essential to prevent these children from becoming fixed in patterns of withdrawal and dependence (5). Medication made it possible to accomplish this necessary step by enlisting the active cooperation of the children. Relieved of symptoms so rapidly, they accepted the reassurance that such feelings were a frequent transient experience at this age, related to "growing up." Psychotherapy could be abbreviated, to minimize dependence on the therapist. The children were able to take responsibility for their own continuing attendance at school and for decreasing their medication and then their visits to the doctor.

The foregoing examples illustrate some of the ways in which medication can increase the child's capacity to organize his own thinking and behavior in a constructive manner during psychotherapy. The aim is to help the child to fulfill his own unique potential for development, and not to apply a chemical strait-jacket to suppress unacceptable behavior. Anxiety is not treated pharmacologically if it is merely the normal accompaniment of acquiring new skills and broadening experiences. Anxiety does require physiological treatment if it is severe enough to distort perception, paralyze reasoning and effective planning, or disorganize behavior. Then it must be reduced, if the child is to mature, and to learn from his experiences in psychotherapy and in the world.

When drugs were used in this way, the limitations of their use were chiefly on the ability to help the children with the most severe psychopathology. The children with schizophrenia and organic brain disease were usually tried on a series of drugs to determine which agent, and which dose, had the optimal effect. In the children with behavior disorders, the desired effect was achieved more quickly, and frequently with mild drugs such as amphetamine and Benadryl.

Early central nervous system signs of excessive drugs were detected on examination and through frequent reports from parents and teachers. Irritability or fatigue appeared before more serious manifestations, such as sleepiness, poor concentration, or confusion. Apathy occurred in only three children. The early symptoms disappeared promptly if medication was reduced, or another agent was substituted. No extrapyramidal symptoms occurred in the dose range employed here, which was lower than that used in hospitalized patients, but was effective for this outpatient group. The only side effects were 5 transient allergic reactions.

DISCUSSION

Since drugs are helpful in the treatment of disturbed children, and can be so benign in their effects when used with the proper precautions, the major question which remains is: How do they affect the subtler interpersonal operations of treatment? I believe that this depends largely on the attitude of the physician who prescribes them. Drugs would destroy therapy, if the doctor used them as a quick expedient to avoid responsibility for the child's complex problems in living, or if he saw drugs as the ultimate weapon of authority to enforce compliance on a problem child, or if he felt drugs were a measure of desperation to be used only after all other measures failed.

As with any other procedure in therapy, the technique draws its meaning from what each participant brings to it, and to the total relationship. Just as therapeutic interpretations can be experienced by the patient as either hostile or supportive, so can drugs. The only difference with children is that they are more acutely aware of the therapist's unconscious intent, and less tolerant of his rationalizations.

Even the very young children could understand that "this is to help the way your stomach feels when you are scared" (or angry or "jumpy"); "we will still have to find out what makes you feel that way." Some needed to be reminded that, magically, friends would not appear, bed-wetting disappear, nor parents stop scolding; but that if they felt better, they might be able to do something about these problems.

The child's distress was made the mutual concern of himself and the therapist; he did not come just to play, nor to be made to behave. He also would not feel better without his active participation. He had the responsibility to report which medicine "worked best," or which made him feel "sleepy" or "jumpy." He had to be the final judge of whether he felt better or not. The way the child reacted to this role was as enlightening as any other aspect of his relationship to treatment and to the doctor. The management of medication between child and therapist became part of the new and constructive experience for the child who was not used to being listened to or taken seriously by an adult.

The children frequently greeted the initial offer of help with skepticism. (One 5 year old scoffed, "I don't see how a pill can take the ghost out of my pocket!") But they were reassured by the information that their "funny feelings" were not unique, and by finding out that these feelings could be helped by medication. This experience contradicts the often expressed fear that medication will make children more worried about their difficulties. On the contrary, when they experienced some relief early in treatment, their hopelessness gave way to more positive feelings about themselves and about their treatment.

The more seriously disturbed children, who needed continued drug therapy, usually began to question the need for this after their acute symptoms subsided. Such children have always needed to understand that everyone has a threshold for anxiety; theirs happens to be somewhat lower, and therefore they tend to be "oversensitive." Maintenance drug therapy was explained as a means of reducing this oversensitivity at various times in their life when this was necessary. These discussions were particularly difficult for the older, brighter and more paranoid schizophrenic children; yet the very fact that their feelings of terrible difference and isolation could be discussed openly helped to reduce them to less frightening proportions.

Even the experience of unpleasant effects from overdosage did not disrupt the children's relationship to the doctor. In the schizophrenic children and those with behavior disorders with very severe anxiety, several drugs usually were tried and the dose of each was pushed up to the maximum amount tolerated, in order to find one with the optimal effect. The children accepted the fact that this was an attempt to help them and that some trial and error was necessary. They understood that their reports of beneficial or unpleasant effects helped the doctor to help them.

The management of medication served similar constructive functions in the relationship between doctor and parent, and between parent and child. From the beginning, the parents were helped to understand the child's symptoms in terms of anxiety or particular disturbances in development. When the parents were drawn into a cooperative relationship with the doctor, aimed at helping the child, the emphasis of treatment was shifted away from blaming the child for being "bad," or the parent for being inadequate. Most parents who were desperate enough to seek psychiatric help, even some extremely disturbed individuals, could take some kind of supporting role with their child with varying degrees of help.

In such a context, the use of medication emphasized the key role of anxiety or developmental disorder in the child's disturbance. The indications for drugs were explained to parents in considerable detail. They had to learn which symptoms of anxiety and which areas of development might improve, and what signs of toxicity to look for. Specific goals were set for increasing the child's functioning, so that medication became a positive tool, and not a way to make the child "behave."

The auxiliary use of drugs need not permit parents to belittle the child's problems, if drug therapy is put into its proper perspective. Parents were forewarned that, at best, drugs produce only quantitative changes, and that the child would not be "cured" or "made over." Discussions with the parents of all the other measures needed to help the child served to emphasize this point. Such discussions of the goals and of the limitations of treatment for a particular child played an important part in helping parents to appreciate and to accept their child's assets as well as his handicaps.

The use of drugs also need not make parents exaggerate the seriousness of their child's disturbance, if the doctor uses drugs for specific indications of varying severity, and does not wait for desperate or hopeless situations to force his hand. The physician can relieve the parent's anxieties about drugs if he himself feels secure in using them; if he is familiar with the effects of drugs, discusses these factually with parents, and is available between appointments to discuss any questionable symptoms.

Certain precautions were taken to prevent the actual giving of medicine from becoming an issue between mother and child. First of all, the medicine was given regularly at specified times; the mother was not to offer it to the child suddenly when he became upset or if he happened to annoy her. Secondly, the dose was changed only by the therapist; the mother reported any change in symptoms but she did not adjust the dose herself, for what might well have been subjective reasons. Both doctor and mother made it clear to the child that the mother acted only as the doctor's agent when she gave medication. Actually many of the older children were made responsible for taking their own medicine, and the mother played an unobtrusive role. If a child objected to drugs, the mother was told not to press the issue. The child's feelings about pills, as about any other aspect of treatment, were a matter for him to discuss with his therapist.

The way a mother participated in drug therapy was used in treatment like any other aspect of her behavior with the child or the doctor. Her objectivity, or her exaggeration, denial or distortion of the child's symptoms, told much about her relationship to the child. Her overenthusiasm, or her belittling of the child's response to therapy, revealed feelings not only about the child but also about the doctor and the treatment. The therapeutic handling of such attitudes was the same as for other phases of the mother's participation in the child's treatment.

SUMMARY

Drug therapy was found to be a safe and useful addition to psychological measures in the outpatient treatment of children whose disorders ranged from severe schizophrenia to mild behavior disorders. Although the underlying pathology was not removed, the quantitative reduction of disorganizing anxiety helped the forces in the child which were striving for re-integration and active mastery. Drugs also promoted more mature patterns of motility, impulse control and attention. These effects enabled many of the children to learn more constructive ways of coping with their interpersonal problems, and to make better use of their schooling. Drug therapy thus facilitated the psychological aspects of treatment, and accelerated the therapy of many of the children. It also provided some help for children who were too disturbed to be candidates for traditional psychotherapy, or who could not participate in such therapy in the absence of drugs.

Drugs were generally accepted by parents and children as simply another way in which the doctor was trying to help the child. The physiological effects of drugs did not interfere with the therapeutic relationships between doctor, child and parent. The regulation of medication introduced additional practical problems and transference complications into these interpersonal relationships, but the management of such problems was no different in principle from the similar problems encountered in the absence of drugs. To this observer, the added problems seemed amply justified by the ability of medication to increase the help available to seriously disturbed children and to accelerate the treatment of many others.

References

1. Psychopharmacology Service Center: Annotated Reference List on Use of Psychopharmacologic Agents with Children. Nat'l Institute of Mental Health, April 14, 1958.
2. BRADLEY, C.: Tranquilizing drugs in pediatrics. Pediatrics *21:* 325–336, 1958.
3. FISHER, S. (Ed.): Child Research in Psychopharmacology. Springfield, Illinois, C. C. Thomas, 1959.
4. FISH, B.: Drug therapy in child psychiatry: Pharmacological aspects. Comprehensive Psychiatry. In press.
5. EISENBERG, L.: School phobia: A study in the communication of anxiety. Am. J. Psychiat. *114:* 712–718, 1958.

Autistic Children in a Day Nursery

Margaret Lovatt

In a research study carried out from 1953–55 at the Hospital for Sick Children in Toronto, over 200 children from the Toronto area were found to be suffering from some form of childhood schizophrenia. Moreover, there was reason to believe that the community contained many more schizophrenic children. No treatment facilities for such children were available.

A large number of the known schizophrenic children were of preschool age and were described as "autistic" because of their isolation

"Autistic Children in a Day Nursery," by Margaret Lovatt. Reprinted from *Children,* May–June 1962, 103–108. U.S. Department of Health, Education, and Welfare, Social Security Administration, Children's Bureau.

and withdrawal from contact with people. Unresponsive even to their own parents, they seemed to live in a dream world of their own, unrelated to reality. They appeared mentally retarded, and most of them lacked speech. They were unable to play. Our child guidance clinics were reluctant to serve such children since experience had shown that play therapy sessions, even when tried over a long period of time with such children, had produced little constructive results.

Authorities had indicated that if a schizophrenic child had not developed speech by the age of 5 or 6 years, the possibility of his improvement was slight.[1] An attempt to help these children in the early preschool years before their patterns of behavior and the family relationship and interaction patterns had become fixed, therefore, seemed urgent. It was urged that the community set up a pilot research and treatment service for them.

About the same time the West End Crèche—a day nursery which provides a modern nursery program for normal children and specialized care for a few handicapped and disturbed children—was eager to provide a special service and research project based on a significant community need. Therefore the director of the Canadian Mental Health Association proposed that the crèche establish the much-needed day treatment center for preschool autistic children. In the center these children would have the benefits of a nursery school environment, the help of the trained nursery staff long experienced in working with preschool children, and the opportunity to be among normal children who would provide both stimulation and an example for them.

The crèche psychiatric advisors made it clear that serving autistic children would be a long-term, demanding, and possibly unrewarding project; that there was little in the way of precedent to follow, and little in the way of success to be expected, for methods of treatment tried elsewhere had not produced any marked degree of success. Nevertheless, the agency accepted the assignment.

We recognized from the first that we could not "cure" these children. Our goal was to find out whether we could be of help to them, and if so, then in what way and to what degree. Could they be helped to experience at least some of the normal satisfactions of life and become in any real way participating members of their families, schools, and communities?

Dr. R. W. Keeler, who had conducted the hospital research, established the new treatment center within the crèche in 1956 with the advisory assistance of members of the Department of Psychiatry of the

[1]KANNER, LEO; EISENBERG, LEON: Notes on the followup studies of autistic children. *In* Psychopathology of Childhood. Paul H. Hoch and Joseph Zubin, eds. Grune & Stratton, New York, 1955.

University of Toronto, and other clinical psychiatrists. Dr. Milada Havelkova took over from Dr. Keeler as medical director later that year.

At the end of the 5-year experimental period, the psychiatric advisors urged the center to continue, and a Provincial-Federal mental health grant was secured. This is supplemented by the United Community Fund, donations, and parents' fees.

The center provides care for 10 children, 5 children in the morning and 5 in the afternoon, each child attending 4 days a week. Because of the nature and severity of the illness, treatment for most of the children needs to be continued for at least 2 years. The age range at the time of admission corresponds with that of the nursery school children—3 or 4 years—so that if the children progress they are ready for kindergarten or first grade when they leave the center.

STAFF ROLES

The psychiatrist, who spends half of each day at the center, directs the total treatment program. This is organized around the usual staff team. However, the roles of the staff members have been somewhat changed.

The direct work with the children is done by the nursery teacher-therapists under the supervision of the psychiatrist, who observes the children regularly and holds a weekly consultation with each teacher. Each child has his own individual teacher-therapist for the 2 hours he attends the center each day, as well as his own playroom.

At least once a week the psychiatrist meets with the caseworker, who works with the parents. The psychiatrist also has periodic interviews with the parents, held jointly with the caseworker, to discuss the child's progress.

The caseworker holds weekly case consultations with each teacher. Two staff conferences are held each week—one for case discussion, and the second for more general purposes such as the discussion of methods, staff education, research, or planning. Neurological, psychological, speech, and some research services are secured when needed from the various health services in the community.

Our recognition that we cannot "cure" these children, is based on the belief that there is a biological factor involved in the illness, and that environmental factors only alter and possibly intensify the expression of the disease. The possibilities of successful treatment, therefore, seem to vary with the relative degree of biological and environmental involvements.

For instance, although treatment may help a child to get along quite well in the community, his personal relationships with people will probably remain restricted. Perhaps for tomorrow's children biochemical or other research will provide an answer to the biological problem and a means of preventing schizophrenia, or at least of controlling it. Meanwhile, the sick children of today must be given every chance to improve through experimental treatment, no matter how costly.

Two primary features of the center which, as far as I know, had not previously been used in treating such children are: (1) its setting in a nursery for normal children where the very gradual integration of the ill child into the normal group can be used as a treatment tool and in some instances as a means of motivating the child toward growth; and (2) the one-to-one relationship between the child and the teacher-therapist. The need for this one-to-one relationship in therapy seems to us implicit in the nature of the illness and the age of the children.

THE CHILDREN

The children's symptoms are numerous and varied, some the opposite of others. For example, 4-year-old George was aggressive, hyperactive, and an expert at getting into difficulties. He would unscrew any electrical fixture in sight, turn on every tap he saw, and at home he would scale his backyard fence and wander off to a dangerous four-lane highway. Raymond, also 4, was an expert at evading supervision and, before coming to the center, had been given hospital treatment several times, after eating glass, drinking a bottle of tranquilizer, and darting into traffic. Rita used to inflict self-injury. Barbara bit, scratched, and kicked others. Mary, age 3, used to sit in a corner at home for an hour or more, her eyes shut tight, rocking back and forth. Attempts to contact her produced only screams and a deeper withdrawal. These are all symptoms which are prevalent among autistic children. Severe anxiety, emotional outbursts with no apparent cause, extreme negativism, and abnormal fears are common.

Although some of the children are of superior intelligence, all are immature, functioning often far below their chronological age. A 3-year old at admission may appear to be at an 18-month level in most functions. On the other hand, in one or more areas he may be more advanced than the average normal child. Jean, for instance, at 3 could pick up a complicated tune at one hearing, but in all else she was below a 2-year level.

These children are "flat" emotionally and do not feel affection for people, even their own parents. Their language and tears are often inappropriate. They relate better to objects than to people, and often carry around an object, perhaps a little box or a bottle, as a sort of emotional prop. Most of them either have not developed speech or do not use it to communicate with others though they may parrot phrases such as television commercials, in a meaningless way. Their play is compulsive or aimless, a mere handling of things, and seems to give them little pleasure. If left to themselves, some children may spend hours just sifting sand or bits of paper through their fingers.

Such symptoms indicated to us the autistic child's need of individual attention. Certainly in the beginning of treatment the child would not be able to make use of the group, nor would the group be able to tolerate his behavior.

As experience in treatment was gained, it became apparent that there were parallels between the treatment and educational needs of the child handicapped by infantile autism and children handicapped by physical conditions or sensory deprivation such as blindness or deafness. Through long-term training each must be helped to understand and accept the limitations which his handicap imposes, and to develop what capacities for normal living he has. Each must be helped to develop an ability to relate to and interact with his environment in a realistic and socially acceptable way.

For instance, some children who are partially isolated from their environment by congenital deafness can be taught in special schools not only to lipread but to develop speech and so become able to communicate with others. Also some children handicapped by congenital blindness, through a persistent long-term program of stimulation and special training can develop a keen awareness of their environment and take a real part in the life around them. Yet the limitations imposed by the handicaps of these children remain very real. Similarly through the development of a dependent trusting relationship and a long-term educational program, the teacher-therapist in our center tries to lead the autistic child into a greater awareness and understanding of his environment (personal and otherwise), to help him accept the limitations imposed by his illness, and through persistent repetitive training and support, to help him learn how to cope with his environment in a more realistic and socially acceptable way.

BEGINNING TREATMENT

When the child first comes to the center, the mother stays in the playroom with him and the teacher-therapist until he feels comfortable about separation. The therapist begins with a very permissive program, feeling her way, following the child's lead, testing out his responses, and adapting her methods to his particular and changing needs—trying to reduce his anxiety with acceptance and reassurance. She uses stimulation to draw him out from his haven of withdrawal, trying to get through to him through the use of whatever objects seem to give him at least some small satisfaction and to focus his attention for at least a moment or two.

The teacher often begins with mechanical objects, for which these youngsters usually have an obsessive fascination, such as anything with wheels—a truck, an eggbeater, rings, or bottle tops. Instead of playing with these as would a normal child, the sick child usually just spins them around or pushes them back and forth endlessly. Through using these objects with him, the teacher tries to rouse him into an awareness of herself, and then to some interest in other playthings and activities. For instance, the teacher might take a truck whose wheels the child is spinning, pile blocks in it and get him to dump them out; or get him to mix soap bubbles in a bowl with his eggbeater, encouraging him to accept a few simple directions. All the while the teacher helps the child to examine and experiment with each new object, to gain at least some slight satisfaction from it, and to learn something of how it can be used.

By keeping the child in his own small playroom in this early period, the distractions are reduced and the teacher is better able to hold his attention on herself and what they are doing together, and thus to keep him from withdrawing into his inner world. Gradually as the child becomes aware of his teacher, and as he develops some sense of confidence in her, more structure can be developed in the program activities and a few more limits set. Generally these youngsters, because of their anxiety and disorganization, are more comfortable and make better progress in a fairly structured program. They need the firm support which routine and structure impose, but these must be planned to meet each child's individual needs.

Throughout the child's attendance at the center the teacher continues the patient, oft-repeated explanation of things which arouse his anxiety, or of concepts which he finds difficult to grasp although they may be grasped quickly by a normal child. The schizophrenic child, for instance, finds great difficulty in distinguishing between the characteristics of inanimate objects and people. It takes time and repeated explanation for him to learn that it hurts a child if you kick him but it does not hurt a ball. Because concepts of space and time are difficult for him, he may try to squeeze himself into a tiny box and fail to understand why things which are to happen in an hour do not happen right now.

When the therapist has been able to establish some degree of relationship with the child so that he trusts and depends on her, she begins to lead him into a wider environment and among other people. He begins to move about the nursery building and playground, but under close supervision. If not closely supervised, the child without a sense of danger might walk heedlessly into moving swings. Another child may be so fearful of everything that for weeks he will venture onto a swing or go down a slide only if he is held firmly on his teacher's knee. Gradually he will find enough courage to go by himself.

IN THE NURSERY SCHOOL

As the child develops an ability to use his therapist's help, to accept some limits and direction, he may begin to visit in one of the normal nursery playrooms for a few minutes—at first perhaps while it is empty and later while a few children are there, but always with his nursery therapist close at hand for support. As he begins to tolerate or respond to this experience, the visits are lengthened and increased in variety. At first he may appear to ignore people who see him and greet him; he may "look right through them." If given free rein he may walk into a playroom, brush from a table whatever the other children are playing with, pile up a lot of toys and knock them down, circle around the room and leave, having looked at no one, child or adult.

When he is being introduced into the nursery school the therapist tells and shows him what is expected of the children there—the basic requirements of the playroom—and he is helped to meet these expectations as far as possible. Naturally there is great flexibility in the demands made on him, but the length of time he visits in the nursery playroom each day is gauged by his ability to conform at least to some extent to its basic requirements. Gradually he begins to "see" the children, to watch them, to begin to imitate them.

Play usually continues for a long time to be of a parallel type—the autistic child copying the other children rather than joining them in their activities—but some of the sick children (though not all) learn very gradually to take part in group activities, such as the music or story circle, although their performance may be erratic. During this integration in the normal nursery, the ill child has an opportunity for practice not only in using play materials and equipment but also in the difficult field of personal relationship. He can learn some of the social skills which the normal child learns, but for him the process of learning is much slower, and his hold on the skill much less sure.

In our nursery's experience the relationship between these children and the normal children has in no instance become very close as is often true of two normal children. However, some of the autistic children have gradually become able to interact with other children, to cooperate in play or in a chore on a more or less surface level, and to gain real enjoyment from the joint activities.

We have frequently been asked how the normal children react to the autistic children, and whether they are affected by the latter's unusual behavior. In order to maintain the "normalcy" of the group (for the sake of both the normal and sick children) we early established a policy allowing no more than one autistic child into any nursery group. Moreover, if the sick child's behavior becomes seriously disruptive, his therapist will take him out of the group to some individual activity. In these circumstances we have not found the normal children adversely affected by the behavior of the ill children. They do observe the strange behavior, and occasionally a child may even consciously imitate it once or twice, but finding therein little satisfaction he soon reverts to his own normal pattern.

The normal children do not show resentment when limits are sometimes stretched a bit for the sick children. In fact they are usually pleased to be helpful to them. While scarcely a day occurs without at least one parent of a normal child observing in the nursery school, we have never had a protest or expression of real anxiety about the influences of the ill children.

Throughout the period of integration into the nursery school, the therapist-teacher continues to work individually with the child for part of each session, very often alone with him in his own small playroom. She continues to help him use his relationship with her to reduce his anxiety and fears, increase his skills, build his self-confidence, develop his speech, and adapt himself to normal social demands.

If the child continues to make progress in fitting into the nursery group, then the therapist begins to refer him to the nursery group teacher for direction and help. If he accepts this, then the new relationship is gradually built up and more and more responsibility for working with him is turned over to the group teacher, and the therapist gradually withdraws. This process takes many months.

Some of the sick children who achieved integration in the nursery school have been ready at the age of 5, others at 6, to test their new-found selves in the more demanding setting of the public school kindergarten. Before the child enters kindergarten, the center seeks the cooperation of the school, interpreting the child's special needs, and offering consultation from its psychiatric director. After the children leave the nursery, we continue our contact with them, their families, and schools for followup study.

All the children who started kindergarten after treatment have so far managed to continue at school, although in some instances despite considerable adjustment difficulty. Four of our first "graduates" are now in the second and third grades and are doing remarkably well. Since they progressed steadily after the difficulties of initial adjustment in kindergarten and grade one, it is hoped that the children now in their first and second years at school will also progress in the educational program. It is, of course, too early and too uncertain to make predictions.

DIAGNOSTIC OBSERVATION

During the past 4 years, the center has also provided a diagnostic observation service. We are now admitting two children each month for observation and have a long waiting list. Autistic symptoms in preschool children may be related to any one of a variety of conditions—childhood schizophrenia, brain damage, visual or hearing impairment, mental defects, or environmental emotional disturbances, or a combination of these. It is important that the causal condition of the autistic behavior be identified at an early age since plans for treatment vary with the basic condition.

Differential diagnosis is sometimes extremely difficult. Psychological tests for such children are of little value because of the child's inability to cooperate in the tests. A history secured from parents often provides baffling or contradictory diagnostic data; and often an examination of a preschool autistic child in the psychiatrist's office may prove quite as inconclusive.

In cases where the diagnostic picture is confused, the child may be referred to the center for a 4-week observation. He attends for 2 hours a day and is cared for by an individual teacher, his program being similar to that of a child in treatment. Some of the values of this type of observation are its length, the opportunity it provides for observing the child in the company of normal children as well as alone, and the long experience of the nursery staff in working with both normal and disturbed preschool children.

After the nursery's psychiatrist observes the child several times and the caseworker has 6 to 8 interviews with the parents, an evaluation is made of the child's ability to respond to people, to react appropriately to his environment, and to benefit from teaching. A conference is held with the referring psychiatrist or agency and a decision is made regarding diagnosis and possible plans for treatment or handling the child. These possibilities are then discussed with the parents and help given to them in planning for the child's care and development. Referrals are made to appropriate services.

THE PARENTS

If the parents can achieve a realistic picture of the child's handicap and capacities, they may be able to prevent the development of further symptoms by reducing their expectations of him.

Much has been written about the "typical" personality structure of parents of schizophrenic, autistic children. Descriptive terms such as "cool," "aloof," "over-anxious," "rigid," "unsocial," and so on, have been used. It has been said that these parental characteristics result in inadequate parent-child relationships and thereby contribute largely to the development of the disease. More recently this theory has been strongly questioned, and it is becoming more generally accepted that the role of environment in the child's illness cannot be so definitely defined. In our experience, there have been parents of autistic children who have not fitted neatly into the classical picture and who have established good relationships with their other children.

Parents are deeply affected by the painful experience they suffer as they gradually become aware that their child is mentally ill. If there is an inadequate parent-child relationship, this traumatic experience probably plays some role in its development. Even in the ill child's early infancy, his parents may feel puzzled and chilled by the child's strange lack of interest in them. As this continues, they feel deeply hurt and rejected.

In infancy and early childhood, schizophrenic children exhibit such problems as severe feeding difficulties, reversal of sleep patterns, rocking, twirling, or headbanging, withdrawal, or bursts of screaming. At times the child may be extremely negativistic. Parents may find themselves almost helpless in dealing with such behavior. As they fail to reach through to their child, they are overwhelmed by feelings of guilt and failure.

One of the primary needs of the parents, following the shock of the diagnosis, is help in accepting the reality of the child's mental illness and the inevitable readjustment that this requires in their family life and their outlook for the future. They need and want to understand the illness, its development, and its effects. What are the child's limitations? What of his future? How can they build a helpful relationship with him? They also need help in recognizing and expressing their feelings, especially toward their child and toward themselves. If they can come to understand and accept the child's limitations and adjust to a realistic level their standards for the child, and for themselves in dealing with him, then they can regain a sense of self-worth and the necessary control of their situation. The caseworker can be of real help in meeting these needs.

The caseworker may also help the parents in gaining some perspective on the often conflicting needs of the ill child and other members of the family. Sometimes where these conflicts are severe and cannot be reconciled, where treatment has not brought significant development and the prognosis is poor, the caseworker can help the parents think through the possibility of institutional care. The fact that treatment has been tried may make it easier for them to reconcile themselves to the necessity of institutional placement. In some instances the parents of ill children are themselves suffering from severe disturbances which are unlikely to respond to casework treatment. The caseworker can, however, support them in strengthening their defenses.

Throughout the child's treatment, the caseworker keeps closely in touch with the child's home experience, and the parents are similarly kept close to his experience in the nursery.

THE MEANING

The role which mental illness plays in crippling and destroying our human resources has long been spelled out plainly. In Canada almost half of all the hospital beds are occupied by patients who are mentally ill,[2] and similar statistics, I believe, exist in the United States. What this means in human suffering we cannot conceive of, nor of what it represents in loss of manpower and in costs of care.

The problem is of such magnitude that it can only be fought with a concerted nationwide effort. This experimental demonstration service in a day nursery setting described here is on a very small scale, but joined to other numerous projects developing across the continent, it may prove to be of some significance in the general attack. Certainly to a number of our children it has given the chance to enjoy their childhood, and may mean for their future a sense of personal worth and a life of purpose.

[2]Encyclopedia Canadiana 1956: Mental health. The Grolier Society, Ottawa, Canada.

The Results of Psychotherapy with Children: An Evaluation

Eugene E. Levitt

A compendium of results of psychotherapy with adults was published a few years ago by Eysenck (16). It included reports from 24 sources on more than 8,000 cases treated by an assortment of psychotherapeutic techniques. The average percentage of cases reported as improved (i.e., cured, improved, much improved, adjusted, well, etc.) is about 65.[1] Eysenck's control or baseline data estimating the remission rate in the absence of formal psychotherapy come from two sources. Those of Landis (32) for hospitalized neurotics, and those of Denker (14) for neurotics treated at home by general practitioners, show similar remission rates of about 70% for a 2-year period. Comparing these figures with the average for the treated cases, Eysenck concluded, ". . . roughly two-thirds of a group of neurotic patients will recover or improve to a marked extent within about two years of the onset of their illness, whether they are treated by means of psychotherapy or not" (16, p. 322). He concludes further that "the figures fail to support the hypothesis that psychotherapy facilitates recovery from neurotic disorder" (16, p. 323).

The difficulties attending an evaluation of psychotherapy have been detailed many times, most recently by Rosenzweig (47) in a critique of Eysenck's findings. Other thoughtful and well-organized delineations of evaluation problems include those of Thorne (50), Zubin (56, 57), and Greenhill (22), among others. It is not within the province of the present paper to repeat these accounts.

The purpose of this paper is to summarize available reports of the results of psychotherapy with children using Eysenck's article (16) as a model.[2] Certain departures will be necessitated by the nature of the data, but in the main, the form will follow that of Eysenck.

[1]The data, however, are not quite as "remarkably stable from one investigation to another" as Eysenck appears to believe. The 19 reports of the results of eclectic therapy differ significantly among themselves when frequencies of improvement and nonimprovement are compared. A chi square is 38.11 with a p beyond the .01 level for 18 degrees of freedom. Eysenck's point is nonetheless basically reasonable; the range of per cent improvement of from 41 to 77 represents considerable stability when one considers the differences in population, chronology, treatment, classification, and terminology among the studies.

[2]Compendia similar to, and overlapping Eysenck's have been published by Zubin (57) and by Miles, Barrabee, and Finesinger (39). These tend to be more detailed and descriptive. Eysenck's work is most concise; in it, descriptions and discussions of individual studies have been subordinated to the presentation of overall results. The present writer feels that this is the most provocative, and hence most fruitful, way of evaluating a collection of psychotherapeutic results.

"The Results of Psychotherapy with Children: An Evaluation," by Eugene E. Levitt, *Journal of Consulting Psychology*, No. 21, 189–196. © 1957, American Psychological Association.

BASELINE AND UNIT OF MEASUREMENT

As in Eysenck's study, the "unit of measurement" used here will be evaluations of the degree of improvement of the patient by concerned clinicians. Individuals listed as "much improved, improved, partially improved, successful, partially successful, adjusted, partially adjusted, satisfactory," etc., will be grouped under the general heading of Improved. The Unimproved cases were found in groupings like "slightly improved, unimproved, unadjusted, failure, worse," etc.

The use of the discharge rate of children's wards in state hospitals as a baseline for evaluating the effects of psychotherapy is not recommended. It is most likely that hospitalized children are initially more disturbed than those brought to the child guidance clinics and family service agencies from which the data on treatment are drawn. Few guidance clinics or family service agencies accept psychotic children for treatment, tending instead to refer them to the state hospital. Furthermore, as Rosenzweig (47) points out, the criteria for discharge from a state hospital are probably less stringent than those leading to an appraisal of Improved by other agencies. For these reasons, available statistics of state hospital populations such as those of Witmer (52), McFie (38), and Robins and O'Neal (46) are not used as baseline data.

Follow-up evaluations of changes in behavior problems in normal children also do not furnish satisfactory control data. Studies such as those of McFie (38) and Cummings (12) report markedly conflicting results, probably as a function of differences in ages of the subjects, and of varying follow-up intervals. More importantly, behavior like nail biting and nose picking can hardly be regarded as comparable to the problems for which children are referred to guidance clinics.

The use of a follow-up control group of cases closed as unsuccessful, as in the study of Shirley, Baum, and Polsky (49), suffers from obvious weaknesses. Such a group is not comparable to an untreated sample; it appears to represent the segment of the treatment population for which a poor prognosis has been already established.

A common phenomenon of the child guidance clinic is the patient who is accepted for treatment, but who voluntarily breaks off the clinic relationship without ever being treated. In institutions where the service load is heavy and the waiting period between acceptance and onset of treatment may range up to 6 months, this group of patients is often quite large. Theoretically, they have the characteristics of an adequate control group. So far as is known, they are similar to treated groups in every respect except for the factor of treatment itself.

Nevertheless, the use of this type of group as a control is not common in follow-up evaluations of the efficacy of treatment. Three studies report follow-up data on such groups. Of these, the data of Morris and Soroker (40) are not suitable for the purposes of this paper. Of their 72 cases, at least 11 had treatment elsewhere between the last formal contact with the clinic and the point of evaluation, while an indeterminate number had problems too minor to warrant clinic treatment.

The samples in the remaining two studies appear satisfactory as sources of baseline data. Witmer and Keller (55) appraised their group 8 to 13 years after clinic treatment, and reported that 78% were Improved. In the Lehrman study (34), a one-year follow-up interval found 70% Improved. The overall rate of improvement for 160 cases in both reports is 72.5%. This figure will be used as the baseline for evaluating the results of treatment of children.

THE RESULTS OF PSYCHOTHERAPY

Studies showing outcome at close of treatment are not distinguished from follow-up studies in Eysenck's aggregation. The distinction seems logical, and is also meaningful in the predictive sense, as the analyses of this paper will indicate. Of the reports providing data for the present evaluation, thirteen present data at close, twelve give follow-up results, and five furnish both types, making a total of eighteen evaluations at close and seventeen at follow-up. The data of two reports (29, 30) are based on a combined close-follow-up rating. Results for the three kinds of evaluations will be presented separately.

The age range covered by all studies is from preschool to 21 years at the time of original clinic contact, the customary juncture for the determination of age for the descriptive data. However, very few patients were over 18 years at that time, and not many were over 17. The median age, roughly estimated from the ranges, would be about 10 years.

The usual psychiatric classification of mental illnesses is not always appropriate for childhood disorders. The writer has attempted to include only cases which would crudely be termed neuroses, by eliminating the data on delinquents, mental defectives, and psychotics whenever possible. The latter two groups constituted a very small proportion of the clinic cases. The proportion of delinquent cases is also small at some clinics but fairly large at others. Since the data as presented were not always amenable to these excisions, an unknown number of delinquent cases are included. However, the outcomes for the separated delinquents are much the same as those for the entire included group.

As in Eysenck's study, a number of reports were excluded here for various reasons. The investigations of Healy and Bronner (24), Feiker (18), Ellis (15), Mann (37), and Giddings (20) were eliminated because of overlap, partial overlap, or suspected overlap of the sample with samples of included reports. Those of Bennett and Rogers (3), Rich (45), Hunt, Blenkner, and Kogan (27), Schiffmann and Olson (48), and Heckman and Stone (25) were not usable either because of peculiar or inadequate presentation of data, or because results for children and adults were inseparable.

The number of categories in which patients were classified varied from study to study. Most used either a three-, four- or five-point scale. A few used only two categories, while one had twelve. Classification systems with more than five points were compressed into smaller scales. The data are presented tabularly in their original form, but the totals are pooled into three categories, Much Improved, Partially Improved, and Unimproved. A summation of the former two categories gives the frequency of Improved Cases.

A summary of results at close is shown in Table 1. Results of follow-up evaluations are summarized in Table 2, while the results from two studies using a combined close-follow-up evaluation are presented in Table 3. In the latter two tables, the follow-up interval is given as a range of years, the usual form of presentation in the studies. An attempt has been made to compute an average interval per case, using the midpoint of the range as a median when necessary. These averages are tenuous since it cannot be safely assumed that the midpoint actually is the median value. For example, in the Healy-Bronner investigation (23), the range of intervals is 1 to 20 years, but the median is given as 2½ years. Since the proportion of cases which can be located is likely to vary inversely with the number of years of last clinic contact, the averages of 4.8 years for the follow-up studies and 2.3 years for the close-follow-up studies are probably overestimates.

Table 1 shows that the average percentage of improvement, i.e., the combined percentages in the Much Improved and Partially Improved categories is 67.05 at close. It is not quite accurate to say that the data are consistent from study to study. A chi-square analysis of improvement and unimprovement yields a value of 230.37, which is significant beyond the .001 level for 17 *df*. However, as in the case of Eysenck's data, there is a considerable amount of consistency considering the interstudy differences in methodology, definition, etc.

The average percentage of improvement in the follow-up studies is given in Table 2 as 78.22. The percentage for the combined close-follow-up evaluations is 73.98, roughly between the other two. The percentage of improvement in the control studies was 72.5, slightly higher than the improvement at close and slightly lower than at follow-up. It would appear that treated children are no better off at close than untreated children, but that they continue to improve over the years and eventually surpass the untreated group.

186   *TREATMENT: attempts to help*

TABLE 1
Summary of Results of Psychotherapy with Children at Close

Study	N	Much Improved	Partially Improved		Unimproved		Per cent Improved
(11)	57	16	18	12	8	3	80.7
(26)	100	13	18	42	26	1	73.0
(28)	70	12	29	19	10		85.7
(44)	250	54	82	46	68		72.8
(34)	196	76	52		68		65.3
(31)	50	15	18		17		66.0
(10)	126	25	54		47		62.7
(53)	290	75	154		61		79.0
(2)	814	207	398		209		74.3
(43)	72	26	31		15		79.2
(33)	196	93	61		42		78.6
(6)	27	5	11		11		59.3
(9)	31	13	8		10		67.7
(8)	23	2	9		12		47.8
(7)	75	35	22		18		76.0
(1)	80	31	21		28		65.0
(35)	522	225			297		43.1
(13)	420	251			169		59.8
All cases	3,399	1,174	1,105		1,120		67.05
Per cent	100.00	34.54	32.51		32.95		

TABLE 2
Summary of Results of Psychotherapy with Children at Follow-up

Study	Interval in Years	N	Much Improved	Partially Improved		Unimproved		Per cent Improved
(33)	1-5	197	49	55	39	38	16	72.6
(5)	2	33	8	11	7	6	1	78.8
(11)	2-3	57	25	17	6	6	3	84.2
(52)a	1-10	366	81	78	106	101		72.4
(28)	2-3	70	21	30	13	6		91.4
(51)	5-8	17	7	3		4	3	58.8
(34)	1	196	99	46		51		74.0
(41)	16-27	34	22	11		1		97.1
(2)	1-20	705	358	225		122		82.7
(4)	5-18	650	355	181		114		82.5
(36)	3-15	484	111	264		109		77.5
(19)	1-4	732	179	398		155		78.8
(13)	5	359	228	80		51		85.8
(21)	1-2	25	6	12		7		72.0
(42)	1-2	25	10	6		9		64.0
(35)	½-1½	191	82			109		42.9
(23)	1-20	78	71			7		91.0
All cases	4.8b	4,219	1,712	1,588		919		78.22
Per cent		100.00	40.58	37.64		21.78		

a Data based on 13 studies originally reported in (54); results of 8 of these are included here.

b Estimated average follow-up interval per case.

TABLE 3
Summary of Results of Psychotherapy with Children Based on Combined Close-Follow-up Evaluation

Study	Interval in years	N	Much Improved	Partially Improved		Unimproved		Per cent Improved
(29)	1-10	339	94	81	76	42	46	74.04
(30)	1-10	30		9	13		8	73.33
All cases	5.5[a]	369	103	170		96		73.98
Per cent		100.00	27.91	46.07		26.02		

[a] Estimated average follow-up interval per case.

This conclusion is probably specious, perhaps unfortunately. One of the two control studies was an evaluation one year after the last clinic contact, the other 8 to 13 years later. The former study reports only 70% improvement while the longer interval produced 78% improvement. The figure for the one-year interval is similar to the results at close, while the percentage of improvement for the control with the 8- to 13-year interval is almost identical with that for the follow-up studies.

The point of the analysis is more easily seen if the results at close and at follow-up are pooled. This combination gives the same sort of estimate as that furnished by the two control groups pooled since one of them is a long-interval follow-up while the other was examined only a short time after clinic contact. The pooled percentage of improvement based on 7,987 cases in both close and follow-up studies in 73.27, which is practically the same as the percentage of 72.5 for the controls.

It now appears that Eysenck's conclusion concerning the data for adult psychotherapy is applicable to children as well; the results do not support the hypothesis that recovery from neurotic disorder is facilitated by psychotherapy.

The discrepancy between results at close and at follow-up suggests that time is a factor in improvement. Denker's report (14) also indicated the operation of a time factor. He found that 45% of the patients had recovered by the end of one year, 72% had recovered by the end of two years, 82% by three years, 87% by four years, and 91% by five years. The rate of improvement as a function of time in Denker's data is clearly negatively accelerating.

A Spearman rank-order correlation between estimated median follow-up interval and percentage of improvement in the 17 studies in Table 2 is .48, $p = .05$. This estimate of relationship should be viewed with caution because of the aforementioned difficulty in determining median intervals. However, it is uncorrected for tied ranks, which tends to make it a conservative null test. It is also, of course, insensitive to the curve of the bivariate distribution.

The percentage of improvement as a function of time interval is shown by the data of Table 4. The studies have been grouped at five time-interval points in the table. There are four studies with estimated median intervals of 1–1½ years, six with intervals of 2–2½ years, three with 5–6½ years, two with 10 years, and two with 12 years.

The data of Table 4 indicate that most of the correlation between improvement and time-interval is accounted for by the studies with the shortest intervals, and those with the largest. The curve is more or less the same as that of Denker's data, negatively accelerating with most of the improvement accomplished by 2½ years. It is peculiar that the improvement after 1½ years is about 60%, less than the 67% improvement at close. However, the difference is not too great to attribute to variations in methodology and sampling among the concerned studies. Another potential explanation will be offered shortly.

This analysis suggests that improvement is in part a function of time, though the mechanisms involved remain purely speculative. Future comparisons of the results of psychotherapy should properly take this factor into consideration.

Inspection of the data in Table 1 discloses another potential factor in the improvement rate. The studies in which only two rating categories, improved and unimproved, have been used, appear to furnish lower percentages of improvement than the average. In the two reports of this kind in Table 1, the average improvement is only 50.5% compared with the overall 67%. A complete analysis of percentage of improvement as a function of number of categories is shown in Table 5. Examination of Table 5 indicates that three-, four- and five-point rating scales produce about the same percentage of improvement. The use of a two-point scale, however, results in over 20% less improvement than the others.[3] This kind of analysis cannot be applied to the data in Table 2 since it will be confounded by the time factor.

Evidently, a certain proportion of the unimproved cases in the studies using two categories would have fallen in partially improved categories if they had been utilized. A number of cases in which a fair amount of improvement was manifested are forced into the unimproved category when central points are not available. A two-point scale thus seems to be overly coarse. It is desirable that finer scales be used in future evaluation studies.

The study of Maas et al. (35), which furnishes three-quarters of the cases in the 1–1½ year interval group in Table 4, used a two-point scale. The percentage of improvement is only 43, which may account for the

---

[3]The marked difference between the two-point scale studies and those using finer scales is reflected in the consistency analysis. The chi square for 17 df was 230.37, but when the two-category studies are eliminated, it falls to 52.66 for 15 df. The value is significant beyond the .01 level, but the original chi square has been decreased by more than 75% with a loss of only two df.

fact that this time-interval group has a lower percentage of improvement than in the studies at close.

TABLE 4
IMPROVEMENT AS A FUNCTION OF THE INTERVAL BETWEEN LAST CLINIC CONTACT AND FOLLOW-UP

ESTIMATED MEDIAN INTERVAL IN YEARS	NUMBER OF REPORTS	TOTAL N	N IMPROVED	PER CENT IMPROVED
1-1½	4	437	261	59.73
2-2½	6	1,167	929	79.61
5-6½	3	742	583	78.57
10	2	1,189	958	80.57
12	2	684	569	83.19
All cases	17	4,219	3,300	78.22

TABLE 5
IMPROVEMENT AS A FUNCTION OF THE NUMBER OF POINTS ON THE RATING SCALE IN EVALUATION AT CLOSE

NUMBER OF POINTS	NUMBER OF REPORTS	TOTAL N	N IMPROVED	PER CENT IMPROVED
2	2	942	476	50.53
3	12	1,980	1,442	72.83
4	2	320	242	75.63
5	2	157	119	75.80
All cases	18	3,399	2,279	67.05

There are a number of different kinds of therapies which have been used in the studies reported here. The therapists have been psychiatrists, social workers, and teams of clinicians operating at different points in the patient's milieu. Therapeutic approaches included counseling, guidance, placement, and recommendations to schools and parents, as well as deeper level therapies. In some instances the patient alone was the focus of attention. In others, parents and siblings were also treated. The studies apparently encompassed a variety of theoretical viewpoints, although these are not usually specified. Viewed as a body, the studies providing the data for Tables 1, 2, and 3 are therapeutically eclectic, a plurality, perhaps, reflecting psychoanalytic approaches.

Thus we may say that the therapeutic eclecticism, the number of subjects, the results, and the conclusions of this paper are markedly similar to those of Eysenck's study. Two-thirds of the patients examined at close and about three-quarters seen in follow-up have improved. Approximately the same percentages of improvement are found for comparable groups of untreated children.

As Eysenck pointed out (17) in a sequel to his evaluation, such appraisal does not *prove* that psychotherapy is futile. The present evaluation of child psychotherapy, like its adult counterpart, fails to support the hypothesis that treatment is effective, but it *does not* force the acceptance of a contrary hypothesis. The distinction is an important one, especially in view of the differences among the concerned studies, and their generally poor caliber of methodology and analysis. Until additional evidence from well-planned investigations becomes available, a cautious, tongue-in-cheek attitude toward child psychotherapy is recommended.

SUMMARY

A survey of eighteen reports of evaluation at close, and seventeen at follow-up, was compared with similar evaluations of untreated children. Two-thirds of the evaluations at close, and three-quarters at follow-up, showed improvement. Roughly the same percentages were found for the respective control groups. A crude analysis indicates that time is a factor in improvement. In the follow-up studies the rate of improvement with time is negatively accelerating. Further analysis contraindicates the use of only two categories in evaluation. This scale tends to give much lower rates of improvement than three-, four-, and five-point scales.

It is concluded that the results of the present study fail to support the view that psychotherapy with "neurotic" children is effective.

References

1. ALBRIGHT, SUE, & GAMBRELL, HELEN. Personality traits as criteria for the psychiatric treatment of adolescents. *Smith Coll. Stud. soc. Wk*, 1938, 9, 1–26.

2. BARBOUR, R. F. Selected surveys prepared for the inter-clinic conference. In J. F. Davidson (Chmn.), Follow-up on Child Guidance Cases. Ninth Child Guidance Inter-Clinic Conference, London, 1951. Pp. 49–59.

3. BENNETT, C. C., & ROGERS, C. R. Predicting the outcomes of treatment. *Amer. J. Orthopsychiat.*, 1941, 11, 210–221.

4. BRONNER, AUGUSTA F. Treatment and what happened afterward. *Amer. J. Orthopsychiat.*, 1944, 14, 28–35.

5. BROWN, JANE L. The follow-up procedure of an intermittent child guidance clinic. Unpublished master's thesis, Smith Coll., 1931.

6. BROWN, MARJORIE. Adolescents treatable by a family agency. *Smith Coll. Stud. soc. Wk*, 1947, 18, 37–67.

7. BURLINGHAM, SUSAN. A quantitative analysis of psychiatric social treatment carried out in seventy-five cases at the Institute for Juvenile Research. Unpublished master's thesis, Smith Coll., 1931.

8. CANADAY, LOUISE J. A way of predicting the probable outcome of treatment of young children who run away. Unpublished master's thesis, Smith Coll., 1940.

9. CARPENTER, JEAN A. Some factors relating to the method and outcome of case-work treatment with the adolescent girl when the girl herself is the focus of treatment. Unpublished master's thesis, Smith Coll., 1939.

10. CHRISTIANSON, EVA, GATES, MARY, & COLEMAN, FAY. A survey of the intake of a mental hygiene clinic with special reference to the outcome of treatment. *Smith Coll. Stud. soc. Wk*, 1934, 5, 211–212.

11. COHEN, MARION, & DAVIS, ELLEN. Factors related to the outcome of treatment in a child guidance clinic. *Smith Coll. Stud. soc. Wk*, 1934, 5, 212–214.

12. CUMMINGS, JEAN D. A follow-up study of emotional symptoms in school children. *Brit. J. educ. Psychol.*, 1946, 163–177.

13. CUNNINGHAM, J. M., WESTERMAN, HESTER H., & FISCHHOFF, J. A follow-up study of children seen in a psychiatric clinic for children. Paper read at Amer. Orthopsychiat. Assn., Chicago, March, 1955.

14. DENKER, P. G. Results of treatment of psychoneuroses by the general practitioner. *N. Y. State med. J.*, 1946, 46, 2164–2166.

15. ELLIS, FLORINE J. A study of one hundred children treated by the Northern New Jersey Mental Hygiene clinics. *Smith. Coll. Stud. soc. Wk*, 1936, 6, 277–278.

16. EYSENCK, H. J. The effects of psychotherapy: an evaluation. *J. consult. Psychol.*, 1952, 16, 319–324.

17. EYSENCK, H. J. The effects of psychotherapy: a reply. *J. abnorm. soc. Psychol.*, 1955, 50, 147–148.

18. FEIKER, HAZEL A. A comparative study of the methods of case work of adolescent boys in the years 1928–1930 and 1938–1940 at a child guidance clinic. Unpublished master's thesis, Smith Coll., 1941.

19. FENTON, N., & WALLACE, RAMONA. Child guidance in California communities, Part 6. Follow-up study of Bureau cases. *J. juv. Res.*, 1938, 22, 43–60.

20. GIDDINGS, ELIZABETH R. Some factors affecting the outcome of treatment of Negro cases in a child guidance clinic. Unpublished master's thesis, Smith Coll., 1940.

21. GOLLANDER, BARBARA. A study of overinhibited and unsocialized aggressive children. III. Later adjustment. Unpublished master's thesis, Smith Coll., 1944.

22. GREENHILL, M. H., *et al.* Evaluation in mental health. *Publ. Hlth Serv. Publ. No. 413*, Washington: U. S. Gov't Printing Off., 1955.

23. HEALY, W., BRONNER, AUGUSTA F., BAYLOR, EDITH M., & MURPHY, J. P. *Re-Constructing Behavior in Youth: A Study of Problem Children in Foster Families*. New York: Knopf, 1929.

24. HEALY, W., & BRONNER, AUGUSTA F. *Treatment and What Happened Afterward*. Boston: Judge Baker Guidance Clinic, 1939.

25. HECKMAN, A. A., & STONE, A. Testing casework results: forging new tools. *Surv. Midmonthly*, 1947, 83, 267–270.

26. HUBBARD, RUTH M., & ADAMS, CHRISTINE F. Factors affecting the success of child guidance treatment. *Amer. J. Orthopsychiat.*, 1936, 6, 81–102.

27. HUNT, J. McV., BLENKNER, MARGARET, & KOGAN, L. S. A field-test of the Movement Scale. *Soc. Casewk*, 1950, 31, 267–277.

28. IRGENS, EFFIE M. Must parents' attitudes become modified in order to bring about adjustment in problem children? *Smith Coll. Stud. soc. Wk*, 1936, 7, 17–45.

29. JACOBSEN, VIRGINIA. Influential factors in the outcome of treatment of school phobia. *Smith Coll. Stud. soc. Wk*, 1948, 18, 181–202.

30. JOHNSON, LILLIAN J., & REID, J. H. An evaluation of ten years work with emotionally disturbed children. *Ryther Child Cent. Monogr.* IV, 1947.

31. LA MORE, MARY T. An evaluation of a state hospital child guidance clinic. *Smith Coll. Stud. soc. Wk*, 1941, 12, 137–164.

32. LANDIS, C. A statistical evaluation of psychotherapeutic methods. In L. E. Hinsie (Ed.), *Concepts and Problems of Psychotherapy*. New York: Columbia Univer. Press, 1937.

33. LEE, P. R., & KENWORTHY, M. E. *Mental Hygiene and Social Work*. New York: Commonwealth Fund, 1929.

34. LEHRMAN, L. J., SIRLUCK, HILDA, BLACK, B. J., & GLICK, SELMA J. Success and failure of treatment of children in the child guidance clinics of the Jewish Board of Guardians, New York City. *Jewish Bd. Guard. Res. Monogr.*, 1949, No. 1.

35. MAAS, H. S., *et al.* Socio-cultural factors in psychiatric clinic services for children: a collaborative study in the New York and San Francisco metropolitan areas. *Smith Coll. Stud. soc. Wk*, 1955, 25, 1–90.

36. MABERLY, A., & STURGE, BRENDA. After-results of child guidance. *Brit. med. J.*, 1939, 1, 1130–1134.

37. MANN, IDA L. Results with child guidance patients diagnosed as psychoneurotic. *Smith. Coll. Stud. soc. Wk*, 1942, 13, 160–161.

38. McFIE, BERNICE S. Behavior and personality difficulties in school children. *Brit. J. educ. Psychol.*, 1934, 4, 30–46.

39. MILES, H. H. W., BARRABEE, EDNA L., & FINESINGER, J. E. Evaluation of psychotherapy. *Psychosom. Med.*, 1951, 8, 83–105.

40. MORRIS, D. P., & SOROKER, ELEANOR. A follow-up study of a guidance-clinic waiting list. *Ment. Hyg. N. Y.*, 1953, 37, 84–88.

41. MORRIS, D. P., SOROKER, ELEANOR, & BURRESS, GENETTE. Follow-up studies of shy, withdrawn children—I. Evaluation of later adjustment. *Amer. J. Orthopsychiat.*, 1954, 24, 743–754.

42. MOSES, JANE. A study of overinhibited and unsocialized aggressive children. Part IV: The later adjustment of unsocialized aggressive children. Unpublished master's thesis, Smith Coll., 1944.

43. NEWELL, N. W. The methods of child guidance adapted to a public school system. *Ment. Hyg. N. Y.*, 1934, 18, 362–373.

44. REID, J. H., & HAGAN, HELEN R. *Residential Treatment of Emotionally Disturbed Children*. New York: Child Welfare League of America, 1952.

45. RICH, G. J. Preschool clinical service and follow-up in a city health department. *Amer. J. Orthopsychiat.*, 1948, 18, 134–139.

46. ROBINS, E., & O'NEAL, PATRICIA. Clinical features of hysteria in children, with a note on prognosis. A two to seventeen year follow-up study of 41 patients. *Nerv. Child*, 1953, 10, 246–271.

47. ROSENZWEIG, S. A transvaluation of psychotherapy—a reply to Hans Eysenck. *J. abnorm. soc. Psychol.*, 1954, 49, 298–304.

48. SCHIFFMANN, FRANCES, & OLSON, ELMA. *A Study in Family Case Work: An Attempt to Evaluate Service*. Evanston, Ill.: Family Welfare Assoc., 1939.

49. SHIRLEY, MARY; BAUM, BETTY; & POLSKY, SYLVIA. Outgrowing childhood's

problems: a follow-up study of child guidance patients. *Smith Coll. Stud. soc. Wk*, 1940, 11, 31–60.

50. THORNE, F. C. Rules of evidence in the evaluation of the effects of psychotherapy. *J. Clin. Psychol.*, 1952, 8, 38–41.

51. WALCOTT, ESTHER. A study of the present adjustment made by solitary children who had withdrawn into an imaginary world. Unpublished master's thesis. Smith Coll., 1931.

52. WILTMER, HELEN L. A comparison of treatment results in various types of child guidance clinics. *Amer. J. Orthopsychiat.*, 1935, 5, 351–360.

53. WITMER, HELEN L., *et al.* The outcome of treatment in a child guidance clinic: a comparison and an evaluation. *Smith Coll. Stud. soc. Wk*, 1933, 3, 339–399.

54. WITMER, HELEN L., *et al.* The later adjustment of problem children. *Smith Coll. Stud. soc. Wk*, 1935, 6, 1–98.

55. WITMER, HELEN L., & KELLER, JANE. Outgrowing childhood problems: a study in the value of child guidance treatment. *Smith Coll. Stud. soc. Wk*, 1942, 13, 74–90.

56. ZUBIN, J. Design for the evaluation of therapy. *Res. Publ. Assoc. Res. nerv. ment. Dis.*, 1953, 31, 10–15.

57. ZUBIN, J. Evaluation of therapeutic outcome in mental disorders. *J. nerv. ment. Dis.*, 1953, 117, 95–111.

section 6

THE CLASSROOM: a place to learn

In the last section we examined attempts to help children grow into emotional maturity through various methods of treatment. We now turn our attention to the classroom, the place our society has especially designated for learning and growing.

Next to the home, the classroom is surely the most potent force in a child's environment. Almost all children spend a very large portion of their waking hours in a classroom during their growing years. What does the child learn there during all of those hours? He learns skills that will help him to satisfy his needs in ways acceptable to our society and thereby master himself and his environment. And he learns his various strengths and their potential roles in shaping his adult life. Hopefully he learns also to take a realistic view of his weaknesses. But *what* exactly are these necessary skills he must learn and *how* does he learn about his particular strengths? Are the three R's sufficient?

The classroom is a place to learn. But how does a child's emotional state influence his experiences in the classroom, and how do these experiences influence his emotional state? We all know from our own experiences in the classroom that one feels joy, anger, affection, rivalry, love, fear, tenderness, and most other human emotions at one time or another. We have seen the child who is so torn by anger that he cannot concentrate on algebra or spelling. We have seen the youngster who feels "dumb" whenever he faces a book but glows with confidence when he sees an automobile engine. And we have seen the none-too-bright child, trusting eyes turned to the teacher, learning almost anything and everything his beloved teacher assures him he is capable of learning.

Where does our hope for the future lie? How can we help our children to learn sufficient skills and confidence to face the world they must master? How can we better ensure a future generation of citizens whose intellectual functioning is not at the mercy of emotions about which they know very little? Where does the teacher's responsibility begin and where does it end? Should the classroom teacher help developing humans find more satisfaction and happiness in adult years? Is this possible? Can some of the time spent in the institution of school make it less likely that time will be spent in other institutions, such as prisons and mental hospitals?

(In Section 7 we shall turn our attention to the role of the school as an institution in our attempt to solve these problems. Perhaps school is our best hope.)

Sex, Social Class, and Anxiety as Sources of Variation in School Achievement[1]

Beeman N. Phillips

Despite the great number of studies which have been reported, it is still difficult to reach definitive conclusions regarding anxiety and its relationships with school attitudes, behavior, and achievement. One of the reasons for this is that sex differences in the consequences of anxiety frequently have been reported (e.g., McGuire, Hindsman, King, & Jennings, 1961; Phillips, Hindsman, & McGuire, 1960; Sarason, Davidson, Lighthall, Waite, & Ruebush, 1960). In addition, it has been found that sex interacts with a variety of factors in these differences in the consequences of anxiety (e.g., Grooms & Endler, 1960; Phillips, Hindsman, & Jennings, 1960; Reese, 1961). Finally, no theory of anxiety seems capable of explaining these multiple results.

In this situation it appears that a further step which needs to be taken is the investigation of factors which have relationships with sex, school achievement, and anxiety. One such factor is social class, which

[1]The research reported here was performed pursuant to OE-2-10-003 with the United States Office of Education, Department of Health, Education, and Welfare. Also, the author wishes to express his appreciation to G. McBee who supervised IBM 650 analyses of data.

"Sex, Social Class, and Anxiety as Sources of Variation in School Achievement," by Beeman N. Phillips, *Journal of Educational Psychology*, No. 53, 316–322. © 1962, American Psychological Association.

is clearly related to all three; and it was the purpose of this study to investigate social class, sex, and anxiety as interrelated factors in school achievement. The investigation was designed to test a general hypothesis, which was that differences in school achievement would be associated with interactions of sex, social class, and anxiety. In addition, the implications of such findings with regard to prevailing conceptualizations of anxiety, and its relationships with school achievement, were analyzed.

METHOD

The 759 subjects of this study were selected from approximately 1,500 seventh grade students in four Texas communities who form the total population of the University of Texas Human Talent Project. The instruments used included the California Test of Mental Maturity (CTMM); the Language Arts, Mathematics, and Reading subtests of the California Achievement Test (CAT); the Social Studies and Science subtests of the Sequential Test of Educational Progress (STEP); and the Castaneda-McCandless Anxiety Scale, with items adapted for use with adolescents. An index of social class based on source of income, occupation, and education of the parents also was computed for each subject (McGuire et al., 1961). In addition, teacher grades were obtained for the subject areas of language arts, mathematics, and social studies at the end of the school year. All of these variables were linearly transformed to stanine values so that each had a mean of 5 and a standard deviation of 1.5.

Basically a fixed 2 × 2 × 2 design was utilized with two levels of social class and anxiety, and two sexes. In order to achieve a clearer differentiation between subsamples, the subjects with stanines of 5 on social class or anxiety were not included in the analyses. Therefore, the "high" levels of social class (middle class) and anxiety included subjects with stanine values of 6 or greater, and the "low" levels of social class (lower class) and anxiety included subjects with stanine values of 4 or less. Thus, there were a total of 8 subsamples drawn from the total population. Another factor, type of achievement measure with two categories, teacher grades and objective tests, was added to the basic design.

Two different approaches to school achievement were employed. The first was based on the *relationship* between intelligence and achievement, which was determined by computing zero-order correlation coefficients between total IQ and each of the eight achievement scores, and then performing an analysis of variance of Fisher z transformations of these correlations.

The other approach was based on the *level* of achievement reached, and for this means and standard deviations were computed on all achievement variables, and t tests and an analysis of variance were performed on these means.

In addition, chi square analyses were made of the distributions of high and low anxiety scores; intelligence means were computed and tested for significance; and differences between intelligence and achievement means were determined.

RESULTS

The analyses of the data are presented in the following order. The results with respect to the correlations are given in Tables 1 and 2. Table 1 gives the actual coefficients and Table 2 shows the result of the analysis of variance of Fisher z transformations. Then in Table 3, the results with respect to the mean differences in achievement between the subsamples are given, while Table 4 presents an analysis of variance of these means. Finally, Table 5 gives the IQ means and standard deviations of the subsamples; Table 6 presents a chi square analysis of the sex and social class distribution of the high and low anxiety scores; and Table 7 shows differences between mean intelligence and mean achievement scores.

TABLE 1
CORRELATIONS OF IQ WITH ACHIEVEMENT VARIABLES

	MALES				FEMALES			
	High social class		Low social class		High social class		Low social class	
ACHIEVEMENT VARIABLES	*High anxiety*	*Low anxiety*	*High anxiety*	*Low anxiety*	*High anxiety*	*Low anxiety*	*High anxiety*	*Low anxiety*
Teacher grades								
Social studies	54	57	29	29	42	37	35	33
Mathematics	66	60	36	21	29	32	36	36
Language arts	54	58	30	24	40	38	34	30
Objective tests								
STEP Social Studies	56	63	60	47	49	57	53	56
CAT Mathematics	69	61	50	34	45	43	43	51
CAT Language Arts	70	63	59	53	41	51	49	52
CAT Reading	70	63	63	51	55	66	52	63
STEP Science	50	57	51	38	49	53	44	47
N	55	99	108	103	58	94	158	84

Note.—*Decimal points have been omitted.*

TABLE 2
ANALYSIS OF VARIANCE OF FISHER z TRANSFORMATIONS OF CORRELATION COEFFICIENTS

SOURCE	SS	df	F
Sex	.17	1	75.09**
Social class	.22	1	96.17**
Anxiety	.00	1	—
Achievement	.56	1	244.39**
Sex × social class	.19	1	81.65**
Sex × anxiety	.04	1	17.09**
Sex × achievement	.00	1	—
Social class × anxiety	.01	1	2.30
Social class × achievement	.07	1	29.04**
Anxiety × achievement	.00	1	—
Sex × social class × anxiety	.00	1	—
Sex × social class × achievement	.04	1	18.61**
Sex × anxiety × achievement	.02	1	7.87**
Social class × anxiety × achievement	.00	1	—
Sex × social class × anxiety × achievement	.00	1	—
Within	.11	48	—

** $p < .01.$

Now, summarizing the results of Table 2, it may be stated that:

1. Three main effects were statistically significant: IQ was more highly correlated with achievement for males than for females, IQ was more highly correlated with achievement in the middle class than in the lower class, and IQ was more highly correlated with objective tests than with teacher grades.

2. Three first order interactions also were statistically significant: an increase in social class resulted in a higher correlation of IQ with achievement for males than for females, an increase in anxiety resulted in an increase in the correlation of intelligence with achievement for males but a decrease in this correlation for females, and an increase in social class resulted in a much higher increase in the correlation of IQ with objective tests.

3. Finally, two second order interactions were statistically significant: for males, an increase in social class resulted in a greater increase in the correlation of IQ and objective tests, while for females, an increase in social class resulted in an increase in the correlation of IQ and teacher grades, but there was no change in the correlation of IQ and objective tests; and for males, an increase in anxiety resulted in an increase in the correlations of IQ and teacher grades, and IQ and objective tests, while for females, an increase in anxiety resulted in an increase in the correlation of IQ and teacher grades but a decrease in the correlation of IQ and objective tests.

TABLE 3

SUBSAMPLE MEANS AND STANDARD DEVIATIONS FOR THE ACHIEVEMENT VARIABLES

	MALES				FEMALES			
	High social class		Low social class		High social class		Low social class	
ACHIEVEMENT VARIABLES	*High anxiety*	*Low anxiety*	*High anxiety*	*Low anxiety*	*High anxiety*	*Low anxiety*	*High anxiety*	*Low anxiety*
	$\bar{X}$ SD	$\bar{X}$ SD	$\bar{X}$ SD	$\bar{X}$ SD	$\bar{X}$ SD	$\bar{X}$ SD	$\bar{X}$ SD	$\bar{X}$ SD
Teacher grades								
Social studies	4.9 1.4	5.3 1.3	4.7* 1.4	3.9 1.7	5.2* 1.3	6.3 1.1	4.0* 1.5	5.3 1.4
Mathematics	4.8 1.5	5.2 1.3	4.7* 1.6	4.0 1.6	5.2* 1.3	6.1 1.3	4.2* 1.5	5.2 1.5
Language arts	4.7 1.4	5.1 1.2	4.6* 1.3	3.8 1.5	5.3* 1.0	6.3 1.0	4.5* 1.5	5.4 1.3
Objective tests								
STEP Social Studies	5.6 1.6	5.5 1.6	4.6 1.3	4.3 1.0	5.6* 1.1	6.4 1.4	4.5* 1.2	4.9 1.2
CAT Mathematics	5.3 1.5	5.2 1.5	4.5* 1.3	4.1 1.2	5.9* 1.1	6.4 1.4	4.6* 1.5	5.2 1.4
CAT Language	5.1 1.5	5.2 1.5	4.5 1.5	4.2 1.4	5.3* 1.2	5.9 1.4	4.2* 1.5	5.0 1.4
CAT Reading	5.5 1.6	5.6 1.5	4.6 1.4	4.3 1.3	5.8* 1.1	6.3 1.3	4.4* 1.3	4.9 1.3
STEP Science	5.6 1.6	5.6 1.7	4.7 1.5	4.4 1.3	5.4* 1.4	6.2 1.1	4.4* 1.3	4.8 1.3

* Difference between this high anxiety subsample mean and the low anxiety subsample mean (in the next column) statistically significant at or beyond the .05 level.

TABLE 4
ANALYSIS OF VARIANCE OF ACHIEVEMENT VARIABLE MEANS

SOURCE	df	MS	F
Sex	1	23947.0	45.9**
Social class	1	154842.0	296.6**
Anxiety	1	5112.0	9.8**
Sex × social class	1	1090.0	2.1
Sex × anxiety	1	27890.0	53.4**
Social class × anxiety	1	3813.0	7.3**
Sex × social class × anxiety	1	8882.0	17.0**
Within[a]	56	522.0	

[a] Based on the eight subsamples and the eight mean achievement scores.
** $p < .01$.

TABLE 5
SUBSAMPLE IQ MEANS AND STANDARD DEVIATIONS

SUBSAMPLE	$\overline{X}$	SD
Male		
High social class, high anxiety	5.7	1.5
High social class, low anxiety	5.8	1.5
Low social class, high anxiety	4.8*	1.4
Low social class, low anxiety	4.3	1.2
Female		
High social class, high anxiety	5.5*	1.4
High social class, low anxiety	6.2	1.3
Low social class, high anxiety	4.3*	1.3
Low social class, low anxiety	4.8	1.3

* Difference between this mean and the mean directly below it statistically significant at or beyond the .05 level.

TABLE 6
CHI SQUARE ANALYSES OF DISTRIBUTION OF ANXIETY SCORES
BY SEX AND SOCIAL CLASS

	ANXIETY		
SUBSAMPLE	High	Low	Chi square
High social class			
Males	55	99	—
Females	58	94	
Low social class			
Males	108	103	9.40**
Females	158	84	
Males			
High social class	55	99	8.64**
Low social class	108	103	
Females			
High social class	58	94	27.88**
Low social class	158	84	

** $p < .01$; $df = 1$.

Referring, now, to Table 4, the following results may be noted:

1. Three main effects were statistically significant: females had higher achievement than males; middle-class subjects had higher achievement than lower-class subjects; and subjects with low anxiety had higher achievement than subjects with high anxiety.

2. Three interactions were statistically significant: an increase in anxiety resulted in lower achievement for females and slightly higher achievement for males; an increase in anxiety resulted in lower achievement for middle-class subjects but had no appreciable effect on the achievement of lower-class subjects; and an increase in anxiety resulted in an increase in the achievement of lower-class males and a decrease in the achievement of lower-class females, while an increase in anxiety resulted in a larger decrease in the achievement of middle-class females than it did in middle-class males.

Next, in reference to Tables 5 and 6, two major findings may be reported: first, an increase in anxiety among females resulted in lower intelligence scores in both social classes, while an increase in anxiety among males resulted in higher intelligence scores in the lower class, and made little difference in the middle class; second, there were proportionately more males and females with high anxiety in the lower class than in the middle class, although in the lower class a larger proportion of females than males had high anxiety.

TABLE 7
SUBSAMPLE DIFFERENCES BETWEEN MEAN IQ
AND THE MEAN OF THE ACHIEVEMENT MEANS

SUBSAMPLE	TEACHER GRADES [a]	OBJECTIVE TEST [b]
Male		
High social class, high anxiety	−.9*	−.3
High social class, low anxiety	−.6*	−.4
Low social class, high anxiety	−.1	−.2
Low social class, low anxiety	−.4*	0
Female		
High social class, high anxiety	−.3	.1
High social class, low anxiety	0	0
Low social class, high anxiety	−.1	.1
Low social class, low anxiety	−.5*	.2

[a] Difference obtained by determining the mean of the three teacher grade means and subtracting the mean IQ.
[b] Difference obtained by determining the mean of the five objective test means and subtracting the mean IQ.
* Difference is statistically significant at or beyond the .05 level.

Finally, from the results of Table 7, it was found that: for males in the middle class, mean teacher grades were lower than mean intelligence in both high and low anxiety groups; for males in the lower class, mean teacher grades were lower than mean intelligence in only the low anxiety group; for females in the middle class, there were no differences between mean teacher grades and mean intelligence in either high or low anxiety groups; for females in the lower class, mean teacher grades were higher than mean intelligence in the low anxiety group, with no mean difference in the high anxiety group; and lastly, differences between standardized achievement and intelligence were insignificant in all subsamples.

DISCUSSION

Viewed in relation to the overall findings of past anxiety research, it is evident that the general results of this study were in agreement on two major points. Sex differences in level of anxiety were obtained, with males having lower anxiety scores than females; and differences in the achievement of subjects with high and low anxiety were found, with high anxiety being associated with lower achievement. However, the significance of these areas of agreement is diminished by the finding that both the level of anxiety and its relationship to school achievement depended on the interaction of sex and social class.

As the first indication of this interaction, sex differences in level of anxiety occurred *only* in the lower social class, where females had significantly higher anxiety scores than males. In addition to this, it should be noted that middle-class and lower-class males differed less in anxiety scores than middle-class and lower-class females.

As a further indication of the interaction of sex and social class, lower-class males with high anxiety had higher intelligence scores than lower-class males with low anxiety, although middle-class males with high anxiety did not differ significantly in intelligence from middle-class males with low anxiety. Furthermore, in both social class levels females with high anxiety had lower intelligence scores than females with low anxiety.

Finally, the interaction between sex and social class was evident in relationships between anxiety and school achievement. In general, anxiety as a debilitating factor was more evident in relation to teacher grades than in relation to achievement tests, with the achievement of lower-class males being less affected than the achievement of other adolescents.

Considering what these findings may mean in terms of anxiety theory, Sarason, Davidson, Lighthall, and Waite (1958) have speculated that males obtain lower anxiety scores than females because they are more reluctant to admit anxiety. As they stated it, anxiety is "ego-alien" to males and "ego-syntonic" to females. In other words, the expression of anxiety is incongruous to the male's conception of himself, and this causes him to be more defensive about admitting anxiety. Accepting this, the results of this study may be explained by assuming that social class is a factor in whether anxiety becomes ego-alien or ego-syntonic. More specifically, the greater differentiation of sex roles in the lower class, particularly with respect to masculinity, causes the ego-alien aspects of anxiety to be more highly developed and delineated in lower-class males.

Although sex and social-class differences in level of anxiety seem to fit into the ego-alien and ego-syntonic rationale, more difficulty is experienced in trying to explain the role of sex and social class in relationships between anxiety and school achievement. According to the rationale, anxiety should have greater disruptive effects on males, due to the greater ego-alien nature of anxiety in males. But, as previously noted, anxiety appeared to interfere less with achievement of males than females, especially in the lower class. Thus, whether anxiety produces responses which are compatible or incompatible with school achievement tasks seems to depend upon social class. More to the point, the social class related experiences of lower-class males appear to be especially significant in whether anxiety has facilitative effects.

Finally, investigators espousing drive conceptions of anxiety have been particularly interested in the performance of highly anxious and less anxious subjects on complex and simple tasks. According to the Hull-Spence drive theory, anxiety should interfere with performance on complex tasks, and if tasks on intelligence tests can be considered complex, the negative relationships usually obtained between anxiety and intelligence appear to be consistent with this view. However, the results of this study did not altogether conform to the prediction of drive theory since lower-class males with high anxiety had *higher* intelligence scores than lower-class males with low anxiety. Apparently, then, the relationship between anxiety and intelligence is not uniformly negative across samples differentiated in terms of sex and social class, which raises the question of whether these factors in some way influence the drive properties of anxiety.

In summary, it is apparent that sex differences are not easily integrated into prevailing theories about anxiety, and that the interaction of sex, social class, and anxiety represents a particular challenge to existing theoretical formulations. Furthermore, it is argued that an integration of research findings concerning anxiety and ego involvement, and social class and school achievement, offers the best opportunity for a conceptualization which will successfully handle such differences. Toward this end, the following facts and speculations are presented:

1. It is known that middle-class subjects have a greater desire to do well in school than lower-class subjects, and that a similar difference exists between females and males, with this difference being greater in

the lower class. As a result, school achievement tasks should be more ego involving to middle-class subjects than to lower-class subjects, and to females more than males, especially in the lower class.

2. There have been studies of the relationship between anxiety and performance under neutral and ego involving conditions, and the gist of these studies is that highly anxious subjects perform better under neutral conditions, while less anxious subjects perform better under ego involving conditions. Therefore, the degree to which anxiety interferes with a subject's performance in a situation depends upon the degree to which the subject is ego involved.

3. Integrating these findings, since school achievement tasks are more ego involving to middle-class subjects, and to females more than males (particularly in the lower class), the degree to which anxiety interferes with school achievement should depend upon both the sex and the social class status of subjects. Taking into account these specific relationships, anxiety should interfere the least with the school achievement of lower-class males, and this is what the overall findings of this study showed.

References

GROOMS, R. R., & ENDLER, N. S. The effect of anxiety on academic achievement. *J. educ. Psychol.*, 1960, **51,** 299–304.

McGUIRE, C., HINDSMAN, E., KING, F. J., & JENNINGS, E. Dimensions of talented behavior. *Educ. psychol. Measmt.*, 1961, **21,** 3–38.

PHILLIPS, B., HINDSMAN, E., & JENNINGS, E. Influence of intelligence on anxiety and perception of self and others. *Child Develpm.*, 1960, **31,** 41–46.

PHILLIPS, B., HINDSMAN, E., & McGUIRE, C. Factors associated with anxiety and their relation to the school achievement of adolescents. *Psychol. Rep.*, 1960, **7,** 365–372.

REESE, H. W. Manifest anxiety and achievement test performance. *J. educ. Psychol.*, 1961, **52,** 132–35.

SARASON, S. B., DAVIDSON, K., LIGHTHALL, F., & WAITE, R. Classroom observation of high and low anxious children. *Child Develpm.*, 1958, **29,** 287–296.

SARASON, S. B., DAVIDSON, K. S., LIGHTHALL, F. K., WAITE, R., & RUEBUSH, B. K. *Anxiety in Elementary School Children.* New York: Wiley, 1960.

The Effects of Direct and Indirect Teacher Influence on Dependent-Prone Students Learning Geometry[1]

Edmund Amidon and Ned A. Flanders

Whether or not a particular type of student can learn when he is exposed to a particular style of teaching has interested a number of researchers. Smith (1955) and Wispe (1951) have both shown that when students are classified by the use of personality test data, they respond differently to highly organized versus loosely organized classroom activities in a college remedial reading course (Smith, 1955) and to college lecturing versus group discussion techniques (Wispe, 1951) in freshman sociology. The present project was concerned with dependent-prone eighth grade students who were exposed to consistently direct versus indirect styles of teaching while learning geometry.

Asch (1951), Kagen and Mussen (1956), and Livson and Mussen (1957) have studied the reactions of dependent-prone persons in various kinds of experimental situations. They concluded that dependent-prone individuals are more likely to comply with authority figures and conform to group pressures than the less dependent-prone. Their results suggest that a dependent-prone student might become overly concerned with following the suggestions and directions of a teacher and more dependent on support and encouragement. The present project was designed to find out if these concerns inhibit or enhance the learning of geometry at the age level represented in the eighth grade.

PROCEDURE

This study employed a laboratory design in order to exercise experimental control of spontaneous behavior. First, the behavior of the teacher was controlled by training a teacher-role player. His statements were classified by an observer to demonstrate that desired differences were great enough for students to notice. Second, those students who

[1]This article is based on the PhD thesis of the first author. It was an adjunctive study of a larger project, the latter supported by a grant from the United States Office of Education.

"The Effects of Direct and Indirect Teacher Influence on Dependent-Prone Students Learning Geometry," by Edmund J. Amidon and Ned A. Flanders, *Journal of Educational Psychology*, No. 52, 286–291. © 1961, American Psychological Association.

scored high on a dependence-proneness test developed by Flanders, Anderson, and Amidon (1960) were selected for the experimental population. Third, control of learning was accomplished by using pre- and post-tests of geometry achievement. And fourth, in half of the experimental groups the basic content material, presented in a tape recording, was so organized that the immediate learning goals were unclear, and in the other half the immediate learning goals were clear.

The four treatments involved were:

Treatment 1. Direct teacher influence: clear goals, 35 dependent-prone students

Treatment 2. Direct teacher influence: unclear goals, 35 dependent-prone students

Treatment 3. Indirect teacher influence: clear goals, 35 dependent-prone students

Treatment 4. Indirect teacher influence: unclear goals, 35 dependent-prone students.

The experimental population of 140 dependent-prone students was part of a larger group of 560 students. The larger group was exposed to the preceding four treatments in groups of 20 as part of a larger study. The 560 eighth grade students were selected at random from Minneapolis and St. Paul public schools. The 140 students were the top 25% in each treatment of the larger population according to their scores on the dependence-proneness test.

The students were brought, 20 per session, to a spare room in a public school. First, a pretest of geometry achievement and a test of dependence-proneness were administered. Second, a tape recording was played introducing the basic concepts of $C = D$, Distance $=$ Speed $\times$ Time, and geometric concepts and formulae concerning inscribed angles. In half of the groups the immediate goals were made clear because the recording explained how this information could be used to solve problems; in the other half, the goals were less clear because the students were warned that they could not be sure how this information could be used. Third, in the direct treatments a teacher gave a 15-minute lecture, with a few questions, explaining the material and illustrating problems that could be solved. In the indirect treatments, a teacher conducted a 15-minute discussion explaining the material and illustrating problems that could be solved. The content coverage was the same in the contrasting treatments. Fourth, the students then had about 15 minutes to practice solving problems at their seats by working on a problem sheet. And fifth, the post-test of achievement was administered. The entire sequence lasted 2 hours.

At appropriate points in this procedure the students' perceptions of goal clarity and their perceptions of the teacher were measured by

paper-and-pencil tests. The reliability of both of these scales was estimated by the use of the Hoyt-Stunkard (1952) analysis of variance
technique. The estimated reliability of the student perception scale was
.64, while the reliability found for the goal perception measure was .93
for the measure administered just before the discussion (Amidon, 1959).
Whenever the teacher talked, an observer classified all teacher and student statements according to Flanders' (1960) system of interaction
analysis. Later the validity and reliability of the observer's judgments
were verified by studying the tape recording that was made of every
experimental session.

RESULTS

Control of Teacher Influence and Goal Perception

The manipulation of direct and indirect teacher influence occurred
right after the tape recording when the teacher first came in contact with
the students. The same role player acted as teacher in all treatments to
avoid differences in personality and appearance. The differences between
the direct and indirect approach are shown in Table 1 according to the
percentage of statements classified into interaction categories.

The figures in Table 1 show that essential differences between the
direct and indirect treatments are: the teacher lectures and gives more
directions in the direct treatments; he asks more questions and gets more
student participation in the indirect treatments; he praises, encourages,
and clarifies student ideas more frequently in the indirect treatments;
and he criticizes students more frequently in the direct treatments.

The fact that the teacher controlled his behavior successfully and
created the two teacher styles is self-evident. A Darwin (1959) chi
square analysis of these same interaction data, after they were tabulated
in a matrix of sequence pairs, was calculated to test the null hypothesis
that there is no difference between interaction data of the direct and
indirect combined treatments. The chi square value found was 702.2 (df
$= 90$). This value, transformed to a z score of 24.1, indicates that the
differences could have occurred by chance with a frequency of much less
than .01.

The reliability of the observers who classified the statements in the
live situation was higher than .90. It can be shown that the errors of
observation, at this level of reliability, are extremely small compared
with the difference shown in Table 1 between the direct and indirect
patterns.

After the lectures and discussions and before the period devoted to
work sheets, the students responded to a number of opinion items combined into a scale which measured their perceptions of the teacher's

behavior. An analysis of variance was made of these scale scores which indicated that the F ratio between the groups subjected to the direct and indirect influence treatments was 78.4 $(df = 1/136)$. This was significant at the .01 level of confidence. The mean scores indicated that students in the direct treatments more often saw the teacher as: "telling us what to do," "firm and businesslike," "making plans for us," "critical of our ideas," "talking more than the students," and "not using student ideas or suggestions." In the indirect treatments, students often marked: "finding out what we know," "relaxed and cheerful," "letting us make our own plans," "letting students talk," "using our ideas," and similar perceptions that were the opposite of the direct pattern. The means and F ratio are presented in Table 2.

TABLE 1
PERCENTAGE OF TALLIES IN INTERACTION CATEGORIES

CATEGORY DEFINITION	TREATMENT			
	1	2	3	4
Teacher talk:				
Praise and encouragement	1.35	1.61	17.04	14.90
Clarification and development of ideas suggested by students	2.48	0.92	15.78	16.10
Asks questions	2.58	1.73	28.07	30.04
Gives own opinions and facts (lectures)	63.10	61.40	13.52	15.97
Gives directions	8.67	10.36	0.28	0.27
Criticizes students	13.03	15.54	1.27	0.94
Student talk	5.07	5.29	16.47	17.17
No one talking	3.49	3.45	7.75	4.69
Total tallies on which the percentage figures are based	889	869	711	746

TABLE 2
STUDENT PERCEPTION OF TEACHER INFLUENCE

GROUP	MEAN	F obs BETWEEN DIRECT AND INDIRECT GROUPS
Direct influence	11.74	
		78.40
Indirect influence	18.84	

TABLE 3
STUDENT PERCEPTION OF THE GOAL

GROUP	MEAN	F obs BETWEEN CLEAR AND UNCLEAR GROUPS
Clear goals	21.40	
		16.98
Unclear goals	26.13	

As expected, an analysis of observation data and of student perceptions of the teacher comparing the clear and unclear goal treatments showed no significant $(p < .05)$ difference in teacher behavior. Also, no significant ($p < .05$) interaction effects were found in the analysis of variance.

The interaction analysis data and measures of the students' perceptions of the teacher did show that the differences between the direct and indirect approach did exist as required by the experimental design, were clearly seen by a trained observer, and noticed by the students.

Paper-and-pencil measures of the clarity of goals were made after the playback of the tape recording introducing the basic geometric concepts. Students responded to items such as: "Can you see all the steps necessary to finish your work?" "Right now can you see what you will be doing clearly?" "Can you picture your work so clearly that you could tell when you will be finished?" and similar items that were combined into a scale. An analysis of variance of these scale scores yielded an F ratio of 16.98 ($df = 1/136$, p $< .01$). An inspection of the means indicated that the results were consistent with the intended goal manipulation. The results show that the immediate response of students to the clear and unclear tape recording was significantly different. The means and F ratio are found in Table 3.

Results of the Geometry Achievement

Since achievement in geometry was the fundamental outcome variable analyzed in this study, the postachievement test was subjected to several analyses. The first analysis was the comparison of postachievement scores between the indirect and direct teacher influence groups. The F ratio found in this analysis was 7.67, which was significant at the .01 level. The means of the indirect teacher influence groups were significantly higher than the means of the direct teacher influence groups on the postachievement measure. In order to reduce unaccounted for error in the analysis of postachievement, two analyses of covariance controlling preachievement scores and intelligence scores were run. The F ratio between direct and indirect teacher influence groups was 10.03 when intelligence was controlled, and 9.62 when pretest scores were controlled. Again, those F ratios were significant at the .01 level, indicating the superiority of the indirect teacher influence group. For each of the analyses of covariance $df = 1/137$.

The analysis of variance and covariance just discussed yielded insignificant ($p > .05$) results when the clear and ambiguous goal perception groups were compared statistically. The interaction of goal perception and teacher influence also did not yield significant ($p < .05$) results. The F ratios found in these analyses are presented in Table 4.

The means of the indirect group were significantly higher than the means of the direct group. This is true when intelligence and preachievement were controlled, and it was also true when they were not controlled. The means of the direct and indirect teacher influence groups are presented in Table 5.

TABLE 4
ANALYSIS OF DIFFERENCES IN THE MEANS OF POSTACHIEVEMENT SCORES WITH
VARIOUS FACTORS CONTROLLED STATISTICALLY

SOURCE OF VARIATION	df	$F\ obs$	NULL HYPOTHESIS
With no measure controlled:			
Interaction	1	—	Not rejected
Teacher influence	1	7.67	Rejected
Goal perception	1	—	Not rejected
Preachievement controlled:			
Interaction	1	2.71	Not rejected
Teacher influence	1	10.03	Rejected
Goal perception	1	—	Not rejected
Intelligence controlled:			
Interaction	1	1.08	Not rejected
Teacher influence	1	9.62	Rejected
Goal perception	1	1.13	Not rejected

TABLE 5
MEANS OF DIRECT AND INDIRECT GROUPS FOR POSTACHIEVEMENT MEASURE

MEAN	NOT ADJUSTED	ADJUSTED BY PRETEST SCORES	ADJUSTED BY INTELLIGENCE
Direct group	9.24	9.31	9.30
Indirect group	10.82	10.76	10.69

DISCUSSION

The measures of geometry achievement indicate that the dependent-prone students learned more in the classroom in which the teacher gave fewer directions, less criticism, less lecturing, more praise, and asked more questions which increased their verbal participation. This finding takes on added significance when compared with Flanders' (1960) findings that the total group of 560 students, those scoring high, average, and low on the dependence-proneness tests, failed to show the same significant differences under the same conditions. Moreover, when the independent-prone students (those in the lower 25% on the dependency scale) were compared separately, no differences were found. Compared with students in general, dependent-prone students are apparently more sensitive to the influence pattern of a geometry teacher.

The authors are disposed to interpret these findings in terms of the probable effects of teacher influence on the dependent-prone student. We assume that dependent-prone students are more sensitive to the

directive aspects of the teacher's behavior. As the teacher becomes more
directive, this type of student finds increased satisfaction in more compliance, often with less understanding of the problem solving steps carried out. Only when he is free to express his doubts, to ask questions
and gain reassurance, does his understanding keep pace with his compliance to the authority figure. Lacking this opportunity, compliance alone
may become a satisfactory goal and content understanding may be subordinated to the process of adjusting to teacher directives. It is interesting to note that this effect occurs even when the material being learned
concerns an orderly, logical system, such as exists in geometry.

One implication of this study is that closer supervision through the
use of direct influence, an all too common antidote to lower achievement, may be more harmful than helpful for dependent-prone students.

SUMMARY

The primary purpose of the study described here was to determine
the effects of direct vs. indirect teacher behavior and of clear vs. unclear
student perception of the learning goal on the achievement of eighth
grade geometry students. A specially trained teacher role played both a
very direct and a very indirect teacher in a laboratory situation involving
140 eighth grade pupils chosen from a larger population on the basis of
high scores on a test of dependency proneness. All students were randomly assigned to one of the following four experimental treatments:
direct teacher influence with clear goals, direct teacher influence with
unclear goals, indirect teacher influence with clear goals, and indirect
teacher influence with unclear goals.

Students in the various classifications were then compared on the
basis of pre- and postachievement tests in geometry. No differences were
found between the clear goal and unclear goal treatments, indicating
that in this study, at least, achievement of dependent-prone students was
not affected by perception of the learning goal. An analysis of the direct
and indirect treatments indicated that the children taught by the indirect
teacher learned more than did the children taught by the direct teacher.

The results of this study take on additional meaning when compared
with the results of Flanders (1960) using the same experimental design.
Flanders found no difference (among the four experimental conditions)
on the total group of 560 students who ranged from very high to very
low on the dependence scale. Apparently dependent-prone students are
more sensitive to types of teacher influence than are independent-prone
students or students who make average scores on the test for dependence
proneness.

References

AMIDON, E. J. Dependent-prone students in experimental learning situations. Unpublished doctoral dissertation, University of Minnesota, 1959.

ASCH, S. E. Effects of group pressure upon the modification and distortion of judgments. In H. Guetzkow (Ed.), *Groups, Leadership, and Men.* Pittsburgh; Carnegie Press, 1951.

DARWIN, J. H. Note on the comparison of several realizations of a Markoff chain. *Biometrika,* 1959, **46,** 412–419.

FLANDERS, N. A. Teacher influence on pupil attitudes and achievement. Final Report; 1960; University of Minnesota; Project 397; United States Department of Health, Education, and Welfare; Cooperative Research Program; Office of Education.

FLANDERS, N. A., ANDERSON, J. P., & AMIDON, E. J. Measuring dependence proneness in the classroom. *U. Minn., Bur. Educ. Res. res. Memo.,* 1960, No. Ber 60–6.

HOYT, C., & STUNKARD, C. L. Estimation of test reliability for unrestricted item scoring methods. *Educ. psychol. Measmt.,* 1952, **12,** 756–758.

KAGEN, J., & MUSSEN, P. Dependency themes on the TAT and group conformity. *J. consult. Psychol.,* 1956, **20,** 19–27.

LIVSON, N., & MUSSEN, P. The relation of control to overt aggression and dependency. *J. abnorm. soc. Psychol.,* 1957, **55,** 66–71.

SMITH, D. E. P. Fit teaching methods to personality structure. *High sch. J.,* 1955, **39,** 167–171.

WISPE, L. C. Evaluating section teaching methods in the introductory course. *J. educ. Res.,* 1951, **45,** 161–186.

The Assessment of Progress in the Treatment of Hyperaggressive Children with Learning Disturbances within a School Setting

Ruth G. Newman

A study was undertaken at the Child Research Bureau of the National Institute of Mental Health, under the direction of Dr. Fritz Redl, concerning the severe disturbances of learning and school adjustment exhibited by hyperaggressive boys with behavior disorders. The subjects were six boys who were especially selected because they were within the normal intelligence range and had an extreme degree of hyperaggressive disorder without perceptible organic damage.

At the outset of the study, in the fall of 1954, the ages of the boys ranged from 8 to 10. At its completion, in the spring of 1957, the range was 11 to 13. During the time of the study the boys lived as inpatients of a closed ward at the Clinical Center of the National Institutes of Health. Subsequently, they moved to a less rigidly protected residence on the grounds of the National Institutes, and are at this time attending public schools in the area. The boys continue to receive intensive individual psychotherapy, which was initiated with their admission to the hospital. Before they entered public schools a complete school program was offered to them. Now, they receive only marginal individual tutoring from the teaching staff on the request of their present schools.

The total therapeutic setting was basic to the treatment and research design. This setting included, besides intensive individual psychotherapy and group work, a complete school program covering group and individual teaching. Thus, interdisciplinary communication and cooperation became an operational necessity. Therefore, the impact of the setting is fundamental to this study on learning disturbances.

Even when organic factors are absent, and adequate intelligence

Essential research information contributed by Mrs. Florence Glaser and Mr. Christopher Faegre, both teachers of the special school at the Child Research Branch, National Institute of Mental Health.

present, the hyperaggressive boy lacking inner controls proverbially presents a problem to himself and to the school. Moreover, the mutual failure experienced by both child and school contributes to the disturbance. Thus, a vicious circle of disorder and defeat is generated. It becomes clear that radical alteration in the school and the personality structure must be set in motion if any degree of school learning and adjustment is to occur. To design an appropriate school program for the hyperaggressive boy implies an awareness of his psychodynamic personality structure. Obviously, how much of his difficulty arises from his personality structure and how much arises from the school program and the teacher personality is a question of major importance if change in the direction of increased learning and adjustment is to occur.

In order to develop a tool which would yield meaningful and useful information concerning the determinants affecting learning and adjustment of these subjects, it first had to be seen whether change in the direction of greater learning and adjustment had occurred at all. Therefore, the daily school records for the 2½-year period were collected. Incidents reporting one complete piece of behavior in school for each day of group school and for each day of individual tutoring were placed under the name of every subject. Samples from this complete set were chosen for every month of the school year, including summer months when only individual tutoring was offered. The samples were selected randomly without regard to whether a given incident pointed up good or bad behavior, dramatic or ordinary activity. The sample was selected from a total of about 700 incidents for each boy and about 4,200 for the entire group.

A behavior scale (Table 1) was devised to evaluate a child's behavior in school for each incident. This instrument was based on the assumption that where a hyperaggressive child's behavior is one of enthusiastic participation in a teacher-directed goal, he has to some extent adjusted to school and is deriving satisfaction and learning from it. Conversely, as his participation diminishes, so do his adjustment and learning. Thus, on this basis, the behavior scale would measure the extent to which learning and adjustment had occurred in a given incident. All the incidents were judged by the author or a colleague on this scale. They were then submitted to four objective judges. However, the incidents had all dates and time sequence notations removed as well as all information concerning what the teacher had done about a given piece of behavior. Thus bias was minimized in order to test the validity of the hypothesis, as well as the reliability of author judgment. Judgments were made three times at spaced intervals. The agreement of judges and examiner was found to be greater than 83 per cent; reliability, greater than 85 per cent.

TABLE 1.
BEHAVIOR SCALE

RATING	DEFINITION	EXAMPLES (EXCERPTS FROM INCIDENTS)
−2	Destructive, disorganized, disintegrative behavior. Subject actively rejects school task or goal.	Ed went around the room asking the other boys to give him their snacks. All refused. He rolled a comic book, began to tap people on the head. He tapped Frank hard. Frank rose and hit him back. Teacher grabbed him as he threw pencil at Frank. Ed fled from teacher's grasp, threw over Frank's desk. Teacher caught hold of him. He screamed at her and bit her, escaped and rushed around the room throwing objects and yelling.
−1	Negative response to school task or goal. Withdrawal from planned or legitimate activity. Refusal to accept legitimate substitute.	Teacher gave Frank a choice of two of his favorite books to read. He refused the first, took the second, threw it down and said the pages were yellow and old. She substituted two other books that he himself had brought from the library. He refused these. She suggested he select an experiment from a science book. He took the book, thumbed the pages, threw down the book, refused to settle on the experiment and left without having settled on any one task.
+1	Interested but detached behavior. Subject able to accept task or legitimate substitute parallel to, but not with the group, or only able to join the group after his need to remain separate has been exhibited.	The group assignment was to place on mimeographed maps the location of Indian tribes and to fill in check lists of Indian objects next to their names. Bob refused this but sat, apart from the group, carefully writing all the things he knew about turtles in a turtle notebook. The other children discussed their maps. Bob stayed removed, got the National Geographic article on turtles, copied the material he wanted into his notebook. Having finished this, he rose and joined the group in filling out the maps and information sheets about Indian objects.
+2	Active, contained, participation in school task or goal for a sustained period.	Each child had chosen an invention to learn about and to make a model of. Cliff had selected a Beebe bathosphere. He found Beebe himself in *The World Book*. He was fascinated that the windows were made of quartz, not glass. He went to the school rock collection and found a piece of quartz. He figured out how the windows must have been made. He planned his model with the teacher and left the room with his arm about the teacher, carrying with him extra material about a bathosphere so that he could begin his model the next day.

The ratings from the Behavior Scale were divided into two parts for each child: the ratings from the first half of a subject's hospitalization were compared with those of the second period of hospitalization. The comparative ratings were then statistically analyzed by means of the Chi Square measure. Change for the total group was significantly different from what could be expected by chance at a .001 level. Change for five of the six subjects was significantly greater than what could be expected by chance at a greater than .05 level. The sixth child had moved in the direction of change, but the change was not statistically significant. (This exception, however, is interestingly explained by clinical occurrences which were not capable of showing up on the Behavior Scale.)

The fact that change had indeed taken place having been established, it became possible to account for the change in a meaningful manner. In order to investigate what had determined the outcome of a given incident, or to observe whether there was a pattern of determinants within each subject, or more generally, in the group, all the same incidents described above were again studied and carefully analyzed in a different way. Initially, descriptive comments were made about every incident for both group school and individual tutoring for each boy. These descriptive comments, drawn from the incidents themselves, were formed into descriptive characterizations and three broad classifications were made. Under the three very general classifications, seven subcategories were derived which covered the material yielded by the analysis of the incidents for all of the boys. These subcategories were carefully defined in terms specifically applicable to the occurrence seen in the incidents. Thus, by a modification of the Critical Incident Technique described by Dr. Flanagan,[1] a range of determinants for all incidents was evolved. A different qualitative rating scale was then devised for each of the subcategories which further described what had occurred in a given incident and created a tool for qualitatively evaluating it.

The three major classifications were Self, Relationships and School. Under Self, the subcategories were the Self-Picture, Inner Drives and Forces, and Infantile Needs and Frustration Tolerance. Under Relationships, the subcategories were Relations to Adults and Relations to Peers; while under the heading School, the subcategories were School Methods, Materials, Subject Matter and Teacher Personality. Without the specific definitions and the attached evaluative scale, these groupings have very little meaning. Therefore Table 2 includes the ratings, definitions and evaluative scale.

These incidents, then, having been submitted to detailed analysis on the basis of the subcategories and their evaluative rating scale, and having been judged by one of the examiners, were given to four objective judges (different from the first set of judges) to be rated independently in order to test the objectivity of judgment. Objectivity was upheld at greater than 85 per cent. Reliability was tested by three separate judgments spaced at intervals and was upheld above 84 per cent. Thus, it was felt that a tool for appraising the determinants of an incident had

---

[1]John C. Flanagan, *The Critical Incident Techniques: Methods of Analysis of School Records* (American Institute for Research and University of Pittsburgh, 1954, 1956). The modification centers largely around the fact that Dr. Flanagan suggests a selection of critical incidents, whereas the incidents selected in this study were random samples.

been devised and that such a tool could be used for other groups of children in other settings in school, or in treatment. For example, such a method might be useful in appraising the learning determinants of a school program for gifted children, or withdrawn children, or hyperaggressive children in nonresidential treatment or it might be used in psychotherapeutic settings as well as school settings.

TABLE 2.

CATEGORIES, SUBCATEGORIES, DEFINITIONS, AND EVALUATION SCALE

CATEGORY	SUBCATEGORY	RATING	EVALUATIVE SCALE
Self	Self-Picture Determinant 1A The way in which a child perceives himself at a given moment	—	Where the child's behavior indicates that he feels helpless, worthless, unlovable, deserted in a hostile world; *or* where he sees himself as magically able to control things, people or events
		0	Where a child finds himself acceptable only if he were something or someone other than himself and his behavior indicates that he has identified with or projected himself onto some object, animal, fictional or real person; *or* if his behavior indicates that he is actively removing himself from situations which might reveal his present self-image
		+	Where a child's behavior indicates that he feels worthy of help, potentially adequate and lovable as a human child, capable of erring and succeeding within realistic limits, and he exhibits a degree of self-acceptance
	Inner Drives and Forces Determinant 2A The way in which a child is driven by his f e a r s, fantasies and anxieties concerning sex, closeness, separation, desertion, inadequacy, etc.	—	Where a child's behavior indicates that he is overwhelmed by his fears, anxieties, fantasies to a point where he has lost self-containment of the ability to perceive the actual situation
		0	Where a child's behavior indicates that he has distorted the material or relationship because of his inner fears, anxieties or fantasies but can maintain a measure of self-containment
		+	Where a child's behavior indicates he has adequately coped with inner fears, anxieties or fantasies *or* where stimuli or situations which previously aroused expression of fears, fantasies or anxieties no longer appear to do so
	Infantile Needs and Frustration Tolerance Determinant 3A	—	Where a child's behavior indicates that his need for immediate satisfaction makes it impossible for him to wait or postpone

TABLE 2. *(Continued)*

CATEGORY	SUBCATEGORY	RATING	EVALUATIVE SCALE
	A child confronts tasks or relationships for immediate satisfaction without ability to postpone gratification or tolerate frustration for a future goal		gratification or to tolerate frustration in a school task or relationship, or makes it impossible for him to perceive the actual situation
		0	Where a child's behavior indicates that he has dealt with his need for immediate satisfaction or intolerance of frustration by negativism, illness, tiredness, baby talk, baby gestures, tears or clinging
		+	Where a child's behavior indicates he has successfully been able to postpone present gratification for a future goal, or to sustain a degree of frustration in a task or relationship and still maintain control and interest
Relation-ships	*Relation to Adults* Determinant 1B The way in which a child relates to an adult in fear of closeness, fear of dependence, rejection, distrust so that accepting help or limits without manipulation becomes impossible	—	Where a child's behavior indicates hostility, rejection, or panic in contacting an adult or where he reacts with extreme withdrawal, denial or detachment to an adult's approach
		0	Where a child's behavior indicates removal, distance or detachment from an adult *or* where to maintain contact he manipulates, maneuvers, controls or demands
		+	Where a child's behavior indicates friendly, warm, unafraid moves toward adults with an ability to accept help, accept limits, and illustrates a nonmanipulative desire to please
	Relation to Peers Determinant 2B The way in which a child can share an adult or another child with a peer or can bear to see another child gratified by praise, time, gifts, skills, concern, or the way in which a child must be the first, best and only or else his rejection of peers, his scapegoating by peer or his manipulation of peers	—	Where a child's behavior indicates jealous, envious, hostile or fearful response toward a peer who was receiving adult attention or attention from another peer or where he becomes the scapegoat or bully as his only means of relating to peers
		0	Where a child's behavior indicates his need to maintain distance from his peers, to belittle their gains, or where he puts himself in a position to be used by his peers for the sake of pleasing or to buy their favor
		+	Where a child's behavior indicates an ability to share an adult, an activity or material with his peer(s) on an equal basis and for a mutual goal

(Continued on following page)

TABLE 2.   *(Continued)*

CATEGORY	SUBCATEGORY	RATING	EVALUATIVE SCALE
School	*Subject Matter, Methods, Material* Determinant 3ABC The way in which a child reacts to method, approach, material, subject matter	—	Where a child's behavior indicated that the school subject matter, or methods, or material was inappropriate, too hard, too easy, belittling, unlimited, unstructured, overstimulating, overfrustrating
		0	Where a child's behavior indicated that the school subject matter, methods or material was dull, poorly planned, unmotivated or lacking in recognition of the child's interests, skills, ability or operating level
		+	Where a child's behavior indicated that the subject matter, methods or material was particularly well suited to the child's needs, appropriate for his operating level, properly structured, properly flexible, containing its own limits, challenging but not frustrating
	Teacher Personality Determinant 3D The way in which a child reacts to a teacher's mode of behavior, handling of his own anxiety, expression by word or gesture of response	—	Where a child's behavior indicated that he was reacting to a teacher's seductive, fearful, rejecting, hostile, ambivalent, uncertain, or withdrawn behavior
		0	Where a child's behavior indicated that he reacted to a teacher's involvement with his own problems or goals without specific awareness of the child's needs
		+	Where a child's behavior indicated that he reacted to a teacher's particularly acute, sensitive awareness of his needs and a teacher's abilities to meet these needs by useful, skillful, constructive or supportive action

One of the more interesting areas that posed itself through the information collected in the manner described above was the weight that could be allotted to personality factors as covered by the Self and Relationship categories on the one hand and that which could be assigned to the School category on the other. (See Table 3.) It is this phase and its implications that we should like to emphasize here. An individual analysis of the proportionate determinants for each child gave some clue as to the type of stimulus which would be most likely to affect his school adjustment and learning processes. Although the weight of different personality categories varied from child to child, it was clear that in each child as in the group, the greatest weight could be allotted to factors arising from forces within the subject.

A detailed analysis of those incidents where the outcome was determined, in part, or in whole, by the subject matter, methods, material and teacher personality of the school, yielded certain information about the school program. It is felt that this information has implications for the planning of school programs for hyperaggressive children in general.

By careful scrutiny of the incidents and their evaluative ratings, it became clear that hyperaggressive boys require an explicit, limited, concrete, carefully defined, brief assignment. Room for doubt, decision, confusion or ambiguity causes disorganization. Emotionally loaded subject matter such as is found in most readers concerning happy family life or charming naughty pranks quite unlike the environment or actions of these children is far too threatening; so is material that is tender—the Bambi story, for example, or the whole cultural impact of the Christmas story. Verbal explanation needs to be specific and minimal. These children have heard too many meaningless, confusing, malevolent or untrue words to be motivated by verbal communication.

TABLE 3.
WEIGHTS OF DETERMINANTS OF SCHOOL INCIDENTS

I. Self		
A. Self-picture	156	
B. Inner drives and forces	170	
C. Infantile needs and frustration tolerance	139	
		465
II. Relationships		
A. Relation to adults	165	
B. Relation to peers	91	
		256
III. School		
(A) School (B) Methods (C)Subject Matter	101	
(D) School teacher personality	50	
		151
Total		872

Activity programs with a great deal of manual emphasis are far more likely to succeed than heavy doses of desk work. Materials need to be laid out and limited so that overstimulation does not break down a school activity. Directions on the use of materials need to be demonstrated step by step, with individual help and without overfrustration from complicated objects or tools. In painting, for example, freedom of expression in line or color leads either to nothing or to disorganization. Two colors are usually the most a hyperaggressive child can deal with at the outset of a treatment program. Free interpretive dancing is far too stimulating to be useful; even formal square dancing with its cooperative demands has to wait until late in the program. Music, although eminently appealing, in the beginning is apt to be successful if it requires passive listening rather than participation. Drumsticks are less successful than a wire whisk broom. Material of the simple game type is most successful for academic subjects requiring routine or memory, even though it may be verbally dismissed by the children as "kid's stuff." The poker game method of teaching fractions, or the dice game method for teaching addition combinations used by one of our teachers was eminently successful where drill was instantly rejected. In remedial techniques, while the kinesthetic methods were diagnostically precisely what was required, to be used at all, they had to be greatly watered down. For children as confused as these, space and time concepts, so basic to comprehension of reading, arithmetic, social sciences and sciences, were far too threatening to be tolerated, let alone assimilated for a long period. When they were introduced, they had to be taught carefully, step by step.

Differences between acceptable and tolerated activities and behavior in the classroom had to be clearly communicated, and a great deal of time and effort had to be spent on transmitting the message that what is tolerated at one period would not be tolerated at a later date. For example, the reading of comics was tolerated in school originally in order to communicate the message that the child was wanted in school and could stay there so long as he was not too disturbing to others. Later, comics were tabooed in school since at this time the message to be communicated was that there were some things appropriate to school and others inappropriate for the best use of schooltime. These children often found very rigid, unimaginative, highly structured methods more acceptable and less frightening than open-ended creative, fantasy-arousing types of tasks, such as play acting or story telling. The arithmetic processes of addition and multiplication were always more acceptable than subtraction and division. There was a distinct implication that this was because of the symbolic attachments connected with the latter processes rather than because of any real greater difficulty within the processes themselves. Subtraction problems could be done when they were rephrased with a "You get" instead of "I take away." Using a child's self-image to the fullest was frequently a means of reaching a core of material from which he could be sufficiently motivated so that he could work for a sustained period and expand his interest, knowledge and skills by doing so. One boy, for example, who closely identified with turtles, could nearly always be drawn into some kind of legitimate work if turtles were the focus of subject matter.

Particularly significant in appraising teacher personality as a determinant of incidents was the proximity-distance scale. That is to say that children who vociferously demanded a close unshared relation with the teacher would frequently become so frightened by the very closeness they had asked for that they would disintegrate in a dramatic fashion. The teacher's problem became one of not feeling rejected, of not demanding closeness from the child, of being able to convey warmth and interest in a carefully removed, undemanding, unstimulating and unseductive manner. Such a detail as how far apart and in what position the teacher's chair and that of the child should be placed in a tutoring session became of primary importance. Occasionally, if the teacher, because of his own needs, or because of a child's distorted perception of him, made a gesture that conveyed a personal demand for closeness, the entire teaching situation might deteriorate to a point where the only way to maintain or rebuild it was to have another neutral adult sitting in the room.

Another area where teacher personality was perceived as crucial was a demand for achievement. When a child became aware that a teacher, perhaps unconsciously, wanted him to achieve in order to gain customarily legitimate and laudable feelings of professional success, the result was bound to be failure for both child and teacher. Since so many unanswerable demands had been placed on these children's shoulders, this reaction was not surprising. From the teacher's point of view, a demand for achievement was equally understandable. A teacher is evaluated by his colleagues, and even more by other disciplines, on the basis of pupil success; thus, frequently, lack of achievement in a child leads to feelings of severe inadequacy, futility and failure in a teacher. Occasionally, in order to overcome the demand for achievement, a teacher responded to the child's learning with pessimism and despair. This also led nowhere, for the children reacted with echoing despair. Thus a neat balance between long-term optimism without personal demand needed to be maintained. This, indeed, is a professional tightrope for most teachers. The ambiguous role demanded of a teacher with hyperaggressive children is a further personality hurdle. The teacher attempts to transmit a message that he is not only available but that he can be useful in helping a child, while at the same time the child is bent on not accepting help even while he demands it. What role to take at a given moment becomes confusing to a teacher and potentially upsets a school goal.

These are samples of the kind of information yielded by an analysis of the incidents which were judged to be determined by school, its methods, materials, subject matter and teacher personality.

To summarize: A part of an overall study on the adjustment and learning difficulties of emotionally disturbed, hyperaggressive children was outlined here. The subjects of this study were six severely disturbed, hyperaggressive boys, living as inpatients on a locked ward at the Clinical Center, Child Research Branch of the National Institute of Mental Health. The study took place in a total therapeutic setting in which individual psychotherapy and a planned school program were included as part of the basic design. The study covered a three-year period and analyzed 872 incidents taken from daily group school and individual tutoring sessions. The incidents were judged on a behavior scale and were then statistically analyzed to determine whether change in the direction of greater learning and adjustment had occurred.

Significant change having been established, the incidents were reanalyzed to investigate what factors had made them come out as they had. A clinically descriptive method was evolved wherein determinants were isolated, classified and categorized. Among other implications of the overall study, it was felt that this method for descriptively analyzing determinants of behavior and change might be used in other settings and with different groups of patients or pupils. This method appears to offer a tool for qualitatively assigning weights to the particular patterns of response of individuals or groups of subjects.

The emphasis in this report was largely placed on those determinants of an incident which arose in part or in whole from the school program itself: its methods, materials, subject matter and teacher personality. Although it was observed by this descriptive method that the large majority of the determinants for incidents arose in the personality of the child himself, it was felt that where the school determined the outcome of an incident the data revealed clues concerning the use of material, subject matter, methods and teacher personality. These clues were felt to have implications for the teaching of hyperaggressive children, in general, even outside the more controlled total therapeutic residential setting reported on in this study.

An Experiment in Educating Emotionally Disturbed Children

E. Lakin Phillips and Norris Haring

One of the strongest considerations of practical school administrators is whether or not the cost of special classes and programs for the education of emotionally disturbed children should be the responsibility of the school. The cause for concern has been real. In many instances the special classes have proved expensive. This has been true even in cases where little improvement has been seen in the child's behavior and academic achievement. It is believed, however, that school administrators could accept special programs if the cost were within reason and if the program could demonstrate its worthwhileness in educational rehabilitation. If educators of exceptional children are to renew their assertions that public school systems can and should assume the responsibility of the education of these children, they must demonstrate that children in these classes can make substantial educational and behavioral gains.

The education methods described in this book were subjected to experimentation for the purpose of objectively testing their effect upon children with disordered emotional development. This chapter is a report of this study, which was initiated four years ago in Arlington County, Virginia, near Washington, D.C.

EXPERIMENTAL PROCEDURE

The experiment was conducted in nine elementary schools in the Arlington County Public Schools.[1] The children in the study were moderately to severely emotionally disturbed and had reflected their disturbance in a wide range of behavior symptoms. These children had provoked frequent hours of case conferences, involving ten to fifteen highly paid professionals, with little improvement resulting in the children. They were children who were selected—by the aid of the files and personal knowledge of the coordinator of special education, principals, supervisors, teachers, visiting teachers, and school psychologists—as children who had presented serious and protracted problems.

[1]John W. Asher of the School of Education, University of Pittsburgh, and John de Jung, Bureau of Child Research, University of Kansas, served as statistical consultants.
From *Educating Emotionally Disturbed Children,* by Norris Haring and E. Lakin Phillips. Copyright © 1962. McGraw-Hill Book Company. Used by permission.

The Arlington County Public Schools assumed the obligations of developing ways to cope with the classroom behavior of these children and of providing an educational program suitable to their needs. The administration and the board of education of the school system had a sincere interest in seeking more practical and effective ways of educating these children and offered their full cooperation. In the effort to study the problems, three different methods of teaching and three grouping situations were utilized.

SELECTION CRITERIA

All of the children were referred on the bases of their behavior and educational performance as observed by teachers, school psychologists, and supervisors. The general diagnosis of emotional disturbance was required before final selection was made. This diagnosis was made by the diagnostic staff, consisting of the coordinator of special education, the school physician, the chief psychologist, the director of speech and hearing, the chief school social worker, and each child's teacher. Each child considered by the diagnostic staff had had complete neurological, speech, hearing, pediatric, and psychological evaluations. The teachers' observations and the psychologist's report were important influences in the final selection of the children. Although the neurological evaluations of the children did not reveal positive signs, the possibility that some of the children in this experiment had organic brain pathology cannot be entirely precluded.

Specifically, the following four criteria were used for selection of the children:

1. Hyperactive, distractible, attention-getting behavior; withdrawn, uncooperative behavior; or tendencies to both
2. Average or near average intelligence (with the recognition, however, that tested intelligence might be an underestimate owing to the emotional disturbance)
3. Presence in the school at least one year (preferably two) before the referral, with educational retardation of one year (preferably two)
4. The likelihood that the parents could and would cooperate, attend parent group meetings, and generally support the school's efforts

Since the study was done with elementary-age children, grade levels 2 to 5, an implicit criterion was that the referred child be in the research study at least one year, preferably two, before going on to junior high, in order that time for follow-up would be available before the child moved from the elementary school level.

TEACHING METHODS AND SETTINGS
FOR THE THREE GROUPS

Description of Group I (structured)

There were three groups of emotionally disturbed children with, for the first year, fifteen children in each group. The children in Group I were placed in two special classes. One was a primary class (aged seven to nine), the other an intermediate class (aged nine to eleven). These classes provided a highly structured, stimuli-reduced educational setting. The teachers closely followed the general aim of increasing order and structure. . . . Preliminary conferences with the teachers were held by the psychologist, and weekly conferences with the teachers and observations of the classroom climates were carried on by the coordination of special education and the project psychologist throughout the first year. As the teachers became acquainted with the structured methods and were settled into the routine, less supervision of their techniques was necessary. The following are some of the educational procedures used with Group I.

Assignments and skill limits of each child. Assignments were determined initially on the basis of intellectual and achievement tests and on the basis of information in each child's personal file. Modifications of assignments were necessary in cases where, for example, a child disliked arithmetic or was especially poor in spelling. The children often tried to postpone work on disliked subjects or acted as if they did not understand directions sufficiently well to proceed on their own. To remedy these conditions, assignments were made very brief and clear; a close, consistent follow-through was then maintained by the teacher. As the teacher got the feel of each child's attitudes and work skills, she gradually gave the child more independence in his work. Piece by piece, day by day, these tolerances and limits were extended.

Seating and movement limits. In addition to regular seats in the classroom, there were two small work tables, about 2½ by 5 feet, and five "offices," or booths. The booths were used to enable the children to work under a minimum of distracting conditions, to increase the tolerance for independent work, and to handle restless, hyperactive, and socially disturbed behavior. The booths, which lined one wall of the classroom, were about 3½ by 3½ feet with a movable chair and fixed table-level desk across the back of each. Sometimes children stored supplies in the booths as well as in the assigned desk each had in the center of the classroom.

Play and recreational limits. Children were held to the completion of assigned work before play or recreational opportunities were available. Most of the academic work was done in the morning; physical education, art, music, and free play periods came in the afternoon *provided* a child's work was up to par. Brief periods allowing for free play with art materials or clay were sometimes sandwiched in during the morning work periods if the child had completed work assigned to him. Care was exercised not to allow the recreational pursuits to crowd out assigned work, and assigned work had a constant, first-order priority at the beginning of each school day.

Free moving privileges. Free moving privileges included access to the rest rooms, moving about in the classroom, moving from group to individual desk work, occasional errands to the school office, and getting in line for lunch. Children asked permission to leave the room. Tasks and errands were distributed weekly among the children, so that all got a chance to carry on "official business" with the school office. The children were free to move from desk to booth to work bench provided a move was closely related to the assigned work. Free roaming about, or movement in lieu of doing work, was kept to a minimum. To preclude the development of fatigue, the group would be taken at appointed times for a walk and thus be allowed a "seventh-inning stretch" during the morning work period. Water in the classroom sink was kept off; art materials were kept under cover so as to minimize distraction. The children knew these materials were available after they qualified to use them, and it did not take long to establish these elementary limits concerning the use of supplies.

Social-emotional conduct limits. Some of the children provoked others unrelentingly, especially at first. Others often came to school "in a bad mood" and hypersensitively interpreted classroom problems personally. They displayed attitudes characterized by refusal to work, to communicate, to participate. In these situations, which were difficult to control effectively and constructively, several guidelines helped. The teachers did early what they would normally be required to do later in the way of setting behavior limits; they did not participate with a child who was upset, i.e., become involved in his upset, but instead gave him time to calm down first, gave one warning, and then acted; isolation was normally the preferred and most effective technique when a child's behavioral disturbance adversely affected others; and a specific emphasis was always placed by the teacher on solution or resolution of a problem in preference to queries as to why the child behaved as he did.

In the conferences each week with the coordinator of special education and the project psychologist, the teachers would discuss accumulated instances of problems they had handled well and those they felt they had not coped with successfully. It was helpful to have contrasting success-failure instances for discussion; in time, this procedure cut down on the failure instances and increased the confidence of the teachers that they could deal with most problems that might be presented. It was simply a matter of successive approximations to more desirable and constructive solutions to problems, both academic and social-emotional. The general guidelines to increasing or firming up structure were held to. The specific solutions to problems fell under this general aim, but it was often necessary to shift and maneuver, to roll with the punches, in order to keep the structure both firm and flexible.

Parent discussion groups. The parents of children in Group I were invited to meet with the teacher and psychologist on an average of once a month for the first year of the study. Only four parent meetings were held in the second year, and only four in the third year. . . .

Description of Group II (regular grades)

The children of Group II were in regular classrooms in six elementary schools in the county. The teachers used methods of teaching emotionally disturbed children generally employed in a regular class setting. The parents were brought into the situation by the teacher as incidents of a child's behavior became disturbing. Nearly all known techniques for coping with behavior problems in a classroom were used from time to time. All school personnel regularly appointed for the responsibility of helping the school with learning and behavior disorders, such as the psychologist, visiting teacher, school physician, nurse, helping teacher, elementary supervisor, and remedial reading teacher, were available for helping the teachers. In addition, regular monthly school staff conferences were held with all school personnel involved in these cases. It was not unusual to have ten to fifteen highly paid professional staff members involved in hours of conference over one child.

Teaching methods and materials. To the extent that was possible, the children assigned to the regular classes were given the regular curriculum used in grades 1 to 5. With this range as a reference base, the teachers made every effort to understand the emotional problems of the children and made all the modifications in their classes which could be permitted. The following considerations were uppermost in the practices of the teachers of the children in Group II:

1. All assigned work was well within the child's ability.

2. Wherever possible, the school work was modified to suit the child's interest.

3. The child was given experiences in which he could find success.

4. The child was given opportunities to find accomplishments and recognition.

5. Extra privileges and responsibilities were provided in order to give the child attention.

6. Punitive responses to the child's aggressive, rebellious behavior were avoided by the teachers.

Description of Group III (permissive)

The fifteen children in Group III were assigned to a special class. The children in this class, like the children in the regular classes, had available the services of the psychologist, physician, visiting teacher, nurse, helping teacher, elementary supervisor, and remedial reading teacher. The teacher of Group III had some experience in and educational background for teaching children with emotional disorders.

The following teaching methods, curriculum, and classroom environment comprised the educational setting for this group:

1.   The curriculum was modified to suit the interests of the children.

2.   The teacher reflected friendliness and warmth with the children.

3.   An atmosphere of relative permissiveness was established, so that the children felt free to express their feelings and anxiety.

4.   The teacher recognized the children's feelings and reflected these feelings back to them.

5.   When limits were set, the teacher still made sure that the children's feelings were accepted and reflected back.

6.   The teacher believed in the importance of meeting the real emotional needs of the child, not only the material, academic needs.

To repeat briefly, Group I was in a highly structured special class environment with a prepared sequence of academic tasks. The tasks were assigned and completed. The structure was relaxed gradually to permit the development of more individual initiative, but a generally firm and nonpermissive structure was held to throughout the period reported on herein. Children in Group II were in fifteen regular classrooms; the necessary modifications were made for teaching these children within that context, but the curriculum and methods were similar to those used with undisturbed children. Group III had a comparatively nonstructured, permissive special class setting. The more conventional educational methods for emotionally disturbed children were utilized. The idea that children must act out their "unconscious conflicts" was prevalent. Thirty emotionally disturbed children were assigned to Groups I and II randomly. The chronological age of the children in these two groups ranged from seven to twelve years. It was not possible to assign the children to Group II completely at random because of the location of the special class. The children in Group III ranged in age from ten to twelve years.

RESULTS SHOWN BY TESTING IN FIRST YEAR

Before-and-after tests of academic achievement and behavior were administered to the three groups in the first year of the program. A testing design involving repeated measurements of the same subjects was employed in comparing the three groups in terms of both achievement scores and behavior ratings. A comparison of the three groups with regard to academic achievement, as measured by the California Achievement Test, will be considered first.

The grade levels reported for the children were assessed at the beginning and at the end of the school year on the CAT. Data on the three groups from this analysis are presented in Table 1.

Both the CAT and the Behavior Rating Scale (BRS) were administered the first week in November and again the first week in May (approximately six months later). The BRS (see Appendix C) was developed by the authors to measure change in overt behavior. The 5-point rating scale consisted of twenty-seven items. The judge rated each child from 1 to 5 on each item of tested behavior. Four teachers were used as judges. The judge observed and rated the children (A) in the classroom, (B) on the playground with supervision, and (C) in play activities without supervision. The ratings in the above three settings were pooled for each item.

Analysis of Academic Achievement

In examining the data, our principal focus was upon gain scores. For academic achievement, gain scores were computed simply by subtracting each pupil's beginning CAT score from the score he earned the following spring The three behavior ratings (A, B, and C) were combined into a total behavior score for both the initial and final testings. The behavioral gain score for each pupil was the difference between his initial and final composite behavioral scores. Moderately low negative correlations between initial and gain scores were found for both the CAT and behavior rating data; correlations of $-.18$ and $-.35$, respectively.

TABLE 1
SUMMARY DATA FOR TESTS OF MEAN DIFFERENCES AND HOMOGENEITY OF VARIANCE FOR CAT GAIN SCORES MADE BY EMOTIONALLY DISTURBED PUBLIC SCHOOL CHILDREN IN THREE DIFFERENT INSTRUCTIONAL SETTINGS

Group	N	$\bar{D}$	$\sigma\bar{D}$	$\sigma\bar{D}_1 - \bar{D}_2$	t	F
I	15	1.973	1.198	.381	2.50*	2.40
II	15	1.020	.773			
I	15	1.973	1.198	.348	3.68†	9.21†
III	14	.693	.394			
II	15	1.020	.773	.239	1.37	3.84*
III	14	.693	.394			

* Significant at the .05 level of confidence.
† Significant at the .01 level of confidence.

Our interest was in comparing the effectiveness of the methods used in each group. The mean differences between each pair of groups in gain scores for the academic (CAT) and for the behavioral (ratings) measures were tested for significance by means of t ratios. The significance of differences between the variances of the gain distributions for each piar of groups was examined in terms of F ratios. These analyses are summarized in Tables 1 and 2.

As is evident in Table 1, Group I pupils achieved the greatest gain scores in CAT over the six-month initial-final testing period. The mean gain score for Group I is significantly higher at the .05 and .01 levels of confidence than are scores for either Groups II or III, respectively. The differences between the mean gain scores of Groups II and III do not differ significantly at the .05 level of confidence. The average gain score of 1.973 for Group I compares very favorably with expected gain scores for normal school children of comparable ages.

The F values in the right column of Table 1 are derived from differences in the variabilities of the gain scores within groups for each of the three comparisons made. There is greater variability of the CAT gain scores among the pupils in Group I than there is among pupils in either of the other groups. Gain scores of pupils in Group III vary the least, significantly less (at the .01 and .05 levels of confidence, respectively) than those for pupils in Groups I or II. Apparently the Group I treatment is more differentially supportive, i.e., though all the pupils made some gain, some made much more than others, resulting in a much larger variance for that group.

The relative gains of the three groups of emotionally disturbed children may be seen graphically in Figure 1. The youngest child in Group III was ten years, two months; in Group I, six years, nine months; and in Group II, seven years. The initial difference in grade level on the CAT between Groups I and III was approximately 3 years and two months. This difference was reduced in six months to just less than two years. The gain in Group II was a year, which is reasonably good considering the lack of modifications and individual attention available in the regular classroom.

The summary data for the analysis of the BRS scores for the three groups of emotionally disturbed children are presented in Table 2. As was the case for the CAT scores, Group I children again exhibited the greatest gains in the six-month interval. The t ratios based on the comparisons of the mean gains in behavioral rating scores of this group with those of Groups II and III were significant in both instances at the .01 level of confidence. The Group II mean behavior rating remained practically constant over the six-month observational period. The mean gain in Group III ratings, somewhat less than half of the gain for Group I, was significantly greater than that for Group II (at the .05 level of confidence).

None of the *F* tests for homogeneity of variance were found to be significant at the .05 level of confidence. Apparently there is approximately the same variability in individual pupil behavioral rating gains within each of the groups. Group II showed a negligible mean gain; approximately one-half of the children in this group received lower behavioral ratings after six months.

FIGURE 1.

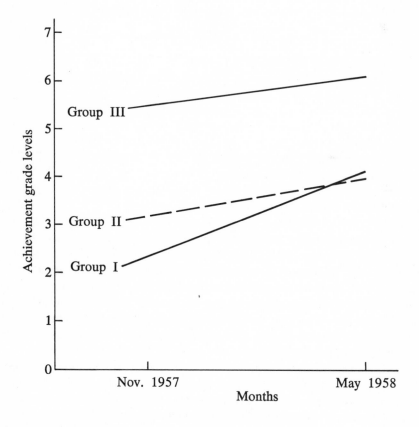

	Pre $\overline{X}$	Post $\overline{X}$	$\overline{D}$
Group I (structured)	2.19	4.16	1.97
Group II (regular grades)	3.03	4.05	1.02
Group III (permissive)	5.36	6.06	0.70

PRE- AND POST-TESTING RESULTS ON CAT TESTS BY GROUPS I, II, AND III

The relative gains of the three groups of emotionally disturbed children are graphically represented in Figure 2. It is to be remembered that the children in Group III are approximately two years older on the average than the children in Groups I and II. The mean initial behavioral rating for Group I was 4.00 rating points less than that for Group III. Six months later the difference in mean behavioral ratings between these two groups was less than one rating point. As is further apparent from Figure 2, the mean behavioral rating for Group II remained practically constant over the six-month period.

TABLE 2

SUMMARY DATA FOR TESTS OF MEAN DIFFERENCES AND HOMOGENEITY OF VARIANCE FOR BRS GAIN SCORES MADE BY EMOTIONALLY DISTURBED PUBLIC SCHOOL CHILDREN IN THREE DIFFERENT INSTRUCTIONAL SETTINGS

Group	N	$\bar{D}$	$\sigma\bar{D}$	$\sigma\bar{D}_1 - \bar{D}_2$	t	F
I	15	5.607	2.717	.985	5.42†	1.19
II	15	.273	2.489			
I	15	5.607	2.717	.888	3.59†	2.37
III	14	2.421	1.760			
II	15	.273	2.489	.835	2.57*	1.99
III	14	2.421	1.760			

* Significant at .05 level of confidence.
† Significant at .01 level of confidence.

SUMMARY AND DISCUSSION

From a practical standpoint, the children who were placed in the structured, academically programmed special class showed an increase in academic achievement and behavior adjustment. It can be argued that these are only overt changes and that the child still has within him the same disturbing feelings, fears, and anxieties, which must be brought out and resolved in order to effect real changes in the child's adjustment. It is not possible to say whether this assertion is true or not. It can be said, however, that the children who were placed in the experimental class showed improvement in that they were (a) more constructive and tractable in the classroom and the home, (b) eager to learn and to accomplish academic tasks, (c) significantly higher in school progress as a whole, and (d) able to complete assigned chores in the home. In general their system of behavior became better organized. They became more goal-oriented with much less meaningless, random behavior.

This experiment demonstrates to public school administrators first that special classes can be productive in the education of emotionally disturbed children and that the cost need not be out of proportion with that of educating these children in regular classes. When one considers the amount of time normally required of the high-salaried professional school personnel by these children when in regular classes, the special program is not markedly more expensive. In addition, the special class is not considered a permanent place for the majority of these children.

FIGURE 2.

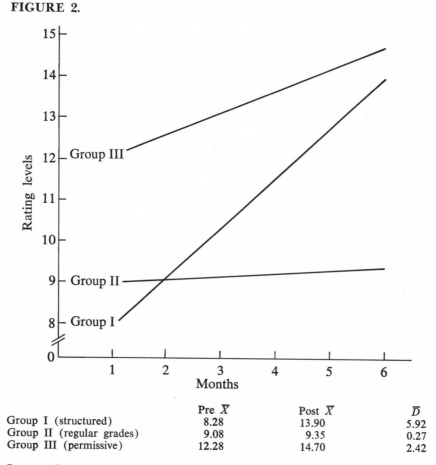

	Pre $\bar{X}$	Post $\bar{X}$	$\bar{D}$
Group I (structured)	8.28	13.90	5.92
Group II (regular grades)	9.08	9.35	0.27
Group III (permissive)	12.28	14.70	2.42

PRE- AND POST-TESTING RESULTS ON BEHAVIOR RATINGS BY GROUPS I, II, AND III

The advantages of a structured type of classroom environment for meeting the needs of emotionally disturbed children exceed those of the other types discussed above, and exceed the expectations of the authors and school personnel involved in this study. Thus, the study also showed that a teacher can successfully teach a class of the type of youngsters studied herein provided she has instruction, direction, and support from experienced psychologists, special educators, and principals. Good teaching is the model to follow; it involves knowledge of each child's potentialities and the ability to give the specific direction necessary for the child's growth and progress. A structured classroom is one in which clear direction, firm expectations, and consistent follow-through are paramount; this is presumably a healthy state of affairs for normal children, as well as necessary for optimal growth of emotionally disturbed children.

section 7

THE SCHOOL:
hope for the future

The preceding section reminded us that the classroom is a place to learn. What the child learns in a classroom is not limited to language arts, mathematics, and social studies. He also learns other skills that hopefully will help him master himself and his environment. He learns attitudes, values, ethics, social behavior, and psychological defenses.

This broad learning that takes place in and around the classroom makes school a potent factor in our effort to build emotional strength into our children. Schools are beginning to respond to the challenge. Fostering mental health does demand additional work from the teacher. It demands that the teacher increase his awareness of psychological factors in the classroom. Behavioral interactions between teacher and student and between student and student must be understood and used by the teacher. Such understanding requires more effort from the teacher and perhaps even more time. But teachers who have begun to take charge of this frequently ignored dimension of classroom experience report that the class eventually becomes more responsive and therefore easier to teach. The children begin to see their classroom as a place where *all* learning is important and useful to them.

Fortunately, many teacher-training institutions are becoming increasingly aware of the need to prepare teachers to guide emotional learning. Perhaps the future will see a corps of teachers who are more adequately trained for this part of their work.

Will the conscious promotion of mental strength by the schools serve our needs sufficiently? Is this the answer to the psychological difficulties that plague modern man? The National Association for Mental Health estimates that one out of ten citizens of the United States suffers from "some form of mental or emotional illness." The school

235

very likely can supply only part of the answer. Answers to complex problems can be equally complex, but finding any part of the answer is crucial in working out the solution. The school alone will not suffice, but it has its part to play.

Prediction of Outstanding Performance, Delinquency, and Emotional Disturbance from Childhood Evaluations[1]

Emmy Werner and Elizabeth Gallistel

This study of special outcomes presents one way of evaluating the predictive effectiveness of pupil responses to inventories and of teacher's ratings in an eight-year study of children's adjustment in a rural county in southwestern Minnesota (1).

PROCEDURE

In 1950 a large number of tests were given to over three thousand school children in this county, all those from grade 4 through grade 12. Inventories to which the pupils responded covered family attitudes, social responsibility, social maturity, home chores performed, range of leisure time activities, pleasant-unpleasant orientation, and psychoneurotic symptoms. In addition, the teachers rated each pupil on 20 personality characteristics (Personality Profile) and on the Havighurst check list of responsible behaviors (Teacher Check List). On the basis of internal consistency, items from these measures were then selected to form a shorter instrument, the Adjustment Inventory. A new responsibility measure was developed from items of the 1950 measure of social

[1]This study has been supported in part by research grant M-690 from the National Institute of Mental Health, U.S. Public Health Service, and in part by funds from the Institute of Child Welfare, University of Minnesota. The principal investigators are J. E. Anderson and D. B. Harris. A major portion of this report was presented at the 1959 meeting of the Society for Research in Child Development.

responsibility and the Teacher Check List which discriminated between young people nominated as very responsible and others thought of as irresponsible. The sentence completion measure, the chores liked, and the Personality Profile were also shortened by including only items which had discriminated in an item analysis.

These revised measures, together with a new Family Attitude scale used by the University of Minnesota's Rural Sociology Department, were given in 1954 to all school children ($N = 3,500$) in grades 4 through 12 in the same county.

In 1958 all youngsters from this population who had become delinquent (146) and all who had received public recognition, special positions, or honors (136) were identified. In addition, social workers, school nurses, the probate judge, and the medical clinic provided the names of 18 young people, 13 girls and 5 boys, who had become emotionally disturbed.

RESULTS

The tentative base rates estimated from these referrals and nominations within the county are low. They are, however, based only on young people in their teens and early twenties. For outstanding performance, they are 32 per 1,000 for females, 28 per 1,000 for males. For delinquency based on the number of *individuals, not* on the number of offenses, they are 15 per 1,000 for females, 85 per 1,000 for males, 20 per 1,000 of these for repeated major delinquencies. For those diagnosed as emotionally disturbed, they are 6 per 1,000 for females and 2 per 1,000 for males. There are two reasons for the small size of the emotionally disturbed group: first, it was impossible to determine how many had sought help through a private physician and/or hospital outside the county; second, most of the young people in our study are still below the age at which severe emotional disorders and the major psychoses commonly have their onset.

The mean scores for each of the special groups on the predictor variables are shown in Table 1. They are stanines or standard scores which permit the comparison of a given youngster in a special group with the average for all pupils in the county of his age and sex. The population mean is 5, and the standard deviation, 2.

Both the outstanding boys and the outstanding girls are differentiated by the largest number of predictors. These young people scored significantly higher than their agemates on measures of intelligence and socioeconomic status, on Family Attitudes, Responsibility, Social Maturity, and the Adjustment Inventory. Their teachers rated them above the average on the Personality Profile and the Teacher Check List.

In contrast, boys and girls in the group who later encountered trouble were differentiated by fewer predictor variables. Those who were to become delinquents, both boys and girls, had significantly lower than average scores on measures of socioeconomic status and on the 1954 Responsibility measure. Delinquent *boys* had, in addition, below average ratings on *all* our teacher instruments and on the 1954 Adjustment Inventory. Boys with a record of repeated major delinquencies (rape, burglary, bodily assault with knife, etc.) had considerably lower scores on more predictors than the other delinquent groups. The teachers' evaluations of the *girls* who became delinquent, though low, were not significant for this size sample. These girls, however, did score significantly lower on the 1950 Family measure describing home practices having to do with trust, sharing decisions, and closeness.

TABLE 1

MEAN STANINE SCORES OF OUTSTANDING, DELINQUENT, AND EMOTIONALLY DISTURBED GROUPS ON PREDICTOR VARIABLES

(Means of all members of sample = 5)

Predictor Measures	OUTSTANDING		DELINQUENT		EMOTIONALLY DISTURBED Girls
	Boys	Girls	Boys	Girls	Girls
IQ (1950)	6.9*	7.2*	5.2	5.3	4.7
SES Measures					
Sewell (1950 SES)	6.7*	6.7*	4.2*	4.3	4.0*
Personal Data (1954 SES) ...	7.3*	7.1*	4.1*	3.3*	4.5
Father's Education	6.6*	6.2*	5.1	3.9*	4.9
Mother's Education	6.6*	6.6*	4.9	3.9*	5.0
Teacher Ratings					
Personality Profile (1950)	5.9*	5.9*	3.8*	4.4	3.9*
Teacher Check List (1950) ...	5.8*	6.0*	4.0*	4.2	5.0
Personality Profile (1954)	6.6*	6.2*	3.8*	4.3	3.4*
Pupil Inventories					
Family (1950)	6.6*	6.2*	4.7	4.1*	5.6
Social Responsibility (1950) ..	6.0*	5.4	4.5	3.8*	4.8
Responsibility (1954)	6.2*	5.8*	4.2*	4.1*	4.1*
Social Maturity (1950)	5.6*	5.8*	4.8	4.8	4.0*
Adjustment Inventory (1954) ..	6.2*	6.0*	4.0*	4.6	4.2
Not Significant					
Leisure Time Activities (1950)	4.7	5.0	4.9	5.8	4.9
Psychoneurotic Indicators	5.1	5.2	4.9	5.0	5.6
Home Chores (1950)	4.7	4.5	5.1	4.8	4.6
Sentence Completion (1954) ..	5.2	4.8	4.9	4.4	4.4
Likes (1954)	4.5	4.4	4.8	4.8	5.4
Family Attitudes (1954)	5.0	5.1	4.7	5.3	5.1

NOTE.—The number of cases varies as follows: outstanding boys 40–61, girls 45–69; delinquent boys 80–97, girls 13–18; emotionally disturbed girls 7–16. There were not enough disturbed boys to test for significance of differences.

* Significant at the .05 level or better.

The emotionally disturbed on whom we have information have significantly lower scores on a measure of rural socioeconomic status. This might, however, have been an artifact of our sampling since we used agency referrals and the county clinic. Table 1 shows only the scores for the girls since the boys' group was not large enough to constitute a sample adequate for statistical analysis. The disturbed girls scored low on the 1954 Responsibility measure and a measure of personal habits, reflecting social maturity. Their teachers rated them significantly lower than their classmates on the Personality Profile, both in 1950 and in 1954.

None of the special groups differed significantly from the population average in the number of chores performed at home and the number of leisure time activities. Fears and worries from the Psychoneurotic Inventory did not predict membership in any of the special groups, not even the emotionally disturbed. We should remember, however, that these tests were taken in middle childhood or early adolescence and that much research needs still to be done to isolate the signs predictive of psychoneurotic behavior in children in contrast with those known of adults.

The 1954 Family Attitude measure did not significantly differentiate any of the special groups, though the 1950 Family measure did. The 1950 Havighurst instrument contained many items of a *specific* nature covering home practices while the 1954 Family measure asked for a *general* expression of positive or negative attitudes toward family members. This evaluation might be more strongly influenced by the temporary emotional state of the youngster, especially an adolescent trying to liberate himself from home.

The differences in the results of these measures point up some of the problems in the evaluation of the relation between certain areas of early adjustment and later outcome. It may be, for example, that there are a number of psychoneurotic signs which can be reliably pinpointed in childhood, but that the form or content of our questions in this area were inadequate. Similarly, it may be that some way of measuring the affect tone of children's responses to a sentence completion measure could be found which would be significantly related to later adjustment, but, though a great deal of research effort was devoted to developing the scoring procedure used for this semiprojective measure, no significant differences were found in these scores for special group members. Both the Sentence Completion and the Likes measures had been found to have diagnostic value, but they had no significant relation to later outcome. There is some indication that they might be unduly influenced by temporary emotions.

Since IQ and SES had differentiated the special groups from the population average, we wondered whether the other measures were significant only because of their relation to those two variables or whether some of the predictors would differentiate members of a special group from agemates of the *same* intelligence and socioeconomic status. Consequently, we tested for significance of difference on all predictors after control for SES and IQ by careful matching and analysis of variance (Table 2).

The Personality Profile proved to be the instrument which most consistently predicted members of special groups after control for IQ and SES, differentiating outstanding members of both sexes, emotionally disturbed girls (no sample for boys), and delinquent boys. It failed to differentiate the delinquent girls whose sample was quite small. The 1954 Responsibility measure differentiated both boy and girl delinquents. A few other variables (parents' education, social maturity) were occasionally significant.

TABLE 2

PREDICTOR VARIABLES WHICH DIFFERENTIATED SPECIAL GROUPS AFTER CONTROL OF INTELLIGENCE AND SOCIOECONOMIC STATUS BY MATCHING AND ANALYSIS OF COVARIANCE

Variables	OUTSTANDING		DELINQUENT		DISTURBED
	Boys	Girls	Boys	Girls	Girls
Personality Profile (1950)	0	0	−	0	−
Personality Profile (1954)	+	+	−	0	−
Teacher Check List (1950)	0	0	−	0	0
Responsibility (1954)	0	0	−	−	0
My Jobs MI (Maturity Index) ..	0	0	−	0	0
Father's Education	+	0	0	−	0
Mother's Education	0	0	−	0	0

+, significant at .05 level or better *above* the mean of control group.
−, significant at .05 level or better *below* the mean of control group.
0 , not significantly different from control group.

Finally, we sought to discover whether these instruments singly or in combination constituted an adequate screening instrument around which a preventive program might be built. Frequency distributions by outcome for all individuals in each stanine on the significant predictors were obtained for the follow-up group graduating in 1957 where we had information for every child. These indicated that combinations of IQ, SES, teacher ratings, and significant pupil measures were not sufficiently discriminating to serve as a screening instrument for each individual child. Though there were no outstanding youngsters in the lower three stanines and no delinquents in the upper three stanines, there were enough of *both* groups in the middle stanines to reduce the predictive accuracy beyond the point of usefulness as an independent screening instrument. This was true for the boys more so than the girls. Both positive and negative outcomes were more clearly separated for the girls.

SUMMARY AND CONCLUSIONS

1. Scores on a number of pupil inventories and teacher ratings of groups of school children later recognized as outstanding, delinquent, or emotionally disturbed were significantly different from the norms for their age and sex. Singly or in combination, however, they did not prove adequate for predicting outcomes for a particular individual. The best predictor instruments would seem more valuable as supplements to IQ and SES information available in school records than as independent screening instruments.

2. A sizeable proportion of the relation between adjustment measures and later outcomes can be accounted for by intelligence and socioeconomic status.

3. After control for IQ and SES, the single predictor which most consistently differentiated special group members from their agemates was a teacher rating scale, requiring ratings of personality characteristics on a five-point scale. As raters, the teachers had the opportunity to compare characteristic behavior of individual children with their agemates and to sample it in different situations over longer periods of time. The personality dimensions covered by the scale were broad enough to characterize both outstanding, disturbed, and delinquent groups and to be meaningful at each developmental stage—late childhood, adolescence, and adulthood.

4. The measure which most effectively differentiated delinquents of both sexes was a pupil instrument measuring social responsibility. It consisted of short descriptive phrases which had been validated empirically against groups known to be high or low on this specific criterion.

5. Measures reporting the range of recreational activities, the number of chores performed at home, the number of experiences liked, the general "affect" as determined from sentence completion tests, and the number of psychoneurotic symptoms all failed to predict membership in any of the special groups.

Reference

1. ANDERSON, J. E., HARRIS, D. B., WERNER, E., & GALLISTEL, E. A survey of children's adjustment over time. A report to the people of Nobles County. Institute of Child Development and Welfare, Univer. of Minnesota, 1959.

The Influence of School Camping on the Self-Concepts and Social Relationships of Sixth Grade School Children

Jerome Beker

Many public and private school systems across the country have introduced school camping programs, held during the regular school year, as part of the regular curriculum. The research reported here was undertaken to test whether the social and emotional growth of school campers over a given period of time could be shown to exceed that of an otherwise equivalent group of school children who had not had a school camping experience. It was hypothesized that the kinds of growth being studied can be stimulated in and by a social climate that makes it possible for children to exert initiative and self-determination within a context of social awareness and clear limits, and with the assistance of sensitive, understanding but not constricting adult guidance and leadership. In addition, it was hypothesized that school camping, because of the very nature of the situation, tends to (but, of course, need not) provide this kind of social climate.

METHOD

Subjects. The members of 17, sixth grade, Long Island public school classes, predominantly from middle and lower middle class suburban homes, served as Ss in the research. Thirteen of these classes participated in a total of seven school encampments during the period of the study, while the members of the other four classes served as a control group. The control classes were from some of the same schools as those which went to camp, and were scheduled to participate in school camping 4–6 months later during the same school year. All classes involved were heterogeneous with regard to the children's intelligence and socioeconomic level. The scheduling of when each class was to go to camp was determined by the two school systems involved, primarily by chance except in a few instances when teachers' preferences were taken into account. There was some attrition of Ss due to absences on days when tests were administered, and other factors. The final data on self-concepts were based on 261 Ss who had participated in school camping, and 96 controls; slightly fewer Ss were involved in the social relationships part of the study, since a number of Ss who did not complete the Social Distance Scale properly were eliminated. The groups were approximately evenly divided between the sexes.

"The Influence of School Camping on the Self-Concepts and Social Relationships of Sixth Grade School Children," by Jerome Beker, *Journal of Educational Psychology*, No. 51, 352–356. © 1960, American Psychological Association.

Research Instruments.[1] A 47-item check list was developed as a means of studying the self-concepts of the Ss at various stages of the research. Most of the items were original, and the others were chosen from about 100 items being used in other studies. Face validity was determined by the judgments of three trained psychologists so as to include items related to a variety of aspects of the self-concept. Items were approximately evenly divided between those concerned primarily with feelings of competence in individual concerns, and those related primarily to feelings of competence as a social being.

Ss indicated for each statement whether: "This is very much like me," "A little bit like me," or "Not like me at all." Twenty-six of the items were worded in a "positive" way, e.g., "I can usually trust my judgment," and 21 items negatively, e.g., "I get upset too easily." The instrument was pretested on a group comparable to the Ss themselves. The task seemed clearly comprehensible to these children, and their interest was maintained throughout. Illustrative items follow:

I enjoy accepting responsibility.
I expect to be a success some day.
I find it hard to get to know people well.
People expect too much of me.

Social relationships were evaluated through the use of the Classroom Social Distance Scale[2] (Cunningham, 1951). On this check list, Ss indicated one of the five categories for each of their classmates, as follows: "Would like to have him as one of my best friends," "Would like to have him in my group but not as a close friend," "Would like to be with him once in a while but not often or for long at a time," "Don't mind his being in our room but I don't want to have anything to do with him," or, "Wish he weren't in our room." This instrument was administered to the Ss together with the check list described above. To encourage honesty on all instruments used, the Ss were assured that their responses would be seen only by the investigator.

A 20-item camp evaluation check list was developed to compare the encampments as they were perceived by the participants. The items were based on the expressed objectives of the participating schools. Each item stated a feeling about or an opinion of some aspect of the camp experience. Campers were asked to indicate whether the item expressed the way they felt "Almost always," "Sometimes," or "Almost never" during the camp period. Illustrative items follow:

I felt like helping when my help was needed at camp.
I felt that I had a real part in planning the trip.
I felt afraid of the teachers and counselors.

The encampments were also rated by two independent adult observers on a five-point scale for each of four specific variables.

Research Design. The self-concept check list and the Classroom Social Distance Scale were administered to each S three times, at school: on the Friday before he

[1]Copies of the instruments used, as well as full details on other aspects of the research are available in the original project report at the Teachers College Library, Columbia University, New York 27, New York. The title of the document is "The Relationship between School Camp Social Climate and Changes in Children's Self-Concepts and Patterns of Social Relationship," by Jerome Beker, 1959.

[2]Used with permission of the Horace Mann-Lincoln Institute of School Experimentation, Teachers College, Columbia University.

left for camp, on the Monday following his return (an interval of 10 days), and between 10 weeks and 3 months later. The same pattern was followed for the control Ss, except that they spent the week between the first and second administrations in their regular classroom program. Thus any effect due merely to the passage of time or to the repetition of the instrument itself would have been roughly equivalent in the two groups. Neither the teachers of the classes involved, who administered the instruments, nor the Ss themselves were informed of the exact purpose of the study, although most were aware that it was related to the school camping program.

Statistical considerations made it necessary to compare the responses made by each S on each item on the three administrations of the self-concept check list. A changed response by an S on any item was recorded as positive or negative. For example, on an item like "I can usually trust my judgment," a given S might have checked "Not like me at all" on the first administration. If he checked "A little bit like me" or "This is very much like me" on the second administration, this would be scored as a positive shift on that item. In each case, responses on the second and third administrations were compared with those on the first. The same procedure was followed for the Classroom Social Distance Scale, using each S's Self Social Distance scores[3] on the three administrations.

The statistics of binomial probability were applied to the data to determine the statistical significance of the proportion of positive shifts to negative shifts noted on each item. The .05 level of confidence was adopted for this purpose. Thus it was possible to compare the camper group with the control group on the basis of the number of self-concept items that showed statistically significant positive or negative shifts from the first administration to the second, and from the first to the third. Limited comparisons could be based on individual items. The shifts in Ss' Social Distance scores were also compared on the basis of the proportion of positive and negative shifts.

The evaluations and ratings of the encampments themselves were introduced in an effort to provide some insight into what it was about the camp experience that produced whatever significant differences were to appear between the campers and the control group. For this purpose, it was hypothesized that the camp "social climate," viewed in terms of several predetermined variables, would be related to changes in campers' self-concepts and Social Distance scores.

The camp evaluation check list mentioned above provided one of the bases on which the encampments were compared. The items were so phrased that the "positive" or "negative" nature of a response was clearly evident. For example, on the item "I felt bored or confused, and didn't know what I could do," the response "Almost always" was considered to be a negative one. Thus the expectation was that an encampment with an overall positive rating (in this sense) relative to the other encampments would produce a greater positive change in campers' self-concepts and Social Distance scores. Each item was given equal weight.

The two adult observers (the camp director and the investigator) were not directly involved in the program but were on the scene during each of the seven encampments. They rated each encampment on the following: (*a*) How "democratic" were the control or discipline patterns used by the leadership? e.g., was respect shown for the rights and dignity of campers as people? (*b*) How involved were the

---

[3]This is a figure indicating each subject's acceptance of his classmates. For details, see Cunningham (1951).

adult leaders with the campers? How interested were the leaders in the program? Did they care, or were they just doing a job? (*c*) How involved were the campers in planning, problem solving, decision making, and other "executive processes" in the camp community? (*d*) What was the overall feeling tone? i.e., how relaxed, friendly, enthusiastic, cooperative was the group? It was hypothesized that the more positive the ratings of a given encampment on the sum of these four variables, the more positive influence would tend to be exerted on campers' self-concepts and Social Distance scores. Here again, composite ratings were developed by arbitrarily assigning equal weight to each of the four variables. Comparisons were made between the independent ratings made by the two adult observers, and between the ratings by the adults and the evaluations by the children.

RESULTS

Self-Concept. The changes noted on the second administration of the self-concept check list, immediately after the experimental (camp) period, markedly favored the campers over the control group. There were significant positive shifts on many more items by campers of both sexes than by the controls. In general, the experimental group shifted on all items on which the control group shifted, and on numerous others as well. Although an increased number of items showing significant positive shifts appeared for both groups on the third administration, the difference between the groups was even greater and in the same direction. The data are summarized in Table 1. The five items on which the experimental group showed the greatest positive change relative to the change shown by the control group on the second and third administrations follow: I am a dependable person, I have trouble making up my mind, I get upset too easily, I worry about what others think of me, and I have some outstanding abilities.[4] Thus it seemed apparent that, as a group, the children who had gone to camp experienced increased feelings of competence as people to an extent that was not matched by children who had not gone. The effect was not a transient one, but was evident in even greater magnitude after a lapse of more than 10 weeks.

Social Relationships. In the experimental group, a statistically significant proportion of the shifts in Social Distance Scores was positive. This was not true for the control group, although the two proportions were not significantly different from each other. The proportion of positive changes on the third administration was slightly lower for both groups, and still significant only in the case of the camper group. Again the proportions were not significantly different from each other. These results suggest that school camping did have some positive influence on

---

[4]A "positive" shift is a shift in the direction of increased feelings of adequacy, of course, and not necessarily in the direction of increased agreement with what a given item states.

campers' Self Social Distance scores, but the differences between the groups seem too tenuous to serve as the basis for any more certain conclusions. These data are summarized in Table 2.

TABLE 1

NUMBER OF ITEMS SHOWING SIGNIFICANT SHIFTS ON SELF-CONCEPT CHECK LIST
(.05 level of significance; signs indicate direction of shifts)

	NUMBER OF ITEMS SHOWING SIGNIFICANT SHIFTS BY			
SHIFTS	Boys	Girls	Entire group, irrespective of sex	N items showing no signif. shift
First to second administration:				
Exper. group[a]	15+	11+	22+	23[c]
Control group[b]	3+	3+	4+, 1−	42
Reliability of the difference	$p < .01$	$p < .05$	$p < .001$	$p < .001$
First to third administration:				
Exper. group[a]	22+	19+	35+	11
Control group[b]	6+	4+	8+	36
Reliability of the difference	$p < .001$	$p < .001$	$p < .001$	$p < .001$

NOTE.—The difference from the second to the third administration shown by the experimental group was reliable at the .01 level for the number of items showing significant shifts by the entire group and for the number showing no significant shift. It was not reliable at the .05 level for either sex alone in the experimental group, or for any of the four categories in the control group.

[a] $N = 261$.

[b] $N = 96$.

[c] The check list consisted of 47 items. The rows total more than 47 because some items shifted in more than one of the three categories listed.

TABLE 2

SHIFTS IN SELF SOCIAL DISTANCE SCORES
(Only shifts of .05 or more in Social Distance scores are included)

	FIRST TO SECOND ADMINISTRATIONS		FIRST TO THIRD ADMINISTRATIONS	
SHIFTS	Exper. group ($N = 247$)	Control group ($N = 85$)	Exper. group ($N = 247$)	Control group ($N = 85$)
Total number	219	76	232	77
Positive proportion	.68	.61	.61	.52
Significance level	.05	ns	.05	ns

NOTE.—The differences between the proportions of the experimental and control groups were not reliable on either the second or the third administrations.

Social Climate. Positive correlations were found between the ratings of the encampments made by the two observers on each of the four variables discussed above, as follows: (*a*) control or discipline patterns, $r = 0.38$; (*b*) involvement of leaders, $r = 0.55$; (*c*) involvement of campers, $r = 0.65$; and (*d*) overall feeling tone, $r = 0.19$. None of these correlations is statistically significant, however, for the small number of ratings involved, seven by each observer for each variable. The seven encampments were also arranged in rank order according to the totals of the ratings by each observer. The correlation coefficient of these two rank orders is equal to 0.71, but this figure is not statistically significant. The ratings of both adult observers were then combined to provide a composite rank order of the social climates of the seven encampments.

The camp evaluation check lists completed by the campers were used as the basis for another ranking of the encampments. For this purpose, each encampment was rated according to the sum of the net percentage of positive responses on each item.[5] The correlation of this rank order with that of the composite of the adult ratings is 0.93, which is significant at the .01 level even for as small a number of cases as is involved here.

The three encampments rated most highly both by the campers and by the adult observers were compared with the three rated least highly. (The encampment which appeared in the middle of both rank orders was omitted for the purpose of this comparison.) The differences between these two groups in changes in campers' self-concepts and social relationships on either the second or third administration were not reliable.

DISCUSSION

The results suggest that school camping can have a marked positive impact on children's self-concepts and, perhaps, on their social relationships as well. The precise nature and depth of this influence and its specific determinants, however, remain obscure.[6] It is suggested that future research on the determinants consider the variable of program content, in addition to those discussed above. If the specific elements in the school camping experience and climate that tend to promote camper growth can be identified, it may be possible to apply them in the classroom and elsewhere, as well as in camping itself. Thus, an understanding of the impact of school camping may suggest ways of increasing the potency of a variety of educational settings.

SUMMARY

A self-concept check list and the Classroom Social Distance Scale were used to evaluate emotional and social growth of 13 school classes

[5]For example, assume that 60% of the campers on a given encampment gave the positive response on a given item, 30% gave the neutral response, and 10% gave the negative response. A "score" of 50 would be credited to that encampment on that item. The rank order was determined on the basis of the sum of these "scores" for each encampment.

[6]This problem is discussed at length in the complete project report (see Footnote 2).

of sixth graders participating in five-day school camping programs as part of their regular school curriculum. Four non-participating classes provided control subjects. Campers, using a check list, and adult observers rated the "social climate" of each encampment. Rank order ratings by the adults and children correlated closely. Significant and marked positive changes in self-concepts were shown by the campers. The control group did not reflect these changes. The differences were even greater after a lapse of 10 weeks than immediately after the camp experience, suggesting the continuation of growth processes started at camp. There also seemed to be a slight positive influence on campers' social relationships, but the gain was not reliably greater than that of the control group. The results were not related to the "social climates" of the encampments, as rated by adult observers and the campers themselves.

Reference

CUNNINGHAM, RUTH. *Understanding Group Behavior of Boys and Girls.* New York: Bureau of Publications, Teachers College, Columbia Univ., 1951.

When the Mentally Ill Child Returns to School

Norma Haan[1]

Since the psychological professions have only recently recognized the widespread incidence of mental illness in children, it is not surprising that the education profession is unclear about the help which schools can give in the treatment of mentally ill children. In the past, such children were apparently labeled "feeble-minded," "brain-injured," "queer," and so on, and they were either kept at home or placed in special classes or institutions. Now, however, increased sophistication and understanding on the part of psychiatrists and psychologists give hope of recovery for many mentally ill children, and a school experience for them is considered an important part of the treatment plan.

In the past several years the Berkeley public schools have successfully integrated a number of formerly severely disturbed children into a

[1]This article was prepared in collaboration with Emory Curtice, principal of the Thousand Oaks School, Berkeley, California, and the following teachers in the same school: Maxine Greer, Margaret Martindale, and John Rozance.

regular elementary-school setting. This integration has been a co-operative venture, and at every step the planning has involved the teacher, the principal, the school psychologist, the child's therapist, and the parents. Although the particular aspects of school plans for mentally ill children will vary in number as greatly as do the number of children involved, there are probably common aspects of such plans that would have general application.

It is not our intention to go into the facts and theories of why children or adults become mentally ill (1, 2, 4). Suffice it to say that mental illness does occur in children and that some of these children now sit in public school classrooms without being recognized as ill. There are others who are never brought to school. Some children may be removed from school during an acutely disturbed phase but will return later after psychiatric treatment and experience in a special school. This article is concerned with the educational experience of these latter children.

The magnitude of the problem of severely disturbed children is indicated by the statistical report entitled *Outpatient Psychiatric Clinics of the California State Department of Mental Hygiene* (3) for the year ending June 30, 1954. Although this report does not include the many ill children who are never brought to psychiatric clinics, it reports accurately the number of mentally ill children who are brought to such facilities. According to this report, 10.6 per cent of the children discharged from California state psychiatric clinics during 1954 were mentally ill. This figure does not include children whose illness or home situation was such that hospitalization was necessary. The children reported on are those whose social, emotional, and intellectual development has been atypical and who have not come to feel at home in the world or with themselves, for reasons known or unknown. Generally, many of them appear to have great areas of inhibition or pseudo dullness, coupled with a few areas of amazingly sensitive insight. For many of them, the body and its co-ordination are involved in their inhibition, and all of them feel uncomfortable with others, particularly strangers.

The school's part in all this is related to the developmental tasks of childhood, and in this respect mentally ill children are no different from other children. The job of childhood, if not of all mankind, is learning, formally and informally, from parents, teachers, and peers. Children who are mentally ill have been unable, for one reason or another, to utilize effectively the earlier informal education given them by their parents or have found it necessary to utilize it in an atypical way. As a result the imparting of society's teachings in the classroom by peers and teachers becomes all the more vital for them. In our work with disturbed children we have seen that the informal learnings which result from peer-peer interaction and teacher-pupil interaction aid disturbed children to normalize themselves. However, socialization has not been our only goal because all humans find inherent gratification and reassurance in being able to master the facts, reading materials, and figures suitable for one's age group.

A neurotic child can loosely be thought of as a child who has assiduously overlearned some aspects of society's "do's" and "don't's" in order to reduce his anxiety, while a mentally ill child avoids anxiety by underlearning most of the "do's" and many of the "don't's." The child psychiatrist can sometimes successfully treat the neurotic child without co-ordinating his work with his patient's classroom experience. But, with children such as ours, the co-ordination of teacher and therapist seems indispensable; for learning to trust the world—the most primitive and earliest learning experience—goes hand in hand with the usual later learning of the elementary-school child; indeed, they appear inextricably intermixed. Such co-ordination between school and therapist was always present in the case of the children with whom we have had these experiences, and we feel this co-ordination has contributed to the success of our venture.

It is recognized that there are many degrees and stages of disturbance. There are children whose disturbance is so great that they do not belong in public school, not only for the sake of the equilibrium of the school, but also for the reason that adjusting to the irreducible minimum of control and standardization necessary in the public school classroom may constitute too complicated a problem for the ill child to handle. However, we are concerned here with children who, though they had been considered at one time too disturbed to attend public school, came to need the experience that a regular classroom can provide. The decision that the children were ready for such an experience was made by those who had the experience to offer (the teacher and the principal) and by those who had previously been responsible for the development of the child (his parents, his psychiatrist, and special school personnel).

We shall examine our experiences from the standpoint of (1) control and permissiveness, (2) relations with other children, and (3) academic work. We shall try to summarize what seems incredibly intangible, that is, the benefits to the disturbed child.

CONTROL AND PERMISSIVENESS

One of the chief sources of anxiety for any teacher who receives mentally ill children in his classroom is the problem of classroom order and management. Each teacher who has had experience with these children has reported an initial period of experimentation in the process of finding out how much conformity can be required and how much permissiveness must be granted. We have come to call this "playing by ear," because there seems to be no way to communicate from teacher to teacher or from therapist to teacher the amount ·of conformity that can be expected from any particular child. This we have found true for all such children, not only in the beginning of their school experiences, but also when they are being passed from one teacher to the next. It is evident that the interaction among the personalities of the child, the teacher, and the group is a complicated process. For the psychiatrist or psychologist to lay down ground rules in advance may make for constriction and artificiality in this interaction, which is most productive when it is genuine and natural. Furthermore, the amount of conformity that can be expected from these children seems to change with the day, the hour, and the situation. One teacher said that on some days she suggested to a primary-grade child that he put a puzzle away; on another she requested that he put the puzzle away; and on other days she demanded that he put the puzzle away.

Another variable that obviously affects the polarities of conformity and permissiveness is the nature of the particular activity involved. Climbing on cupboards can be dangerous, but talking to one's self is not and only becomes important as a long-range indicator of one's social growth. The question is obviously related to the values placed on classroom behavior, not only in terms of the individual child's safety, but also in terms of his growth, when growth is seen as his increasing ability to relate himself harmoniously and meaningfully to others. Rules and controls are to be learned, not imposed, as part of growth, and the fact that abiding by the rules brings greater adult peace of mind is one of the happy facts of life. We are focusing this discussion largely on the disturbed child and are not thinking of conformity in terms of the group's standard because we have discovered that the group, even when composed of kindergarten children, does not demand conformity from the disturbed child which is identical to that demanded of the group.

Underlying the ups and downs of the disturbed child's conforming or his failure to conform are the slow-moving, but persistent, gains in being willing to do what the teacher asks. Many of these children have found survival in inexorably thwarting the educative attempts of their parents, but in the schoolroom the teacher has powerful allies, not possessed by the parents, in the form of thirty-five children of the same age. Time and again we have seen the other children expect conformity and accomplishment, and win, where an adult would fail. It is evident that the children's unabashed astonishment at nonconformity cannot be effectively operative in a teacher-centered classroom. The effect of other children on the disturbed pupil is somewhat stronger in the upper grades. This fact is related to the older children's stronger orientation toward their peers and weaker orientation toward their teachers. At the same time, the children are generous in their recognition of gains made by the disturbed child; we have heard many comments about how "So-and-so is getting much better." One cannot escape the impression that these comments are not directed merely to the disturbed child's increased conformity but are also astute and sensitive observations of increased psychic well-being.

There is no doubt that a disturbed child can utilize the pressure from his normal peers for a multitude of reasons; the cultural, wide, and impersonal expectation that all children shall go to school to learn is a powerful lever. Our disturbed children have been incredibly pleased and gratified when they knew that they were to attend public school "like other kids." Mentally ill children know that they have problems and that they are disturbed, and the increased normality and health that are implied by regular school attendance must be a reassurance of no small importance. The demands of other children and of that somewhat more impersonal and different adult, the teacher, can sometimes be met a little differently, perhaps, from the way in which the demands of parents have been met. One teacher persuaded a child to give up wearing his rubber pants to school and to use the school lavatory, although previous attempts by the home had been rebuffed. No doubt, too, the inevitable competitiveness in the situation and the meeting of new competitors of one's own age hasten accomplishment through imitation.

Almost all these children have some unusual and eccentric symptoms. For the most part, these symptoms are self-directed; that is, they have personal meaning for the child but are not too obnoxious socially, although they may be irritating. We have in mind such things as making funny noises, rocking back and forth, and being obsessed with prehistoric times, cars, television programs, etc. These seem to operate from the very depths of the child's being. Some symptoms appear when things are unusually upset at home or at school, and they disappear when things are again more comfortable. We do not interfere with the symptoms, but sometimes we try to distract and redirect the child. The symptoms are weather vanes, and, as growth progresses in the school and in therapy, the symptoms disappear.

RELATIONS WITH OTHER CHILDREN

As school is a standardized group situation for the most part, one of the first and most inevitable things a teacher needs to consider is the group's attitude toward the unstandardized, and sometimes unusual, disturbed child. In almost all classrooms we have found it necessary to structure for the group, at some time, something of the nature of the mentally ill child's difficulty and the role of the group members in relation to him. The explanation is best given after the pupils have had some experience with the child. The structuring needs to be done within the specific and limited frame of reference of the particular child and his unusual behavior that is causing anxiety in the group. As seems to be generally true of adult society's fantasized preconceptions about mentally ill people, children's fantasized preconceptions sometimes are far beyond the bounds of reality. Always the teacher's explanations to the group seem best when they are simple, convey his acceptance of the child, and indicate the need for a helping role toward the disturbed child. We have given calm, matter-of-fact explanations, such as, "We are all different, and he hasn't had the chance to learn some of the things, or as many things, as you have yet. Sometimes he gets unhappy, and, when he gets unhappy, he may scream. We must help him."

We have found that intermediate-grade pupils demand more explanations, particularly in regard to their own role, than do primary-grade pupils, who require almost no structuring at all. At the same time, intermediate-grade children play a more active role with the disturbed youngster. One teacher found that other children in the room were much more successful in quieting the disturbed child after an anxiety attack than was the teacher himself. Older children can be used, too, as protective companions for the child when he must temporarily escape the confines of the room.

We have come to believe that the involvement of other pupils with the disturbed child is a most valuable curriculum experience from a number of standpoints. One teacher said that the effect on the other pupils had been one of producing "better citizens because of the real need to share, practice tolerance, show consideration, and realize the worth of each individual. Not many children have this experience made so real to them." Certainly, the concept of the worth of the individual, upon which our democratic philosophy rests, can be made no more clear to children than it is when a teacher accepts a disturbed child and his behavior because the teacher knows that he can do no other in the school situation—a situation which has been constructed and arranged by cultural agreement to produce a modicum of, and an opportunity for, basic cultural uniformity. One teacher said, "I notice the wonderful attitude they have toward me. I can't help but feel that they appreciate the allowances that I have made for the disturbed one. They seem to have this attitude in all activities, and not just those around the disturbed child, which conveys a feeling that they are all working with me and not just for me." To us there seems to be no dichotomy here between disturbed and normal children with regard to making allowances. Rather, the emotional growth of each child is regarded in the same way that intellectual growth has been for so long: "You take the child where he is and go on from there."

Children seem to sense, sometimes more quickly and accurately than do adults, that the child's disturbed behavior comes because he cannot help it. When a teacher scolded one of our disturbed children for not finishing his work, a little girl said, "But, Miss Jones, Tom is much better about finishing than he used to be." Another value for all the children, although probably more subtle, is the reassurance, implicit in the disturbed child's presence and treatment in the classroom that, if they themselves should find themselves in a situation where they can do no other, people will treat them protectively and kindly. Basically, this is a prophylactic principle, because much disturbance in modern society is, in part, the fear of losing control rather than the actual loss of control. No doubt, too, the presence of mentally ill children in ordinary classrooms will aid in the reduction of the stereotypes and fantasies surrounding psychological handicaps, as has been the result of integration programs involving physically handicapped children.

We have had some parental reaction to the presence of these children in classrooms. The parents' questions have been answered satisfactorily in terms of the gains for the class as a whole. Some parents, to judge from their children's comments, have apparently utilized the opportunity to help their children understand differences in people and to suggest an attitude toward the child based first on his being an ordinary person and only secondarily on consideration of his handicap. Most parents have been satisfied with the teacher's explanations, and seem to believe they need feel no concern as long as the teacher and the principal have had no cause to believe that the majority was suffering. Some parents have, without suggestion, fitted into the school's plan by inviting the disturbed child to accompany their own child in out-of-school activities.

ACADEMIC WORK

When a neurotic child has an emotional difficulty which affects his school learning, one can hope that, once his emotional problems are resolved through psychiatric treatment, he will quickly catch up. However, with the sort of child we are discussing, the fact of not learning at all is, in a sense, the primary difficulty. He is in some ways a thing unblossomed, and whatever gains he can make in formal learning at school will aid the blossoming and normalizing process. Furthermore, the recovery process, even under the best conditions, is much longer than for a neurotic child, perhaps four or five years, so that a disturbed child could be hopelessly behind and suffering secondary complications if all academic learning were delayed until his recovery. It is a question whether complete, or even partial, recovery could be obtained without the accompaniment of school learning. However, academic learning is secondary to the group experiences. Learning cannot be forced, although, after some experiences with a particular child, we have found that a little judicious pressure pays dividends.

Disturbed children will not learn unless they are emotionally able, at a particular time, to do so. Inducing them to learn requires the greatest persistence and timing. However, most of these children learn a great deal without seeming to have learned anything. For example, one of them reported at home in great detail and accuracy the content of a social-studies lesson but was seemingly not listening or not understanding at school. One day when a primary-grade child felt in a particularly communicative frame of mind, his teacher asked him to respond to a number of flash cards. He knew all the words that had been taught and none of the others. His teacher had thought he had absorbed nothing up to that point.

ROLES OF OTHER ADULTS

The principal of the school plays a vital role in the school's plan for the mentally ill child. It is he who, first and maybe for some years, has helped in establishing a climate of easy and frank human interaction between himself and staff and between staff and children. This quality of human understanding is characterized in one principal's observation: "If we understood enough about any one child, we would then understand that what he is doing is normal for him in terms of the history of his experiences." The principal's influence is first exercised in selecting teachers who will feel challenged by dealing with these children. It is probably true that being a good teacher is not necessarily synonymous with being an effective interactor with mentally disturbed children.

Our principal was sometimes able to give the teacher assistance. For some children the principal's office can become a haven when on a particular day the group is too stimulating and anxiety-provoking. During the early stages of adjustment to school by one upper-grade child, the child and a classmate arrived in the principal's office. The child was obviously severely agitated, and his classmate said that they would like to talk to the principal. A more or less innocuous conversation followed. After a bit, the two left. The child was calm again, and his classmate gave the principal the Churchillian "V for victory" sign as the two went out the door.

The certain assurance that the authority of the principal will set things straight is useful in reassuring frightened children. Some mentally disturbed children become acutely agitated over minor scratches and injuries. Knowing and understanding the child, the principal and the nurse are able to understand and reduce his terror over this body violation. We have seen our children progress from acute agitation over a sliver to casual indifference.

The secretary and the janitor in our school also have known something of the mentally ill child who is just learning that the world is essentially a safe place, and they have, when occasion demanded, dealt with him as an individual. Other teachers, too, who direct special activities have played roles in helping our children widen their horizons of participation and achievement. Some of the children have gone to other classrooms when they could not or would not participate in the necessary activities (an excursion, for example) in their home rooms.

SUMMARY

We feel that we have had the privilege of sharing in an unusually gratifying and stimulating experience. We have seen growth processes at work that are not different from, but perhaps more clearly basic than, those ordinarily seen in an elementary school. Our participation in them and our contribution to them have seemed great. We shall continue to work with mentally disturbed children. We feel that we have hardly scratched the surface in finding methods and techniques of providing a public school experience for such youngsters.

References

1. BETTELHEIM, BRUNO. *Love Is Not Enough.* Glencoe, Illinois: Free Press, 1950.
2. BETTELHEIM, BRUNO. *Truants from Life.* Glencoe, Illinois: Free Press, 1955.
3. CALIFORNIA STATE DEPARTMENT OF MENTAL HYGIENE. *Outpatient Psychiatric Clinics of California State Department of Mental Hygiene.* Sacramento, California: State Department of Mental Hygiene, June 30, 1954.
4. CAPLAN, GERALD. *Emotional Problems of Early Childhood.* New York: Basic Books, 1955.

Changes in Student Teachers' Attitudes Toward Childhood Behavior Problems

George A. Pinckney

Educators have long been aware of the difficulty teachers have in judging pupil behavior in its true psychological perspective. Teachers have a tendency to overrate the seriousness of behavior problems related to sex, dishonesty, and disobedience, while underrating shyness, sensitiveness, fearfulness, and other behavioral manifestations which do not express pupil antagonism toward authority in the classroom.

Wickman (1928) found that teacher ratings of the seriousness of 50 behavior problems correlated negatively with ratings given by 30 clinicians. Rank-order correlation between the ratings of 28 teachers in Cleveland and the clinicians was found to be −.22, while a group of 511 Minneapolis teachers correlated −.11 with the same 30 clinicians.

This, and similar studies (Amos & Washington, 1960; Gage & Suci, 1951; Gronlund, 1950; Hunter, 1957; Thompson, 1940), have drawn attention to the need for more understanding and education on the part of student teachers concerning the behavior problems of young children. Teacher training institutions have expended considerable quantities of both time and money investigating the most suitable coursework and supervised experience programs to include in their respective curricula.

Twenty years after Wickman's study, Schrupp and Gjerde (1953) replicated the Wickman rating procedure to determine what, if any, progress had been made in teachers' ability to interpret psychological problems manifested in child behavior. They found that differences were still present in teacher-clinician ratings, but that the magnitude of these differences was not as great as it had been in the earlier study.

This closer agreement between the classroom teacher and the clinician can be assumed to have been brought about, in part at least, by the general increase in public knowledge of basic psychological concepts, as well as by the adoption of curriculum policies which require one or more courses in psychology in teacher education programs.

The present study was designed to investigate the extent to which changes in rating of childhood behavior problems are related to the experience in psychology courses for teachers college students.

"Changes in Student Teachers' Attitudes Toward Childhood Behavior Problems," by George A. Pinckney, *Journal of Educational Psychology*, No. 53, 275–278. © 1962, American Psychological Association.

METHOD

Subjects

The experimental group for this study consisted of 203 undergraduate students enrolled in six sections of an introductory educational psychology course in Teachers College, University of Nebraska. The control group was composed of 58 students enrolled in the same college, but who had not taken coursework in any area of psychology. All of the subjects in both the experimental and the control group were planning for careers in the teaching profession.

Procedure

At the first meeting of each section of the educational psychology courses the subjects were presented with a list of 32 behavior traits selected from Wickman (1928). Instructions were given to rank these traits from the most serious to the least serious using a nine-point Q sort technique after Stephenson (1953). A list of the behavior traits under consideration in the present study may be seen in Table 1.

Subsequent course material was presented in the usual manner for the remainder of the semester, with no further mention of the ranking being made. All reference to the Wickman (1928) study was carefully removed from lecture notes, and reading assignments were screened to avoid, as much as possible, any reference to it or similar work.

The subjects in the control group were chosen at random from sections of courses in history and principles of education, and were administered the Q sort with the same instructions as the experimental group.

The same procedures were followed with both the experimental and control groups during the final week of the school year. The Q sorts were scored on a nine-point basis, with the trait ranked as least serious receiving no points. A rank order of trait seriousness based upon mean Q sort scores was established for precourse ratings by both the experimental and the control groups, and a correlational analysis of these was made.

RESULTS

The rankings of the 32 behavior traits, together with mean rating for the experimental and control groups, are shown in Table 1. The results of the correlational analysis of the precourse and postcourse rankings for both the experimental and the control groups are shown in Table 2. A ranking of the 32 behavior traits based on the earlier work of Wickman (1928) and Gage and Suci (1951) was made for the 1928 teachers, 1928 clinicians, and the 1951 clinicians. These results are also included in Table 2.

The precourse ranking of the control group was found to correlate .939 with the experimental groups' precourse ranking of the behavior traits. The precourse ranking of the control group correlated .854 with their own ranking of the traits at the end of the course. The postcourse ranking of the experimental group, however, correlated only .555 with the control groups' postcourse ranking and .608 with their own ranking made prior to the course.

TABLE 1
RANKING OF 32 BEHAVIOR TRAITS

TRAITS	EXPERI-MENTAL PRERANKING		EXPERI-MENTAL POSTRANKING		CONTROL PRERANKING		CONTROL POSTRANKING		1928 TEACH-ERS	1928 CLINI-CIANS	1951 CLINI-CIANS
Stealing	1	(6.48)	5	(6.12)	1	(6.67)	2	(5.94)	2	11.5	11
Cheating	2	(5.52)	14	(5.14)	2	(6.06)	3	(5.87)	7	18.5	20
Destructiveness	3	(5.29)	3	(6.45)	6	(5.35)	5	(5.53)	8	29	14
Untruthfulness	4	(5.28)	8	(5.73)	3	(5.43)	4	(5.59)	5	18.5	19
Cruelty	5	(5.24)	1	(7.45)	4	(5.41)	1	(6.84)	6	6	3
Heterosexual activity	6	(5.11)	9.5	(5.50)	16	(3.87)	6	(5.25)	1	20	21
Disobedience	7	(4.97)	16	(5.08)	5	(5.38)	7	(4.84)	9	26.5	24
Obscene notes	8	(4.96)	22	(4.70)	12	(4.61)	12.5	(4.34)	4	22.5	25
Temper tantrums	9	(4.94)	6	(6.06)	8	(5.12)	16	(3.84)	10	15	10
Profanity	10	(4.94)	23	(4.43)	7	(5.29)	8	(4.65)	11	30	30
Masturbation	11	(4.62)	18	(5.00)	11	(4.64)	15	(3.93)	3	26.5	28
Selfishness	12	(4.56)	15	(5.09)	9	(4.83)	14	(4.03)	19	14	22
Impudence	13	(4.33)	21	(4.75)	13	(4.38)	9	(4.59)	12.5	24	27
Unhappiness	14	(4.15)	2	(6.80)	10	(4.68)	23	(3.30)	17.5	3	2
Overcritical of others	15	(4.10)	17	(5.05)	23	(3.19)	11	(4.47)	29	8	9
Resentfulness	16	(4.07)	7	(5.92)	14	(4.22)	10	(4.50)	20	4	13
Unsocialness	17	(4.03)	4	(6.26)	18	(3.64)	17	(3.72)	26	1	1
Smoking	18	(3.76)	30	(2.85)	27	(2.90)	29	(2.62)	14	32	31
Domineering	19	(3.76)	19	(4.92)	20	(3.51)	12.5	(4.34)	23	10	17
Suspiciousness	20	(3.68)	13	(5.17)	19	(3.55)	18	(3.66)	25	2	5
Easily discouraged	21	(3.56)	9.5	(5.50)	17	(3.68)	19	(3.62)	17.5	7	7
Laziness	22	(3.39)	27	(3.79)	15	(3.90)	24	(3.22)	12.5	25	23
Tattling	23	(3.33)	28	(3.34)	22	(3.29)	21	(3.47)	30	22.5	29
Enuresis	24	(3.13)	25	(4.21)	24	(3.16)	26.5	(2.90)	15	21	16
Nervousness	25	(3.09)	12	(5.30)	25	(3.03)	28	(2.87)	16	16.5	6
Cowardliness	26	(2.98)	24	(4.24)	21	(3.42)	20	(3.61)	22	13	18
Fearfulness	27	(2.93)	11	(5.34)	30	(2.01)	25	(2.97)	24	5	4
Interrupting	28	(2.84)	32	(2.61)	26	(2.97)	22	(3.37)	28	31	32
Tardiness	29	(2.71)	31	(2.68)	28	(2.80)	26.5	(2.90)	21	28	26
Sensitiveness	30	(2.62)	20	(4.91)	29	(2.42)	31.5	(2.03)	31	9	15
Shyness	31	(1.85)	26	(3.81)	31	(1.61)	30	(2.34)	32	11.5	8
Dreaminess	32	(1.53)	29	(3.19)	32	(1.32)	31.5	(2.03)	27	16.5	12

NOTE.—Mean scores on the Q sort are shown in parentheses.

The control group correlated −.152 with the 1951 clinicians on the precourse rankings and −.029 with the postcourse ranking. The experimental group, on the other hand, correlated −.069 with the 1951 clinicians on the precourse ranking and .663 on the postcourse ranking.

The significance of the change of the experimental group from a correlation of −.069 with the 1951 clinicians in the precourse ranking to a correlation of .663 on the postcourse ranking was determined by transforming the rho's to Z values and expressing the differences as a relative deviate of the normal curve as suggested by Wert, Neidt, and Ahmann (1954). This change was found to be significant at the .001

level of confidence. The same change for the control group was found to be nonsignificant.

DISCUSSION

It is apparent from Table 2 that the attitudes of the experimental group toward childhood behavior problems changed to a significant degree. A correlation of $-.069$ was found between this group and the 1951 clinicians on the precourse rankings. The rankings at the end of the course correlated .663, indicating a change was significant at the .001 level of confidence. No such change was apparent in reference to the control group. The precourse and postcourse correlations of the controls with the 1951 clinicians were $-.152$ and $-.029$, respectively.

TABLE 2
INTERCORRELATIONS AMONG GROUP RATINGS ON 36 BEHAVIOR TRAITS

GROUP	1928 CLINICIAN	1951 CLINICIAN	1961 CONTROL (PRE-COURSE)	1961 CONTROL (POST-COURSE)	1961 EXPERI-MENTAL (PRE-COURSE)	1961 EXPERI-MENTAL (POST-COURSE)
1928 teachers	−.340	−.220	.764**	.650**	.816**	.394*
1928 clinicians		.860**	−.063	−.017	−.107	.557**
1951 clinicians			−.152	−.029	−.069	.663**
1961 control (precourse)				.854**	.939**	.603**
1961 control (postcourse)					.901**	.555**
1961 experimental (precourse)						.608**

  * Significant at .05 level.
 ** Significant at .01 level.

The data would tend to substantiate the hypothesis that psychology courses may play a significant role in the formulation of teachers' attitudes toward childhood behavior problems. An integral part of this educative process must certainly be the attitudes which the instructor himself feels are important. These may be expressed formally in class lectures or may be interpreted by students from the less overt behavior patterns of the instructor. Their relative contribution to the total change in attitudes is not known, but it must be assumed that they exert a larger influence on the experimental group than on the controls. This must be kept in mind when interpreting the data of the experimental group.

It may be noted that of the five traits rated as most serious by the 1951 clinicians (unsocialness, unhappiness, cruelty, fearfulness, and suspiciousness) four were among the traits registering the greatest change from precourse to postcourse rankings of the experimental group. The greatest disagreement between the clinicians and the experimental group of the postcourse ranking was found on the traits of shyness, dreaminess, and heterosexual activity.

In conclusion, it seems apparent from the results of this investigation that introductory courses in psychology can meet the needs of student teachers for better understanding of the basic principles of behavior.

References

AMOS, R.T., & WASHINGTON, R. M. A comparison of pupil and teacher perceptions of pupil problems. *J. educ. Psychol.*, 1960, **51**, 255–258.

GAGE, N. L., & SUCI, G. Social perception and teacher-pupil relations. *J. educ. Psychol.*, 1951, **42**, 144–152.

GRONLUND, N. E. The accuracy of teachers' judgments concerning the sociometric status of sixth grade pupils. *Sociometry*, 1950, **13**, 197–225, 329–357.

HUNTER, E. C. Changes in teachers' attitudes toward children's behavior over the last thirty years. *Ment. Hyg., N. Y.*, 1957, **41**, 3–11.

SCHRUPP, M. H., & GJERDE, C. M. Teacher growth in attitudes toward behavior problems of children. *J. educ. Psychol.*, 1953, **44**, 203–214.

STEPHENSON, W. *The Study of Behavior.* Chicago: Univer. Chicago Press, 1953.

THOMPSON, C. E. The attitude of various groups toward behavior problems of children. *J. abnorm. soc. Psychol.*, 1940, **35**, 120–125.

WERT, J. E., NEIDT, C. O., & AHMANN, J. S. *Statistical Methods in Educational and Psychological Research.* New York: Appleton-Century-Crofts, 1954.

WICKMAN, E. K. *Children's Behavior and Teachers' Attitudes.* New York: Commonwealth Fund, 1928.

An Analysis of the Work of the School Mental Health Unit of a Community Mental Health Board

Margaret Morgan Lawrence, Irene J. Spanier, and Mildred W. Dubowy

The School Mental Health Unit, a consultative service to the schools of Rockland County, has been in operation since the fall of 1957. A pilot project in the state of New York, it is county and state supported, and the second agency organized and sponsored by the Rockland County Community Mental Health Board, the first being a treatment center.

"An Analysis of the Work of the School Mental Health Unit of a Community Mental Health Board" by Margaret Morgan Lawrence, M.D., Irene J. Spanier and Mildred W. Dubowy, *The American Journal of Orthopsychiatry*, Vol. 32, 99–108. Copyright 1962, The American Orthopsychiatric Association, Inc., reproduced by permission.

While the Rockland County Center for Mental Health was providing treatment services to children, many situations required communication between Center and school staff. The Center, at that time, was unable to provide adequate communication of this sort. Some of the questions raised which anticipated the need of a consultation service to schools were: What is happening to a troubled child in the classroom? How can we find opportunities to communicate with principals and teachers about this child? How can we help children who need guidance but something less than a therapeutic experience? How can we provide psychiatric, psychological, and casework consultation to school psychologists, school nurse-teachers, and school administrators who ask for it? School administrators, the Vocational Board director, school psychologists, the directors of Rockland State Hospital and of its child guidance clinics, the directors of the Mental Health Center, the Rockland County Community Mental Health Board, and the Community Services Division of the State Mental Hygiene Department, all cooperated in the plans for a mental health consultation service to schools.

In September 1957, the School Mental Health Unit began operation with a half-time psychiatrist, and a full-time clinical psychologist, psychiatric social worker, and secretary.

The School Unit staff had had previous experience in consultation to schools. The Unit thought neither in terms of case finding, nor diagnosis, nor even treatment—but in terms of consultation. It had as its chief concern not even the most seriously disturbed children but all of the children. The Unit's goal was to assist school staff in their work of emotional education, to the end that the level of emotional health of all children would be raised. This was to be accomplished chiefly by helping school staff to a better understanding of the assets and needs of individual children during their development, and of the relationship of teacher attitude to the child's school functioning. The School Unit's services were to be available to the school community of 30,000 children in 9 districts and 54 schools.

The kind of service offered by the School Mental Health Unit was related, as has been described, to the needs of the school community. More specifically it sought to support and catalyze existing psychological programs and provide opportunities for these, through their contact with the work of the Unit, to develop ways of functioning which would contribute more than they had in the past to the emotional health and good performance of the majority of the children. Well-established psychological programs in schools and related to schools provided school psychologists, monthly child guidance clinics (of the Rockland State Hospital and under the able direction of Dr. E. R. Clardy), guidance counselors in high schools, and a testing program offered by the Vocational Education and Extension Board. Psychotherapy under private auspices and publicly supported treatment were available.

In addition to a concern for the early treatment and prevention of mental illness in children, the School Unit hoped to touch the lives of the majority of the county's children in the support of their emotional health. The progress desired was the raising of the individual child's level of emotional health to the end that he might utilize his gifts to best advantage. The Unit said:

We are not satisfied with the functioning of our "normal" children in school. Were we to offer our children's teachers help in becoming aware of the individual child's hidden feelings, strengths, and needs as each makes his hazardous journey along the developmental road, would those who instruct our young be better able to assist them to a higher level of emotional health? Would teachers who join us in the study of children and their assets and needs discover the relationship between their own feelings and attitudes and the ability of children with differing temperamental patterns to be productive in their classrooms? Would a prevailing classroom atmosphere of self-knowledge and responsiveness to the deeper and often subtly expressed needs of the child bring about greater creativity in thought and perform-ance on the part of children? Would the consultants themselves become enriched in their knowledge of the child in the school setting, through their intimate exposure to the ideas and know-how of skilled persons in the educational field?

These and other questions were asked by the staff of the School Unit as it began to consult with school people. One further question was immediate: How could a "team" approach apply to the needs of consul-tation in schools? A psychiatrist could have diagnostic interviews with children referred to the Unit; a psychologist similarly could test these children and consult with school psychologists; a psychiatric social worker could interview parents if this seemed advisable and could give counsel to school nurse-teachers in their family casework roles. Func-tions related to the training and experience of each Unit staff member would indeed prove valuable. Equally vital for mental health consulta-tion to schools, however, was the communication which might involve any combination of the three staff members, making use of the training and experience background of each, the interaction products of these three backgrounds, the psychodynamic orientation resident in their pro-fessional insights, and the common knowledge of the immediate situa-tion. Each consultant, therefore, was prepared to communicate with various school people; administrators, guidance counselors, teachers, and the like. The choice of a particular staff member as consultant was often unrelated to the preparation of the Unit staff person for the task, but was dependent upon circumstances related to school or community. Usually it was judged apropos to send the director of the agency to consult with a chief administrator although the Unit psychologist might subsequently be called in to counsel on some testing procedures used in the district.

Hierarchical matching has become less important as schools and Unit have become better acquainted with one another. Any one of the team members might observe an 11-year-old boy in a classroom who responds to his teacher's repeated requests that he write a story by grimacing and delaying for most of the class period. Each one of the team would relate the boy's inability to begin his work to his fear that he would not be able to perform, and further, to his poor self-image as well as his identification with the picture of inadequacy provided by his father. All three staff persons would see help for the child through contact of teacher and boy at the moment of the difficulty. This contact might provide firm support of the child's awareness that he could hurdle his understandable fears and grapple with the task. Each worker would arrive at similar insights by somewhat different routes. These insights would have been previously enriched by discussions among the three Unit staff members of material garnered from all sources on the child.

Although consultation is accomplished almost entirely in the schools themselves, the Unit office is the *sine qua non* of its activities. The team members, who most often travel their separate ways in the nine Rockland school districts, must have regular and frequent opportunities to report their observations and responses are checked by other observations and the general knowledge of the staff of three. Essential to the use of case study as a tool of consultation is the Unit staff conference. Here the full findings of the social worker, the psychologist, and the psychiatrist in turn are brought to the consulting staff. From these findings is extracted material suitable and useful for communication to teachers in their group conference. In the meantime the child's assets and needs as seen in the light of the study are systematically listed. This list is methodically matched by recommendations which might be useful to the teacher and the school in guiding the child in his classroom and school. Each staff member accepts the responsibility for transmitting to the teacher group concepts that are germane to her usual sphere of activity. It will be seen that the teacher group conference thrives on free participation by all present in relatively informal discussion. However, the Unit staff soon became aware that careful planning prior to the teacher group conference makes for free and effective participation on the part of the Unit staff in the teacher group conference. This planning includes the delegation of responsibility for the transmission of specific concepts regarding the child's strengths, needs, and indicated aid.

Unit staff conferences are held at least twice a week for an hour or more. They provide for administration and planning, coordination of activities, preparation for consultation, and research. The Unit's home office also screens requests for services and makes referrals to the proper agencies. It thus educates the community concerning its functions and offers limited referral services in a county where this activity is remarkably lacking. Important in this role is the Unit's secretary, who must represent the School Unit for those who visit and call on the many occasions when all other staff members are working in schools.

Outside of the School Unit office and in the world of the school the proper functioning of a mental health consultation service requires continuous interpretation of its work to the schools' administrators. Without these essential contacts consultative work with teachers and other school staff has little meaning. Teachers in a group may study with a consultant the needs of children for many weeks, only to have all that they have learned denied by an administrator's decision concerning the handling of a child. Contact with the administrator must be an integral part of the work with the child and his teachers. The School Unit is rendered more useful to the entire school when the principal is comfortable in the knowledge of every movement of the consulting team and himself fulfills a significant role in the coordinated activities of school and Unit. It is an almost invariable rule that the school principal is the chairman of the teacher group conference, which is the highlight of each study. The question of whether or not teachers feel inhibited in the presence of their administrator may be answered by the statement of the fact that those teachers and other school staff present in the conference have all been seen in individual interviews with one or the other consultant. Private feelings, ideas, and theories have been ventilated and teachers have been encouraged to present their unique offerings. It can be said, therefore, that they have been prepared for their contact with the Unit and their own principal in the group meeting.

Important to our consideration of the relationship between School Unit and school administrators is the knowledge that the organization of a consultation service to schools was not in response to requests for this service from chief executives. It cannot be said, therefore, that they conceived of the School Unit's goal, that of raising the level of emotional health of all children, as their own. Resistance to the offerings made by the Unit to the schools through their executives would be expected. The Unit, too, in its initial contacts with chief administrators was in the position of selling a program which was not completely formulated and surely not yet of proven value. Administrators, therefore, were often reluctant to become involved in the new mental health activity, protective against any possible invasion or invidious comparison of their already existing programs, and desirous of having the new agency diverted away from contact with teachers to work with some of the most seriously disturbed children for whom they had not yet found assistance.

The Unit consultants in turn experienced feelings of rejection of their program which could in some instances extend to the point of personal rejection. Here, with administrators, as in every other consultative situation in schools, it was imperative that the consultant recognize that both consultant and consultee function to some degree both on a level of awareness and on a level of unawareness, that is, that they are motivated both consciously and unconsciously. It was important for the consultant to have sufficient background information on the school and its community to have easily available insights into motivating factors in the executive's behavior. Similarly, the consultant in his immediate contact with the administrator needed thoroughgoing awareness of his own response to nonacceptance on the part of the school representative. In the early days of consultation to schools it appeared that the needs of the administrator often required an initial period of contact with the consultant during which the Unit could be totally rejected. This seemed akin to a period of catharsis. The consultant often thought that he needed to "sit it out" and that when this revoking period was over an obstruction to communication would suddenly disappear. The consultant could then, in the same interview, interpret the offered program. The progression was storm, calm, and easier sailing. For the most part the calm persisted. However, at times, subsequent to the initial interpretation, the catharsis on the part of the consultee was repeated. By then, fortunately, communication would have increased to such a degree, because of repeated contacts between consultant and administrator, that the causes of the new break in communication could quite frequently come to light and present themselves for open discussion.

Consultation with administrators holds in common with work with other school persons the need for constant awareness of and alertness to the consultee's personal and professional strengths. Gerald Caplan (1), out of his six years' experience supervising mental health consultants in schools, believes that "the consultant may become not only an accessory ego figure, but also an accessory super-ego and ego-ideal figure." This is certainly true in some instances. However, it would appear that dramatic and more durable positive movement is to be expected when the consultant is able to bring to awareness and vigorously support the consultee's own ego strengths which are certain to be there. This would almost seem to require some self-effacement on the part of the consultant, and does demand a ready sensitivity to the point where the consultee should be permitted to "go it alone." It is better, through one's attitudes, not to ask him to recall that his successful maneuvers needed temporary support.

One of the creators of the School Mental Health Unit was a school psychologist. He had been on the forefront of the community mental health movement in Rockland County since its inception and had contributed to its advance from the stage of community education through the organization of treatment facilities to the most current period of concern with prevention and better emotional health for all. On September 1, 1957, when the School Mental Health Unit opened its doors, a meeting of all school psychologists was held. They expressed their enthusiastic anticipation of a consultative service which would provide consultation by each Unit staff member concerning the psychologists' work in the schools. There were at that time nine school psychologists. Dr. R. Gaston Scott, who had worked so assiduously in community mental health, was also an informal supervisor of the school psychologists. All nine were hired by the County Vocational Education and Extension Board. The schools contracted with this Board for their services. Dr. Scott became an important liaison person between the group of school psychologists, who had not existed as a functioning group until that time, and the School Unit. It was also clear that the small Unit team of three had the possibility of extending its work and increasing its effectiveness many times through the nine school psychologists, each of whom had a specific assignment in one or more school districts. Thirty-nine meetings of school psychologists were held in the Unit's first school year. There was an average attendance of twenty psychologists per month and five each meeting.

The group character of these meetings is of interest and importance. The Unit staff knew the school psychologists well through previous cooperative endeavors in county mental health, through individual contacts, principally between Unit and school psychologist, and by a detailed study of the training and experience of the school psychologists made by the Unit psychologist. The group meeting, held once a week, had two leaders, the director of the Unit and the supervisor of the school psychologists. The two met for collaborative conferences at frequent intervals. There was soon an amazing "openness" on the part of the participants of the group, and all communications there were considered confidential. The Unit office also became a place where individual conferences between psychologists from different schools could be held. Communication within the entire group was enhanced, and group goals were developed by the school psychologists. Early meetings were concerned with interpretation of the Unit's goals and methods as well as with the means by which the schools, represented by the psychologists, could become acquainted with these. Members of this group also helped the Unit to achieve intimate knowledge of their schools and the strengths and problems of the latter. There were discussions of specific school situations, giving particular attention to the feelings and attitudes of school persons and changes in their responses. General school matters were considered. A discussion of the function of the school psychologist as consultant in the teacher-psychologist relationship included consideration of the ways to support the interest of teachers in emotional health as well as emotional illness, means of helping the teacher to achieve an awareness of his own strength and creativity, and the opportunities for proving themselves teacher allies rather than judges. Six case studies were made during 14 group meetings. They included investigation of the problems of a slow learner, a bright underachiever, and an adolescent involved in the court.

Important in the development of Unit staff and school psychologists was the "feeling" for the right time to move out and leave the consultee on his own. This insight became valuable to the psychologist-consultant in the school, the Unit in its relations with the school psychologist, and the Unit with the entire group of school psychologists. Their close contact with the Unit had been vital to the psychologists and life-giving to the Unit. Separation, with the benefit of continued close cooperation and integrated activities, had in the second and third years of the Unit's life, its own rewards. The number of school psychologists had increased, on the demand of the various school districts, from 9 in 1957 to 14 in 1959.

In the Annual School Mental Health Unit Report for January through December 1958 to the Rockland County Community Mental Health Board, the following specific attempts were made to clarify the terminology used by the Unit staff to describe its activities in schools:

The overall method used by the School Mental Health Unit is *consultation*. Unit staff members communicate to educators their knowledge of individuals and their development, including individual functioning on intellectual, emotional, and attitudinal levels. This knowledge is practically useful to school persons in their relationships with children. Consultation is a two-way communication and Unit staff members learn from the educator of the behavior of children in school groups. This information increases the usefulness of the Unit staff in further consultations. Consultation has been used as a general term to include all forms of communication between Unit staff and school staff. It describes brief communications concerning general school problems as well as a child under study. It may refer to the work of a staff member with a group of teachers for an entire evening on a once-a-month basis, or the activity of a Unit staff person in leading a Parent-Teacher Association discussion.

A *limited consultation* is a communication concerning a school child between school person and Unit over a period of a few minutes to several hours, which is less complete or thoroughgoing than a case study.

Contact is the word used to describe any specific communication between Unit staff and individuals related to schools. It assumes that the communication has meaning for the work of the School Unit. It has been used synonymously with *consultation*.

A *case conference*, or teacher group conference, is a group meeting of school administrator, teachers, other school staff and one or more School Unit staff members for the purpose of discussing the problems, the findings, and the recommendations of the group concerning a child under study. The meeting is chaired by the administrator and planned with the school psychologist and other staff persons.

The process of consultation is in essence communication. One referral of a child with school phobia to the Unit was initiated by the psychologist after consultation with the elementary supervisor of the district. The referral was accepted by the Unit psychiatric social worker. The psychologist was free to communicate to the Unit, in his referral, the fact of involvement of the local village, grandparents and parents, superintendent of schools, elementary supervisor, principal, school nurse-teacher, as well as the interacting attitudes of all. The next move on the part of the Unit was to "check in" with the elementary supervisor. This move was based on the knowledge of the relationship between the supervisors, other school persons, and the village, between the supervisor and the psychologist, and the role of the supervisor in the district's total structure. This contact then proved an "open sesame" to the child's family, the principal, the teacher, the school nurse-teacher, and the child. There were 13 contacts with 7 individual school staff persons prior to a teacher group conference of all school staff participating in the study.

In this consultation with the school district and its parts, knowledge of the school's structure, its relationship to the village, the freedom permitted each consultee in his specific role and, above all, each consultee's strengths and needs in the particular situation were essential. There was, implicit in this consultation, respect for each consultee's expertness and the fact that he functions on the same level in his field as the consultant does in his, his own insight into the immediate situation, and his desire to cooperate in finding a solution to the problem. In the contact of consultant with consultee were new demands for discovery of personal strength to support positive movement in the situation and for attitudinal changes toward child, parents, and other staff members. The Unit operates on the premise that such attitudinal changes can occur and that such strength is resident in the individual, although the consultee may not immediately become aware that this is true. Resistance and even hostility to the proffered demands are to be expected. The consultant gives little attention to expressions of anger and resistance, as compared with a therapeutic approach, except to permit catharsis of the same. In such an instance, the consultant may discontinue the consultation for the time being, only to provide other opportunities for future contact with the same consultee after the need for the attitudinal change and the recognition of his strength have percolated through to consciousness. In other situations, it has been necessary for the Unit to ground itself at the point of resistance and make an opportunity of what might have been considered a failure to achieve effective communication. This was true when the Unit was limited to contact with a single school in a large district. The Unit then put all of its efforts and time, which it expected to allocate to the district, into the work with the one small kindergarten-sixth grade school. This became a demonstration project in which the efficacy of consultation to schools could be fully tested.

More specifically, contact between consultant and consultee provides an opportunity for the school person to bring into the open his ideas and his concerns. He hears these and often discovers that he has been accomplishing "more than he knew." The consultant always emphasizes the positive aspect of the school person's communication and points to elements which could well lead to a solution. The consultant raises questions which provoke further thought on the part of the consultee and provides analogies from casework, testing situation, and playroom which match the problem situation and point to particular needs for response. He remains aware of the validity of what is spoken and unspoken by the consultee and remains supportive, nonjudgmental, and accepting of rejection of his contributions. The consultant increases his own knowledge within the contact. All communications remain confidential.

Consultation, in Unit terms, is an appeal to strength. In one kindergarten-sixth grade school, principal, school nurse-teacher, school psychologist, the child's teacher, former teacher, and special reading teacher were gathered with the Unit team for a teacher group conference. Twenty-three school contacts had been made with eight individual persons by four Unit staff members. (This includes the Unit's first interne psychologist.) In what ways was strength elicited in this group?

The child under study belongs to a relatively poor family which lives not far from the school. This family is a rare member of the low income group in a predominantly middle-class community. The father, a steady worker, has lived a withdrawn life since his youth because of a marked physical deformity. The school nurse-teacher was eager to function as a family caseworker in this situation and tended to follow her natural inclination to give fully, not only of herself, but of goods and services which the family appeared to need. She also found communication with her principal easy and was in a position to interpret to him the family's needs. Eliciting the school nurse-teacher's strengths consisted of encouraging her demonstrations of the principal's concern for the family and its child to the family, and helping her to a greater awareness of how it feels to be a child from the lower economic group in a middle-class setting. This insight demanded that she and her teachers refrain from a sentimental sympathy which would offer the child three ice cream cones. There appeared instead opportunities for the nurse to ask both parents, who are basically able and intelligent people though depressed, to share in the work of the Parent-Teacher Association as well as in some emergency repair for the school.

The nurse was guided in making a referral to a family agency outside of the school. She was able, then, to desist from using the school for extensive charitable enterprises for the family. Having become aware of the nuances of self, despite anger, fear, and resistance on the part of the family members toward the community, the school, and each other, the nurse has used herself effectively in this situation. Her role in the school has through this study achieved a new perspective.

The principal, prior to the conference, had visited the child's father in his home. The principal wisely opened the conversation with some talk about their mutual hobby—fishing. The father, habitually withdrawn, began to talk eagerly of his fishing experience when suddenly he stopped, saying, "You don't want to talk about that. Get to the point." The principal naturally experienced great feelings of rejection and wondered if further contacts were possible with this parent. Within the case study conference he was able to relate the father's attitude to his own fear of rejection and feelings of lack of worth. The principal could then make plans for further contacts with this father in which his knowledge of this parent would sustain him in the demonstration of the strengths of both father and son, and the possibility of each finding value in the other.

Each teacher present at the teacher group or case study conference had had one or more interviews with a Unit team member. The strengths of the child under study and his family had been stressed. Their own knowledge of his strong points and how to assist him in making use of them had been underlined. In the group conference the child's last year's teacher, having indicated her awareness in retrospect of much that was good in the boy, finally commented on the importance of "the little things that count" in observing a child and determining needs that are not readily apparent. The boy's current teacher readily admitted her displeasure with his apparent laziness and unpleasant mien. With the help of the psychologist's interpretation, she could understand his difficulty in starting a task and his need for assistance at that point. She had been hiding from her colleagues the fact that she had, a little while before, begun to keep him after school to "start" him on his homework. It was clear, in the light of the Unit's detailed classroom observation of the child, this was exactly what he needed. The school psychologist was newer to the school than the Unit's contact with this district and school. The case study team, which included the school psychologist, developed, within the conference, knowledge of many strengths in the school that were quiescent and even unknown.

To complete the picture of consultation to discover strength, the small 13-year-old boy himself responded to the spoken question "What do you like best about yourself?" in the psychiatric interview, as well as to the school's unspoken new attitude to him which asked the same thing, with combed hair, neat clothes, and increased endeavors in the classroom.

It is our belief that this concern for strength and need should be exerted for our "normal children," who comprise most of the school population. Studies of normal children prove profitable when administration, teachers, and other school staff are able to develop an eye for what each child has to use in his own fulfillment. These studies provide insights into the needs, both surface and hidden, which must be answered at each step in his developmental ladder if he is to profit fully by his educational experience. The Unit, therefore, although recognizing the need to initiate activity in schools at a point where the schools find the work of the Unit acceptable, keeps clearly in view its goal to assist in raising the level of emotional health of all children. To that end, it begins with a consideration of the needs of emotional ill health only to educate school persons to a fuller understanding of what is to be gained by applying our concerns also to the healthier and vastly larger group. Here are all of our children in whom lie our hopes.

We believe firmly that the object of a child's training is "the full development of each of the principal elements of his nature: the mind, the body, and the heart." It is surprising to note that this quotation is a statement of a principle held by one Vittorino da Feltre, the master of a school for sixty or seventy boys and girls in the dominion of Mantua, in 1423. He himself stated, "Whatever our own predilections may be, we recognize that we must follow nature's lead." He declared that "Everyone has some gift, if only one can discover it," and in the words of Iris Origo, "he, therefore, bestowed especial pains upon the dullest boys, trying to find some subject or skill to meet his needs." Perhaps a final comment should be, "There is nothing new under the sun."

SUMMARY

The development of the School Mental Health Unit, a consultative service to schools in Rockland County, New York, is described. Its goal is to assist school staff in their work of emotional education of all the county's children. The School Unit seeks to support and catalyze existing psychological programs offered by the school community and to aid the school in raising the individual child's level of emotional health.

Each member of the Unit team provides services consistent with his training and experience; each is able to practice communication with schools with a common approach because of the integration of the experiences, knowledge and insights of all three team members.

The proper functioning of a mental health consultation service to schools requires continuous interpretation of its work to the schools' administrators. School psychologists play an essential role in the total functioning of the School Unit.

The process of consultation as experienced by the School Unit is elucidated. The consultee's awareness of his own strength is the chief response sought.

References

1. CAPLAN, GERALD. "Mental Health Consultation in Schools," in *The Elements of a Community Mental Health Program.* New York: Milbank Memorial Fund, 1956.
2. GINSBURG, ETHEL L. *Public Health Is People.* Cambridge, Mass.: Harvard Univ. Press, 1950.

3. HAY, LOUIS. *A New School Channel for Helping the Troubled Child.* Am. J. Orthopsychiatry, **23:** 676–683, 1953.

4. LAWRENCE, MARGARET MORGAN. *The Application of Psychiatric Techniques to Teaching.* Nerv. Child, **10:** 378–386, 1954.

5. _____. *The School Mental Health Unit of Rockland County Community Mental Health Board: The Work of Its First Year.* Presented at Third Annual Conference of New York State Assn. of Community Mental Health Boards, Syracuse, May 21, 1958.

6. STILLEY, J. R., R. A. SIM, and E. W. LOOSLEY. *Crestwood Heights.* New York: Basic Books, 1956.

CONCLUSION

This is a small book about a big question. We realize that the question of emotional disturbance in relation to school learning would not be covered completely in a book many times the size of this. We hope it has been of help to the reader in defining the question for himself. In addition, we hope that it has served as a sampler of the literature and a casebook for examining case histories and research methodology.

Emotional disturbance is difficult to define at any age, but it presents even more resistance during childhood and adolescence. One learns his adult behavior by trying out new behavior that is frankly experimental, changing, and often inappropriate. Research to date indicates that "normal" children exhibit transient "symptoms" of "mental illness."

Problems and difficulties, internal and external, serve both as threats to emotional growth *and* as the necessary challenges that produce it. There can be little psychological growth without the stimulus of a problem. It is time to stop thinking of the *problem child* and start thinking in terms of children experiencing problems. All children have problems. Some children have more than others, but any child has more at special points in his life. A child must be helped to solve these problems and use the exercise to develop emotional muscles that will better prepare him for the future.

Some children develop sturdy muscles more easily than others. But if there has been insufficient practice or exercise, emotional muscles may well prove inadequate in a period of stress. The child will not surmount his problem; he will stumble and fall before it. It will block his path of growth.

At such times we must offer him special help. Whether we call that help "psychotherapy" or use another name, it calls for a large amount of

274

learning. Help is offered by a special "teacher" called a therapist, who relates the special help to the child's experiences in school and elsewhere in his normal environment. He guides the child's learning in a concentrated manner.

When we think of guiding a child's learning, we think of parents—but we think also of teachers and their classrooms. Parents are responsible for their child's learning, but they delegate much of this responsibility to a trained expert, the teacher. As in any profession, these teachers vary considerably in their trained competence and in their natural talent, but it is their responsibility, nonetheless, to guide the development of succeeding generations.

And here is where we must define "school learning" and permit ourselves some crystal-ball gazing. A teacher's job has been seen differently in various cultures and ages. Today, in the United States, it seems to be changing. We are abandoning our concept of the teacher as a technician who oversees a child's learning of a limited number of skills, such as reading or arithmetic. We are returning to a broader view of the teacher as a professional who assumes the delegated responsibility of the parent and of society to guide intellectual, moral, and emotional growth. In past ages and today, this enormous responsibility has been taken on by teachers with varying degrees of awareness. Much of the guidance has been done haphazardly and by accident. The teacher often has been unaware of the moral and emotional lessons delicately interwoven in a geography lesson. Great teachers of all ages, however, have been aware that these lessons are inseparable.

But where does the responsibility begin and end? There must be some limits. We suggest that the limits are placed by the individual teacher's intellectual and emotional resources. Limits are only partly drawn by school walls. The school is a place where teachers help children to learn. The school is also a part of the community and a teacher is aware that much learning is begun or shaped outside the school. A teacher who is interested in helping his students grow must be familiar with their lives in the community surrounding the school. But the teacher does his teaching inside the school building for the most part. Happenings outside of school are brought into the school by the students. To the best of his ability, a teacher uses all of these experiences to promote learning.

Sometimes a teacher may seem to act like a psychiatrist, a psychologist, or a social worker. Anyone who has observed in a classroom knows that a teacher will also, at times, act like a mother, a carpenter, a secretary, a policeman, a nurse, a fireman, or a judge. The moment dictates the role. The difference is one of purpose. A teacher takes on any role for the moment if it helps to get the job of teaching done—if it helps children learn.

We do not ask whether the teacher is a properly trained and qualified carpenter or judge. We understand that he does the best he can with the borrowed role because he is a properly trained and qualified teacher. He does not attempt to "psychoanalyze" a student, nor does he attempt to apprehend bank robbers or put out three-alarm fires. He knows he is a teacher, and he learns as part of his training and early supervised experience when to apply a Band-aid with love, when to call the ambulance, and when to do nothing at all. But just as there *is* an ambulance or a policeman to call when the teacher believes a situation is beyond his competence, there must be mental health consultants available also. Many school districts today have school psychologists, social workers, psychiatrists, or a mental health team. Shamefully, many more have no such expert help and the teacher must do the best he can, because he knows that turning his back on a problem never makes it go away.

School is a place where most of our children spend many hours during their most formative years. In the classroom they attempt to acquire *any* skill that promises down-to-earth usefulness in facing the probable demands of their future lives. Part of the help they require of the teacher is in developing emotional skills to solve emotional problems.

Many teacher-training institutions are reawakening to this responsibility. If a teacher is to take on a full job, he must be fully trained. Teaching the rules of grammar will probably become a job for an efficient teaching machine in today's efficient world. Guiding a child's growing ability to interact with facets of a widening world is and will remain a job for a teacher. Perhaps the future will see teaching become a more highly respected, better-paid profession. If the complexity of the job is finally understood, carefully supervised internship and residency requirements will surely be increased. This will help the better new teachers who are frequently frightened by the responsibility they encounter in a classroom. School learning is not simply learning the three

R's; it is learning to master one's life through understanding many things as diverse as arithmetic, hostility, spelling, and tenderness. Schools have always represented our hope for the future; they do so no less today.

And where in all this is the role of research? Research must be a guide to those of us who are the professional guides, or teachers. Through research we learn the changing needs for what must be taught and the changing ways in which it can best be taught. This role of research is equally important to the classroom teacher and to that special "teacher" who calls himself a psychotherapist.

But perhaps the greatest lesson that research can teach is the lesson of patience and tolerance. We do not have *the answers* and we never shall. We use the tool of research to study the changing contours and moods of life. We must tolerate unanswered questions while trying to answer them. We must act according to the answers we have now, knowing full well that many will prove false tomorrow. An open mind is not an empty one.

Profiles of Contributing Authors

ACKERMAN, NATHAN W.—Clinical professor of psychiatry, Columbia University; director of Professional Program, The Family Institute; supervising psychiatrist, Family Mental Health Clinic, Jewish Family Health Service of New York. Dr. Ackerman is the author of *The Psychodynamics of Family Life* (Basic Books, 1958) and numerous articles in professional journals. His current focus of interest is family psychotherapy.

ALLEN, LUCILE—Parent educator and nursery school teacher. Miss Allen has been associated as interviewer with the Guidance Study research program at the University of California, Berkeley. It was she who obtained the behavioral and personality data on the subjects of the study.

AMIDON, EDMUND—Associate professor of educational psychology, Temple University. Dr. Amidon is a staff associate of the National Training Laboratories, an NEA affiliate which conducts human relations workshops at Bethel, Maine. He has done extensive research and writing on the application of group dynamics and social psychology to education. He is particularly concerned with the application of this research to the improvement of preservice and in-service instruction. Dr. Amidon is the author of a number of journal articles and of *The Role of the Teacher in the Classroom*. He is coauthor of *Student Teaching: Cases and Comments*.

BEKER, JEROME—Senior research assistant, Syracuse University Youth Development Center. Dr. Beker's areas of concentration are school integration, classroom climate, and the educational implications of camping. Formerly he was research psychologist at the Berkshire Farm for Boys in Canaan, New York. Dr. Beker has contributed a number of articles to professional journals and is the author of *Training Camp Counselors in Human Relations* (Association Press, 1962).

BOARDMAN, WILLIAM K.—Associate professor, Emory University School of Medicine. Dr. Boardman's research interest is in the effects of subliminal stimuli and psychopathological states on perceptual and judgment processes. He has contributed many articles to professional journals.

CLANCY, NORAH M.—Supervisor of teacher education in the School of Education at the University of California, Santa Barbara. Dr. Clancy has been director of several child care centers and director of the Child Development Laboratory at the University of California, Santa Barbara.

DISTLER, LUTHER S.—Clinical psychology supervisor, University of California, Berkeley. Mr. Distler's research projects have included the prediction and response of schizophrenics to treatment and the effects of the treatment, both in the short term and in a two-year follow-up. He is currently doing his thesis research on the patterns of parental identification in college students.

DUBOWY, MILDRED W.—Psychiatric social worker for the Rockland County Organization for Mentally Ill Children Day Care Center and the Happy Valley School, Pomona, New York. Miss Dubowy is also a discussion leader for parent education groups cosponsored by the Rockland County Mental Health Association and the Rockland Community College.

EKSTEIN, RUDOLF—Director, Project on Childhood Psychosis, Reiss-Davis Clinic for Child Guidance. Dr. Ekstein is also a training analyst at the Los Angeles Institute for Psychoanalysis. He is the author of about one hundred publications on psychoanalysis, psychotherapy, professional teaching, and childhood psychosis. With Robert S. Wallerstein, he is coauthor of *The Teaching and Learning of Psychotherapy* (Basic Books, 1958).

EPPERSON, DAVID C.—Assistant dean, School of Education, University of California, Santa Barbara. Dr. Epperson's research interests involve those sociological and psychological factors that influence learning in educational institutions. His current project (in collaboration with Richard A. Schmuck) is "Political Socialization in the Classroom: A Cross-National Study of How Attitudes Toward Authority Are Developed and Maintained in the Classroom." He is the author of a number of journal articles.

FISH, BARBARA—Psychiatrist-in-charge of the Children's Services of Bellevue Psychiatric Hospital and associate professor of psychiatry at New York University School of Medicine. For the past twelve years Dr. Fish has been working in child psychiatry, studying psychopharmacologic agents in children, and developing behavioral measures for psychopathologic disorders from birth to puberty. She is currently directing the Children's Psychopharmacology Unit of the Children's Service under a grant from the National Institute of Mental Health. This unit has been adapting developmental methods for the systematic evaluation of drugs in children.

FLANDERS, NED A.—Professor of education and research consultant at the University of Michigan. Dr. Flanders' special interests are in techniques for observing classroom behavior, laboratory experiments in group dynamics, and influence theory.

GALLISTEL, ELIZABETH—School psychologist for the Wayzata (Minn.) Public Schools. Miss Gallistel is continuing her study of the problem of predicting students' later difficulties from tests and observations in the early school years. She is also studying what can be done to prevent more serious problems from developing in children who display early maladjustment.

GOWAN, JOHN CURTIS—Professor of education at San Fernando Valley State College. Dr. Gowan is the author of numerous articles on gifted children, teacher evaluation, and measurement, and is a coauthor of *Education and Guidance of the Ablest* (Charles Thomas, 1964). He is a consultant on gifted children for Los Angeles and a number of other cities in southern California.

HAAN, NORMA—Assistant research psychologist at the Institute of Human Development, University of California, Berkeley. Miss Haan also has a private practice in psychodiagnostics and psychotherapy. She was formerly associated with the University of Utah Guidance Center, the Child Guidance Division of the Hawaiian Department of Public Instruction, and the Berkeley Public Schools. Her publications include a number of journal articles.

HARING, NORRIS G.—Director of special education, University of Kansas Medical Center, and formerly professor of education at the University of Maryland. He is coauthor of *Assistance for Teachers of Exceptional Children; Discipline, Achievement and Mental Health; Attitudes of Educators Toward Exceptional Children;* and *Educating Emotionally Disturbed Children.*

HERZAN, HELEN M.—Psychiatrist-in-chief, Wellesley Human Relations Service, Inc., Wellesley, Mass.

HONZIK, MARJORIE P.—Lecturer in psychology and associate research psychologist at the Institute of Human Development, University of California, Berkeley. She has spent the greater part of the past thirty years analyzing the findings on the growth and development of the normal children in the continuing Guidance Study. Miss Honzik has authored a number of publications on mental growth and the behavior of normal children.

KANNER, LEO—Author of six books and more than 250 articles on psychiatry, psychology, education, and the history and folklore of medicine. In his forty years of professional life, Dr. Kanner has lectured in Europe, Canada, Mexico, and throughout the United States. He has been on the editorial boards of many journals, including the *American Journal of Psychiatry* and the *Journal of Child Psychiatry.* In 1958 at Lisbon, he was the honorary president of the Fourth International Congress of Child Psychiatry. Among his many other honors, Dr. Kanner was the recipient of the first annual award for outstanding contributions in the field of medicine from the Association for the Help of Retarded Children.

LAKOS, MARCILLE H.—Formerly research assistant for the Oregon State Board of Health. Mrs. Lakos practices psychotherapy in New York, specializing in work with children, in family diagnosis, and group therapy.

LAWRENCE, MARGARET M.—Member of the department of psychiatry at Harlem Hospital (an affiliate of the College of Physicians and Surgeons of Columbia University), medical director of the Rockland County Organization for Mentally Ill Children Day Treatment Center, and a practicing psychiatrist and psychoanalyst. Articles by Dr. Lawrence have appeared in a number of professional journals. She is writing a book on mental health consultation to schools under a grant from the New York State Department of Mental Hygiene.

LEVITT, EUGENE E.—Professor of clinical psychology, Indiana University Medical Center. Dr. Levitt is the author of three books and more than eighty journal articles. He is a member of the editorial board of *Child Development Abstracts* and advisory editor of the *International Journal of Clinical and Experimental Hypnosis.*

LOVATT, MARGARET—Executive director of the West End Crèche, Toronto, Canada. Miss Lovatt was formerly a social worker with the family division of the Department of Public Welfare in Toronto, and in the foster home supervision and intake departments of the Protestant Children's Homes, a voluntary child placement service.

LUSZKI, MARGARET B.—Research associate at the Center for Research on Utilization of Scientific Knowledge, Institute for Social Research, University of Michigan, and clinical psychologist at the Ann Arbor Veterans Administration Hospital. Dr. Luszki is the author of many articles and of *Interdisciplinary Team Research: Methods and Problems* (New York University Press, 1958). Her major interests are mental health, vocational rehabilitation, and group relations.

MACFARLANE, JEAN W.—Professor of psychology and research psychologist, emeritus, University of California, Berkeley. Miss Macfarlane has been in charge of a continuing research program, known as the Guidance Study, for three and a half decades. The research has followed the biosocial behavior and personality development of a normal sample of subjects from their birth to the present time. The subjects are now in their mid-thirties. She is the author of several journal articles.

MANN, EDNA B.—Member of a Bureau of Child Guidance team working in New York high schools with disturbed teen-agers, and a privately practicing therapist working with adults and teen-agers. Miss Mann has published articles in newspapers and professional journals and has contributed a chapter on the emotional climate in the classroom to the New York Board of Education Bulletin.

MURPHY, LOIS BARCLAY—Research psychologist and therapist in the Children's Services of the Menninger Foundation. Dr. Murphy has a background of research and teaching in child psychology. She is the author of several books, including *The Widening World of Childhood* (Basic Books, 1962), which is an outgrowth of her work as principal investigator for the U.S. Public Health Service on a study of normal children.

MUSSEN, PAUL H.—Professor of psychology at the University of California, Berkeley. Dr. Mussen's particular research interest is personality development, with emphasis on its dependence on parent-child interactions. He is the author of *Child Development and Personality* and *The Psychological Development of the Child,* and the editor of *The Handbook of Research Methods in Child Psychology.*

NEWMAN, RUTH G.—Codirector of the School Research Program of the Washington School of Psychiatry. A practicing clinical psychologist, Dr. Newman has also taught in public and private schools in New York City. She has written a number of journal articles and is coauthor of *Conflict in the Classroom,* to be published.

PHILLIPS, BEEMAN N.—Associate professor, Department of Educational Psychology, University of Texas. Dr. Phillips is the director of the Child Development in School Project sponsored by the U.S. Office of Education; the project is a study of school anxiety during a two-year period. He is the author of *Psychology* (Steck, 1959) and a coauthor of *Psychology at Work in the Elementary School Classroom* (Harper, 1960), and has written numerous articles for professional journals.

PHILLIPS, E. LAKIN—Professor of psychology, director of Psychological Clinic, George Washington University, Washington, D.C. Dr. Phillips' interests are in behavior change, the experimental study of clinical problems, and the application of cybernetic theory to behavior. He has published books and articles on clinical, child, and adolescent psychology; psychotherapy; behavior change; and clinical-theoretical topics.

PINCKNEY, GEORGE A.—Associate professor of psychology, State University of New York, College at Brockport. Dr. Pinckney formerly taught at the University of Nebraska. He has published materials on learning, both animal and human, in several journals. His current interest is in human problem solving, and he is researching various parameters of anagram solution.

SCHMUCK, RICHARD A.—Study director with a joint appointment in the Research Center for Group Dynamics and the Center for Research on the Utilization of Scientific Knowledge, Institute for Social Research, the University of Michigan. Dr. Schmuck is also assistant professor of psychology and lecturer in education at the University of Michigan. Previously he has done research on children and classrooms at the Institute for Social Research. His major research interests are interpersonal processes in children's peer groups, classroom socialization processes, sibling relationships, political extremism, and social change and education.

SMITTER, FAITH W.—The late Dr. Smitter was professor of education at the University of Punjab. Formerly she was assistant head of the Education Extension at the University of California, Los Angeles, and director of guidance for the Santa Barbara County Schools.

SPANIER, IRENE J.—Senior psychologist with the Jewish Child Care Association, New York. Miss Spanier's special interests are projective techniques, intelligence testing, and child therapy and guidance.

SZASZ, THOMAS S.—Author of *Pain and Pleasure* (Basic Books, 1957), *The Myth of Mental Illness* (Hoeber-Harper, 1961), *Law, Liberty and Psychiatry* (Macmillan, 1963), and more than one hundred articles and book reviews. Dr. Szasz was a member of the Chicago Institute for Psychoanalysis and is currently professor of psychiatry at the State University of New York, Upstate Medical Center, Syracuse.

WERNER, EMMY E.—Assistant professor of child development at the University of California, Davis. Dr. Werner has published articles dealing with the personality development of exceptional children, such as the gifted, the underachiever, and those who underwent prolonged stress in their formative years. She has participated in longitudinal studies at the Institute of Child Welfare, the University of Minnesota, and the National Institutes of Health.

WYATT, GERTRUD L.—Department of Psychology, Boston University. Formerly Dr. Wyatt was clinical associate and supervisor of graduate study in the Graduate School of Education at Harvard University.

Bibliography

DEFINITION: emotional disturbance, mental illness, and other labels

ADAMS, A. A. "Identifying Socially Maladjusted School Children," *Genetic Psychology Monographs,* 1960, **61**, 3–36.

AMOS, R. T., and WASHINGTON, R. M. "A Comparison of Pupil and Teacher Perceptions of Pupil Problems," *Journal of Educational Psychology,* 1960, **51**, 255–58.

ANDREW, OWEN L., and LOCKWOOD, HILDA. "Teachers' Evaluations of the Mental Health Status of Their Pupils," *Journal of Educational Research,* 1954, **47**, 631–35.

BAHN, ANITA K., and NORMAN, VIVIAN B. "First National Report on Patients of Mental Health Clinics," *Public Health Report,* 1959, **74**, 943–56.

BEILIN, H. "Teachers' and Clinicians' Attitudes Toward the Behavior Problems of Children: A Reappraisal," *Child Development,* 1959, **30**, 9–25.

BLOCK, D. A., and others. *A Study of Children Referred for Residential Treatment in New York State.* Albany, N.Y.: Departmental Health Resources Board, 1959.

EISEN, N. H. "Some Effects of Early Sensory Deprivation on Later Behavior: The Quandam Hard of Hearing Child," *Journal of Abnormal Social Psychology,* 1962, **65**, 338–42.

EISENBERG, L. "Emotionally Disturbed Children and Youth," *Children and Youth in the 1960s.* (Survey of papers prepared for White House Golden Anniversary Conference on Youth.) Washington: 1960.

FOOTE, E. J. *Six Children.* Springfield, Ill.: Thomas, 1956.

GILBERT, G. M. "A Survey of 'Referral Problems' in Metropolitan Child Guidance Centers," *Journal of Clinical Psychology,* 1957, **13**, 37–42.

HUNT, R. G., ROACH, J. L., and GURRALIN, O. "Social-Psychological Factors and the Psychiatric Complaints of Disturbed Children," *Journal of Consulting Psychology,* 1960, **24**, 194.

KVARACEUS, W. C. "Behavior Problems," *Encyclopedia of Educational Research,* ed. C. W. HARRIS, 1960, 137–43.

LEVY, J. "A Quantitative Study of the Relationship Between Intelligence and Economic Status as Factors in the Etiology of Children's Behavior Problems," *American Journal of Orthopsychiatry,* 1931, **1**, 152–62.

McGINNIS, M. "The Wellesley Project Program of Preschool Emotional Assessment," *Journal of Psychiatric Social Work,* 1954, **23**, 135–41.

MADDY, N. R. "Comparison of Children's Personality Traits, Attitudes, and Intelligence with Parental Occupation," *Genetic Psychology Monographs,* 1943, **27**, 1–65.

MOWRER, O. H. " 'Sin,' the Lesser of Two Evils," *American Psychologist,* 1960, **15**, 301–4.

OLSON, W. C. *Problem Tendencies in Children: A Method for Their Measurement and Description.* Minneapolis: Univ. of Minnesota Press, 1930.

PHILLIPS, B. N., and DEVAULT, M. V. "Relation of Positive and Negative Sociometric Valuation to Social and Personal Adjustment of School Children," *Journal of Applied Psychology,* 1955, **39,** 409–12.

REMMERS, H. H. "Cross-cultural Studies of Teenagers' Problems," *Journal of Educational Psychology,* 1962, **53,** 254–61.

ROGERS, C. A. "Mental Health Findings in Three Elementary Schools," *Educational Research Bulletin* (Ohio State Univ.), 1942, **21,** No. 3.

SERBIN, T. R. (ed.). *Studies in Behavior Pathology.* New York: Holt, Rinehart & Winston, 1961.

STOUFFER, G. A. W. "Behavior Problems of Children as Identified by Today's Teachers and Compared to Those Reported by E. K. Wickman," *Journal of Educational Research,* 1955, **48,** 321–31.

TAYLOR, C., and COMBS, A. W. "Self-acceptance and Adjustment," *Journal of Consulting Psychology,* 1952, **16,** 89–91.

ULLMAN, C. A. "Identification of Maladjusted School Children," *Public Health Monograph,* No. 7. Washington: Federal Security Agency, Public Health Service, 1952.

ANTECEDENTS: why troubles grow

ALLEN, F. H., and PEARSON, G. H. J. "The Emotions of the Physically Handicapped Child," *British Journal of Medical Psychology,* 1928, **8,** 212–35.

BEDOIAN, W. H. "Mental Health Analyses of Socially Over-accepted, Socially Under-accepted, Over-age and Under-age Pupils in the Sixth Grade," *Journal of Educational Psychology,* 1953, **44,** 336–71.

BENDER, L., and PASTER, S. "Homosexual Trends in Children," *American Journal of Orthopsychiatry,* 1941, **11,** 730–44.

BOWLBY, J., AINSWORTH, M., and ROSENBLUTH, D. "The Effects of Mother-Child Separation: A Follow-up Study," *British Journal of Medical Psychology,* 1949, **29,** 211.

BROWN, G. D. "The Development of Diabetic Children, with Special Reference to Mental and Personality Comparisons," *Child Development,* 1938, **9,** 175–83.

BUSWELL, M. "The Relationship Between the Social Structure of the Classroom and the Academic Success of the Pupils," *Journal of Experimental Education,* 1953, **22,** 37–52.

CLARK, K. B. and MAMIE P. "Emotional Factors in Racial Identification and Preference in Negro Children," *Journal of Negro Education,* 1950, **19,** 341–50.

COMMOSS, H. H. "Some Characteristics Related to Social Isolation of Second Grade Children," *Journal of Educational Psychology,* 1962, **53,** 38–42.

COOK, L. A. "An Experimental Sociographic Study of a Stratified Tenth Grade Class," *American Sociological Review,* 1945, **10,** 250–61.

DAI, B. "Some Problems of Personality Development Among Negro Children," in *Personality in Nature, Society, and Culture,* eds. C. CLUCKHOHN and H. A. MURRAY. New York: Knopf, 1953. Pp. 545–66.

FIELD, M. "Maternal Attitudes Found in Twenty-five Cases of Children with Primary Behavior Disorders," *American Journal of Orthopsychiatry,* 1940, **10,** 293–312.

GATES, M. F. "A Comparative Study of Some Problems of Social and Emotional Adjustment of Crippled and Non-crippled Girls and Boys," *Journal of Genetic Psychology,* 1946, **68,** 219–44.

GOFF, R. M. *Problems and Emotional Difficulties of Negro Children.* New York: Columbia Univ. Press, 1949.

GOLDFARB, W. "Variations in Adolescent Adjustment of Institutionally Reared Children," *American Journal of Orthopsychiatry,* 1947, **17,** 449–57.

GOODLAD, J. I. "Some Effects of Promotion and Nonpromotion upon the Social and Personal Adjustment of Children," *Journal of Experimental Education,* 1954, **22,** 301–27.

GRONLUND, N. E. "Personality Characteristics of Socially Accepted, Socially Neglected, and Socially Rejected Junior High School Pupils," *Educational Administration and Supervision,* 1957, **43,** 329–38.

_____ and HOLMLUND, W. S. "The Value of Elementary School Sociometric Status Scores for Predicting Pupils' Adjustment in High School," *Educational Administration and Supervision,* 1953, **44,** 255–60.

HOLLINGSHEAD, A. B., and REDLICH, F. C. *Social Class and Mental Illness: A Community Study.* New York: Wiley, 1958.

JONES, H. E. "The Environment and Mental Development," in *Manual of Child Psychology,* ed. L. CARMICHAEL. New York: Wiley, 1954.

KLEIN, D., and ROSS, A. "Kindergarten Entry: A Study of Role Transition and Its Effects on Children and Their Families," in *Orthopsychiatry and the School,* ed. M. KRUGMAN. New York: American Orthopsychiatric Assn., 1958.

MYERS, J. K., and ROBERTS, G. H. *Family and Class Dynamics in Mental Illness.* New York: Wiley, 1959.

POLLACK, G. H., and RICHMOND, J. B. "Nutritional Anemia in Children: Importance of Emotional, Social, and Economic Factors," *Psychosomatic Medicine,* 1953, **15,** 477.

SCHONFELD, W. A. "Inadequate Masculine Physique," *Psychosomatic Medicine,* 1950, **12,** 49–54.

SPRINGER, N. N. "A Comparative Study of the Behavior Traits of Deaf and Hearing Children in New York City," *American Annals of the Deaf,* 1938, **83,** 255–73.

_____. "The Influence of General Social Status on the Emotional Stability of Children," *Journal of Genetic Psychology,* 1938, **53,** 321–28.

VOGEL, E. F. "The Marital Relationship of Parents of Emotionally Disturbed Children: Polarization and Isolation," *Psychiatry,* 1960, **23,** 1–12.

_____ and BELL, N. W. "The Emotionally Disturbed Child as a Family Scapegoat," *Psychoanalytic Review,* 1960, **47,** 21–42.

WALDFOGEL, S., COOLIDGE, J. C., and HAHN, P. B. "The Development, Meaning, and Management of School Phobia," *American Journal of Orthopsychiatry,* 1957, **27,** 754–80.

WALKER, R. N. "Body Build and Behavior in Young Children, II: Body Build and Parents' Ratings," *Child Development,* 1963, **34,** 1–24.

WERNER, E., and GALLESTEL, E. "Predictions of Later Behavior from Childhood Evaluations," *Child Development,* 1961, **32,** 255–60.

TROUBLED STUDENTS: case histories

APPLEBAUM, A. W. "The Meaning of External Control to a Schizophrenic Adolescent Girl," *Bulletin of the Menninger Clinic,* 1957, **21,** 140–51.

BARTLET, DEONE, and SHAPIRO, M. B. "Investigation and Treatment of a Reading Disability in a Dull Child with Severe Psychiatric Disturbances," *British Journal of Educational Psychology,* 1956, **36,** 180–90.

BUTTERFIELD, VIRGINIA. "School Phobia: A Study of Five Cases," *American Journal of Orthopsychiatry,* 1954, **24,** 350–80.

SIEGEL, L. "Case Study of a Thirteen Year Old Fire-Setter: A Catalyst in the Growing Pains of a Residential Treatment Unit," *American Journal of Orthopsychiatry*, 1957, **27**, 396–410.

TREATMENT: *attempts to help*

ABRAHAMSON, D., and others. "Status of Mental Hygiene and Child Guidance Facilities in Public Schools in the United States," *Journal of Pediatrics*, 1955, **46**, 107–18.

AXLINE, VIRGINIA M. "Nondirective Therapy for Poor Readers," *Journal of Consulting Psychology*, 1947, **11**, 61–69.

BAKER, B. H., and others. "Further Report on Experimental Evaluation of Mental Hygiene Techniques in School and Community," *American Journal of Psychiatry*, 1957, **113**, 733.

————. "Preliminary Report of a Controlled Mental Health Workshop in a Public School System," *American Journal of Psychiatry*, 1955, **112**, 199.

BILLS, R. E. "Non-directive Play Therapy with Retarded Readers," *Journal of Consulting Psychology*, 1950, **14**, 140–49.

————. "Play Therapy with Well-Adjusted Retarded Readers," *Journal of Consulting Psychology*, 1950, **14**, 246–49.

DAVIDSON, SUSANNAH. "Social Phobia as a Manifestation of Family Disturbance: Its Structure and Treatment," *Journal of Child Psychology and Psychiatry*, 1961, **1**, 270–87.

D'EVELYN, KATHERINE E. *Meeting Children's Emotional Needs*. Englewood Cliffs, N.J.: Prentice-Hall, 1957.

EATON, M., WEATHER, G., and PHILLIPS, B. N. "Some Reactions of Classroom Teachers to Problem Behavior in School," *Educational Administration and Supervision*, 1957, **43**, 129–39.

FITZSIMONS, M. J. "The Predictive Value of Teachers' Referrals," in *Orthopsychiatry and the School*, ed. M. KRUGMAN. New York: American Orthopsychiatric Assn., 1958.

GRONLUND, N. E. *The Accuracy of Teachers' Judgments Concerning the Sociometric Status of Sixth Grade Pupils*. New York: Beacon House, 1951.

LEHRMAN, L. J., and others. *Success and Failure of Treatment of Children in the Child Guidance Clinics of the Jewish Board of Guardians*. New York: Jewish Board of Guardians, 1949.

McCORD, W., McCORD, J., and ZOLA, I. K. *Origins of Crime: A New Evaluation of the Cambridge-Somerville Youth Study*. New York: Columbia Univ. Press, 1959.

McKEACHIE, W. J., POLLIE, D., and SPEISMAN, J. "Relieving Anxiety in Classroom Examinations," *Journal of Abnormal Social Psychology*, 1955, **50**, 93–98.

POWERS, E., and WITMER, HELEN. *An Experiment in the Prevention of Delinquency*. New York: Columbia Univ. Press, 1951.

ROGERS, C. A., and others. "The Role of Self Understanding in the Prediction of Behavior," *Journal of Consulting Psychology*, 1948, **3**, 174–86.

ROSENFELD, H., and ZANDER, A. "The Influence of Teachers on Aspirations of Students," *Journal of Educational Psychology*, 1961, **52**, 1–11.

SCHEIDLINGER, S. "Group Factors in Promoting School Children's Mental Health," *American Journal of Orthopsychiatry*, 1952, **22**, 394–404.

WITMER, HELEN, and TUFTS, EDITH. *The Effectiveness of Delinquency Prevention*

Programs. (Children's Bureau Publication No. 350.) Washington: Department of Health, Education, and Welfare, 1954.

THE CLASSROOM: a place to learn

ANDERSON, H. H., and others. "Image of the Teacher by Adolescent Children in Four Countries: Germany, England, Mexico, United States," *Journal of Social Psychology,* 1959, **50,** 47–55.

BOYNTON, P., DUGGER, H., and TURNER, M. "The Emotional Stability of Teachers and Pupils," *Journal of Juvenile Research,* 1934, **18,** 223–32.

CALVIN, A. D., McGUIGAN, F. J., and SULLIVAN, M. W. "A Further Investigation of the Relationship Between Anxiety and Classroom Examination Performance," *Journal of Educational Psychology,* 1957, **48,** 240–44.

COOPER, S., RYAN, W., and HUTCHESON, B. R. "Classroom Screening for Emotional Disturbance," *American Psychologist,* 1959, **14,** 340.

DAVIDS, A., and WHITE, A. A. "Effects of Success, Failure, and Social Facilitation on Level of Aspiration in Emotionally Disturbed and Normal Children," *Journal of Personality,* 1958, **26,** 77–93.

DAVIDSON, K. S., and SARASON, S. B. "Test Anxiety and Classroom Observations," *Child Development,* 1961, **32,** 199–210.

DEUTSCH, M. "Minority Group and Class Status as Related to Social and Personality Factors in Scholastic Achievement," *Society for Applied Anthropology Monograph,* 1960, No. 2.

FENTON, N. *Mental Hygiene in School Practice.* Palo Alto, Calif.: Stanford Univ. Press, 1943.

GNAGE, W. J. "Effects on Classmates of a Deviant Student's Power and Response to a Teacher-Exerted Control Technique," *Journal of Educational Psychology,* 1960, **51,** 1–8.

HARING, N. G., and PHILLIPS, E. L. *Educating Emotionally Disturbed Children.* New York: McGraw-Hill, 1962.

HATTWICK, B. W., and STOWELL, M. "The Relationship of Over-attentiveness to Children's Work Habits and Social Adjustment in Kindergarten and the First Six Grades of School," *Journal of Educational Research,* 1936, **30,** 169–76.

LEVY, M. M., and CUDDY, J. M. "Concept Learning in the Educationally Retarded Child of Normal Intelligence," *Journal of Consulting Psychology,* 1956, **20,** 445–48.

MACCOBY, ELEANOR E., LEVIN, H., and SOLYA, B. M. "The Effects of Emotional Arousal on the Retention of Film Content: A Failure to Replicate," *Journal of Abnormal Social Psychology,* 1956, **53,** 373–74.

MEYER, W. J., and THOMPSON, G. C. "Sex Differences in the Distribution of Teacher Approval and Disapproval Among Sixth-Grade Children," *Journal of Educational Psychology,* 1956, **47,** 385–96.

MORGAN, E. F., and STRUCKER, G. R. "The Joplin Plan of Reading *vs.* a Traditional Method," *Journal of Educational Psychology,* 1960, **51,** 69–75.

PRATT, E. "Experimental Evaluation of a Program for the Improvement of Listening," *Elementary School Journal,* 1956, **56,** 315–20.

SEARS, PAULINE. "Levels of Aspiration in Academically Successful and Unsuccessful Children," *Journal of Abnormal Social Psychology,* 1940, **35,** 498–536.

WITTY, P. "Reading Success and Emotional Adjustment," *Elementary English,* 1950, **27,** 281–96.

THE SCHOOL: *hope for the future*   /

Bower, E. M. *Early Identification of Emotionally Handicapped Children in School.* Springfield, Ill.: Thomas, 1962.

————, Tashnovian, P. J., and Larson, C. A. *A Process for Early Identification of Emotionally Disturbed Children.* Sacramento: California State Department of Education, 1958.

Murphy, Lois B. "Learning How Children Cope with Their Problems," *Children,* 1957.

Schrupp, M. H., and Gjirde, C. M. "Teacher Growth in Attitudes Toward Behavior Problems of Children," *Journal of Educational Psychology,* 1953, **44,** 203–14.

Stiles, F. S. "Developing an Understanding of Human Behavior at the Elementary School Level," *Journal of Educational Research,* 1950, **43,** 516.

Ullman, C. A. "Teachers, Peers, and Tests as Predictors of Adjustment," *Journal of Educational Psychology,* 1957, **48,** 257–67.

Zinberg, N. E., and Shapiro, D. "A Group Approach in the Contexts of Therapy and Education," *Mental Hygiene,* 1963, **47,** 108–16.

Additional References

Berkowitz, Pearl H., and Rothman, Esther P. *The Disturbed Child: Recognition and Psychoeducational Therapy in the Classroom.* New York: New York Univ. Press, 1960.

Bovet, Lucien. *Psychiatric Aspects of Juvenile Delinquency.* Geneva, Switzerland: World Health Organization, 1951.

Cloward, R. A., and Ohlin, L. E. *Delinquency and Opportunity: A Theory of Delinquent Gangs.* Glencoe, Ill.: Free Press, 1960.

Cohen, A. K. *Delinquent Boys: The Culture of the Gang.* Glencoe, Ill.: Free Press, 1955.

Coleman, J. S. *The Adolescent Society.* Glencoe, Ill.: Free Press, 1961.

Conant, J. B. *The American High School Today.* New York: McGraw-Hill, 1959.

————. *Slums and Suburbs.* New York: McGraw-Hill, 1961.

Erikson, E. H. (ed.). *Youth: Change and Challenge.* New York: Basic Books, 1963.

Friedenberg, E. Z. *The Vanishing Adolescent.* Boston: Beacon Press, 1959.

Glueck, S. and Eleanor T. *One Thousand Juvenile Delinquents.* Cambridge: Harvard Univ. Press, 1934.

Jackson, L. A. "Emotional Attitudes Toward the Family of Normal, Neurotic, and Delinquent Children," *British Journal of Psychology,* 1950, **41,** 35–51.

Kvaraceus, W., and others. *Delinquent Behavior.* Vols. 1 and 2. Washington: National Education Assn. Project on Delinquency, 1959.

Wirt, R. D., and Brown, W. F. "The Relation of the Children's Manifest Anxiety Scale to the Concept of Anxiety as Used in the Clinic," *Journal of Consulting Psychology,* 1956, **20,** 462.

Glossary

Analysis of covariance——A complex form of analysis of variance, in which the operation of certain factors is controlled statistically.

Analysis of variance——A statistical device used to determine whether a set of discovered *differences* is too strong to be due to chance alone.

Anxiety——An extremely unpleasant feeling that is similar to fear but usually more vague and oppressive than a simple fear *of* something.

Autistic——Seeing the world in terms of one's own inner needs and not in terms of the reality that most of us agree upon. This term is most often applied to children who are seriously disturbed and who would be identified as troubled even by untrained observers.

Case conference——A meeting or conference of interested parties in which a case (i.e., client or patient) is discussed. Such a conference may have the purpose of deciding diagnosis and treatment. Usually the mental health team (psychiatrist, psychologist, and social worker) make up the core of the conference.

Caseworker——*See* Social worker.

Chi square——A test applied to determine whether findings differ sufficiently from those expected by chance to be considered statistically significant.

Clinician——A psychologist or other professional who works directly with patients or clients—for instance, a clinical psychologist as opposed to an experimental psychologist.

Control group——A group of people chosen to match as closely as possible an experimental group. The control group is not subjected to the experimental conditions and therefore serves as a base line from which changes in the experimental group may be determined.

Correlation coefficient——A statistical estimate of the degree of relationship between two variables; theoretical range is from $+1.00$ (a perfect positive relationship) to -1.00 (a perfect negative relationship).

df——*See* Degrees of freedom.

Decile——One of ten equal parts of a ranked distribution of scores.

Defense mechanism——A device, such as forgetting or distorting, used by an individual to protect himself against psychological hurt or pain. This defensive maneuvering often operates unconsciously.

Degrees of freedom——Used in measuring statistically the similarities and differences between groups.

Dynamics——*See* Psychodynamics.

E——Experimenter.

Ego-alien——Something the person does not associate with himself because it does not fit his self-picture.

Ego-syntonic——Opposite of ego-alien. Something that fits easily with a person's picture of himself. He can easily claim the attitude, behavior, or whatever, as his.

Endopsychic——Occurring *within* the psychological sphere or mind as opposed to an event occurring *outside* a person's psyche.

F-ratio——A statistical device used to determine whether or not a difference is statistically significant. (*See* Probability.)

IQ——*See* Intelligence quotient.

Identification——The adoption of another's behavior, mannerisms, values, attitudes, etc.

Intelligence quotient——A score on a test designed to measure intellectual ability or intelligence.

Mann-Whitney U Test——A nonparametric test applied to determine the statistical significance of differences between means.

Mean——One form of the statistical average. If there are six scores of 5, two scores of 15, and one score of 30, the mean would be 10 (the total of 90 points divided by nine cases).

Median——That point in a distribution of scores that is exactly in the middle (half the scores are higher and half are lower).

N——The number of subjects in a study.

NS——Not statistically significant.

P——*See* Probability.

Percentile——A point in a ranked distribution of scores that indicates the percentage of the population that obtained lower scores (e.g., 85th percentile indicates a score higher than 85 percent of the population).

Probability——The evaluation of much psychological research data rests on the degree of certainty that a given result has not occurred because of chance alone. In these articles one often sees $p. < .05$ (meaning that there are fewer than five chances in a hundred that the finding is due to chance) or $p. < .01$ (less than one chance in a hundred) or $p. < .001$ (less than one chance in a thousand).

Psychodynamics——Psychological processes that serve as explanations for observed behavior or experienced feelings.

Psychologist——One who has done advanced graduate work in psychology. Various state laws define the degree of training and experience that qualifies one as a psychologist. Those who work as part of a mental health team have specialized in clinical psychology.

Psychiatrist——A physician who has specialized in mental health work. Various state laws prescribe the amount of education and experience required to qualify as a psychiatrist.

Psychoanalysis——One type of psychotherapy. In its original form as elaborated by Sigmund Freud, the patient talked to the psychoanalyst five or six times each week. The patient spoke freely of anything that entered his mind while lying on a couch; the analyst sat out of view of the patient and used the free communication to help the patient understand himself psychologically.

Psychotherapy——A treatment for psychological discomfort involving verbal communication between a professionally trained mental health worker (e.g., a psychiatrist, psychologist, or social worker) and a client or patient.

Q sort——A test in which a subject is given a stack of cards. Each card contains a statement. The subject sorts the cards into piles according to how true or applicable they are to him or to whatever he is being asked to judge.

r——*See* Correlation coefficient.

Rank——The arrangement of items in some sort of systematic order (e.g., putting scores in order from highest to lowest).

Reliability——This term has approximately the same meaning when used in reference to numbers in statistics that it has in reference to people. It indicates the degree to which one can count on a number to remain the same and be relatively free from error.

S——Subject. A person or animal studied in an experiment.

SD——*See* Standard deviation.

SES——Socioeconomic status. Indicates one's position in a community. Ordinarily related to one's education, income, residence, employment, and family history.

Schizophrenia——Implies severe difficulty in understanding and operating in terms of agreed-upon reality. There are many types of schizophrenia; most cases that are referred to as *psychotic* (operating according to ground rules that differ drastically from those guiding others in their culture) are today diagnosed as schizophrenic.

School phobia——The fear displayed by a child who is unable to attend school and who often becomes physically ill if forced to attend. It is believed that this is related to a usually unconscious wish of the child's mother to keep him a baby at home with her.

Social worker——A person trained in a graduate school of social work, usually with a master's degree. Those who are trained to work with individuals are usually referred to as caseworkers; those trained to work as part of a mental health team are called psychiatric social workers.

Standard deviation (SD, σ)——An index of distance from the mean or arithmetical average. For instance, approximately 68.26 percent of all scores for a population fall between one SD below the mean and one SD above the mean.

Standard score——A score determined by the distance (in terms of standard deviation) of one's raw score from the mean. It is possible to compare standard scores when their raw score equivalents are not comparable (e.g., a score on an arithmetic test and a score on a test of grip strength).

Stanine——A statistical unit determined by converting the scores of a distribution into standard scores and then dividing the distribution into nine equal parts.

Statistical significance——A measure of the likelihood that an observed outcome did not occur on the basis of chance alone, but that it reflected the influence of some particular factor(s) or variable(s).

Symbolism——Making use of one thing (e.g., an image) to stand for something else. It is supposed that this is especially prevalent in dreams, for instance, where people and objects represent needs pressing from the unconscious for expression.

T——*See* Standard score.

t test——A test to determine whether or not a difference may be considered statistically significant. Indicates the probability that the observed difference could have occurred by chance alone.

Therapy——*See* Psychotherapy. In addition to verbal interchange, the term may include other means such as drugs and electroshock.

X——*See* Mean.

x²——*See* Chi square.

σ——*See* Standard deviation.